I0473319

THE TALLY

An Artist's Book
By Sydney Cardew

A record of the deaths during the 1st
year of the Coronavirus pandemic in the UK

Our leaders have blood on their hands.

9 781008 992375

© Sydney Cardew for Idle Toil Press, 2021

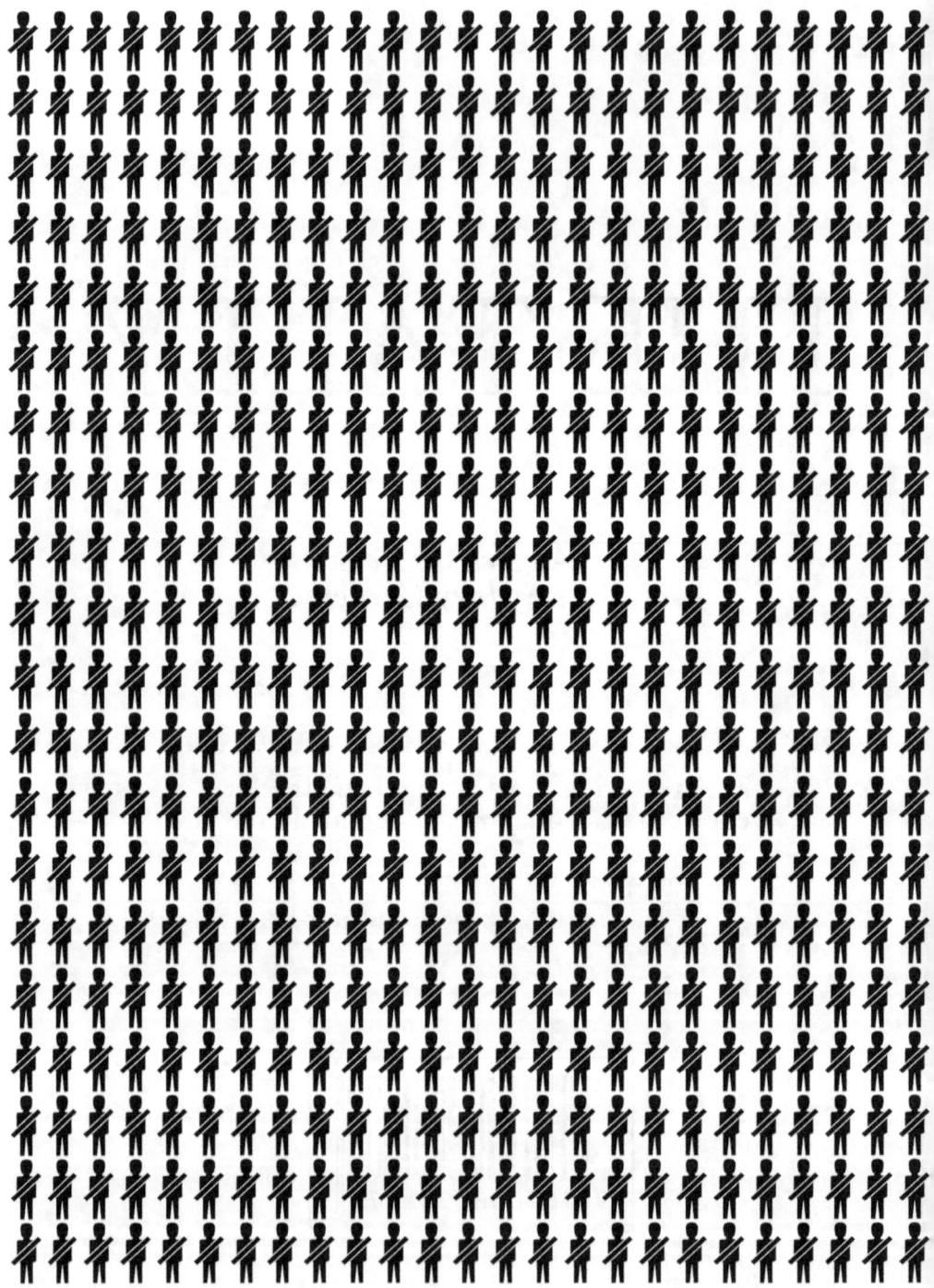

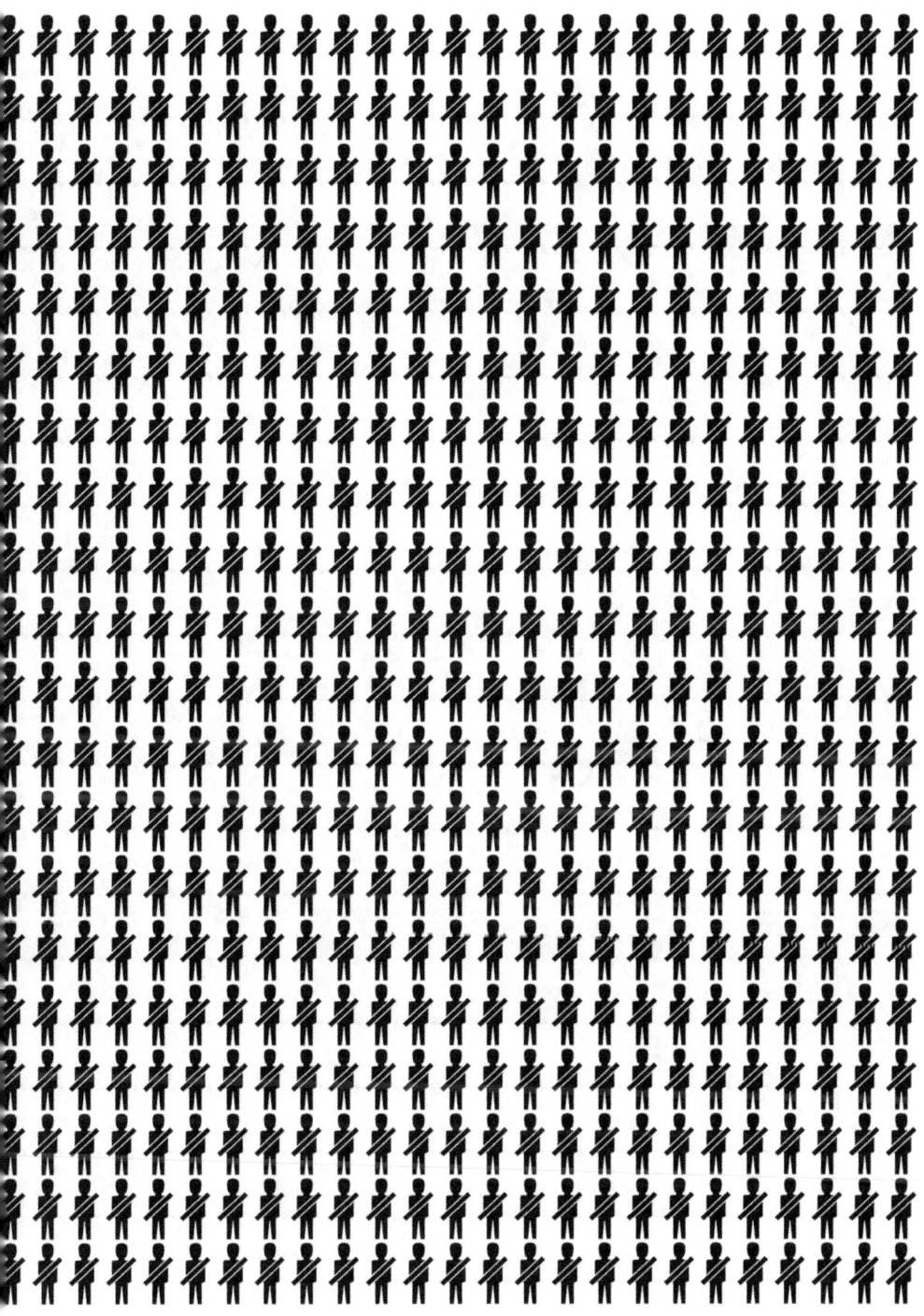

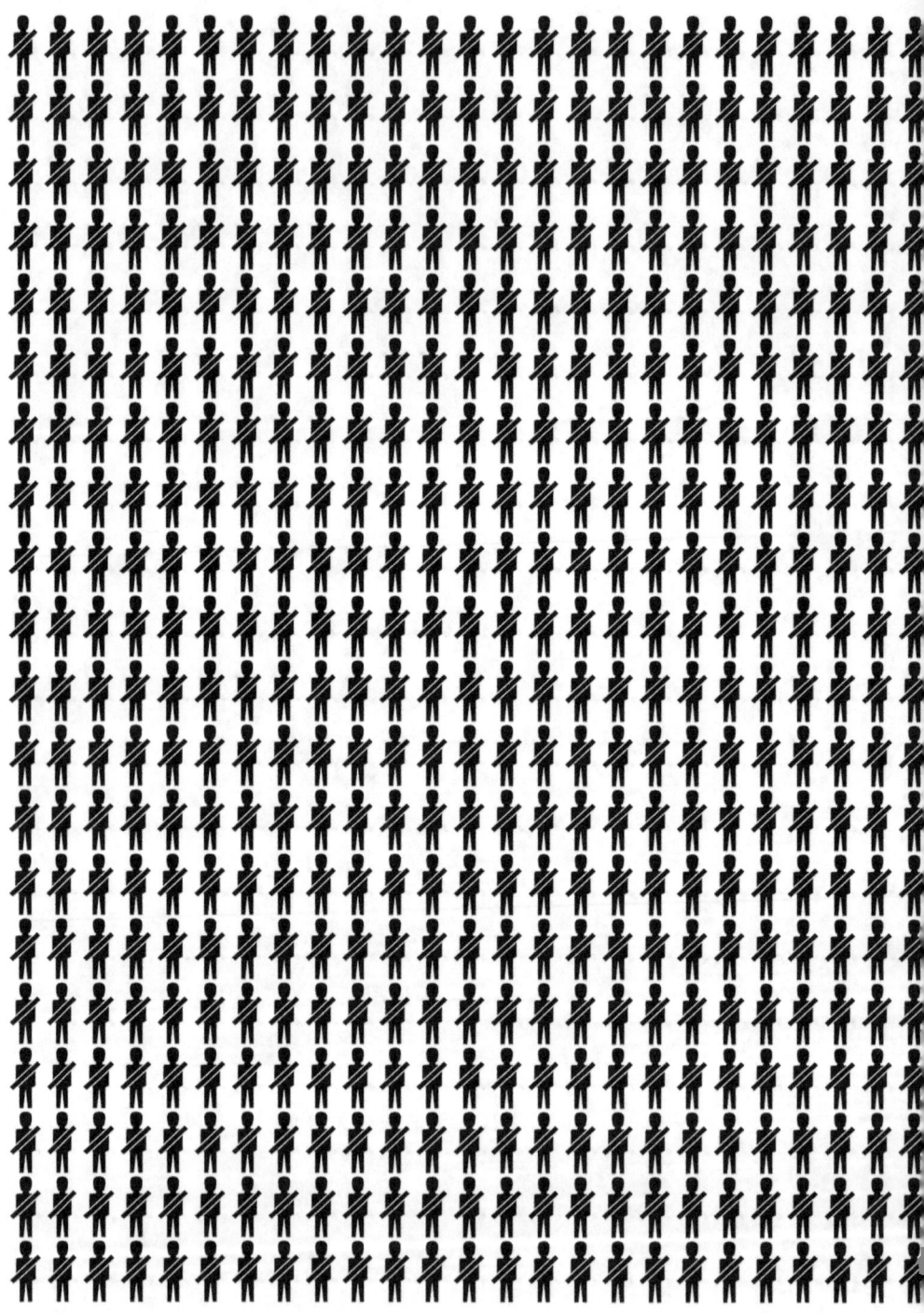

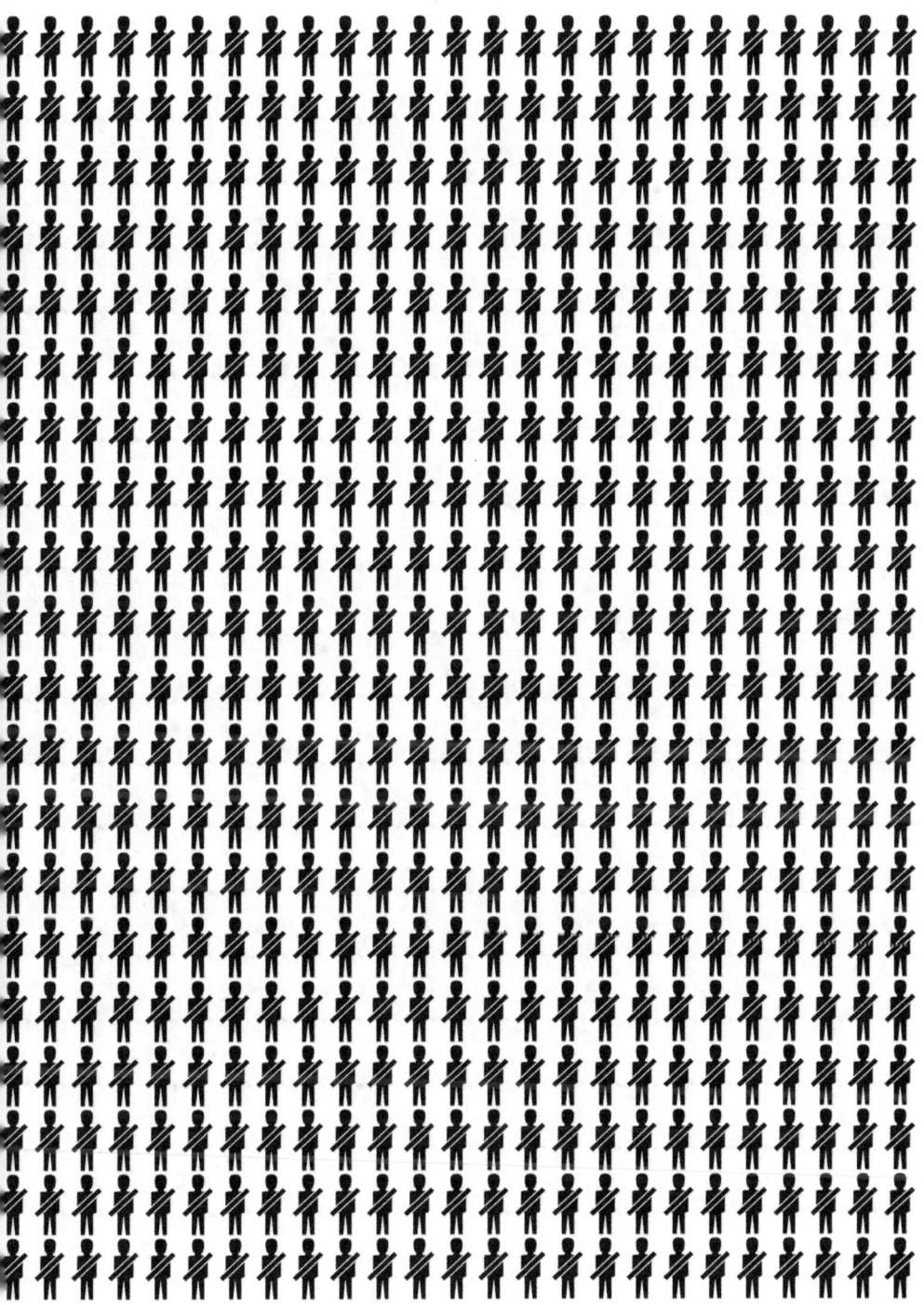

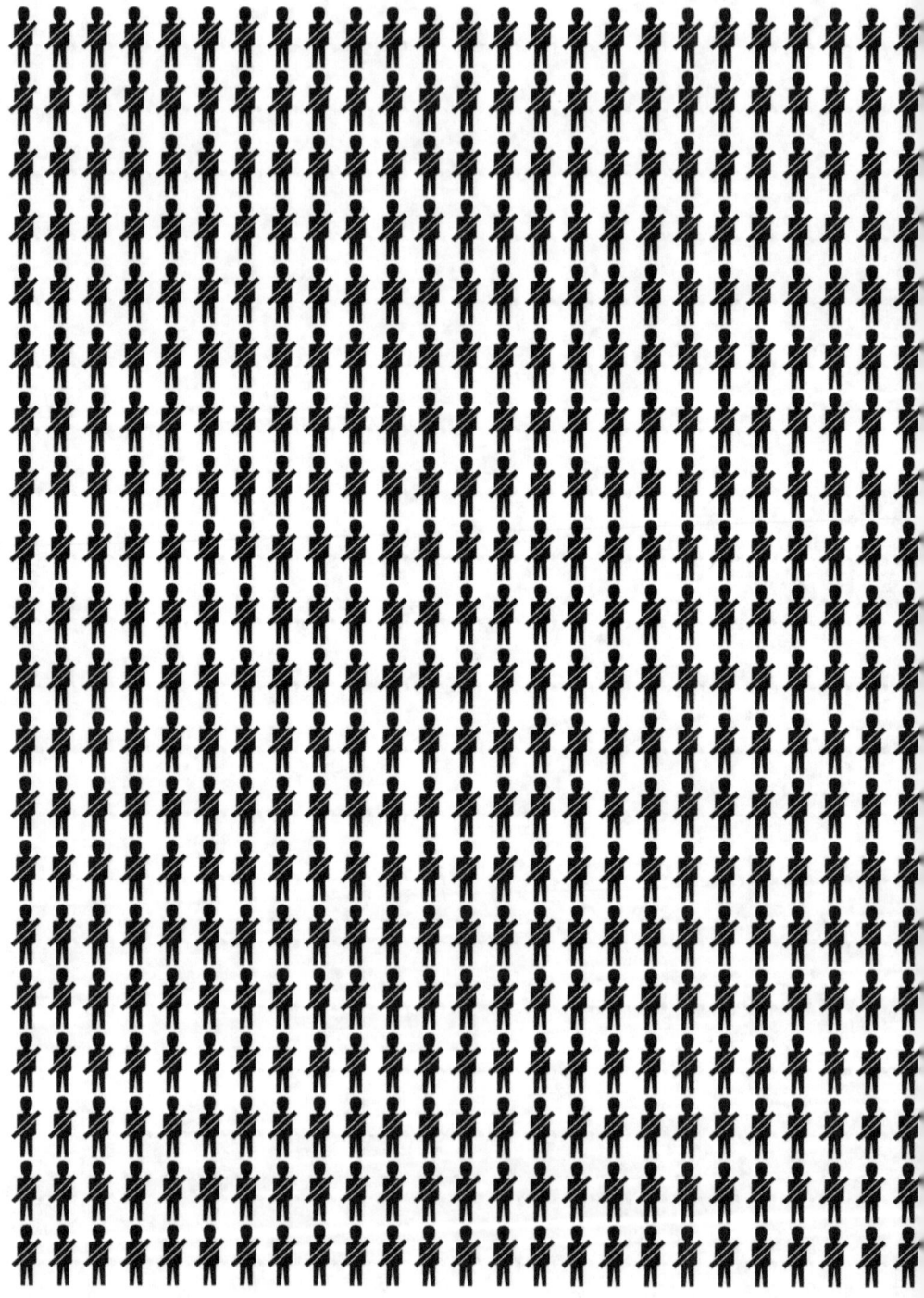

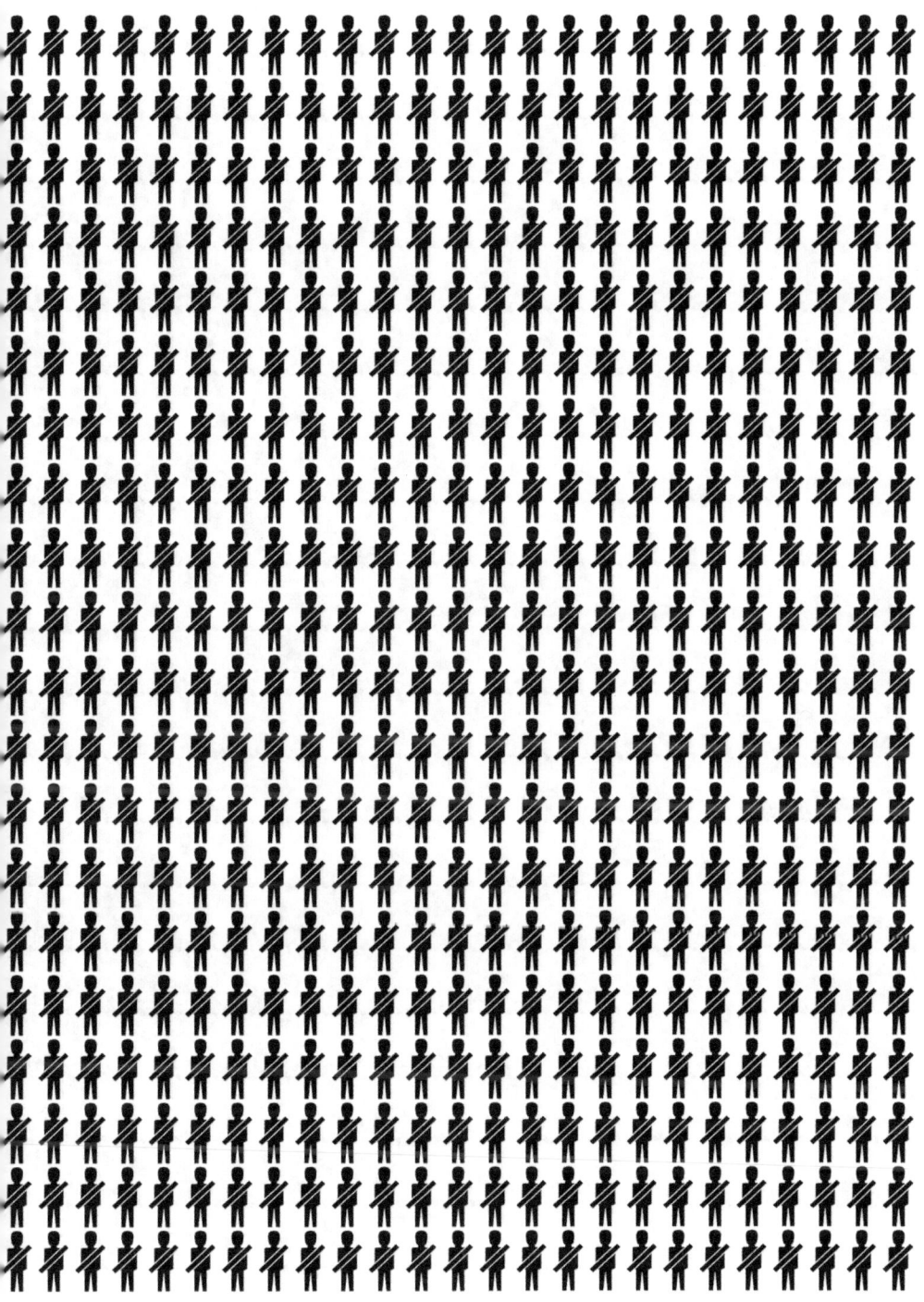

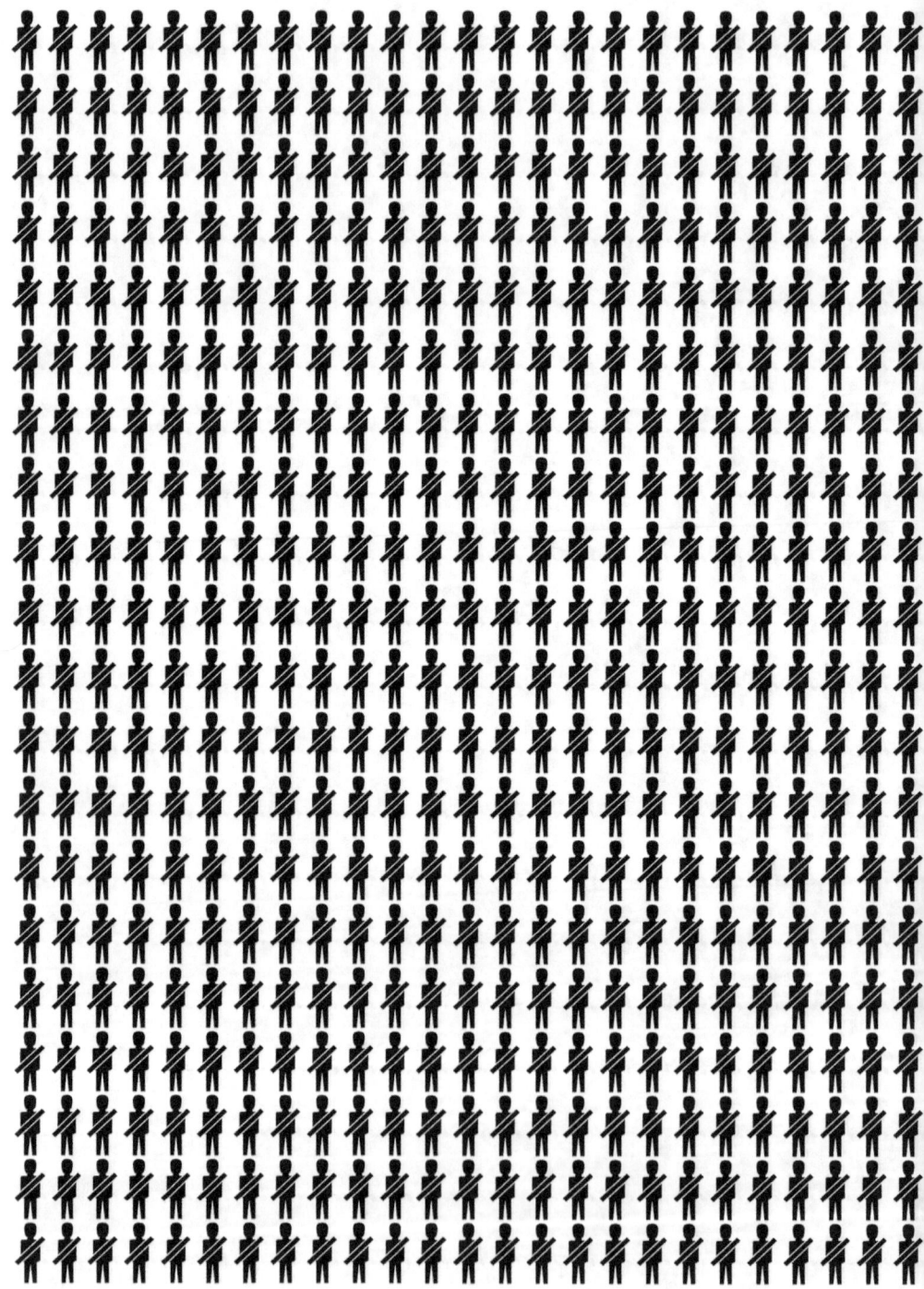

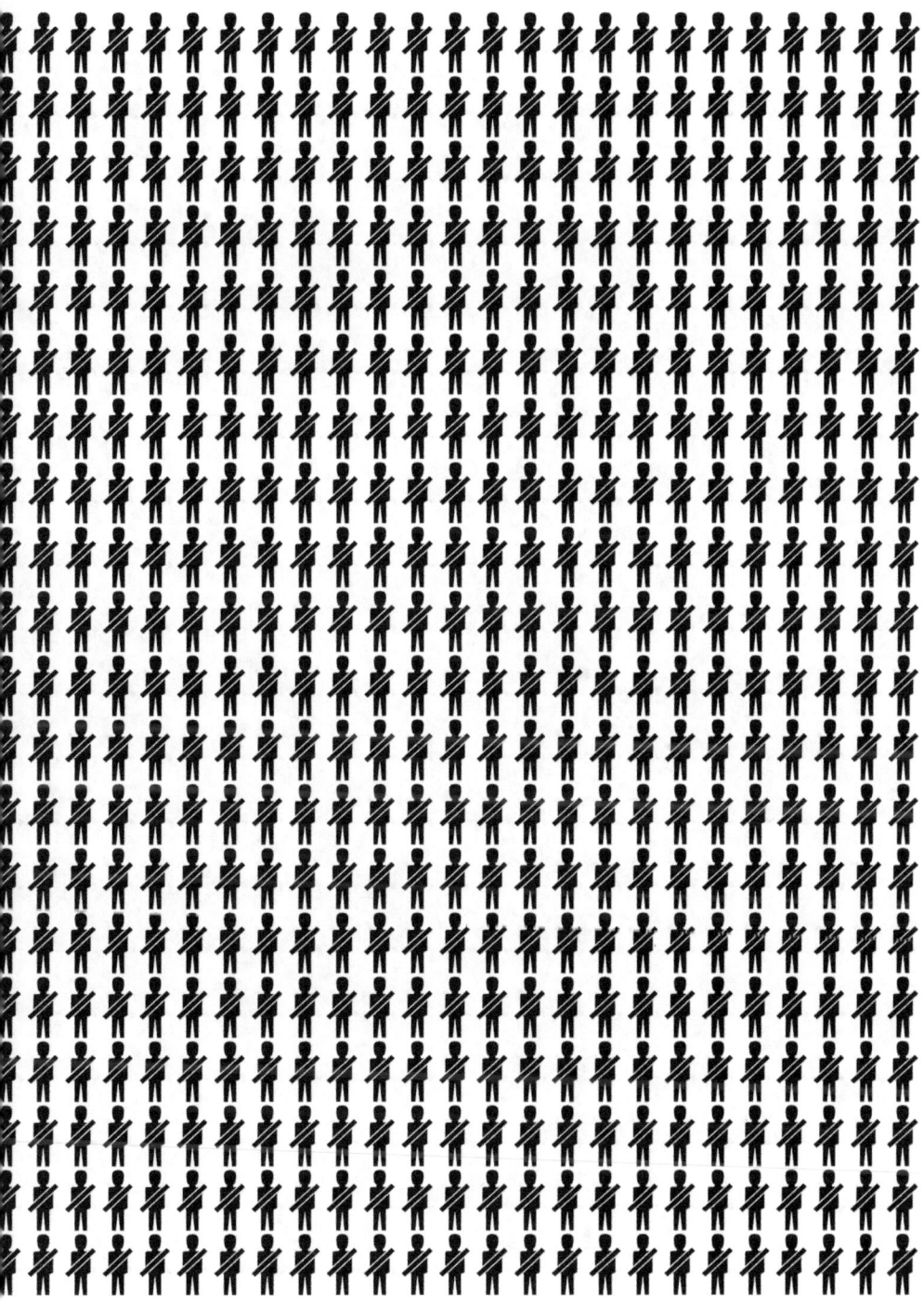

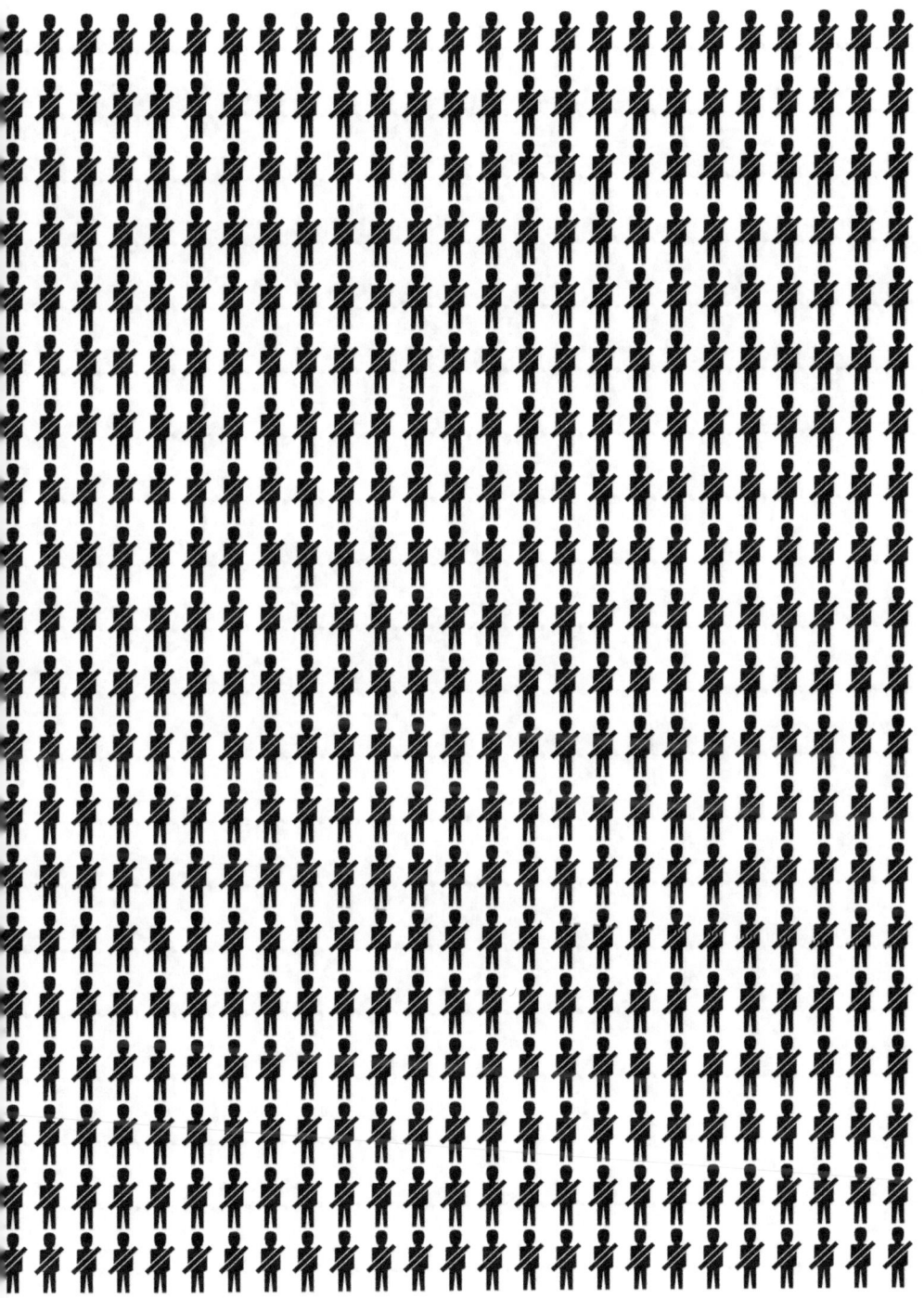

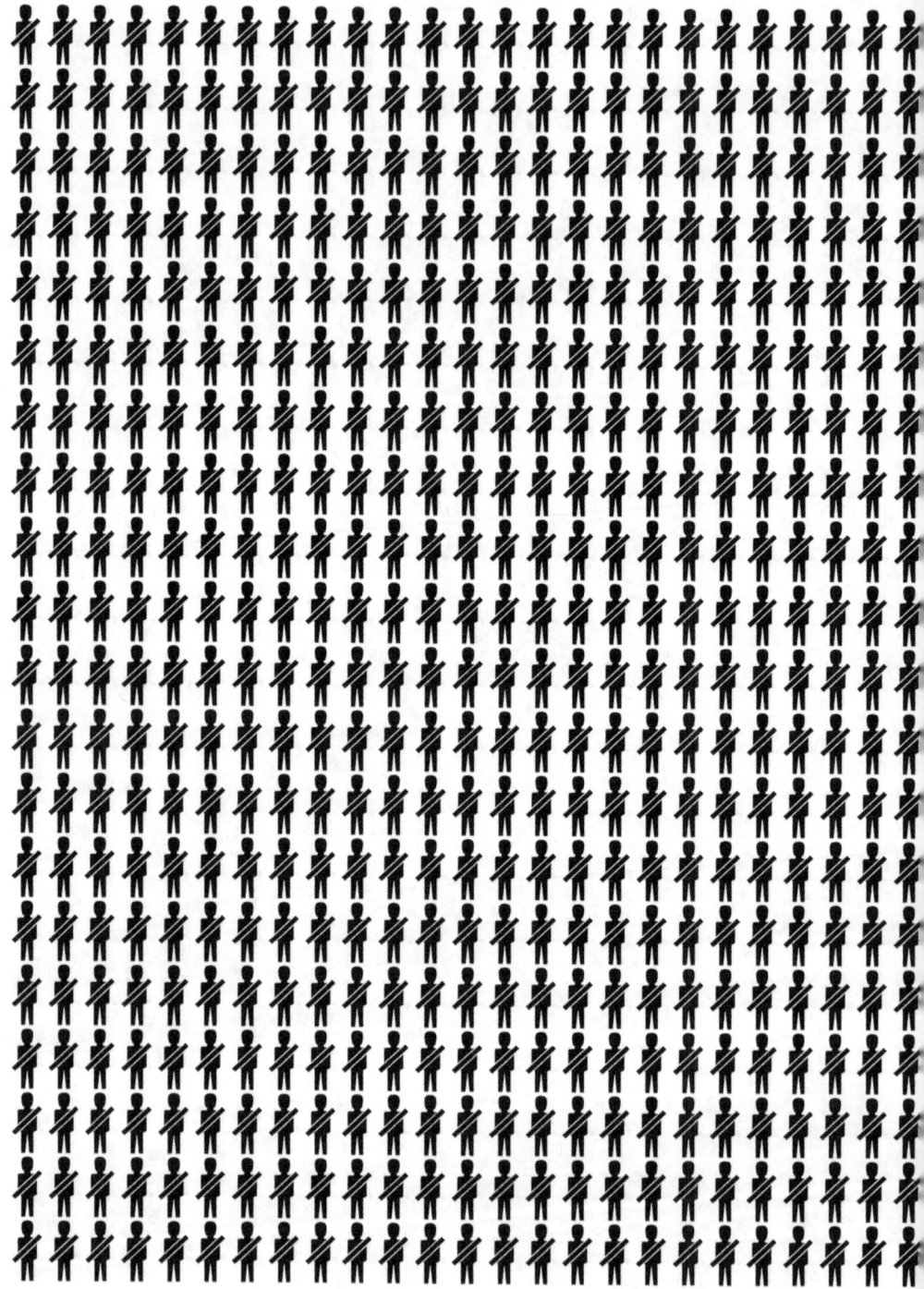

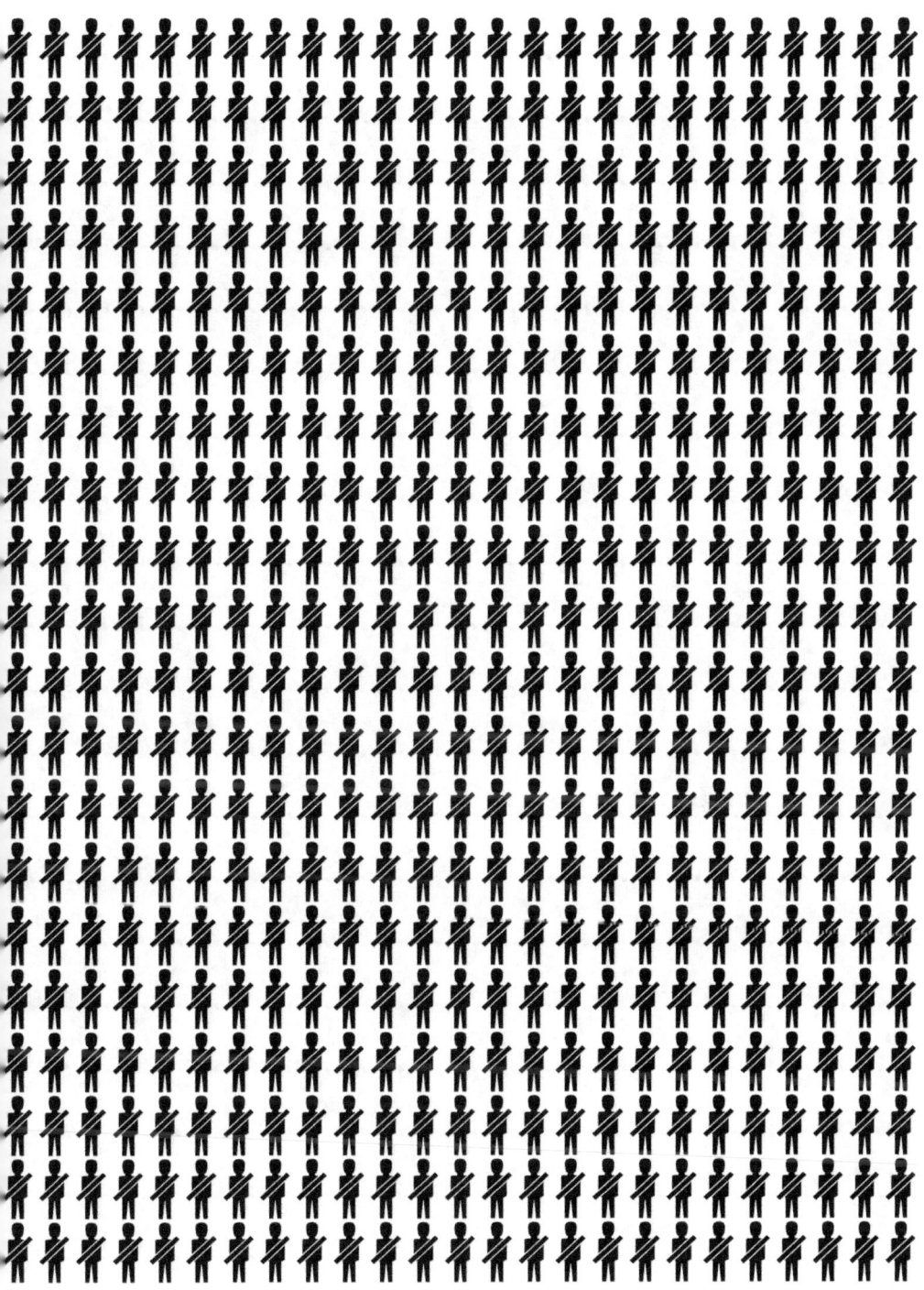

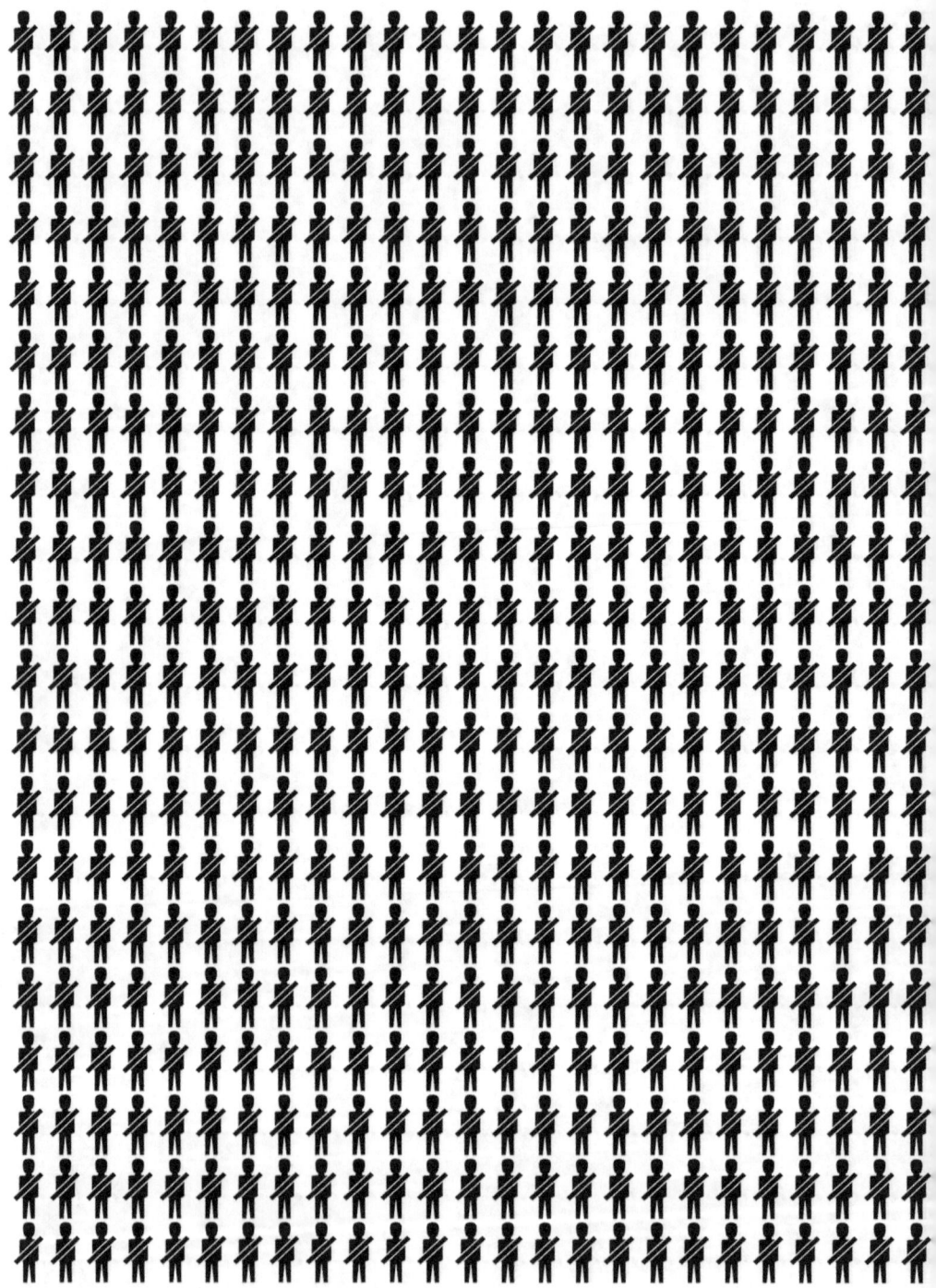

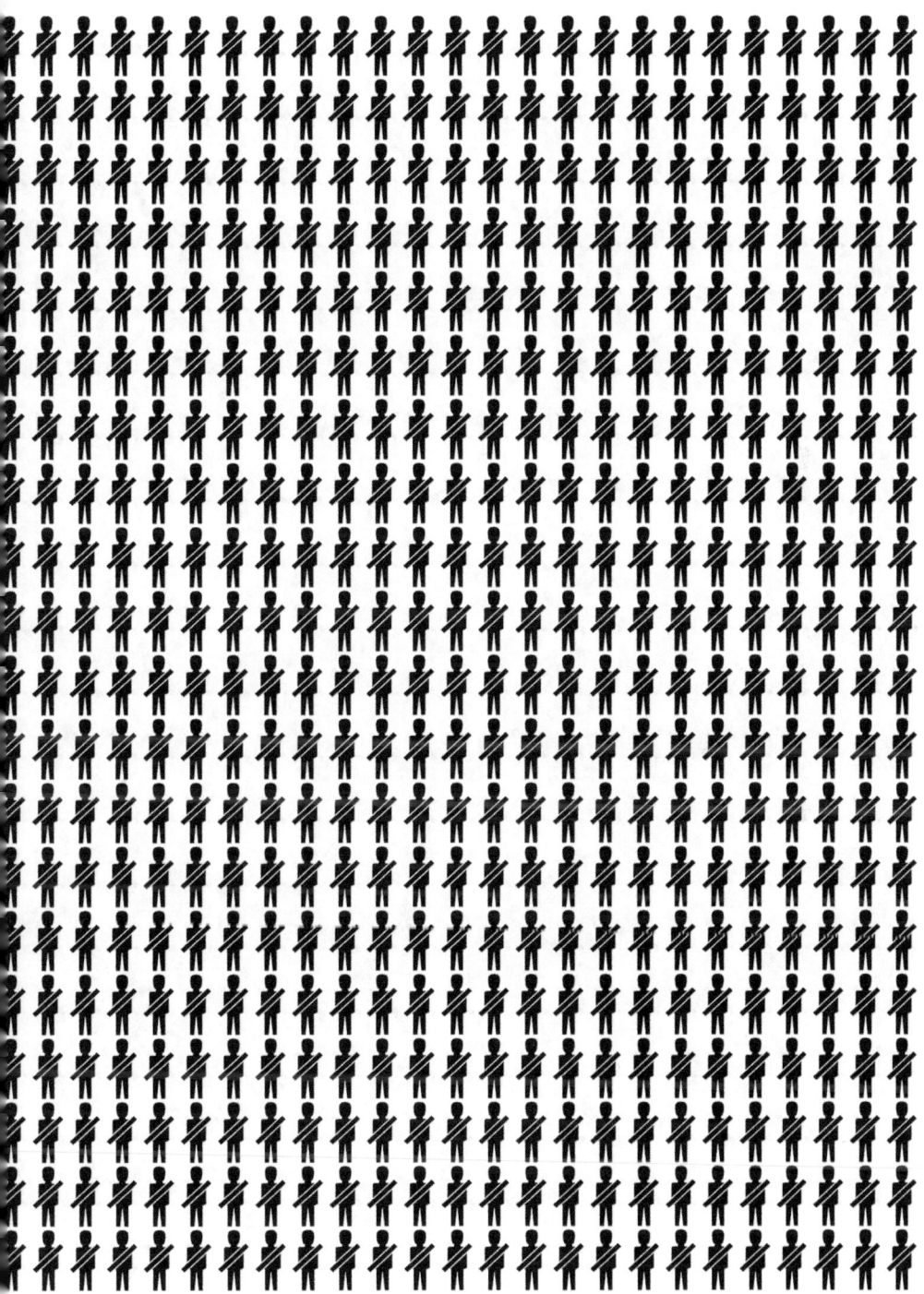

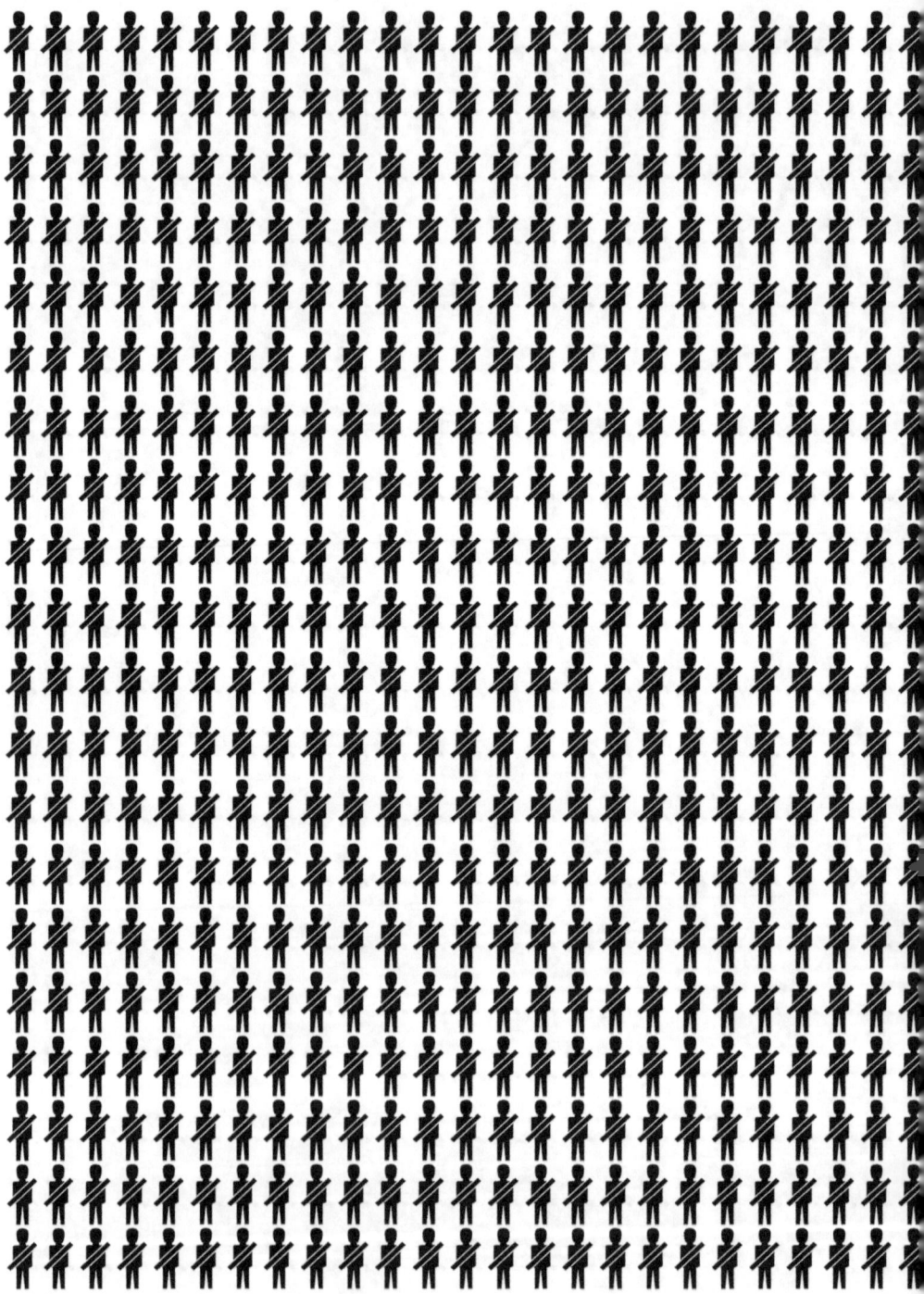

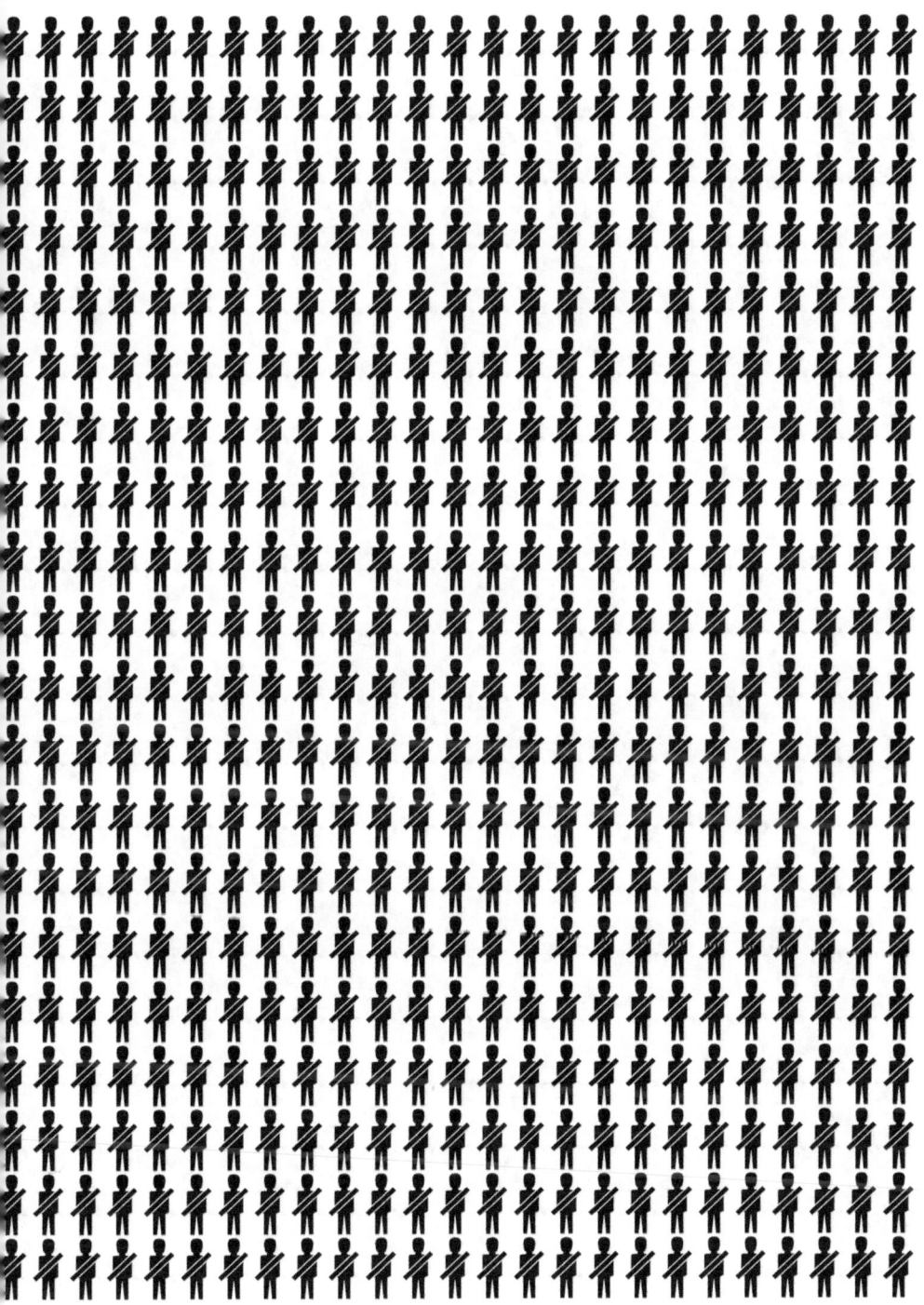

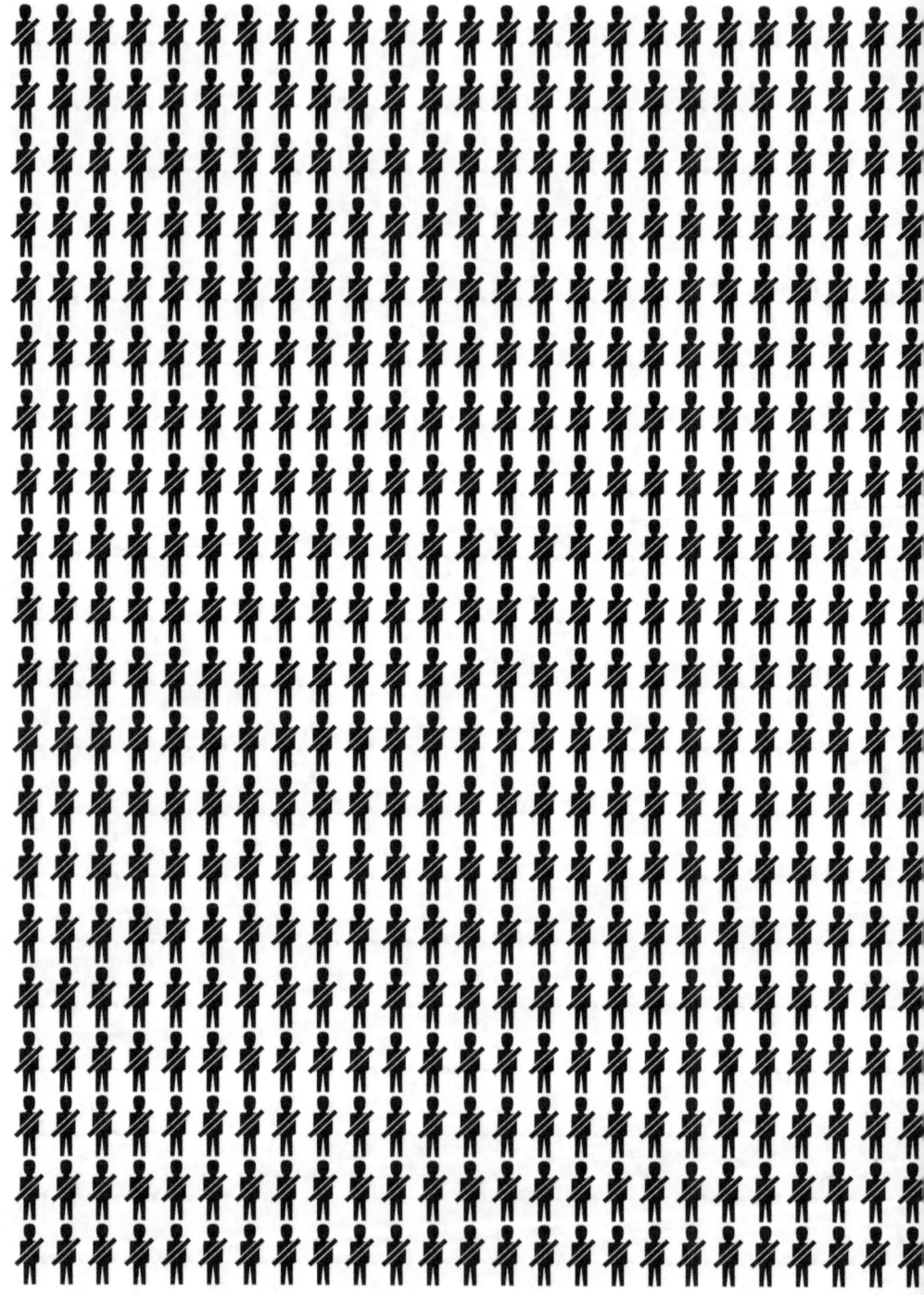

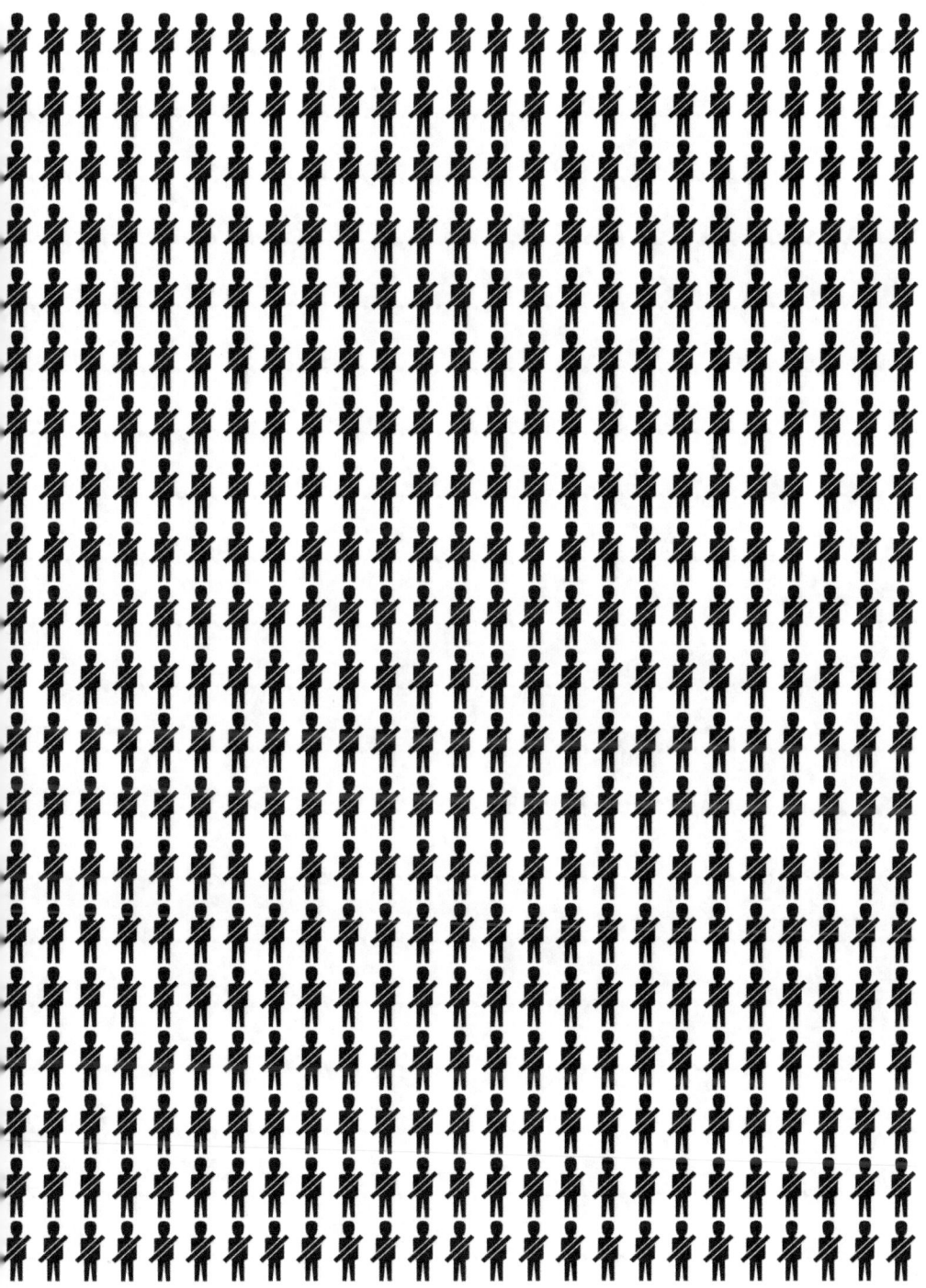

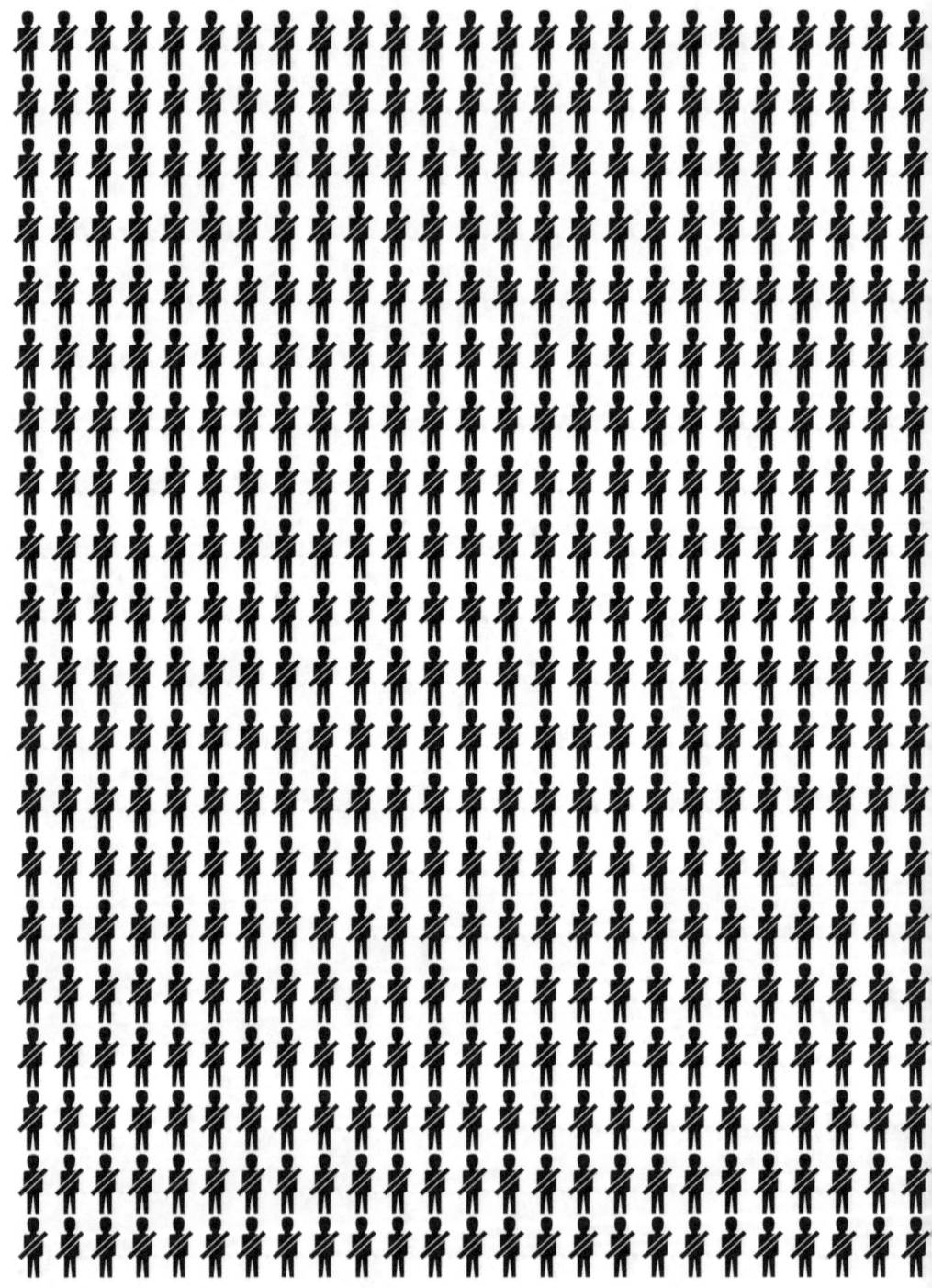

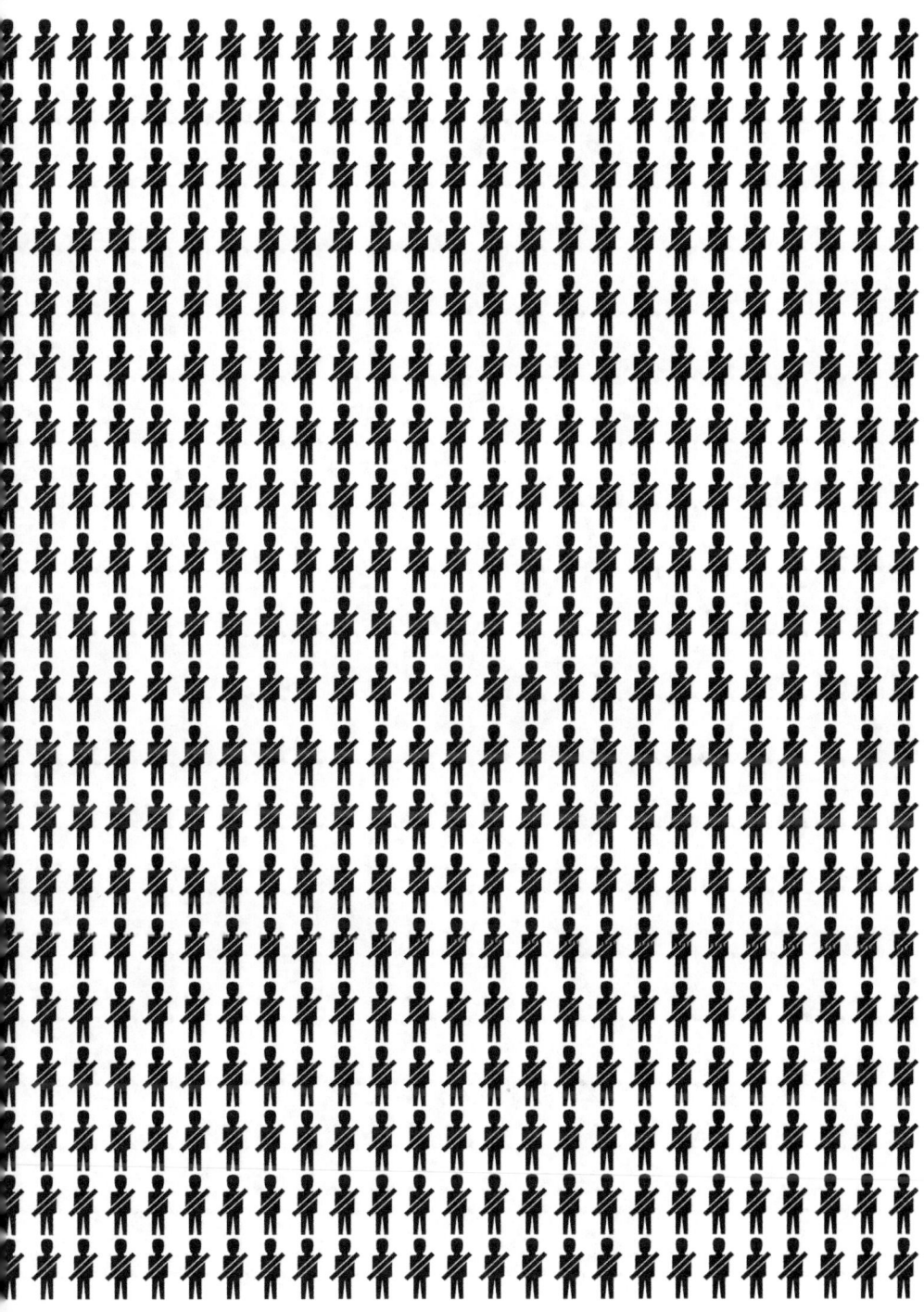

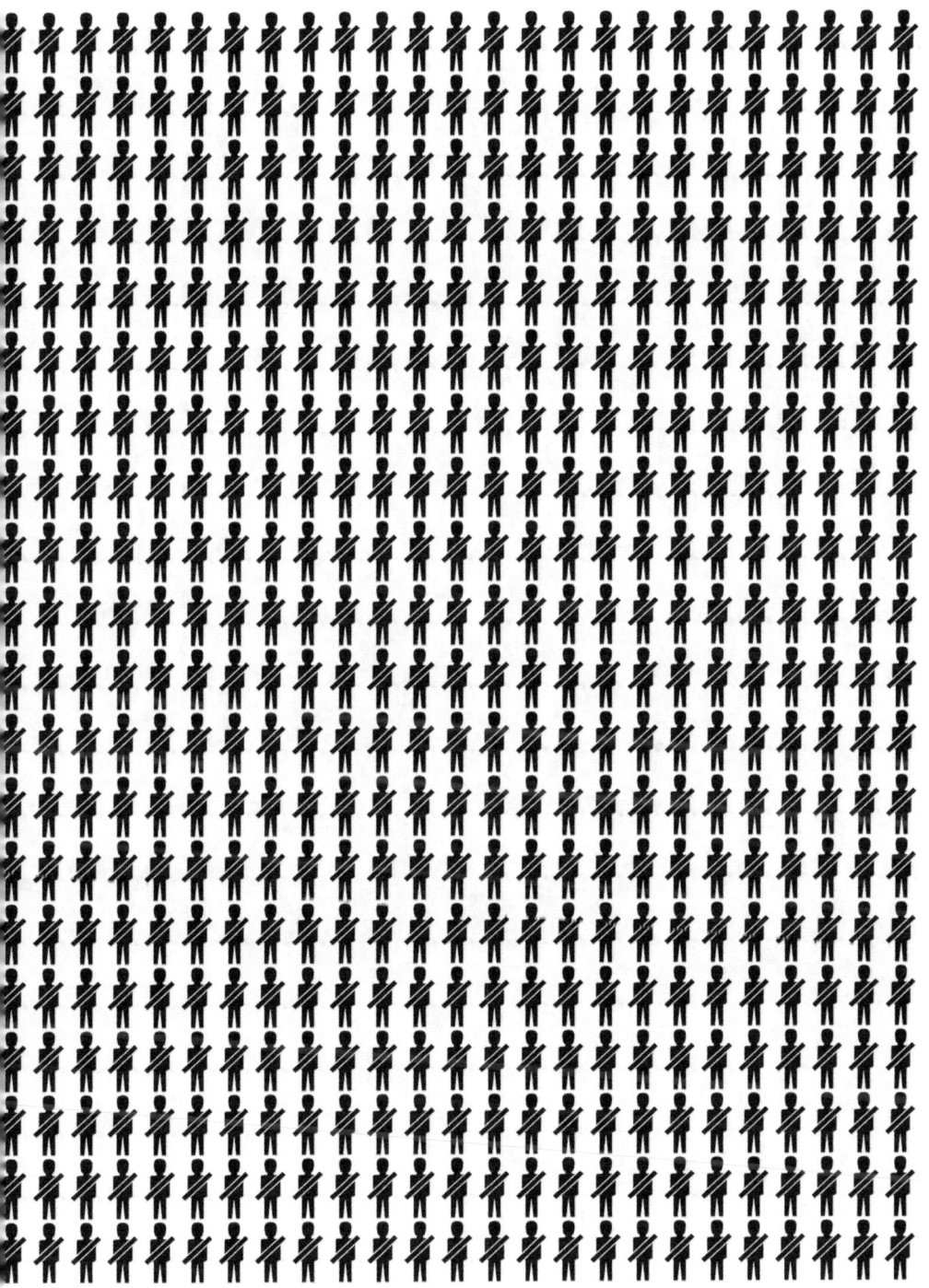

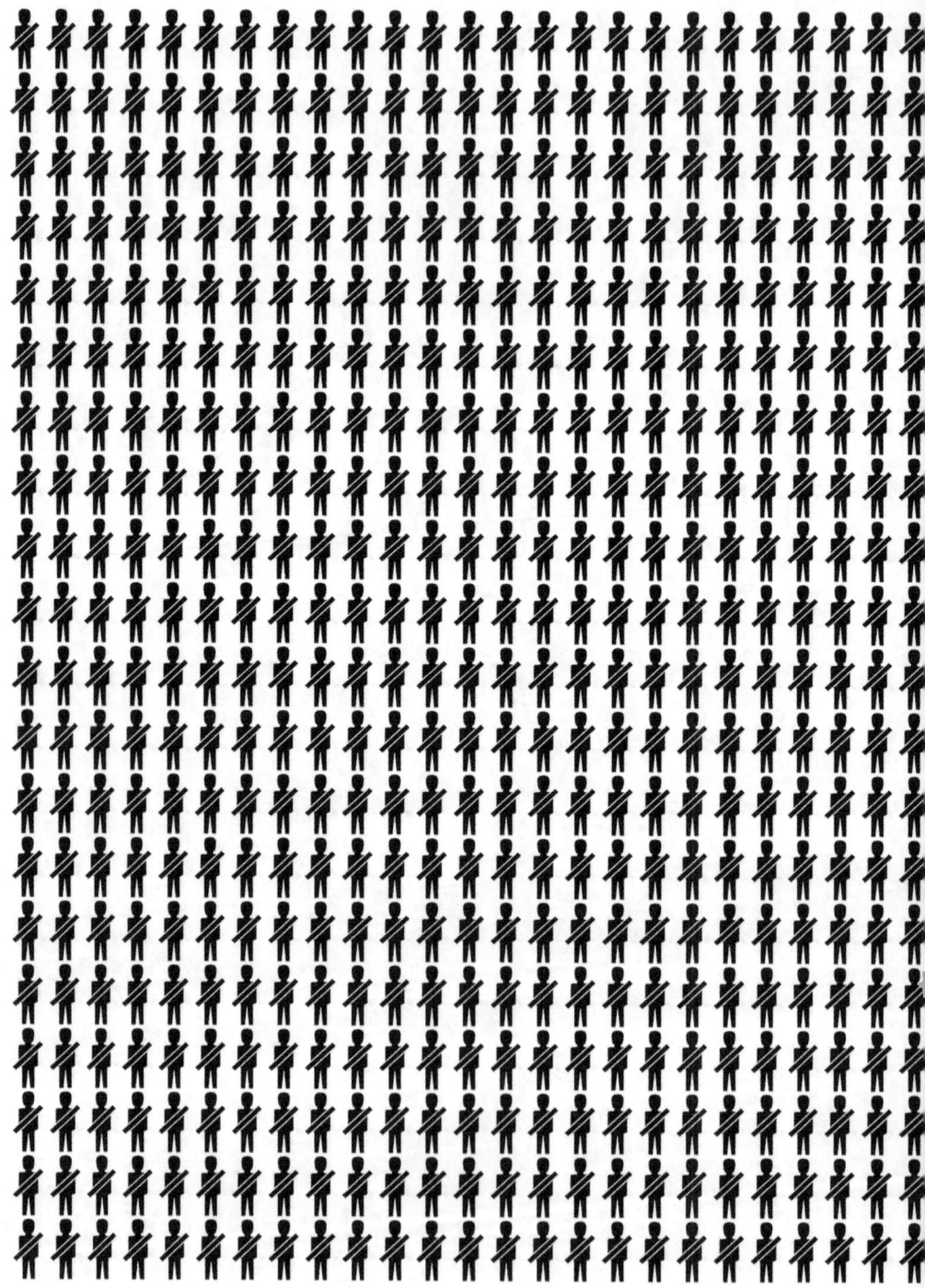

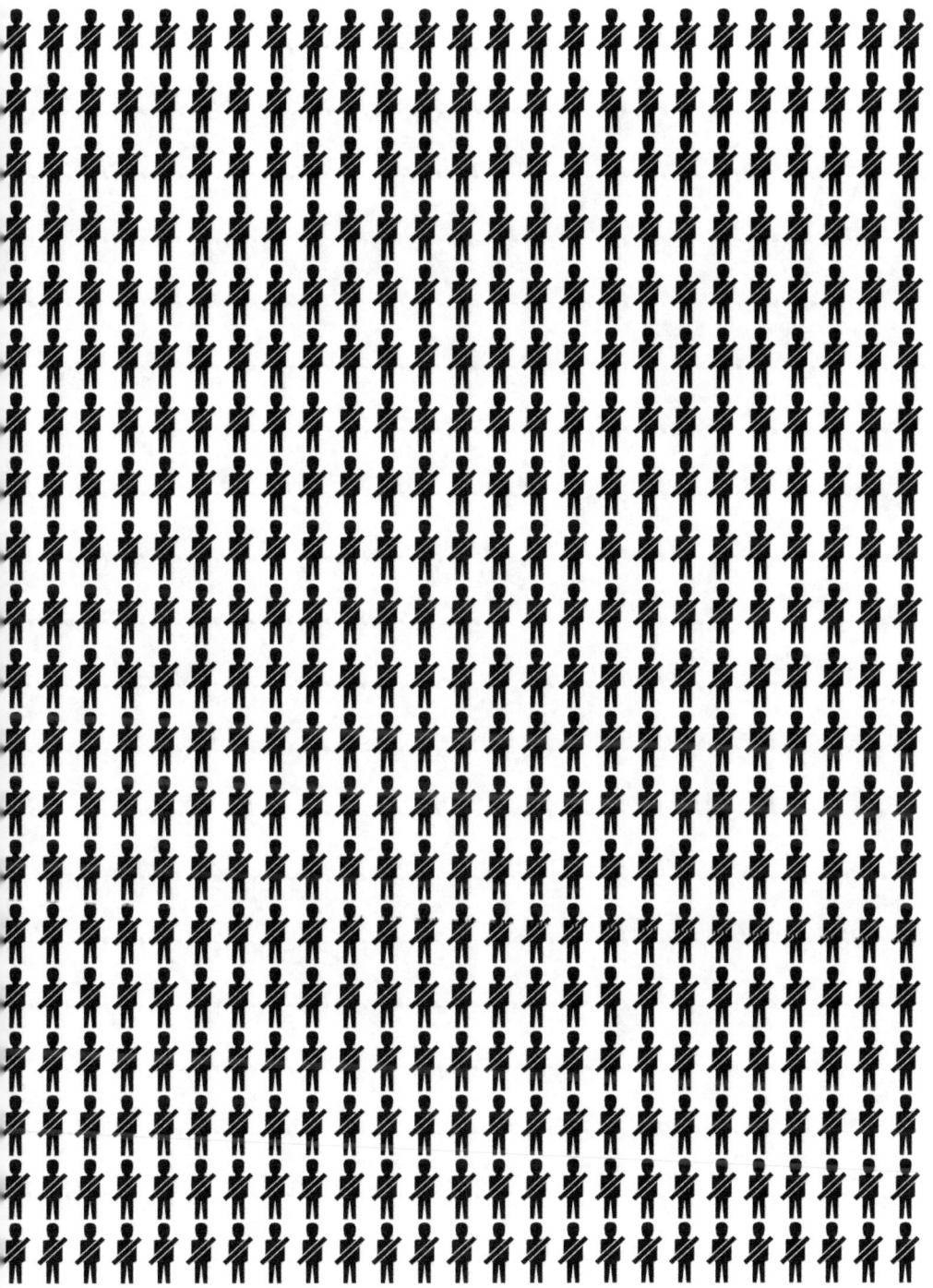

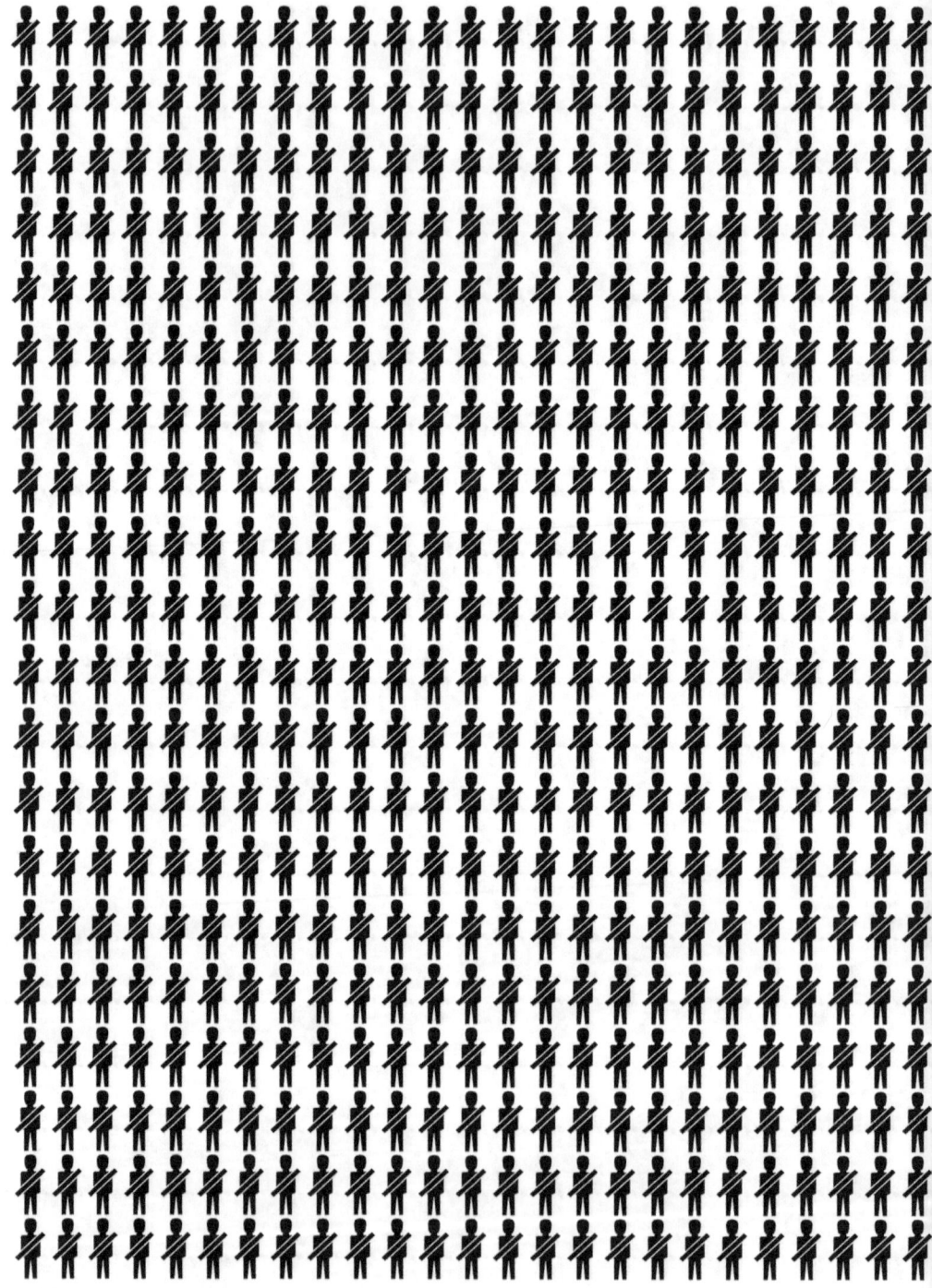

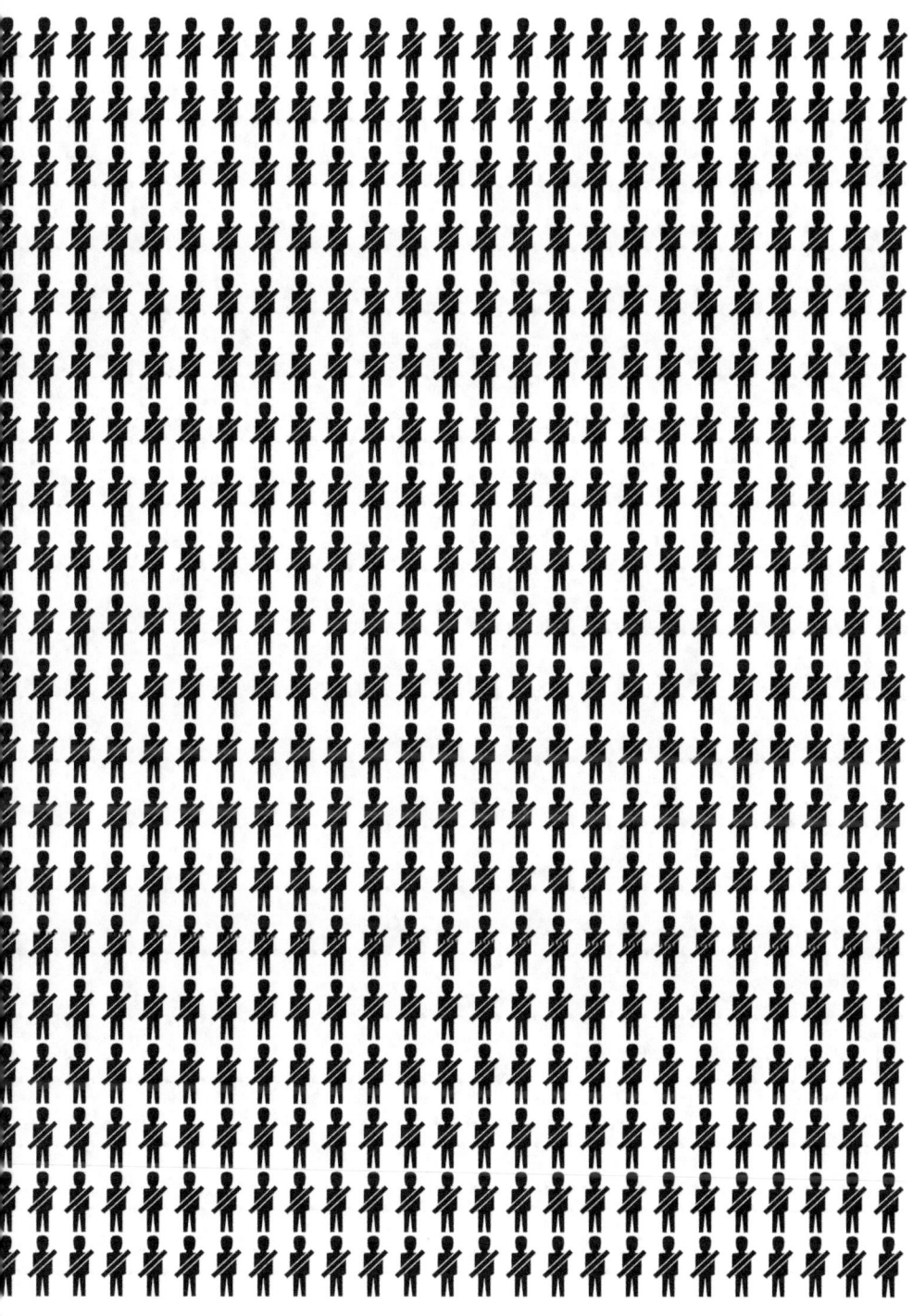

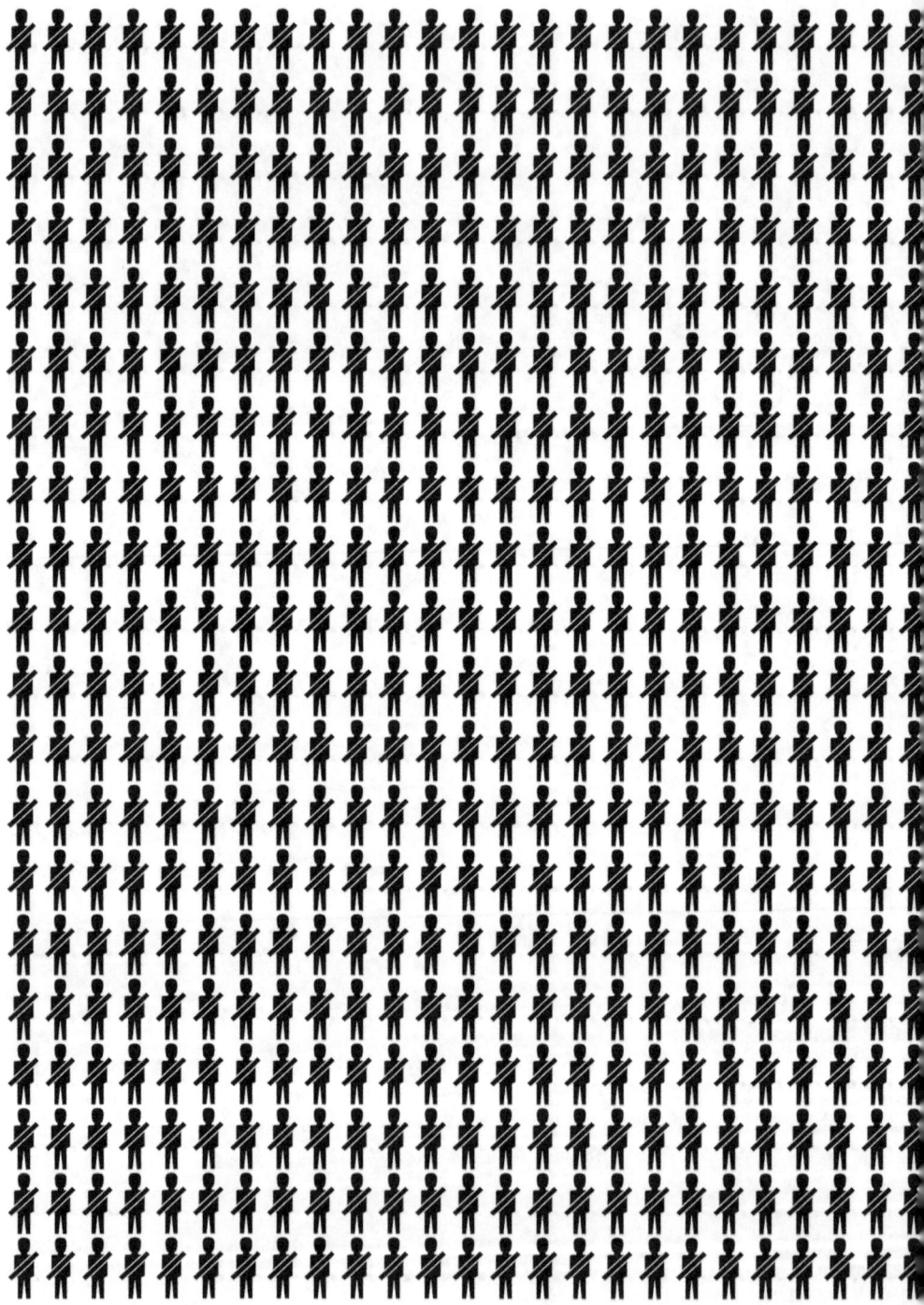

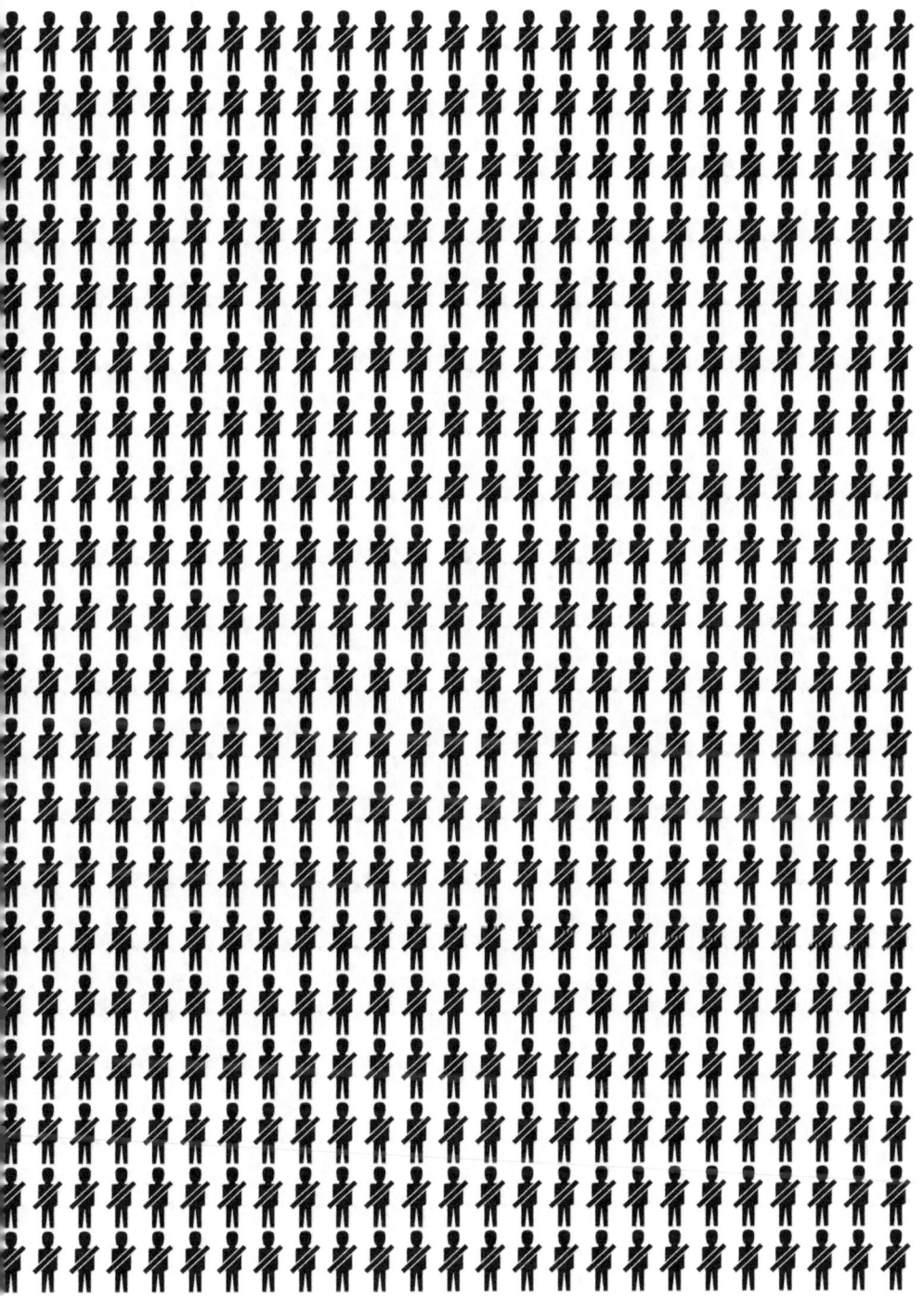

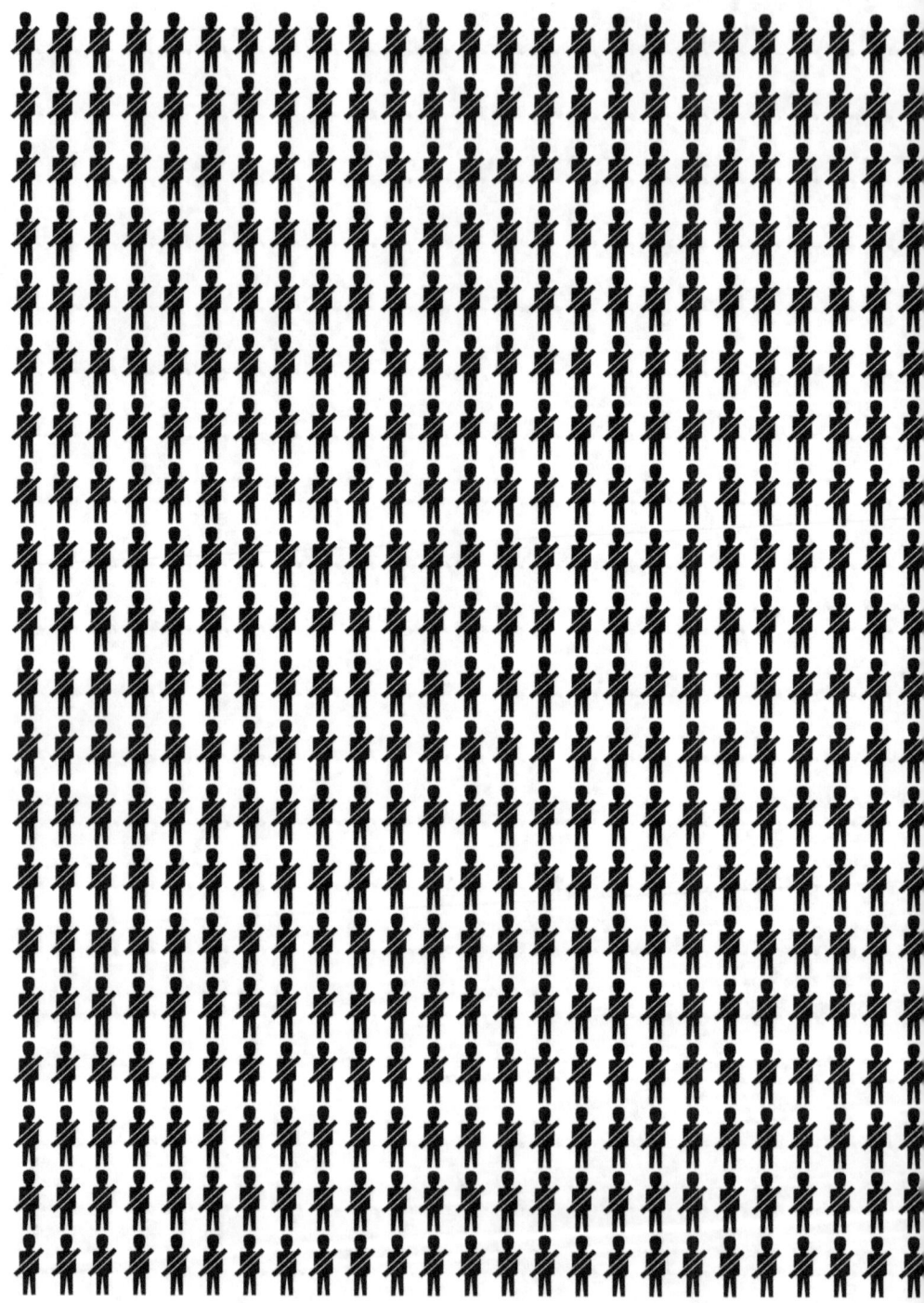

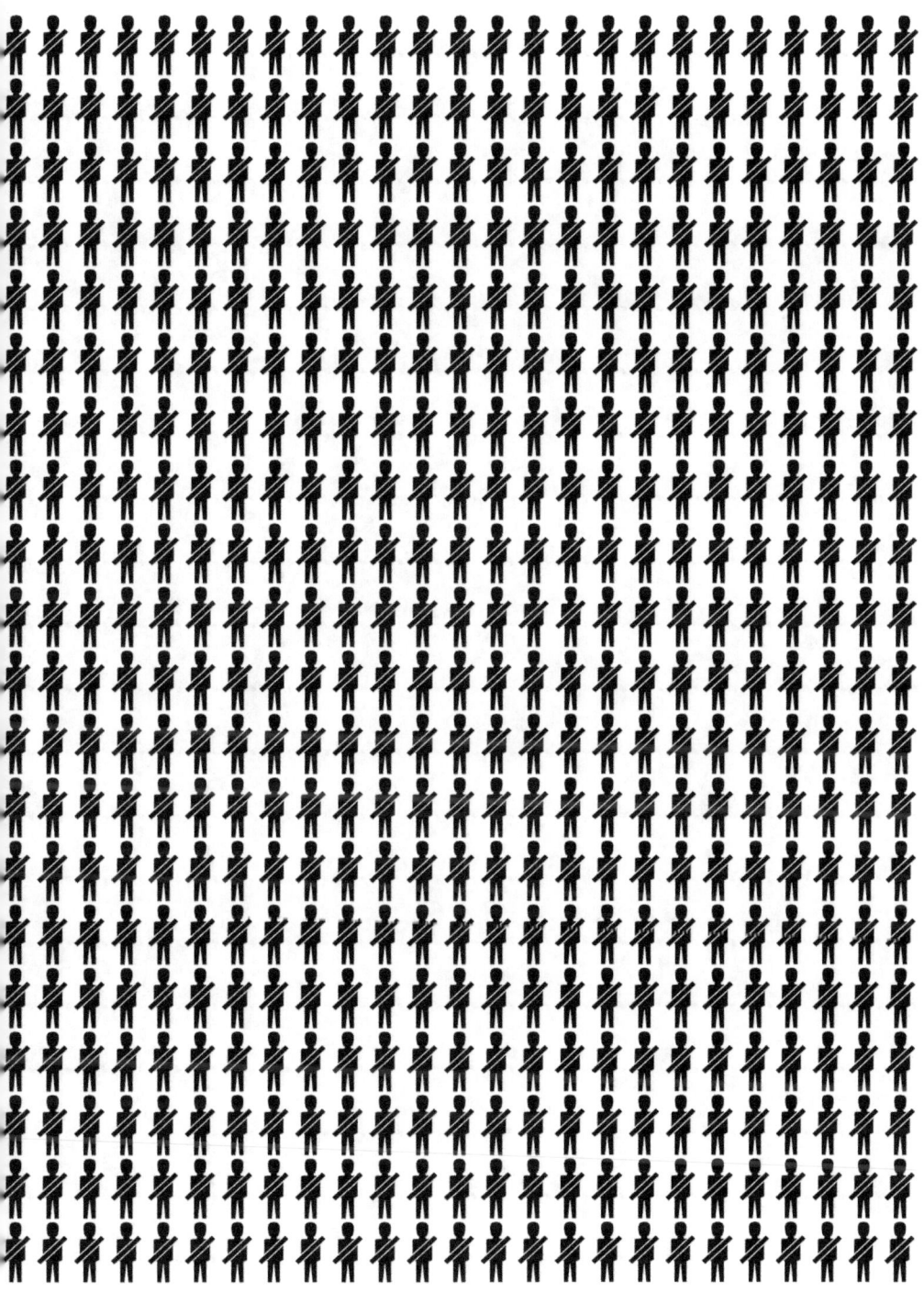

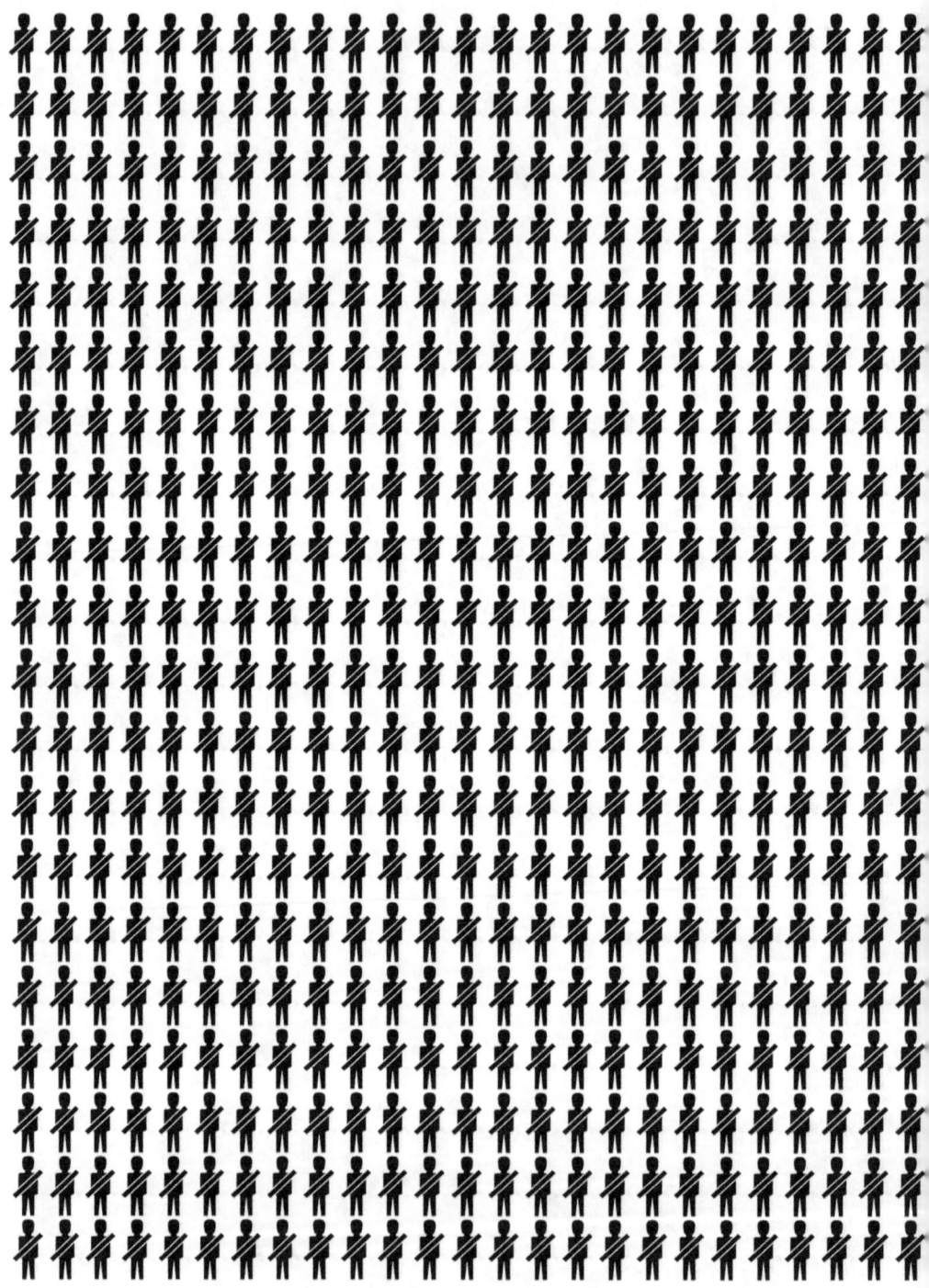

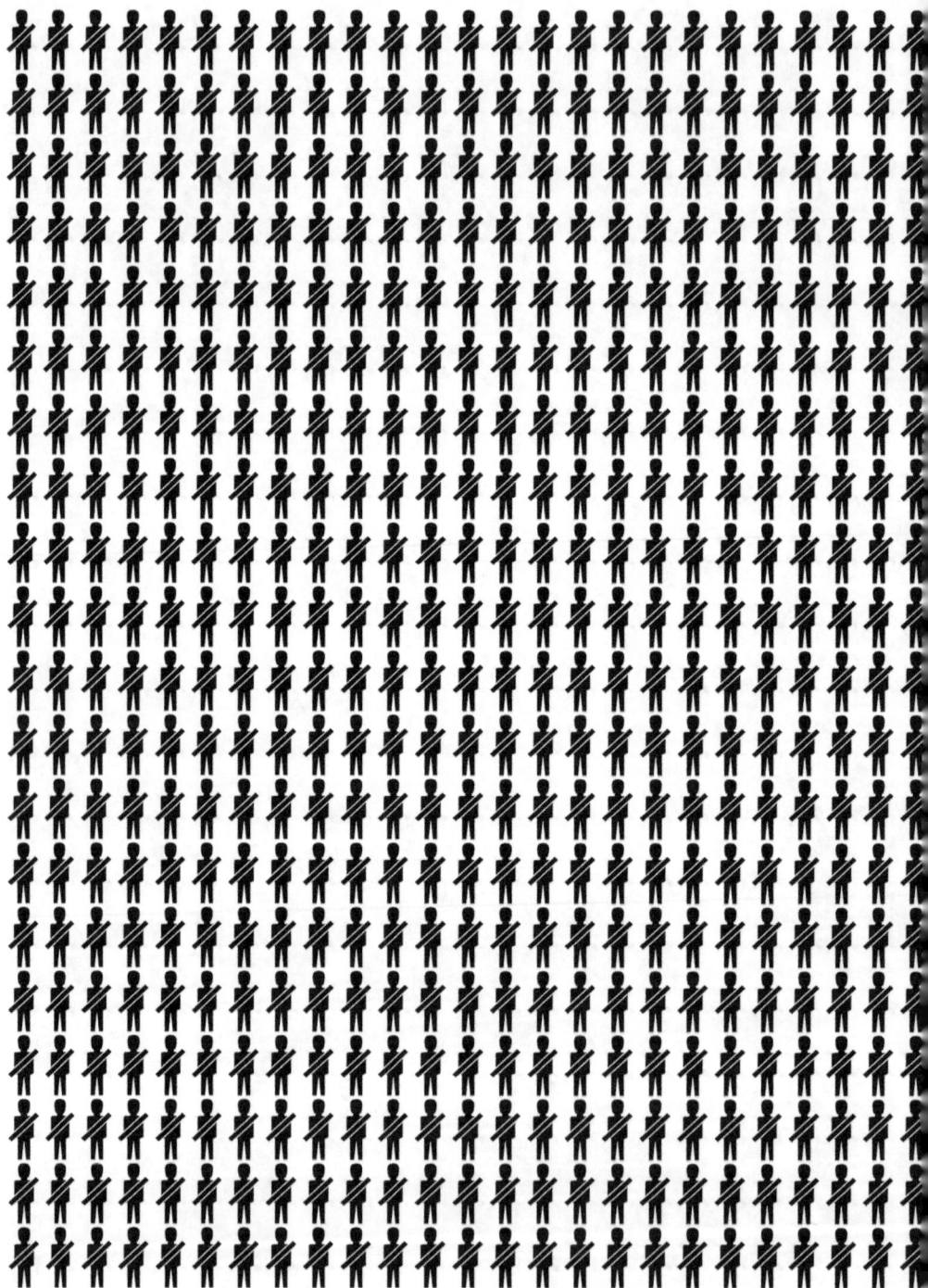

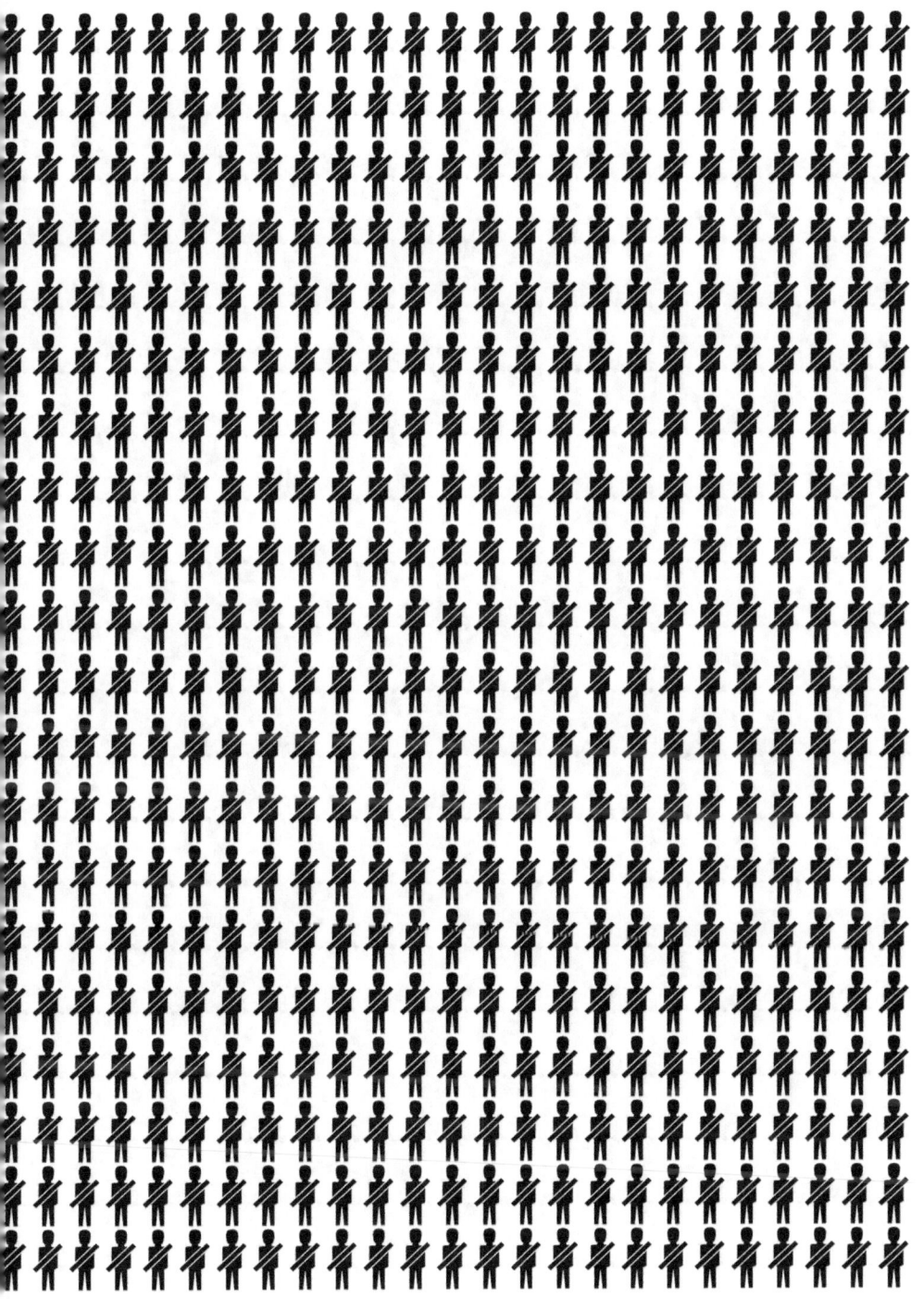

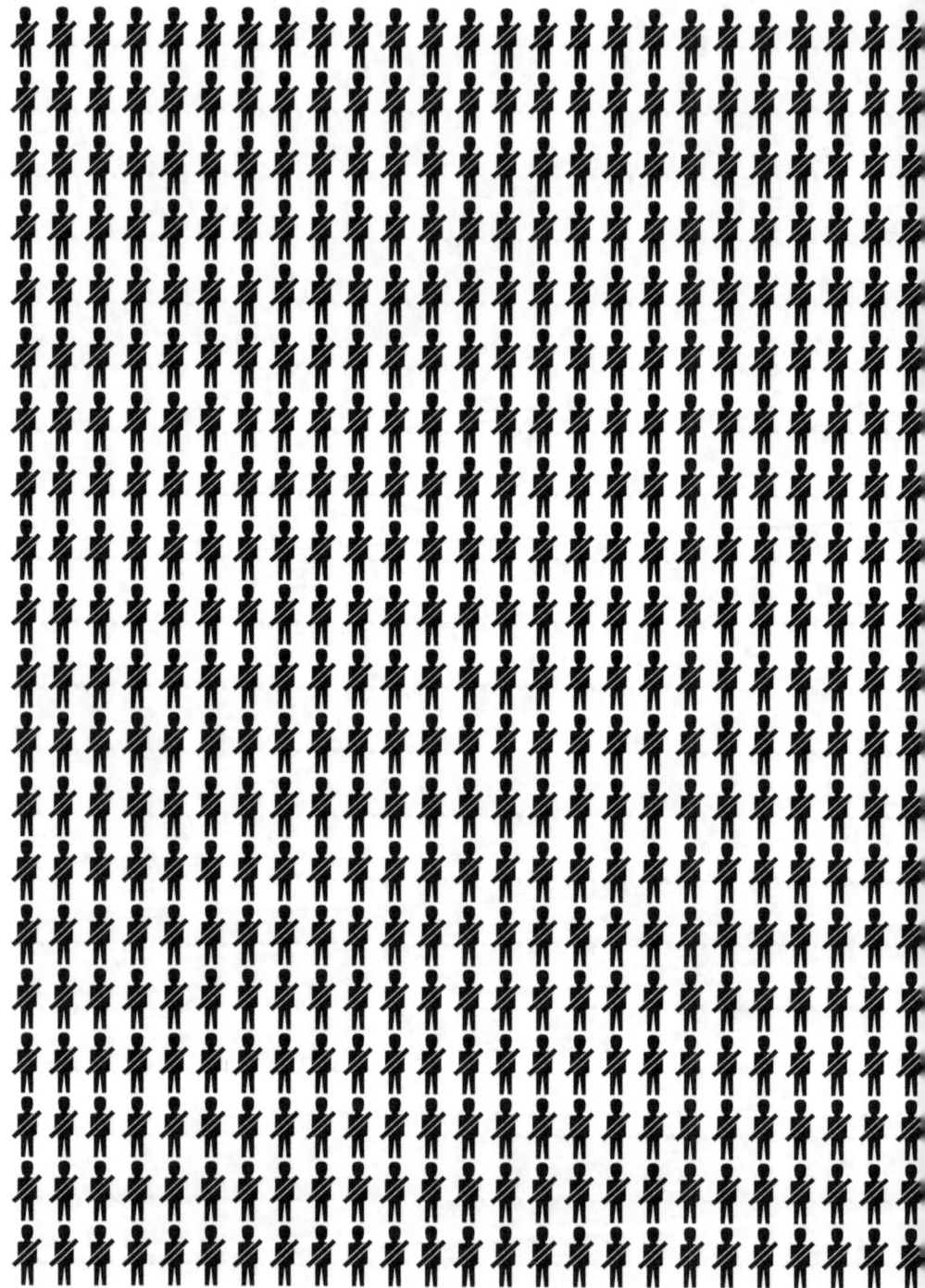

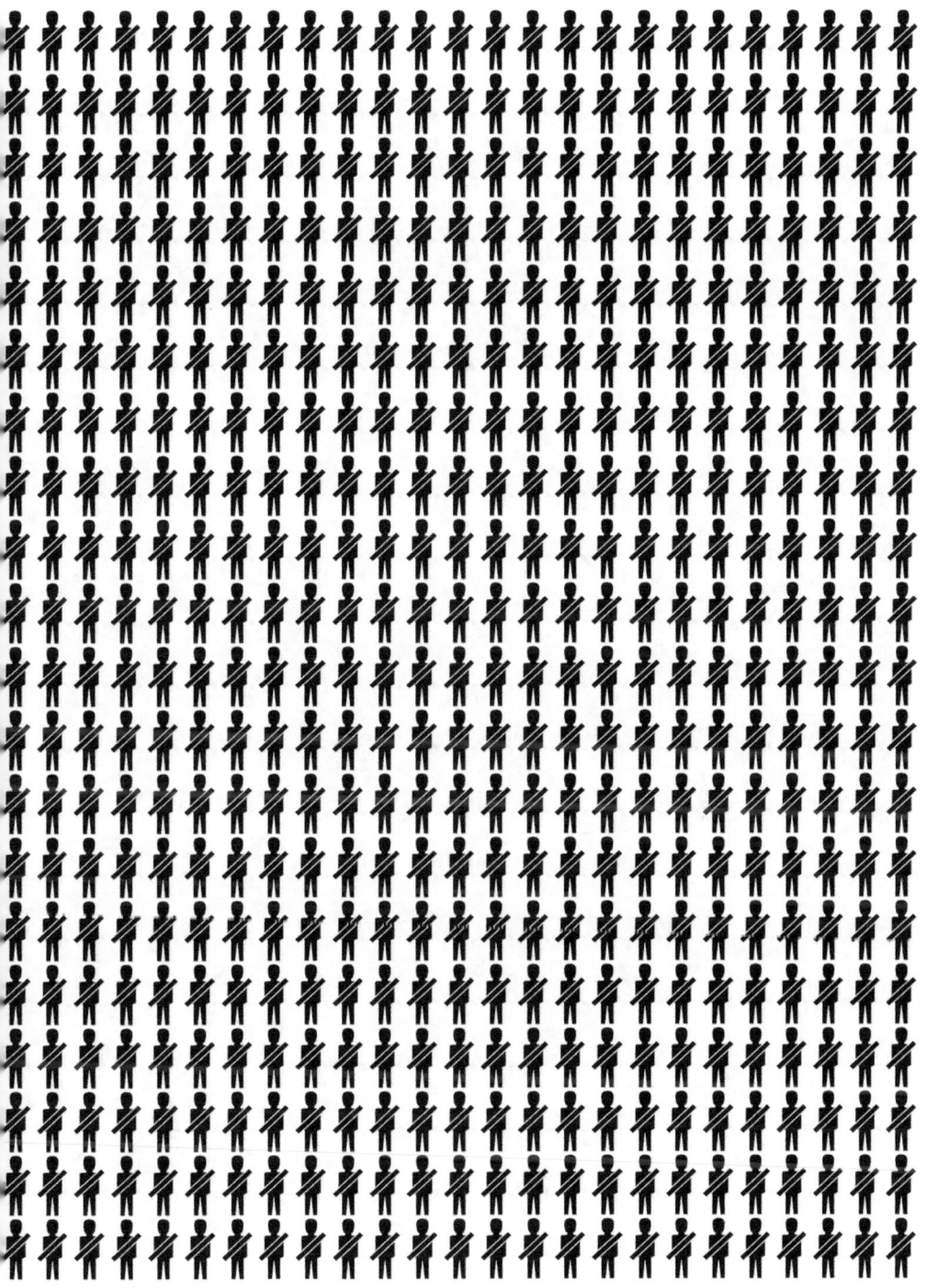

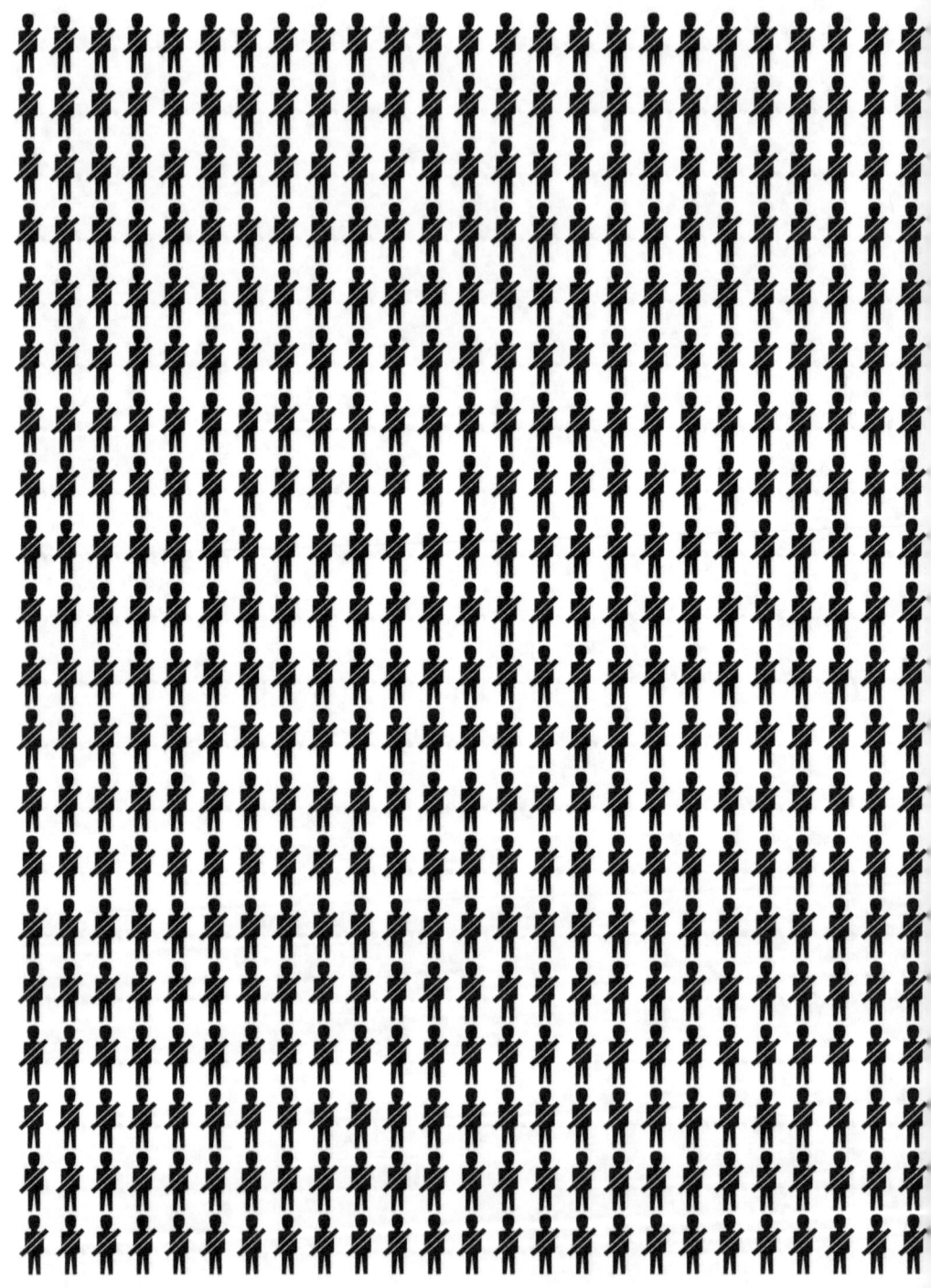

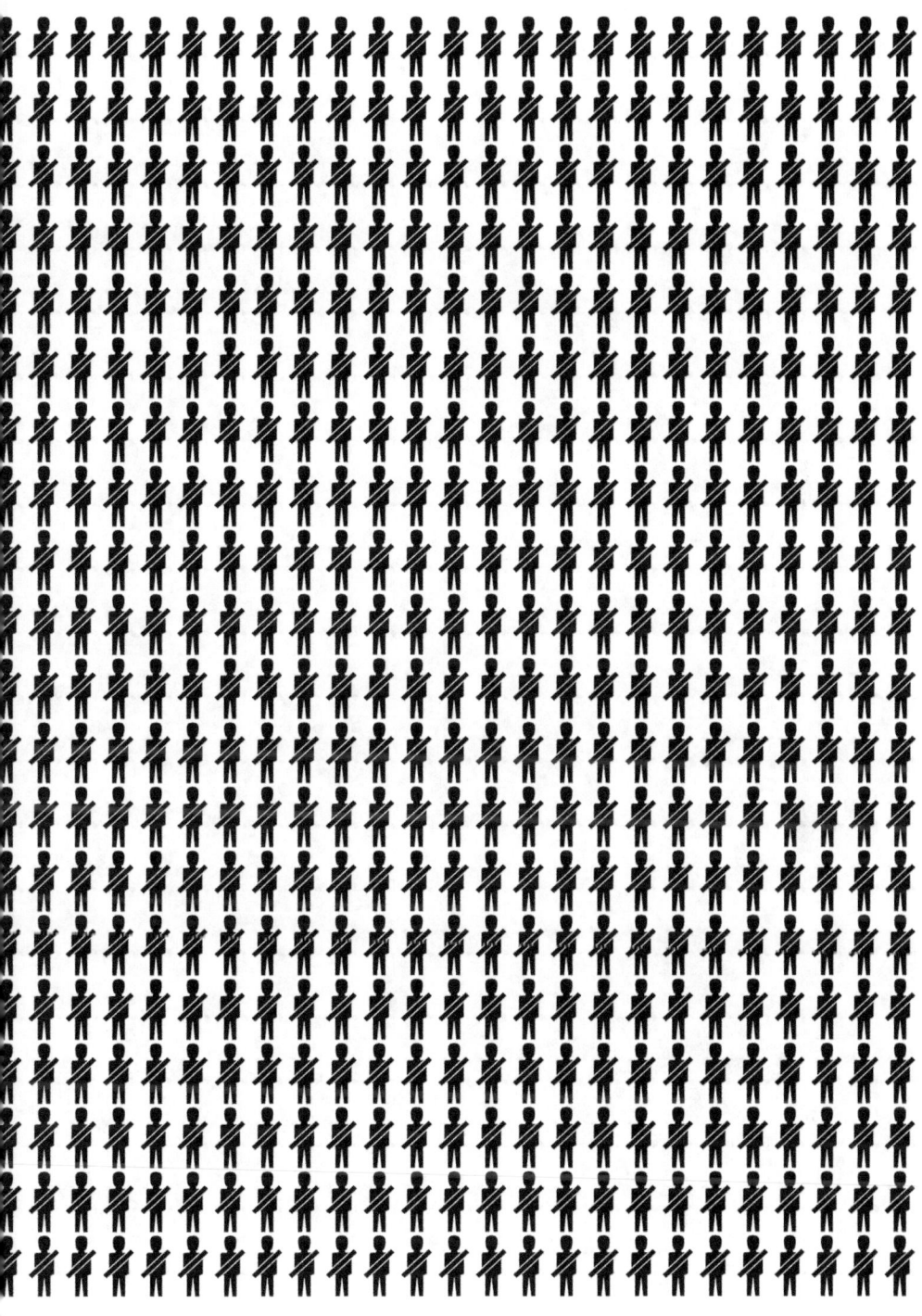

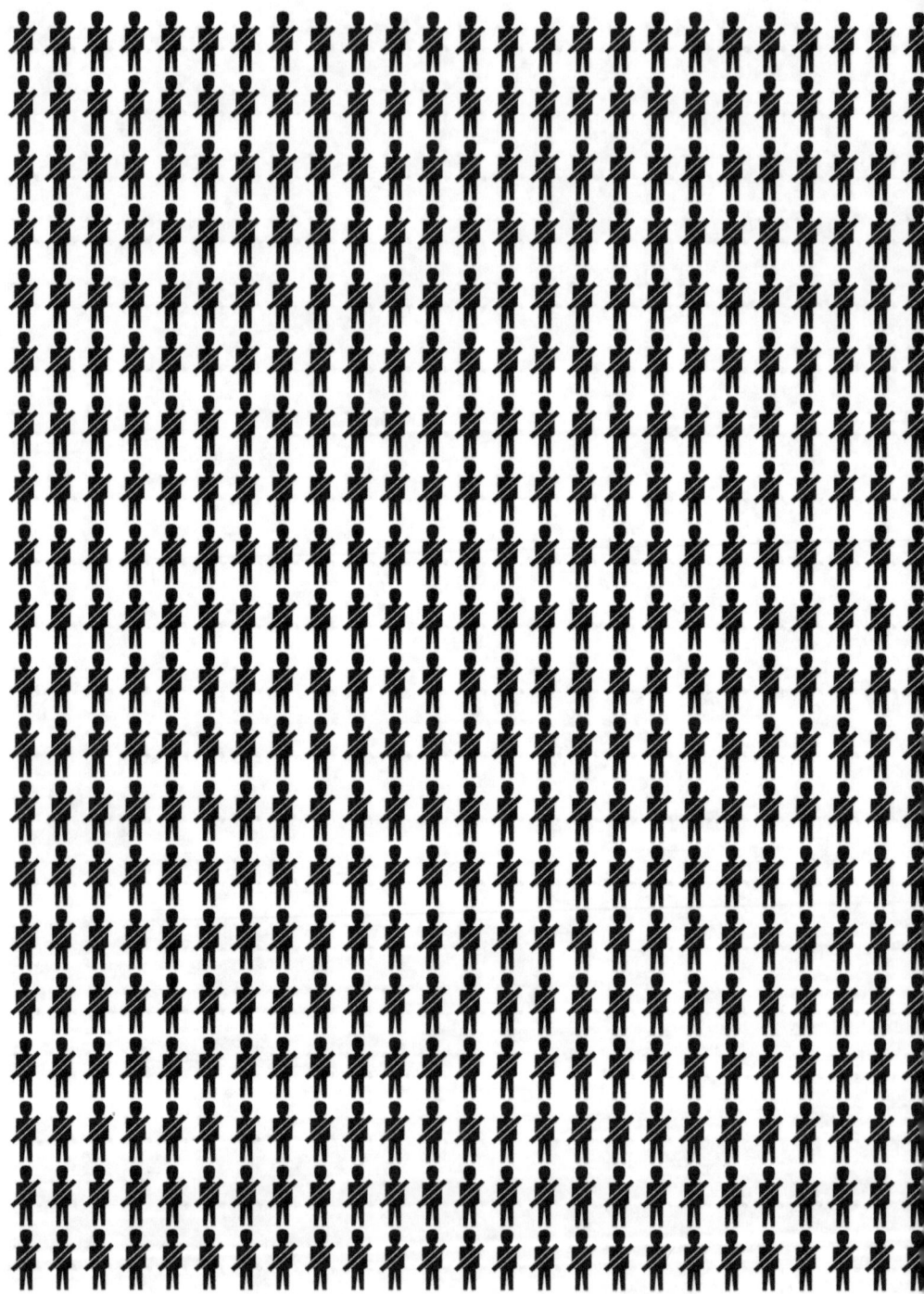

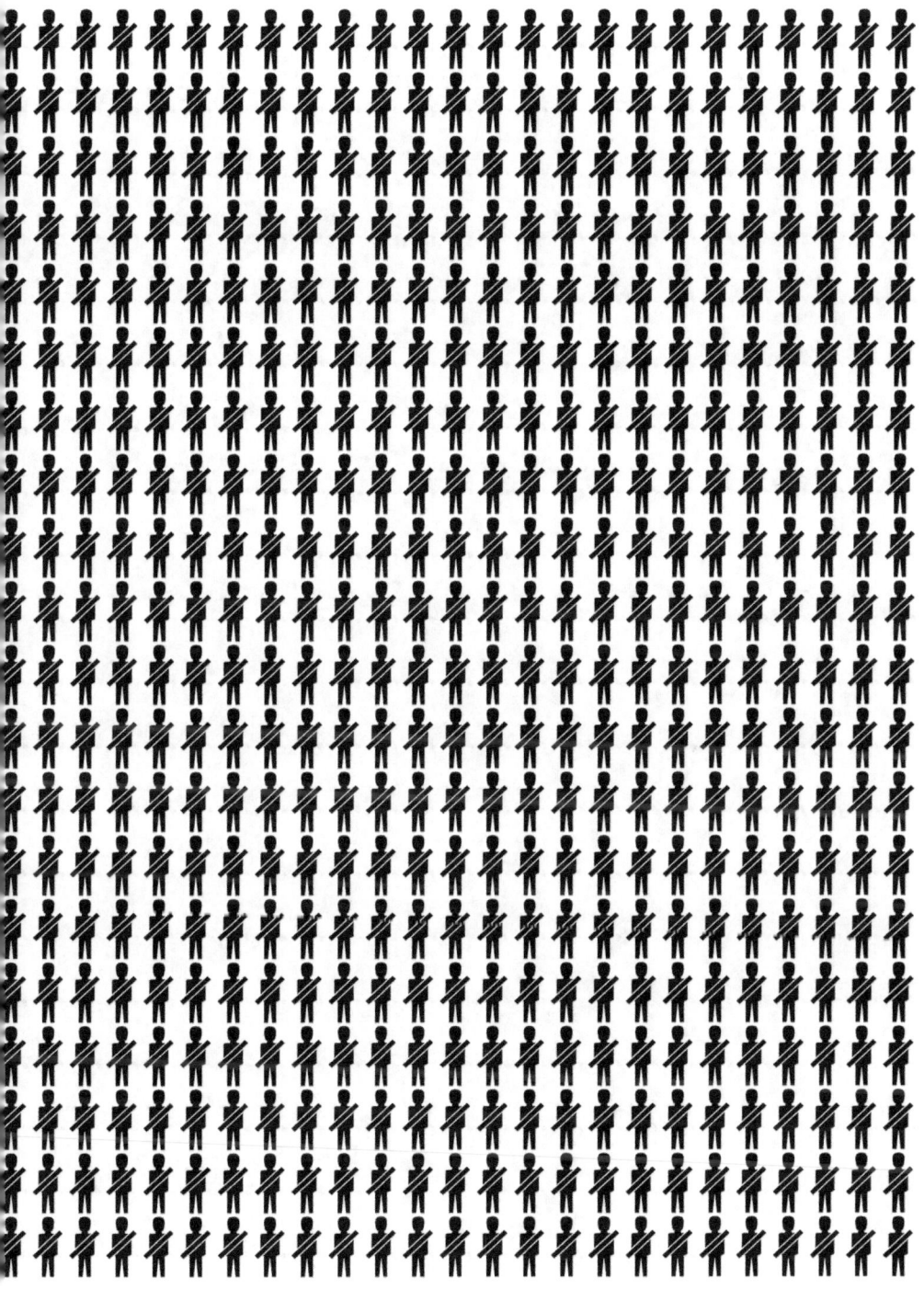

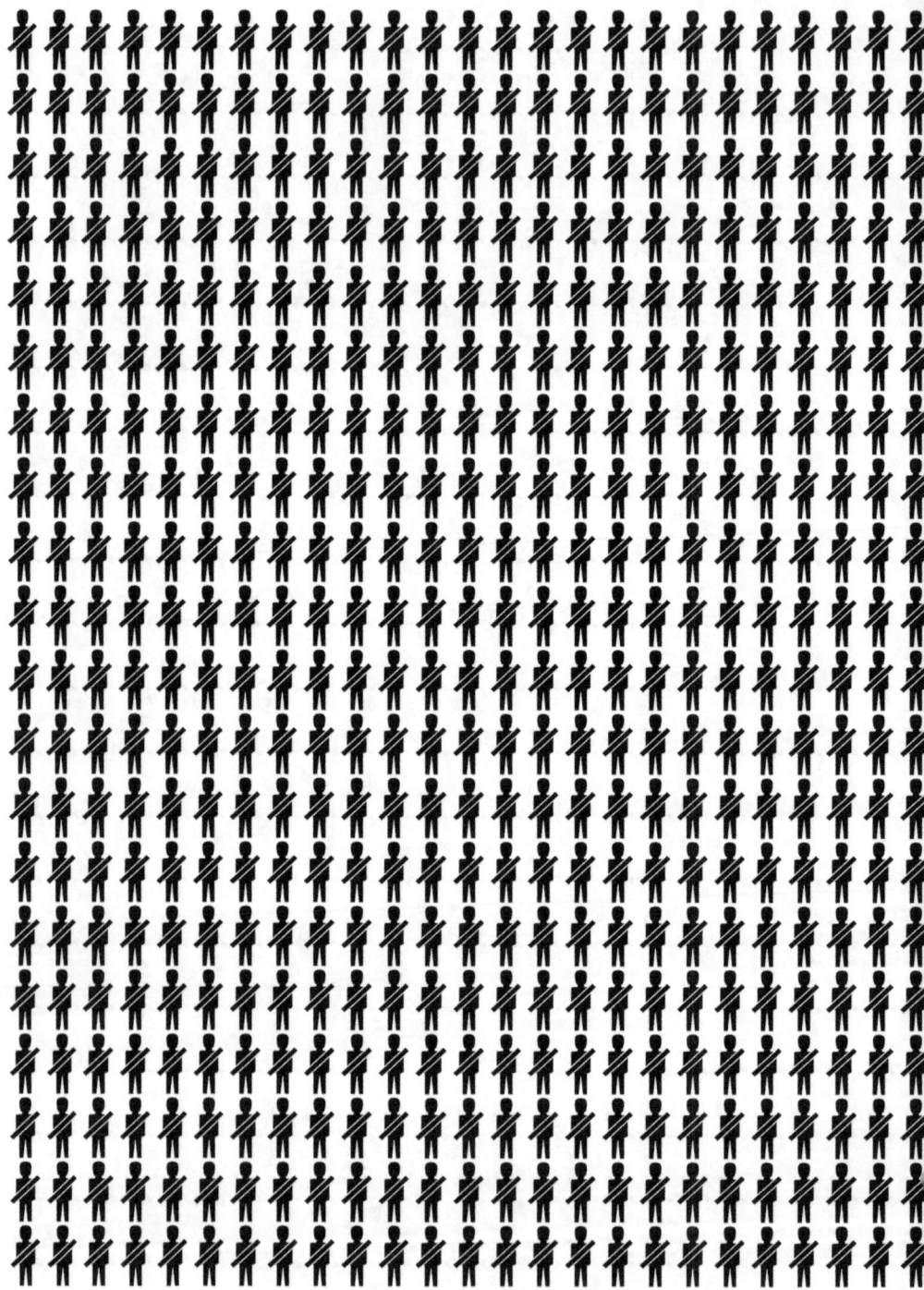

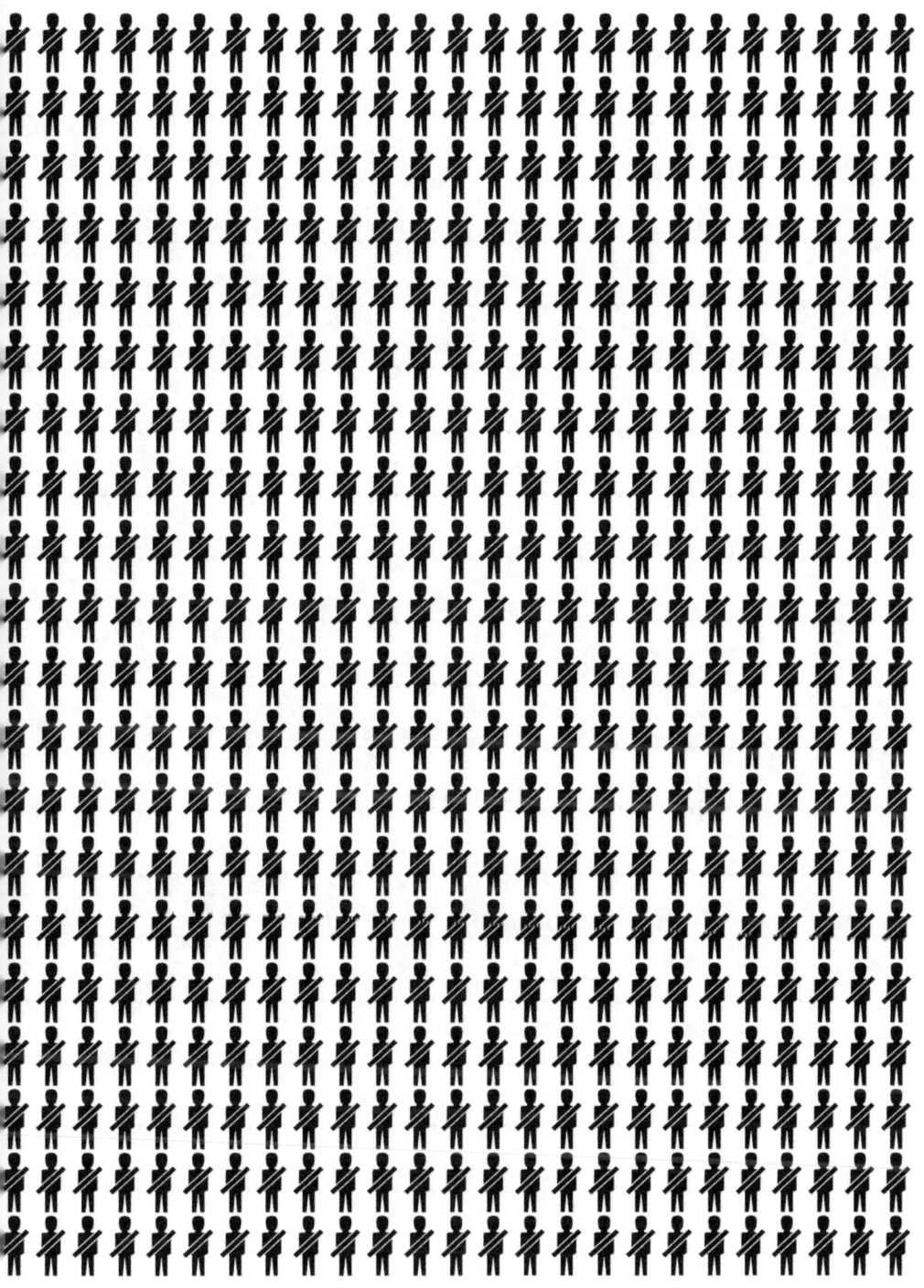

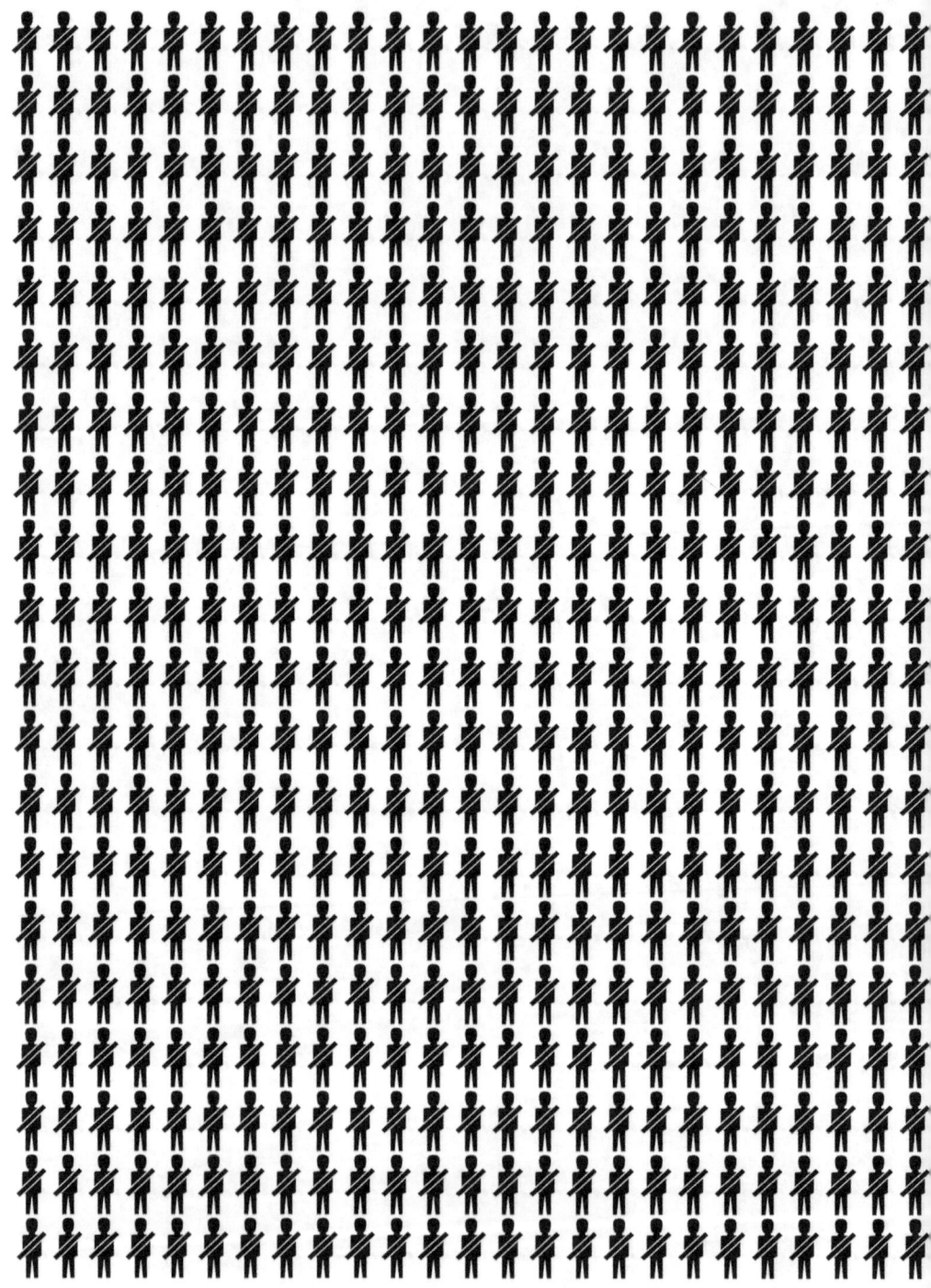

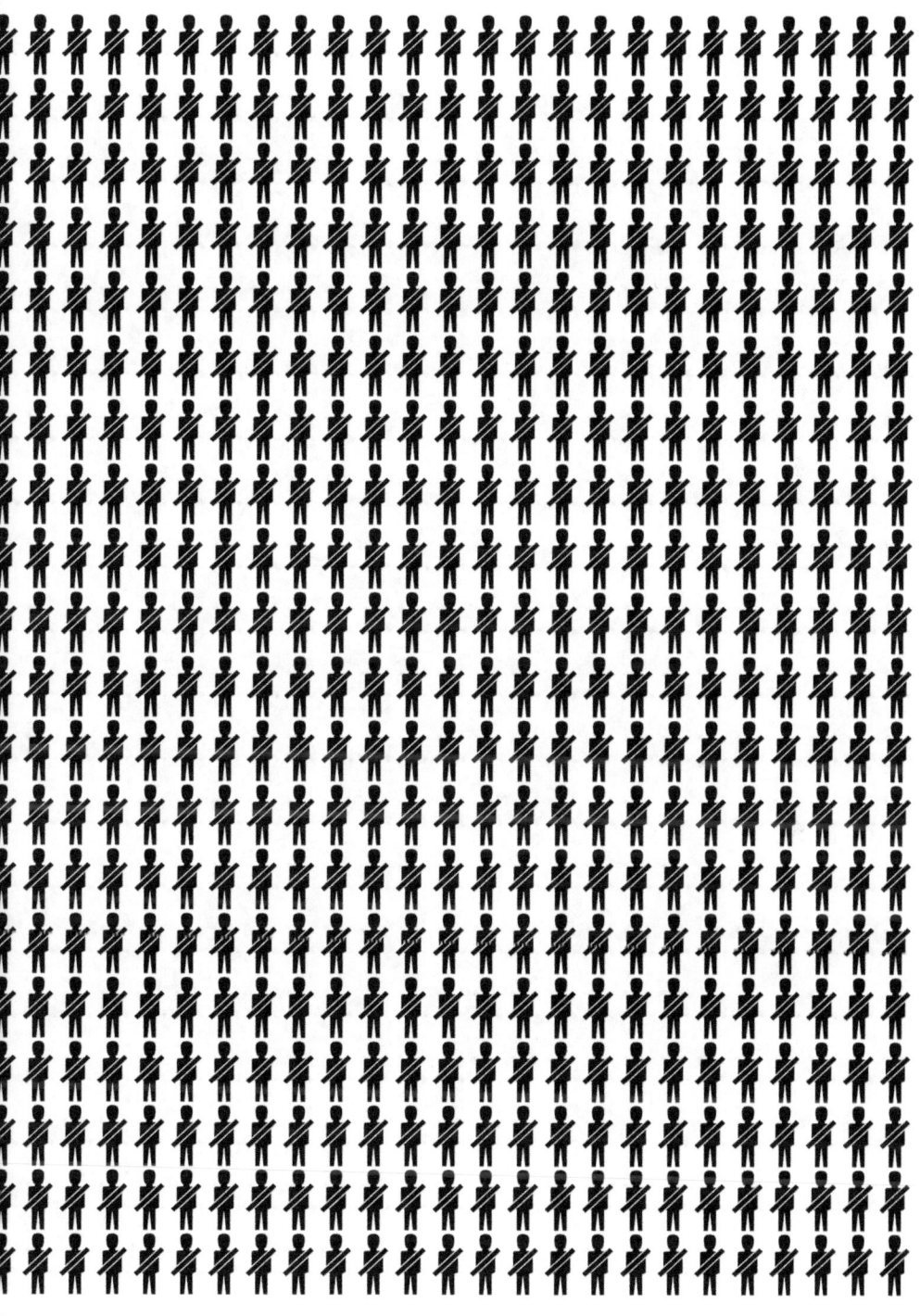

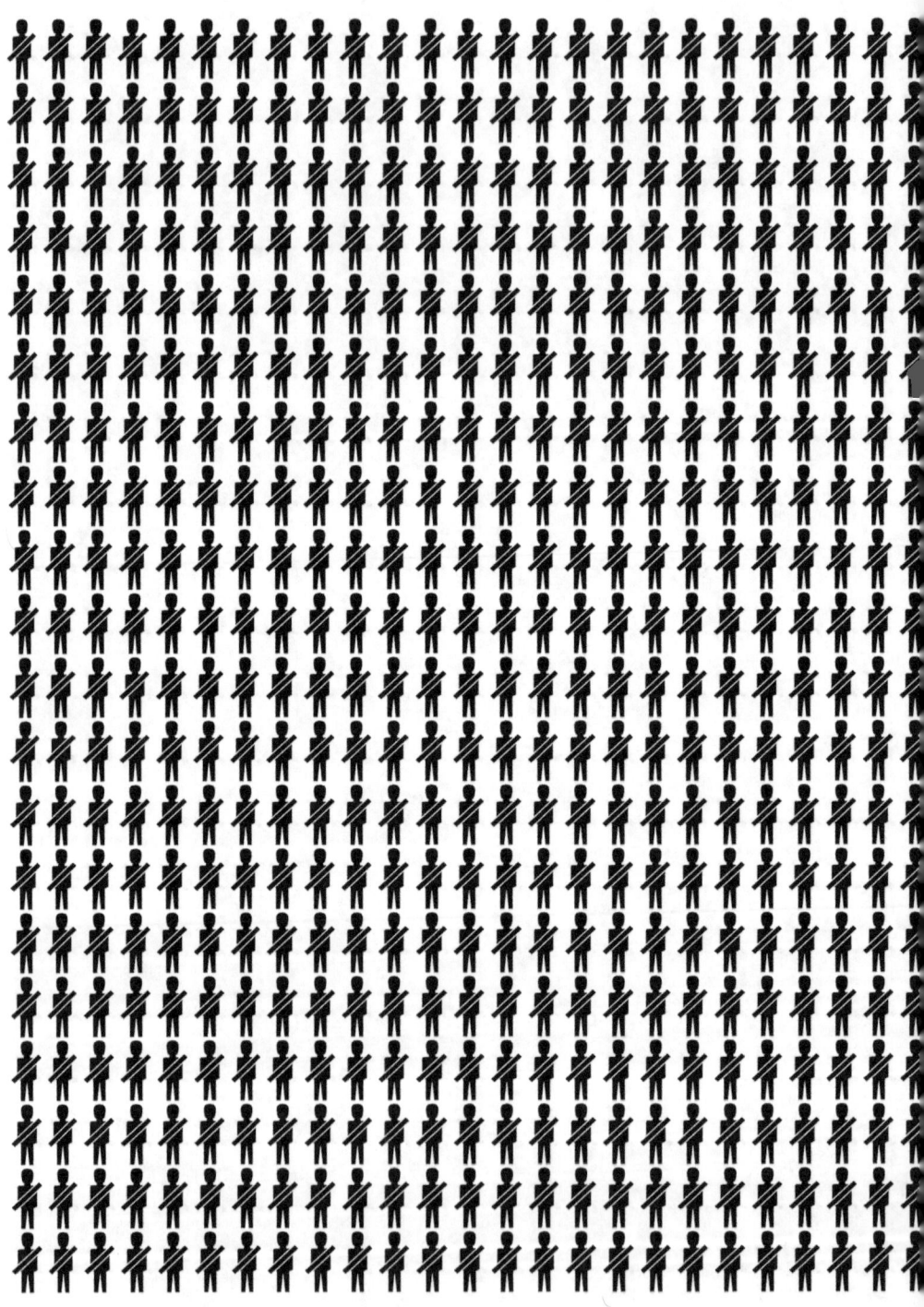

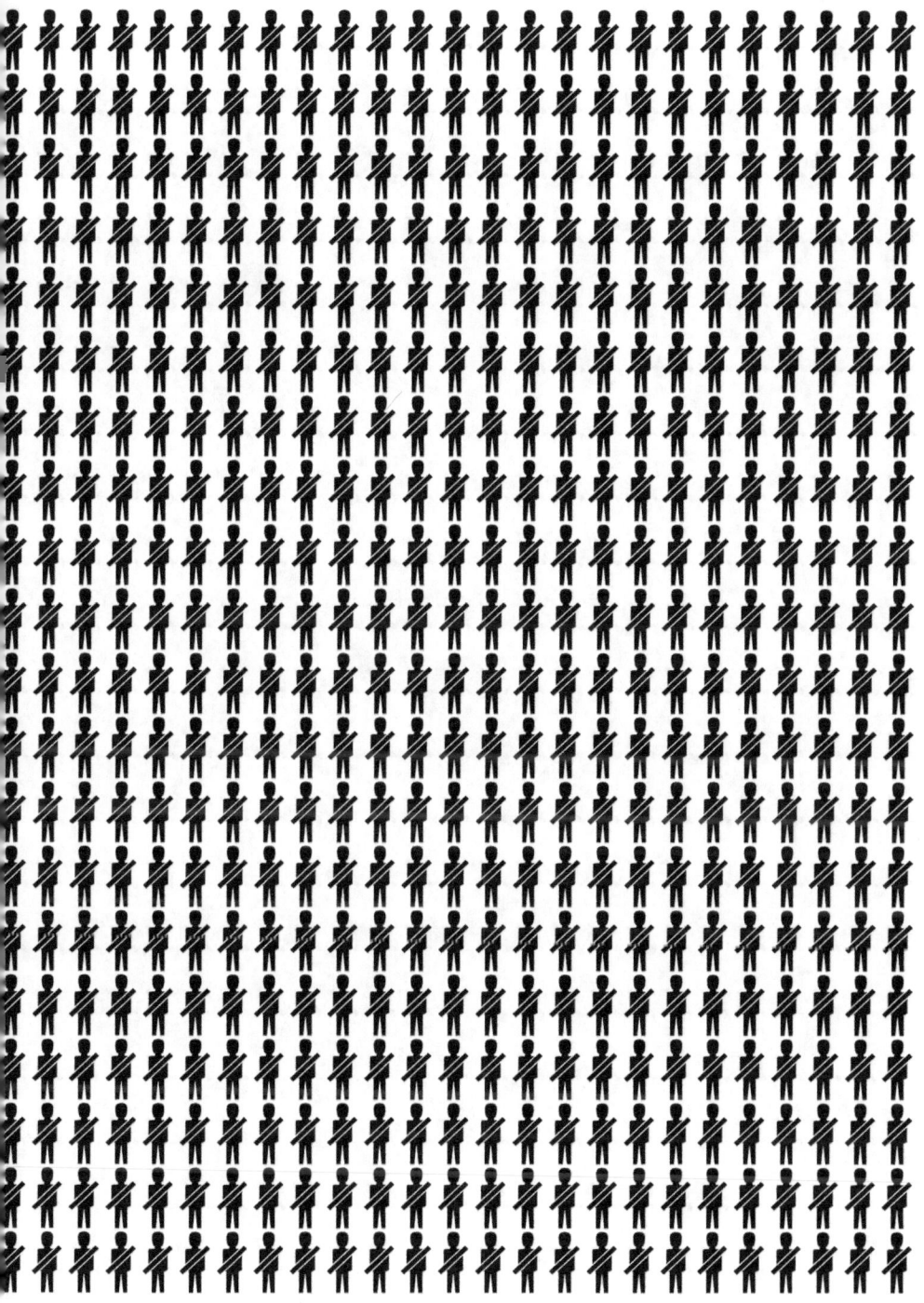

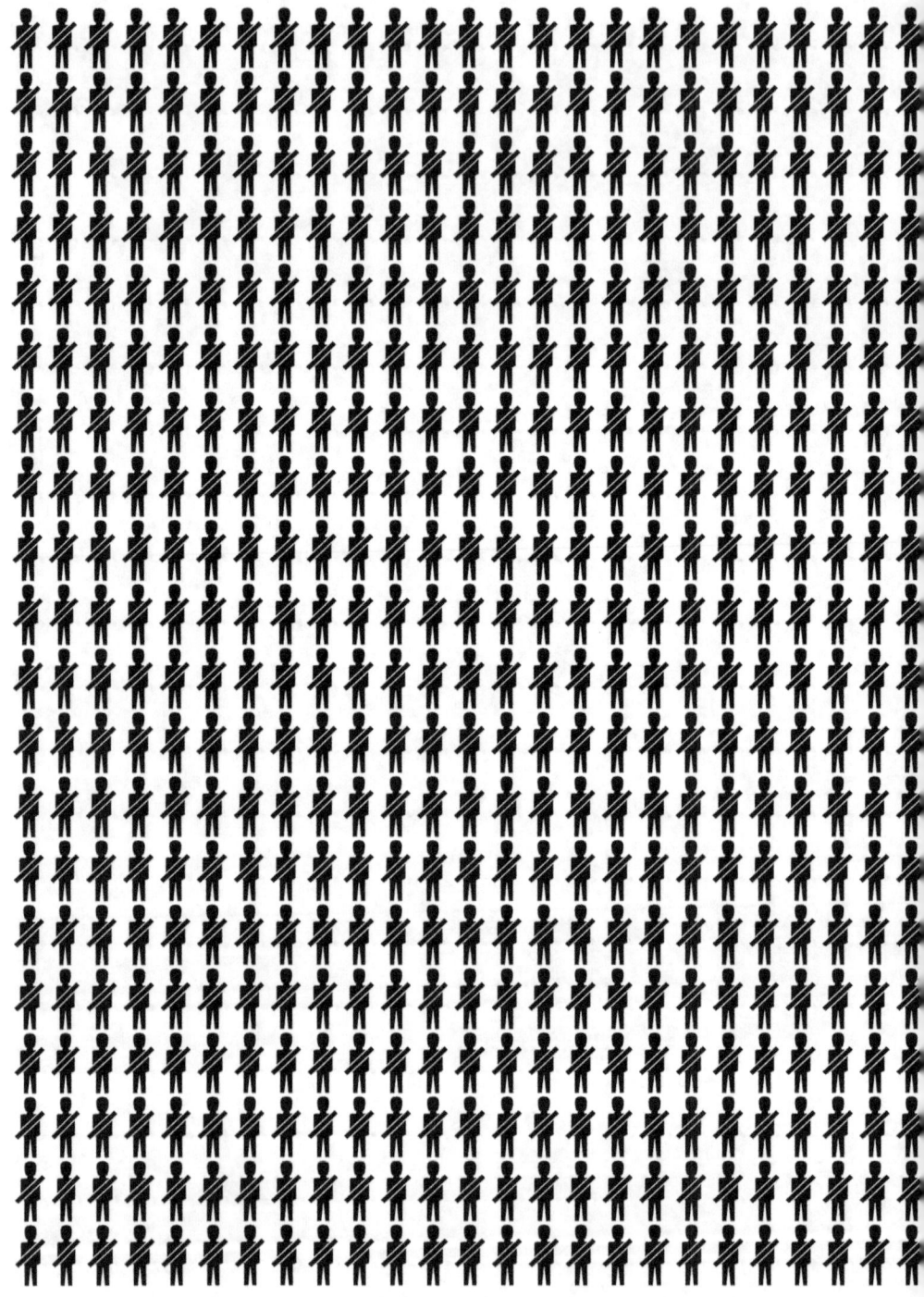

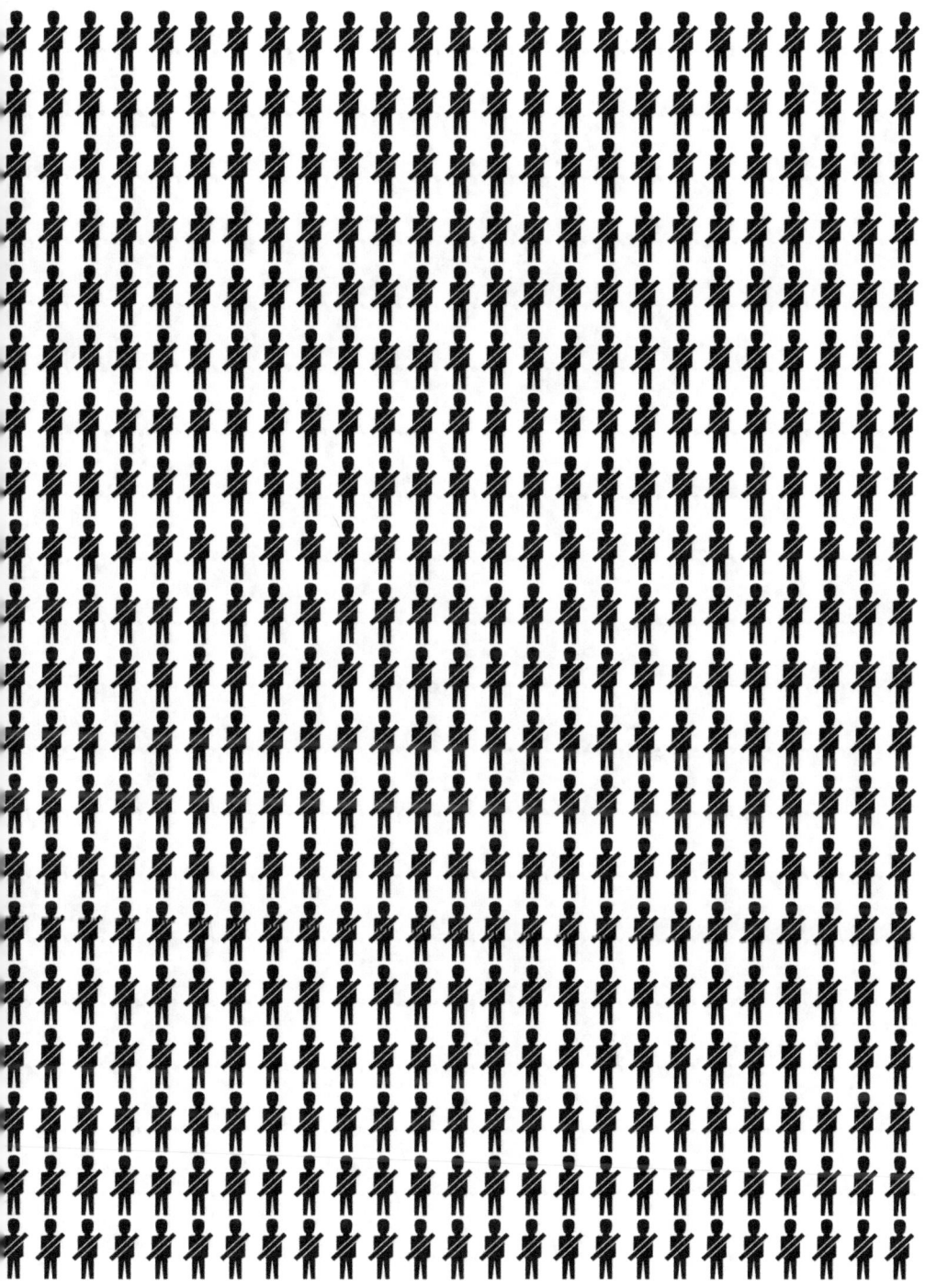

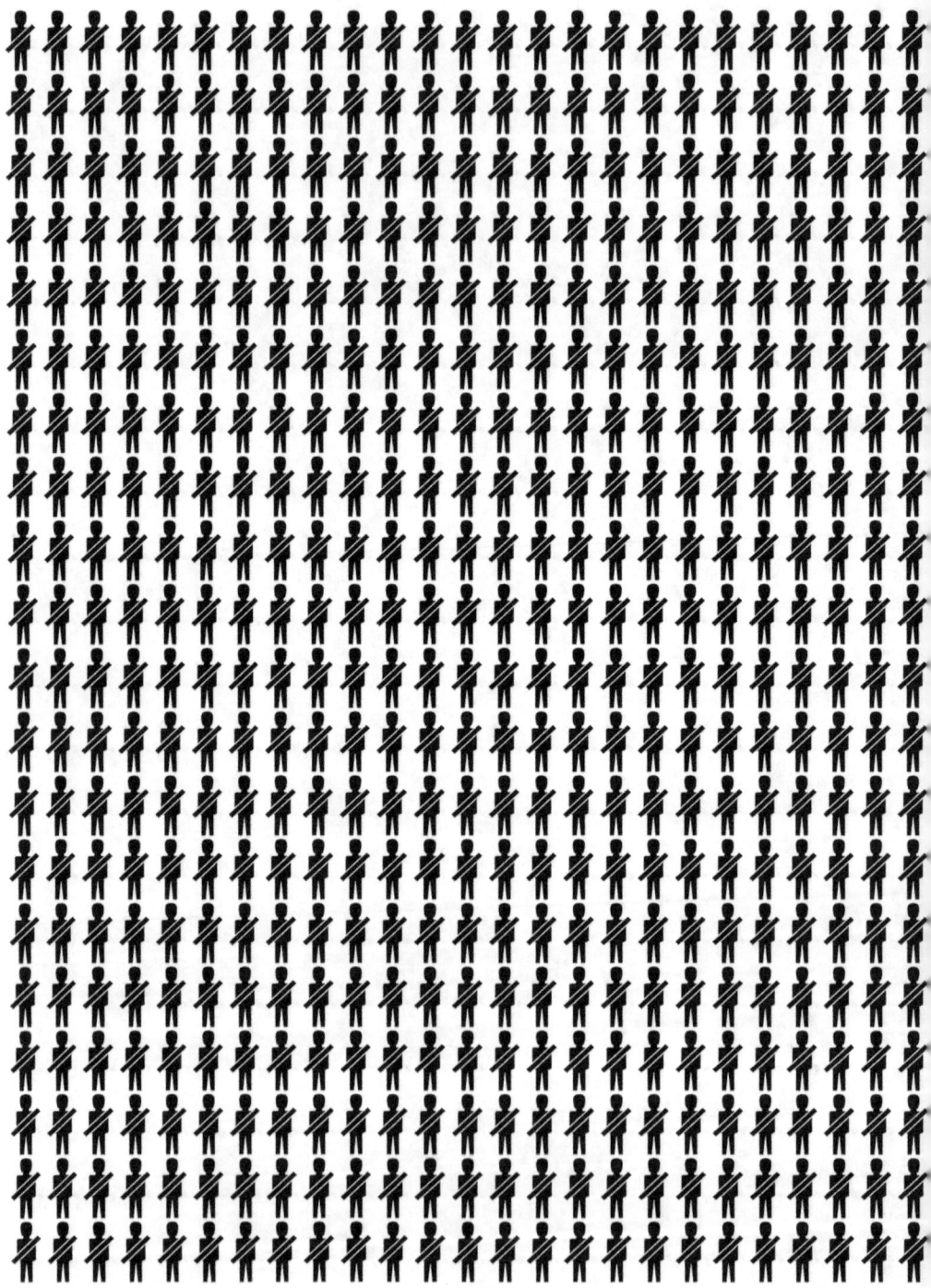

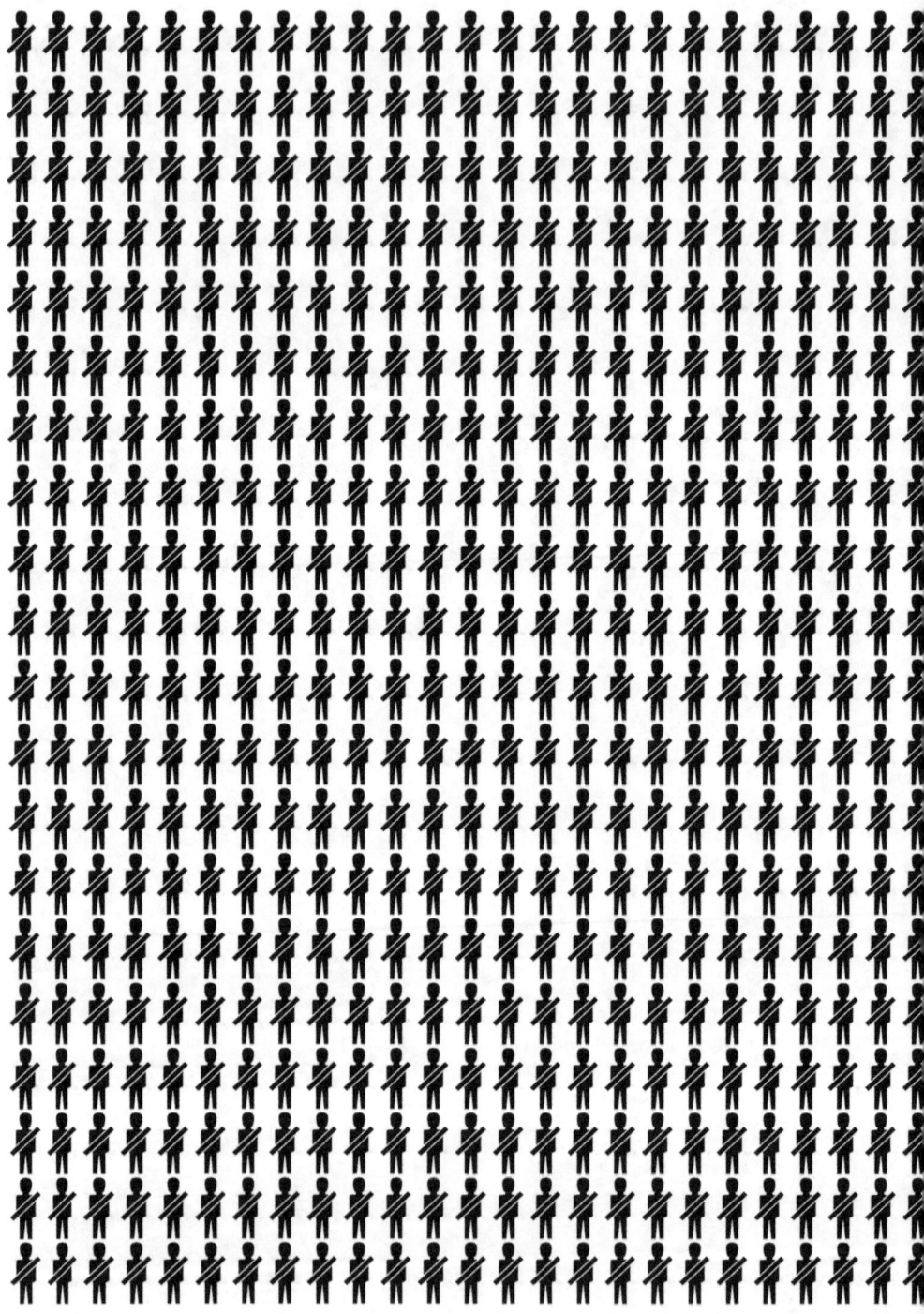

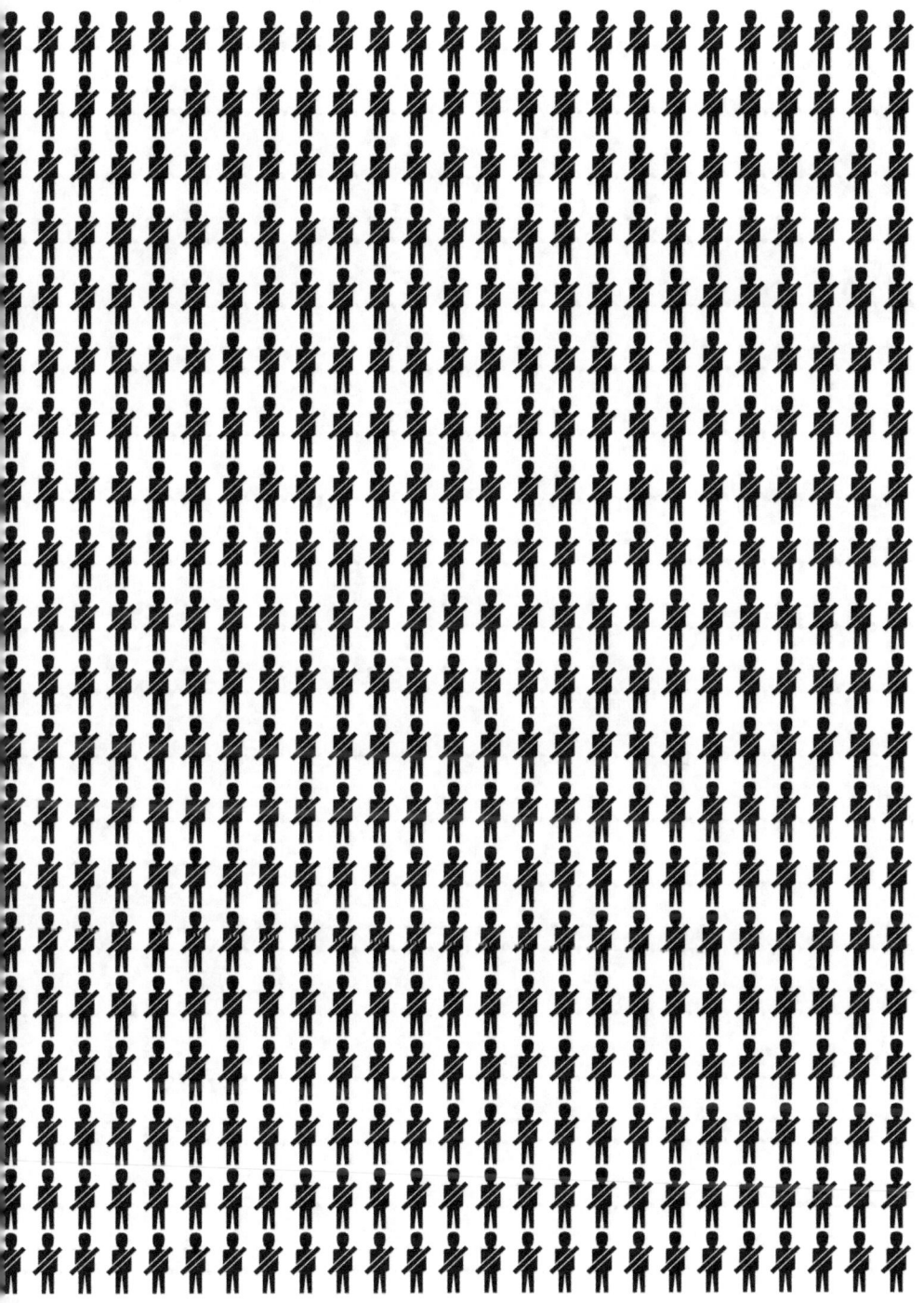

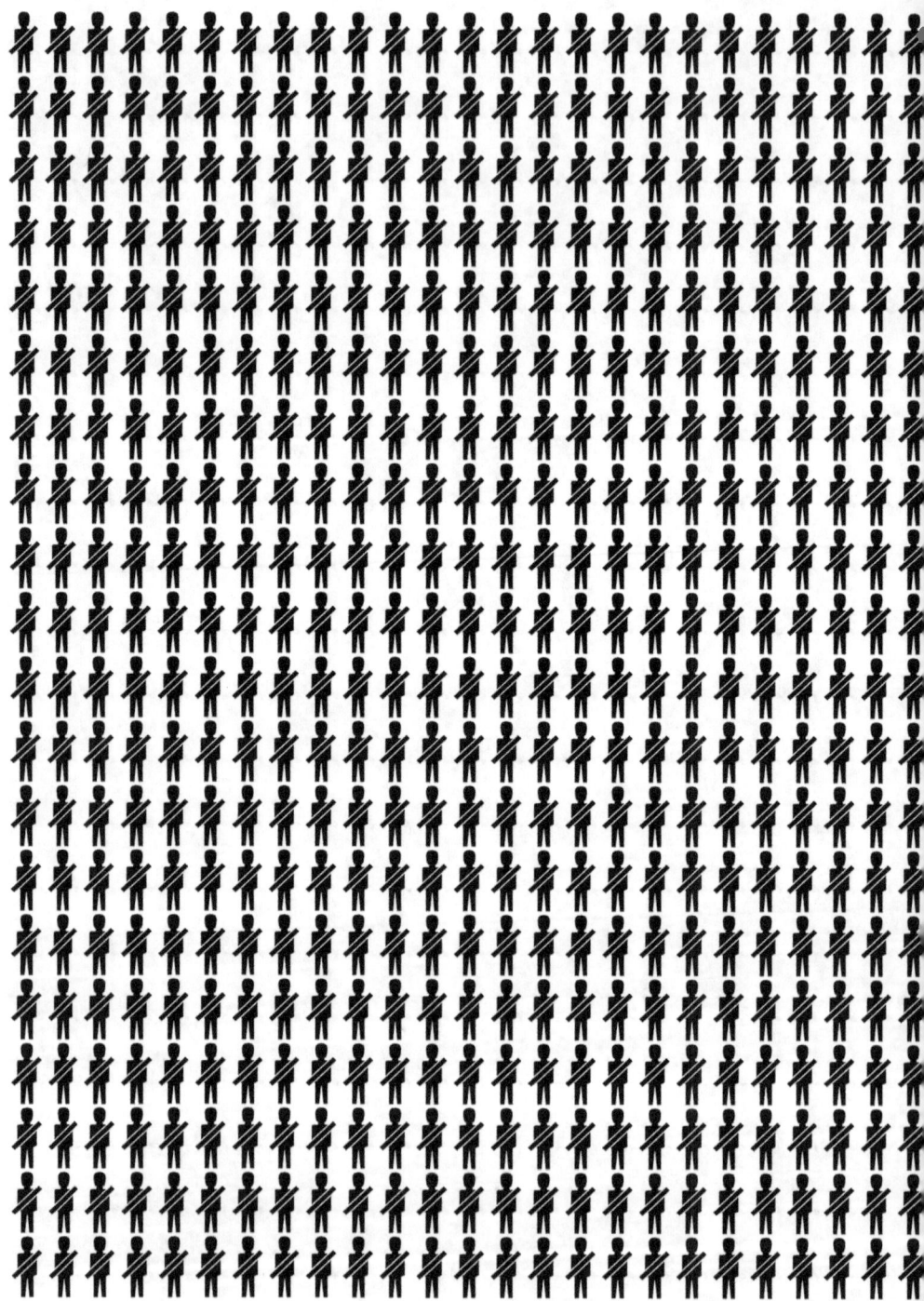

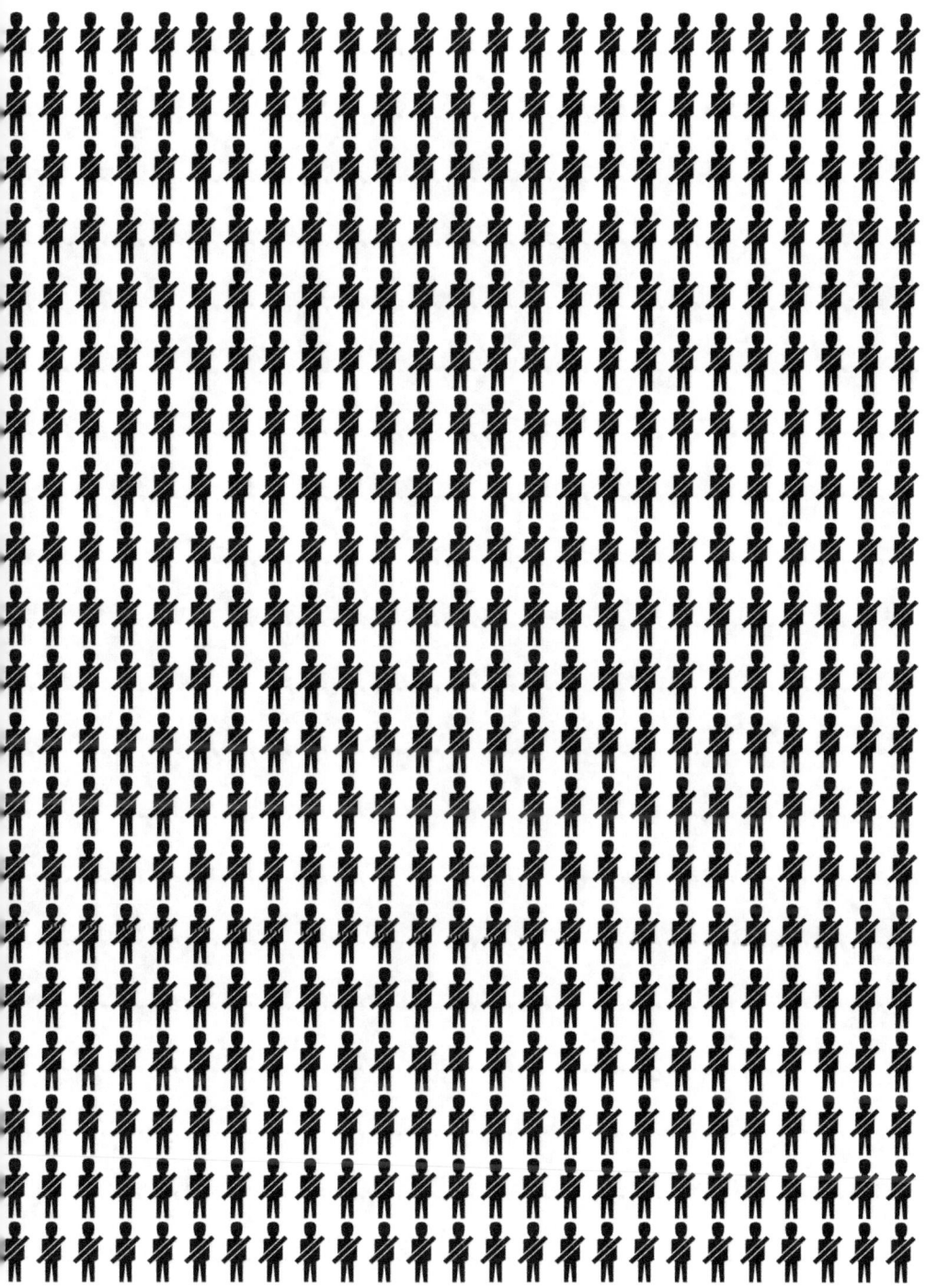

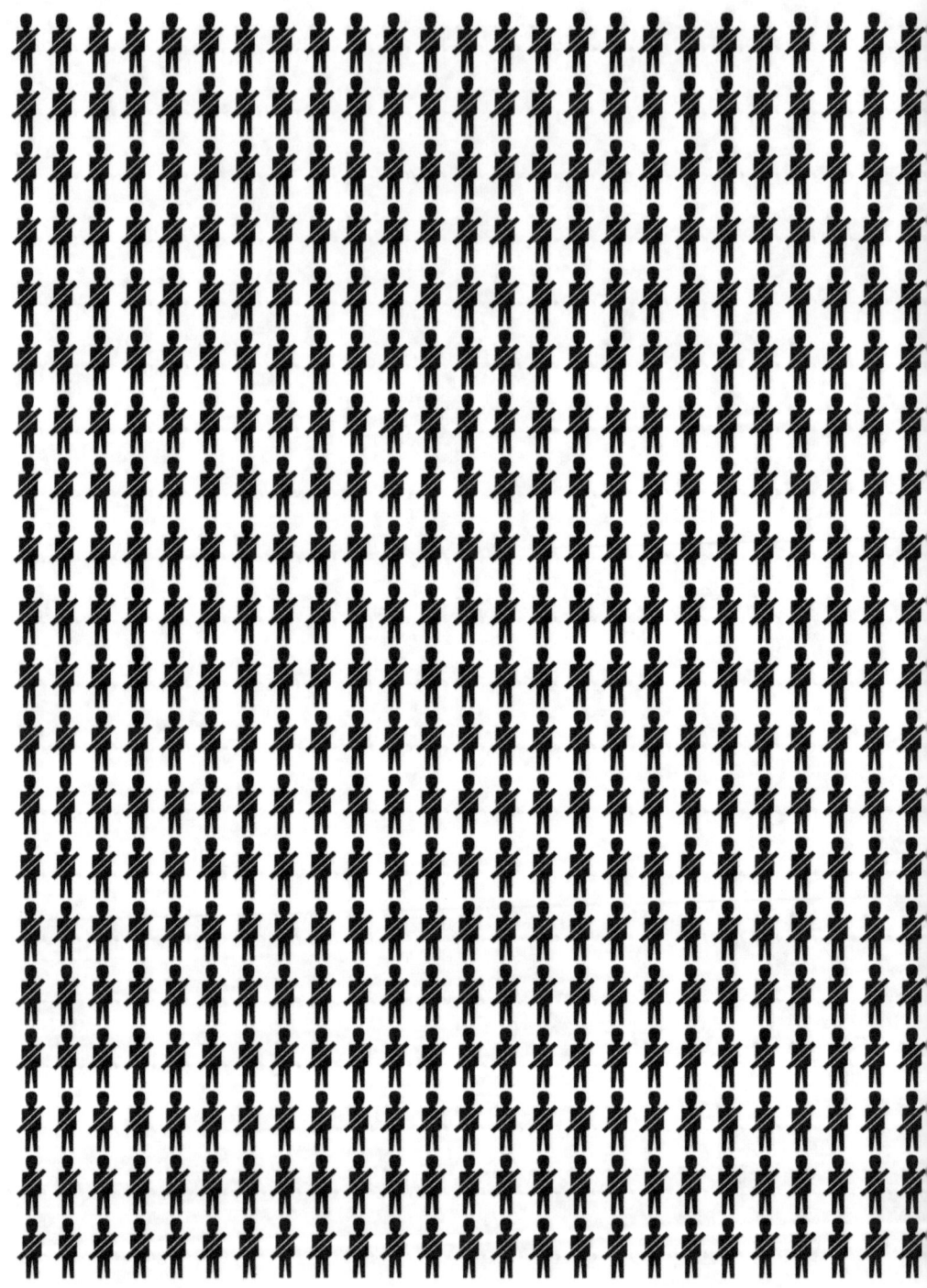

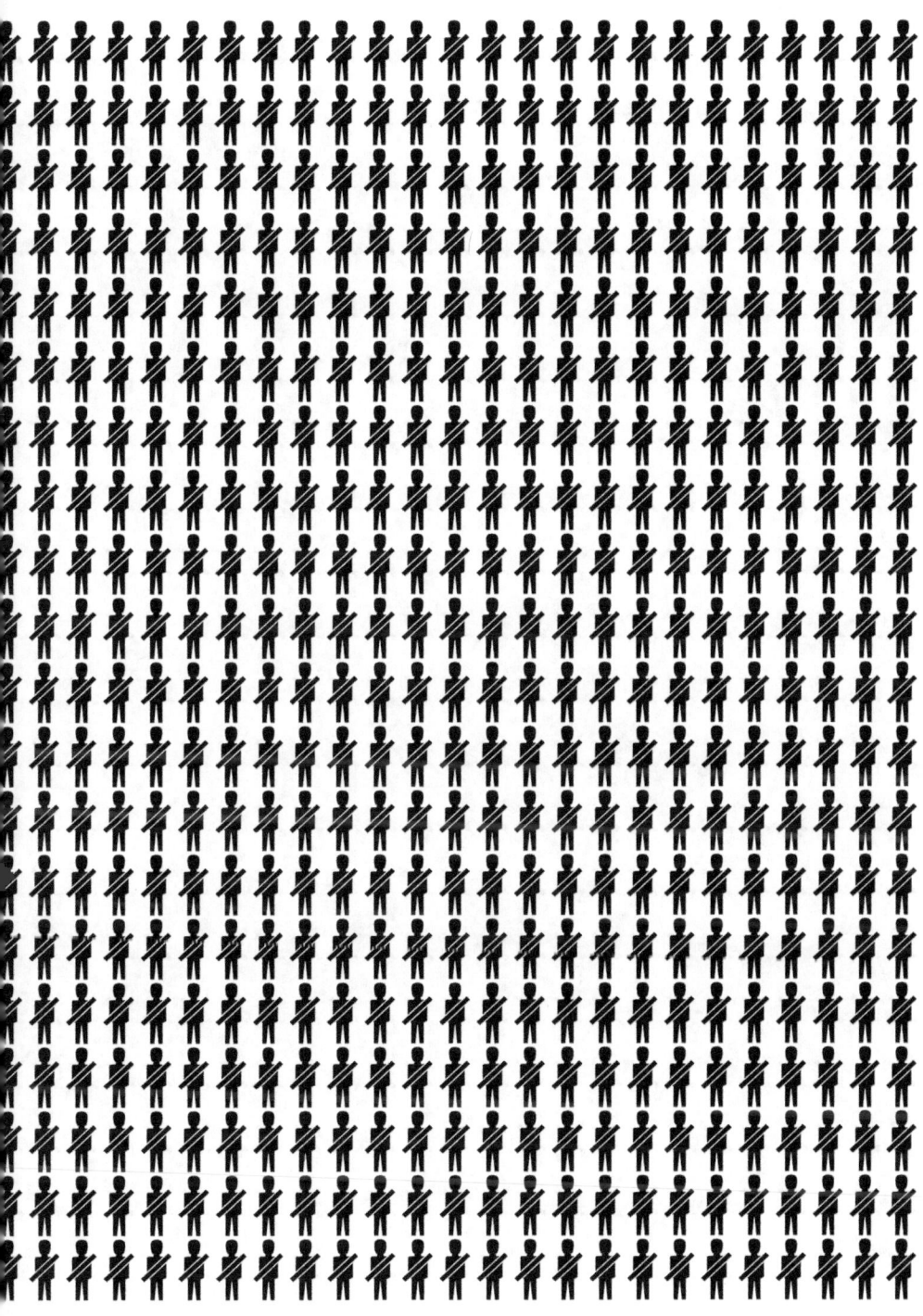

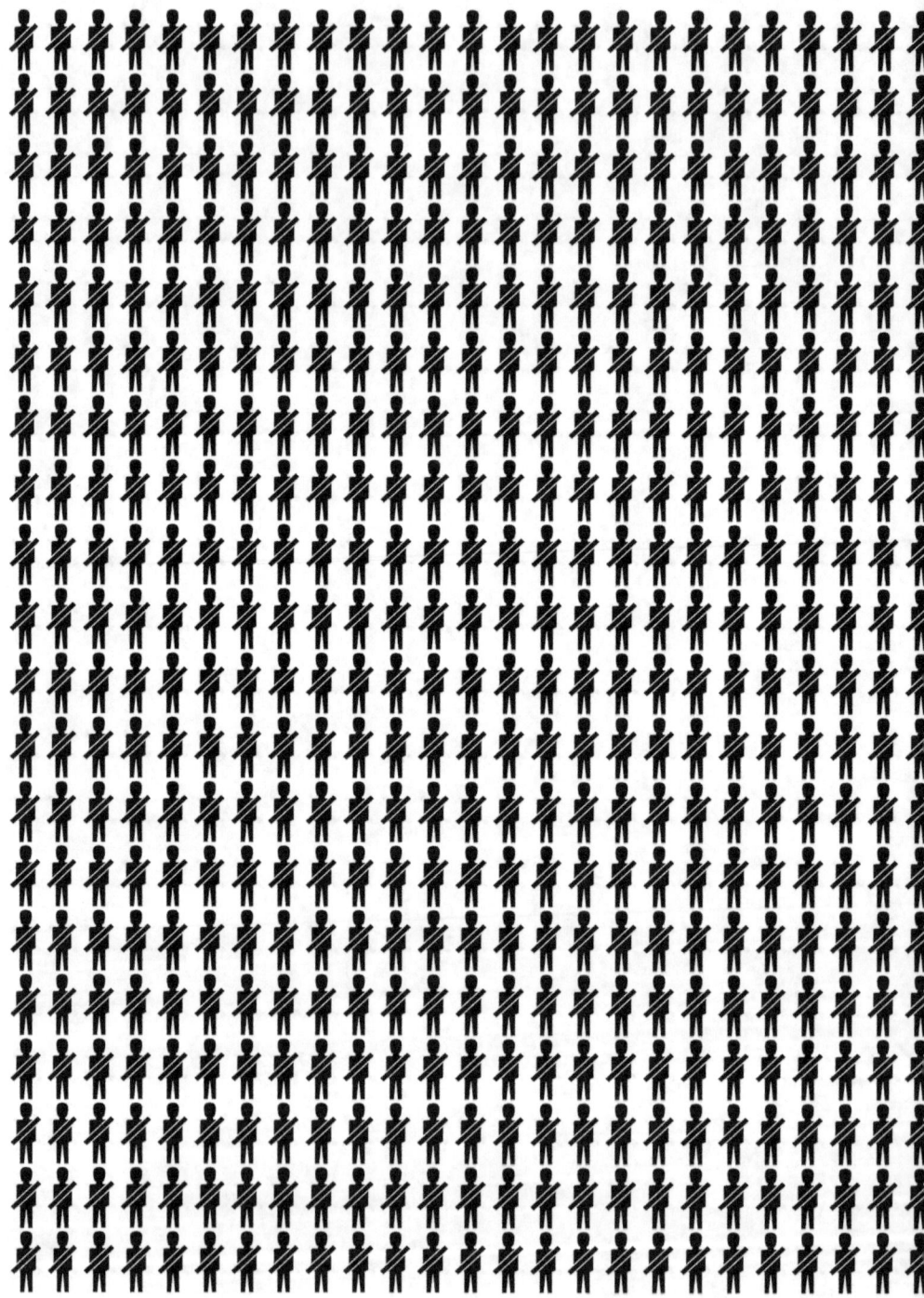

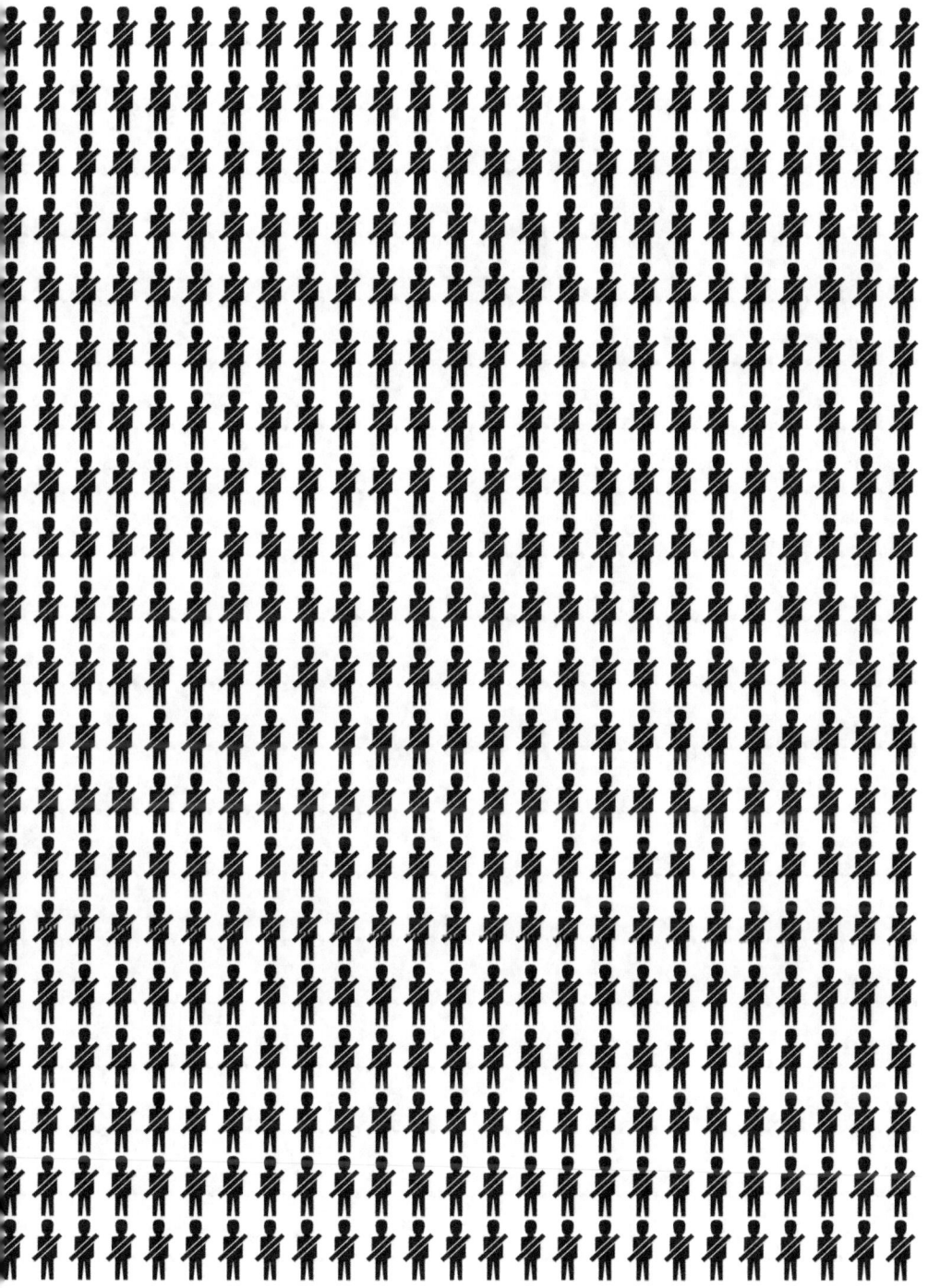

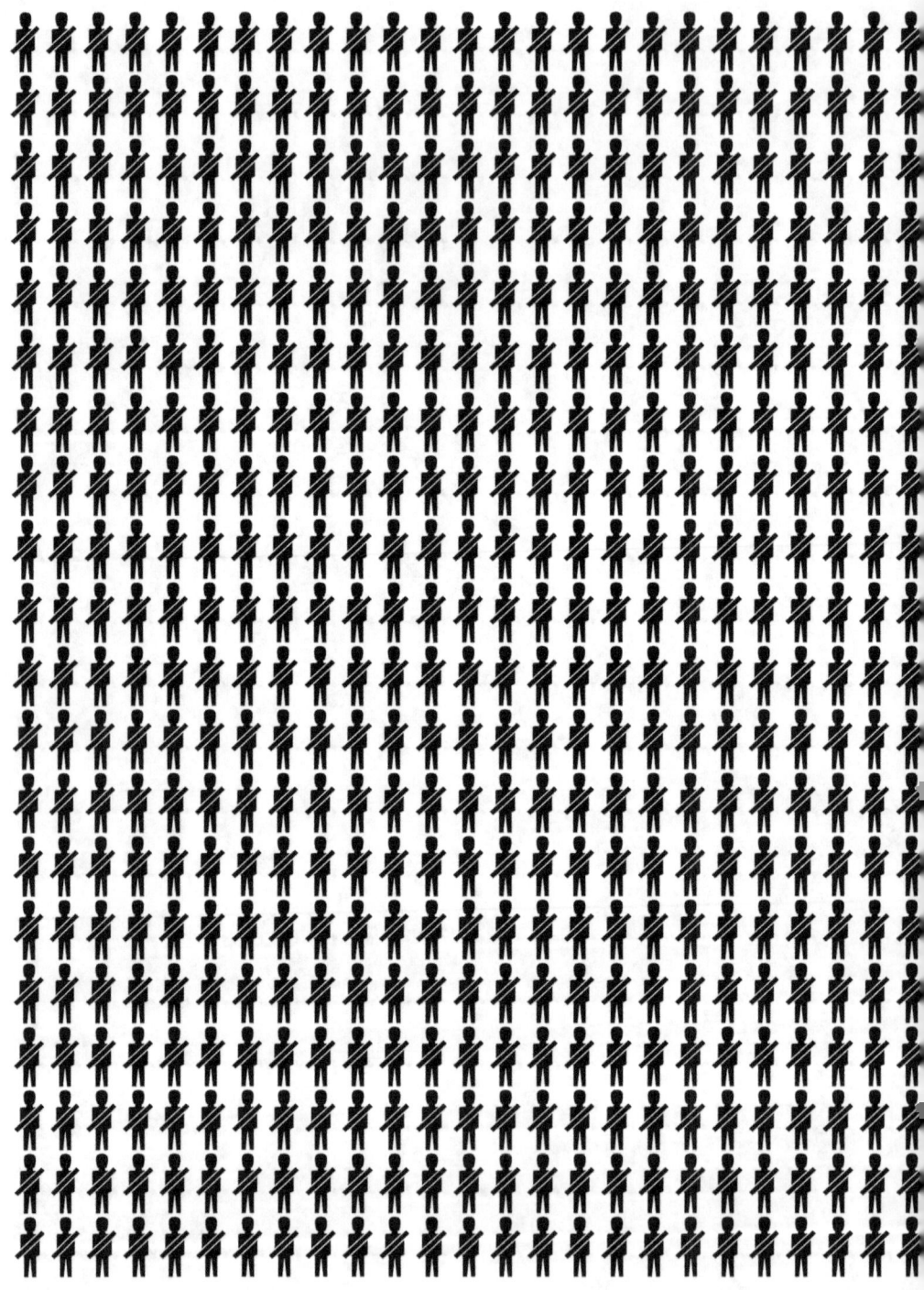

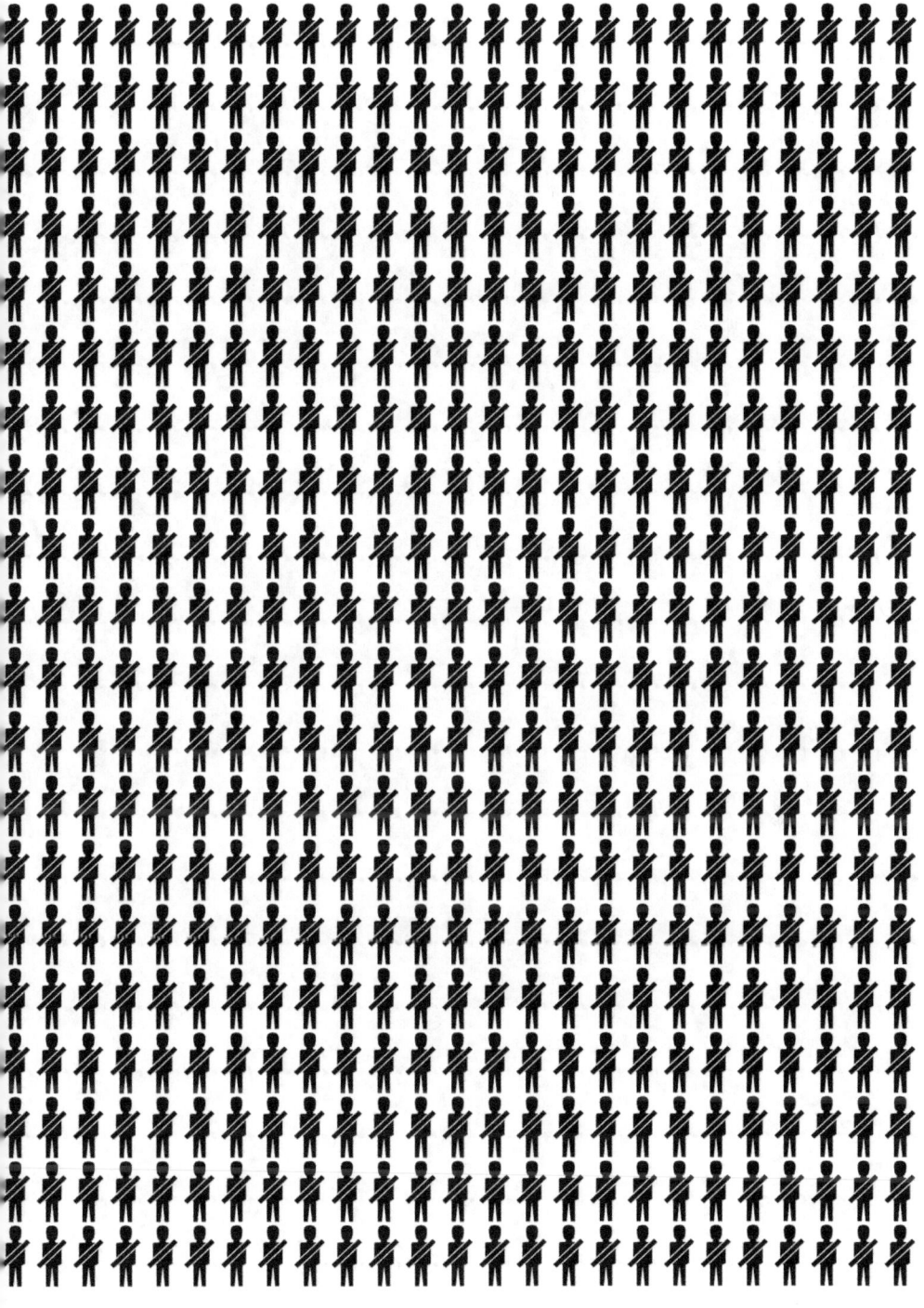

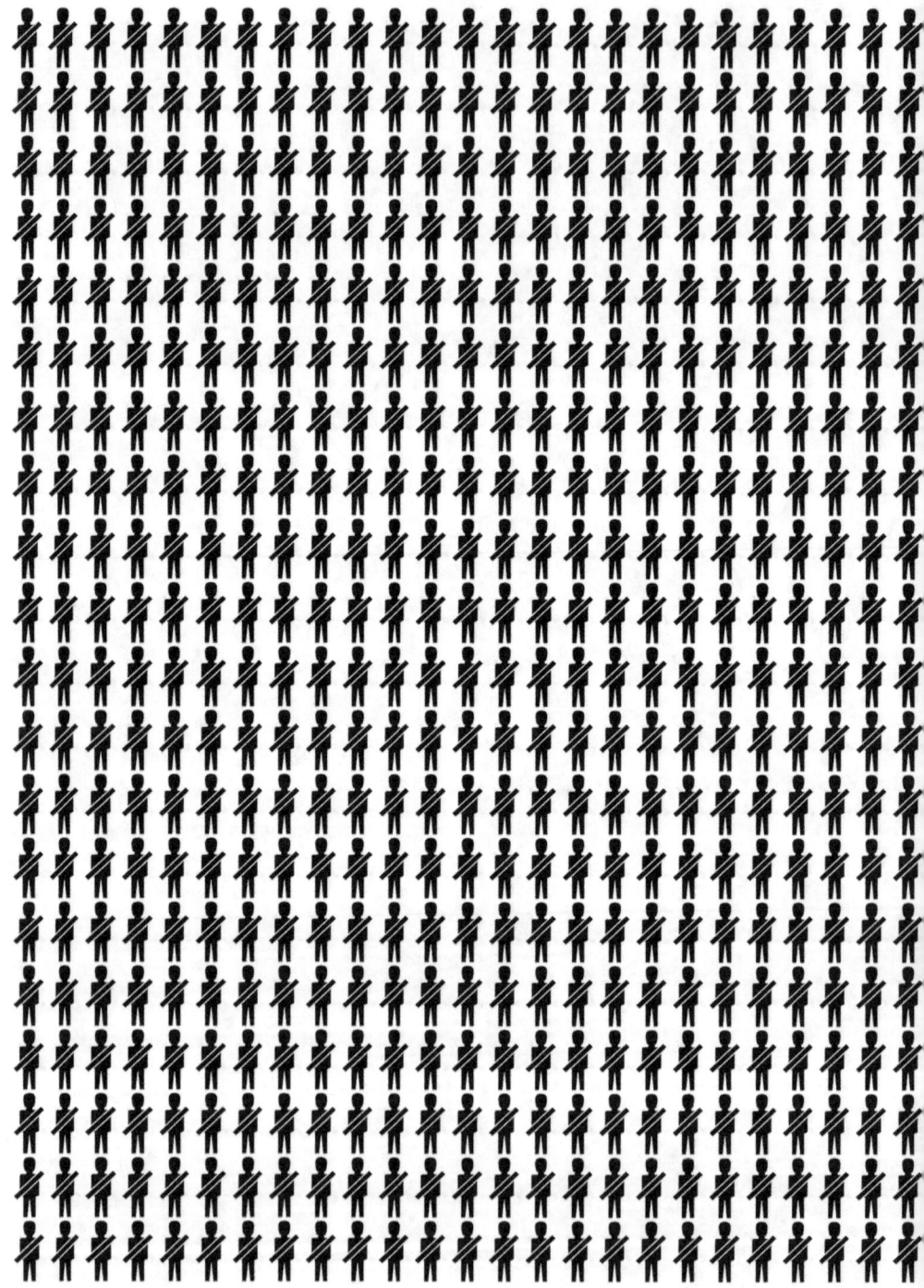

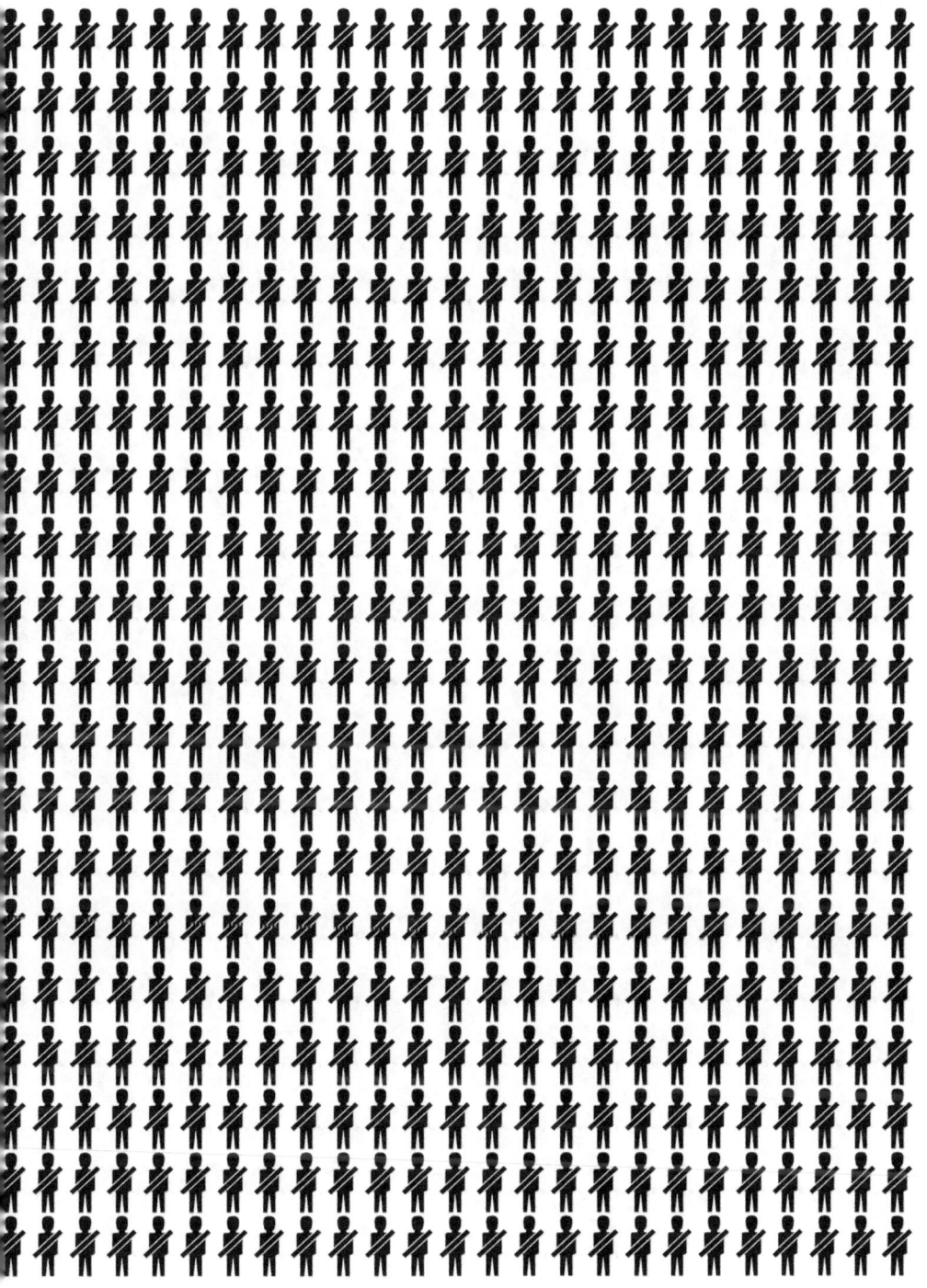

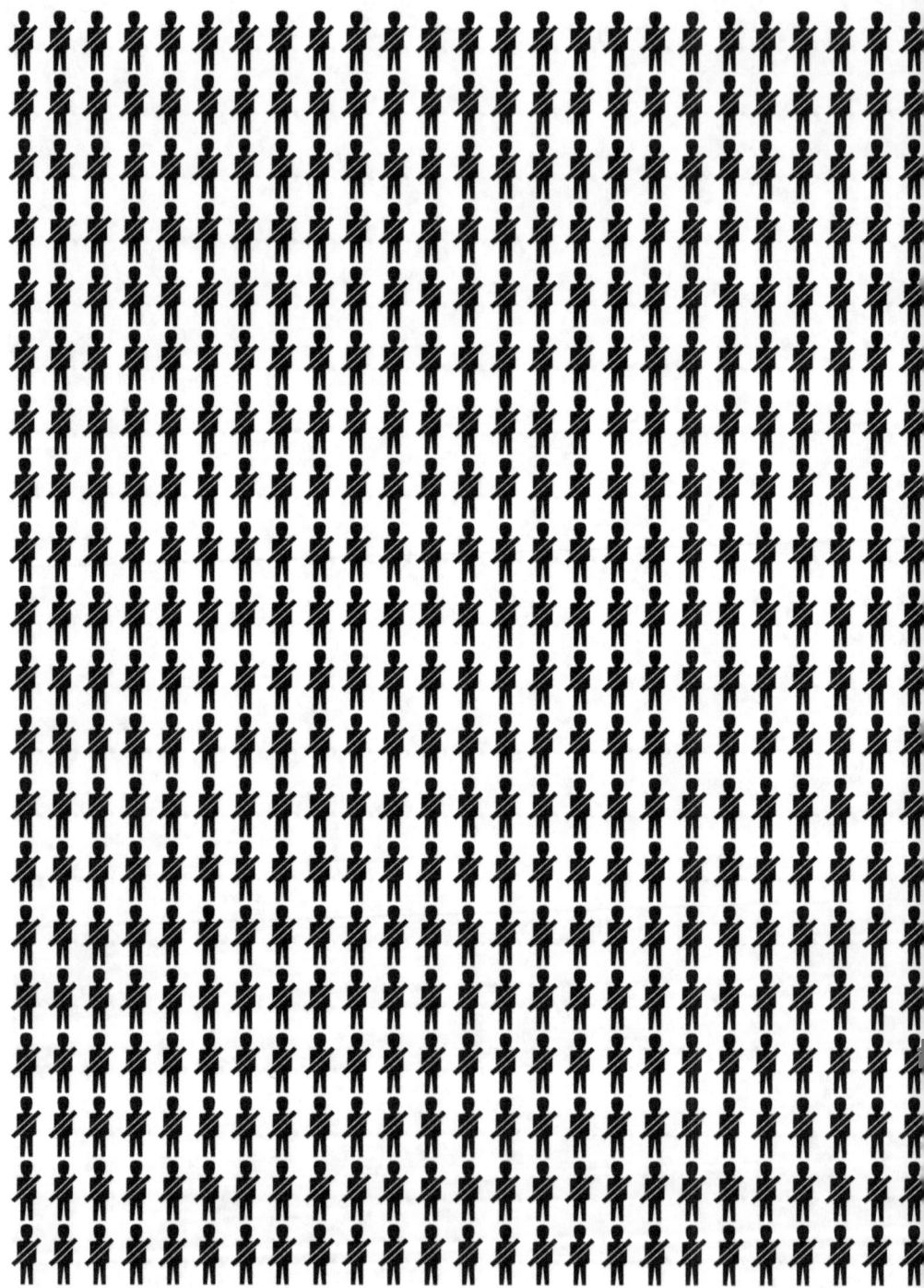

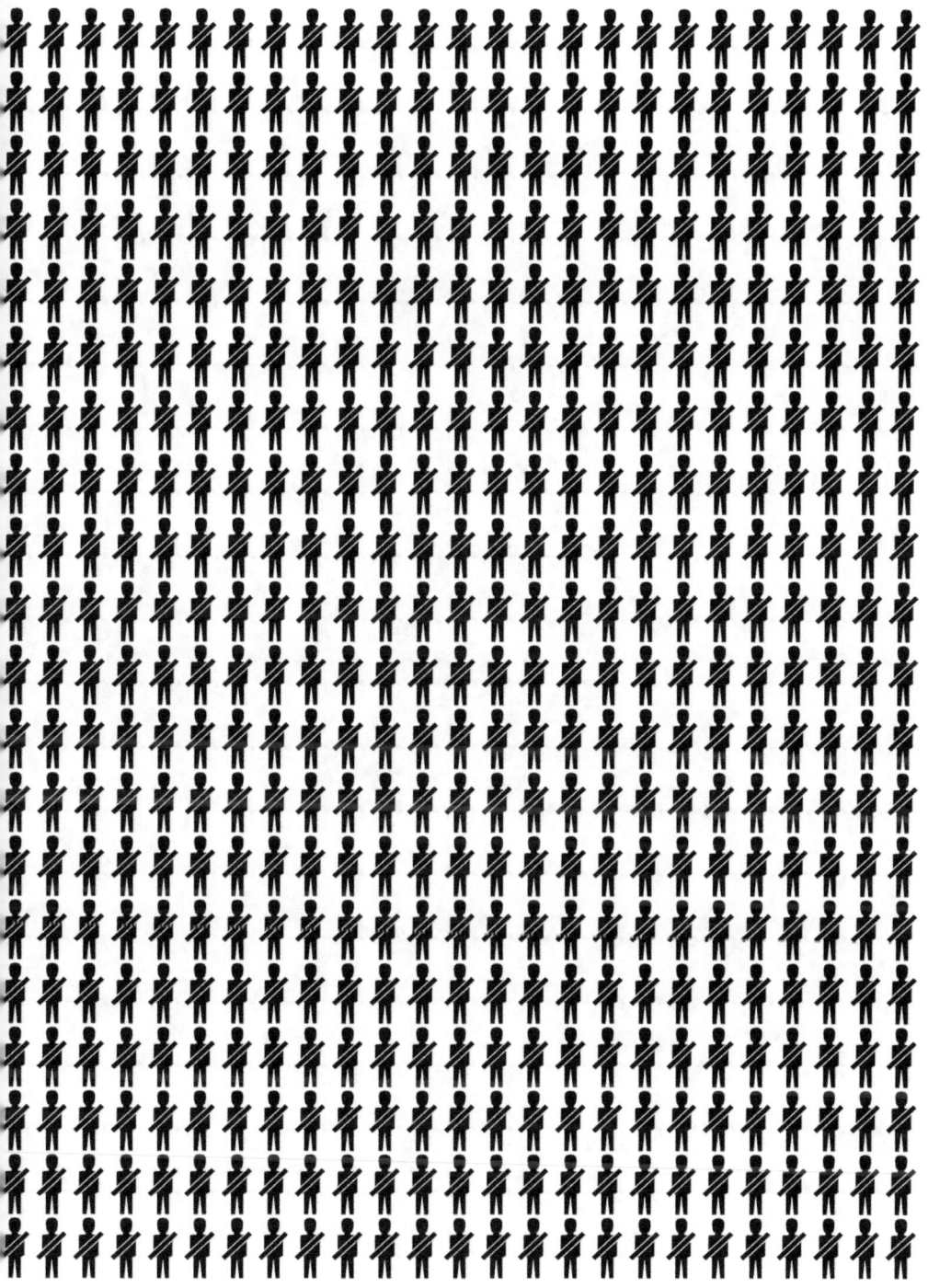

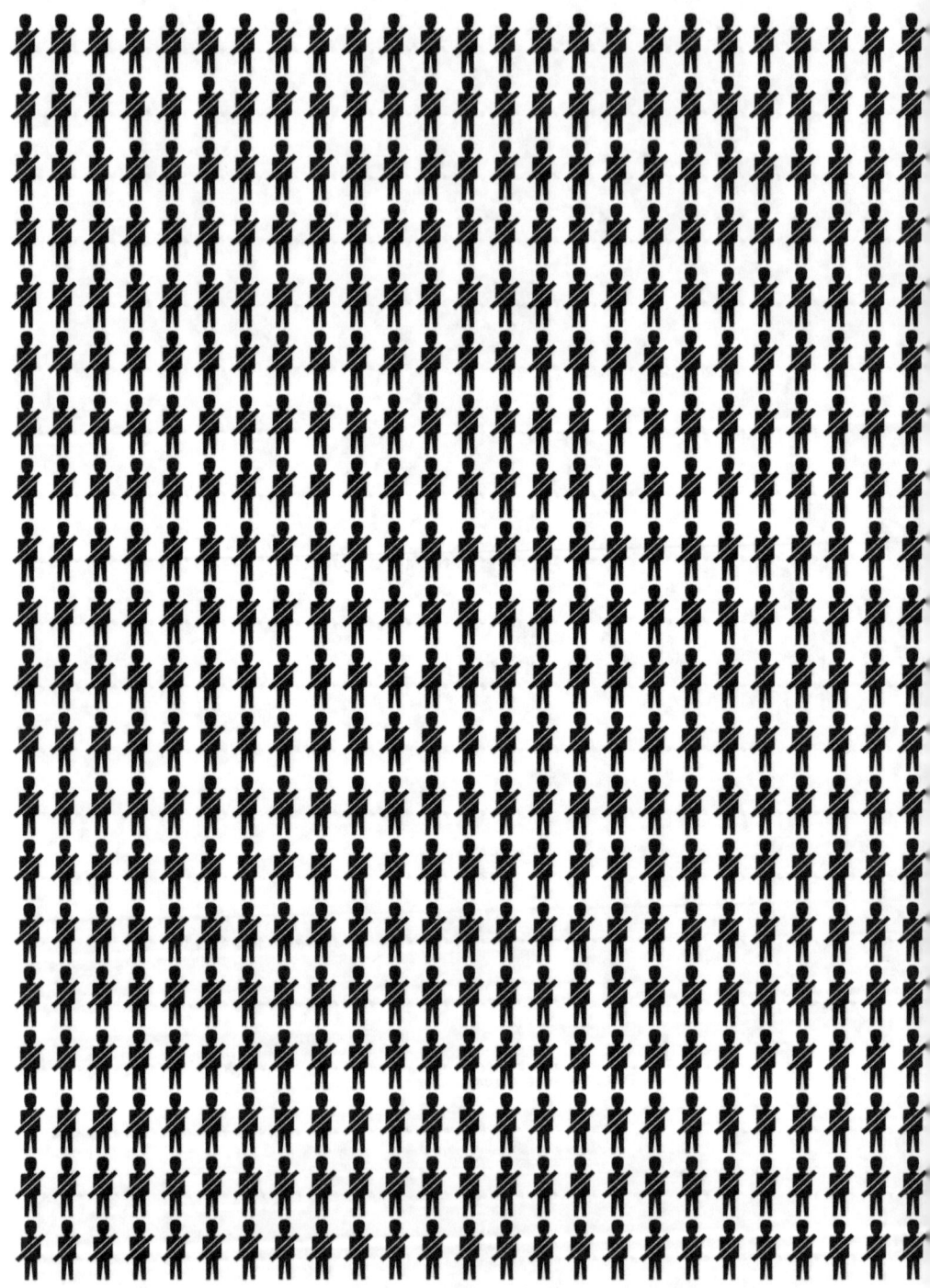

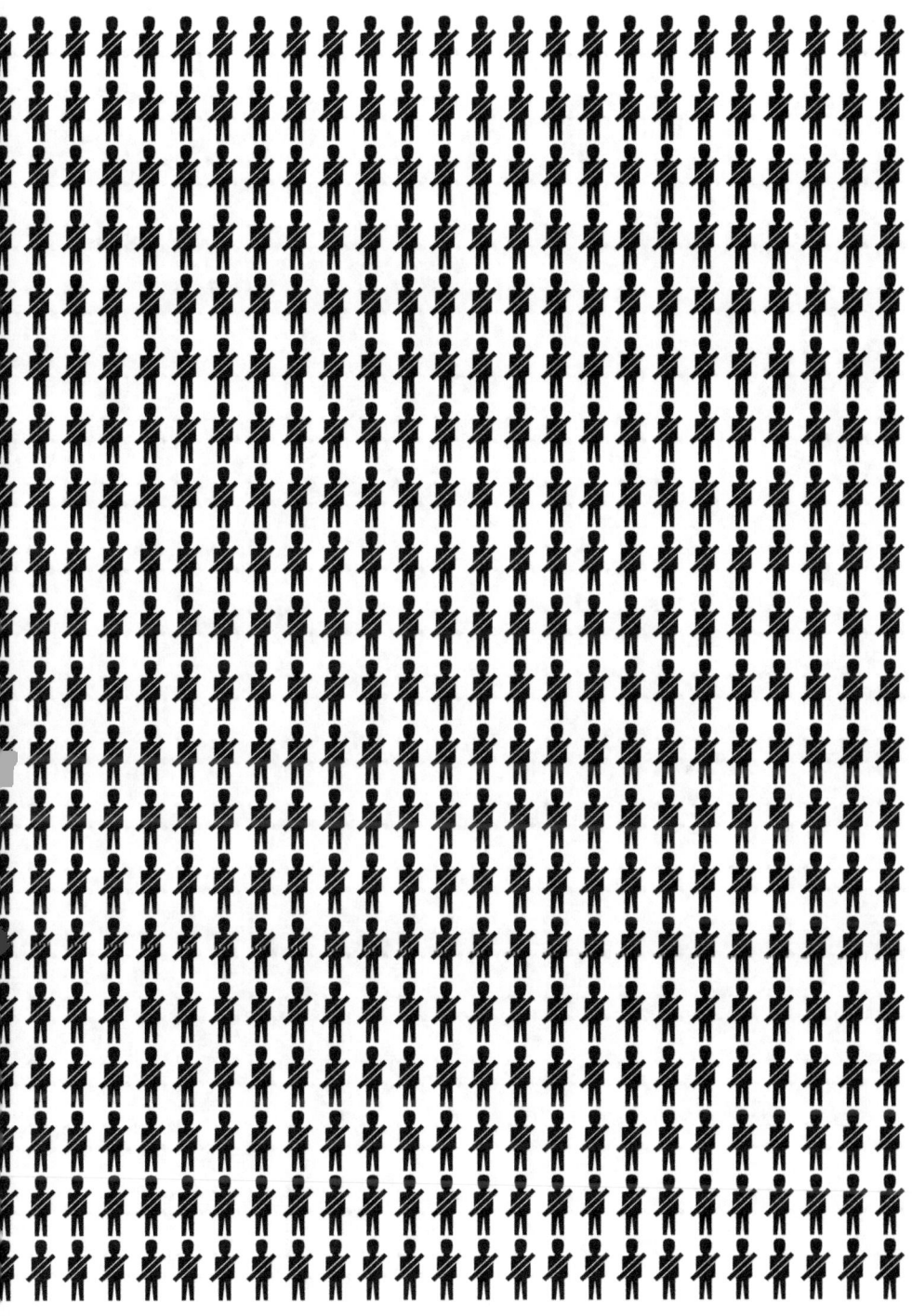

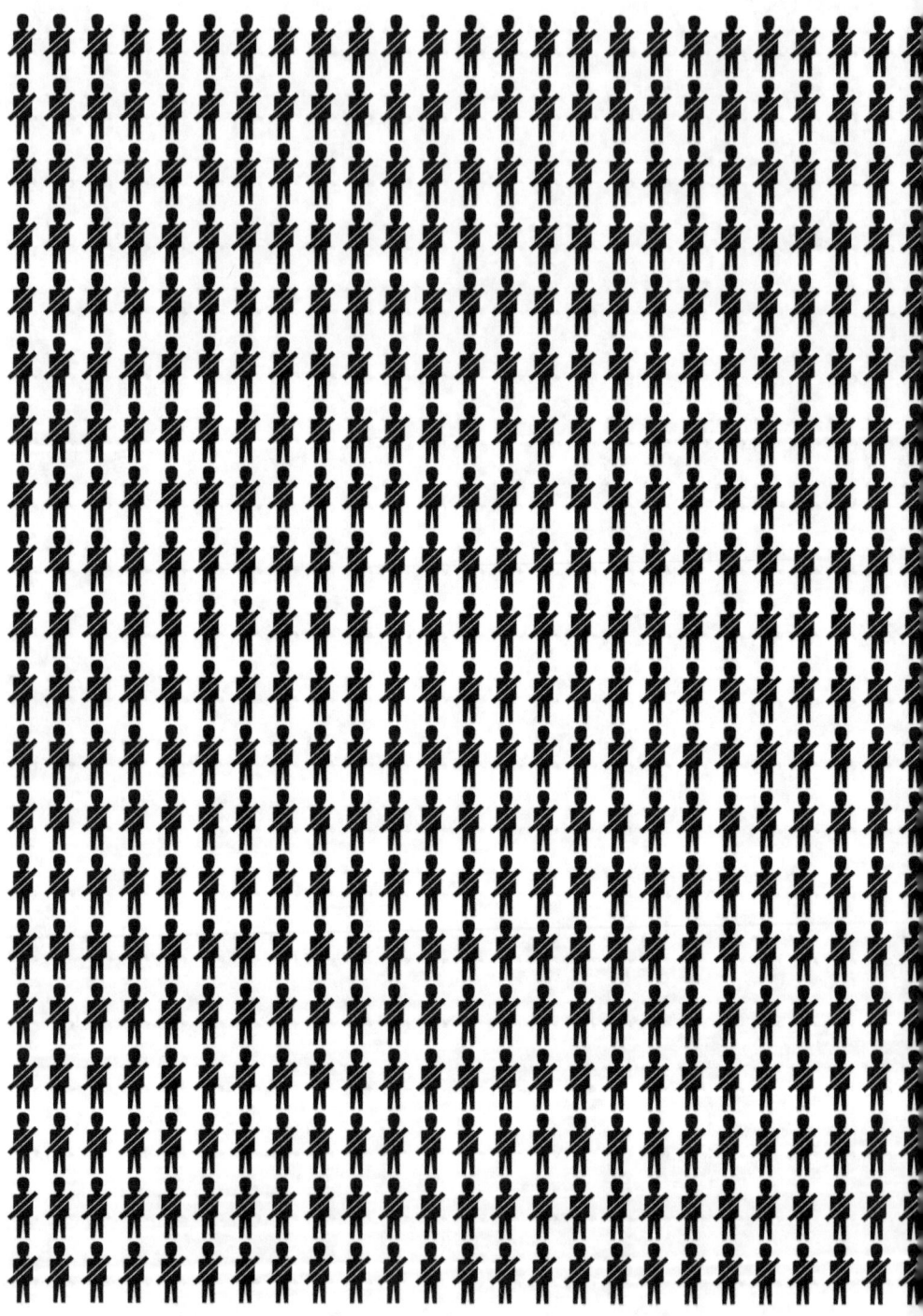

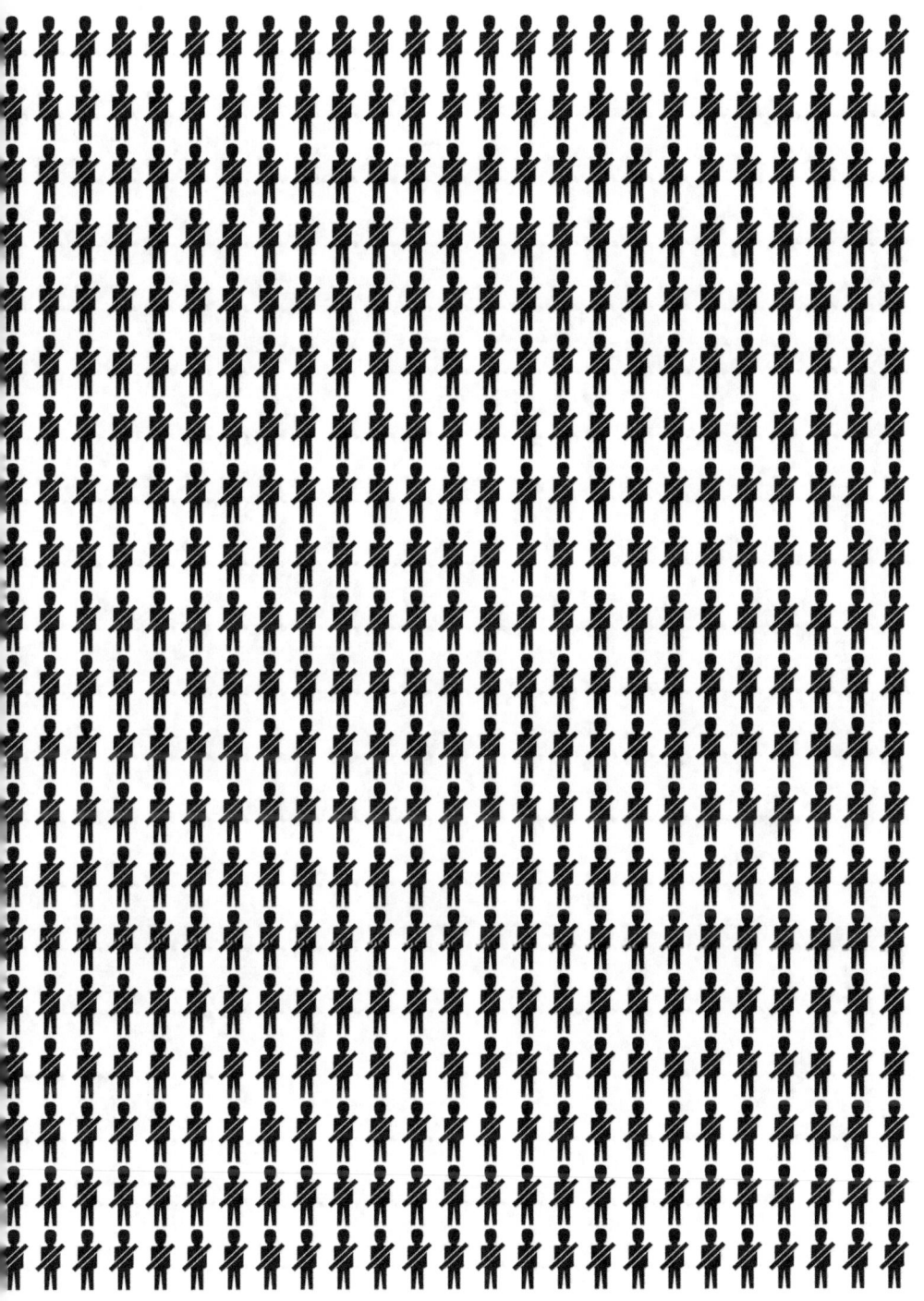

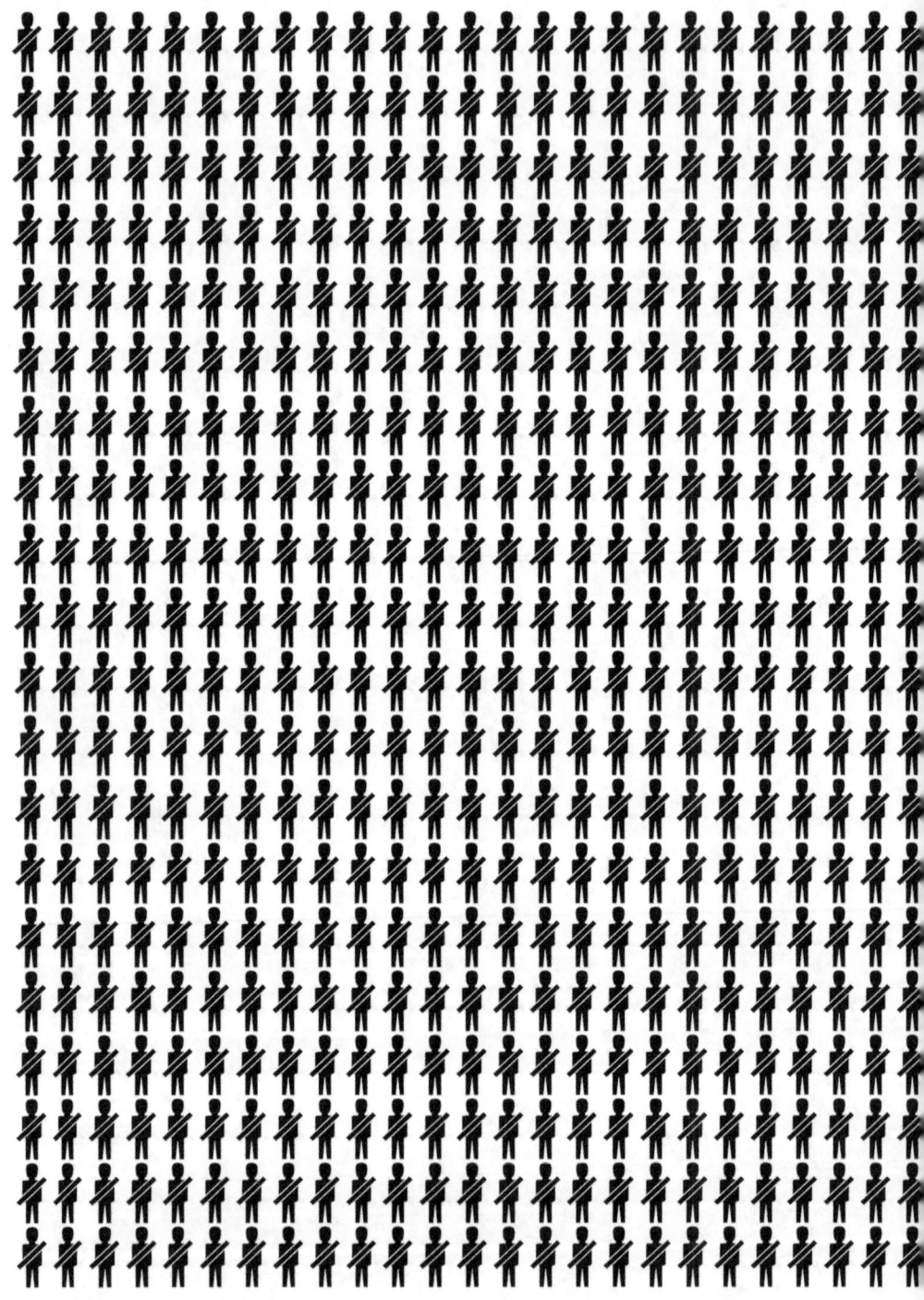

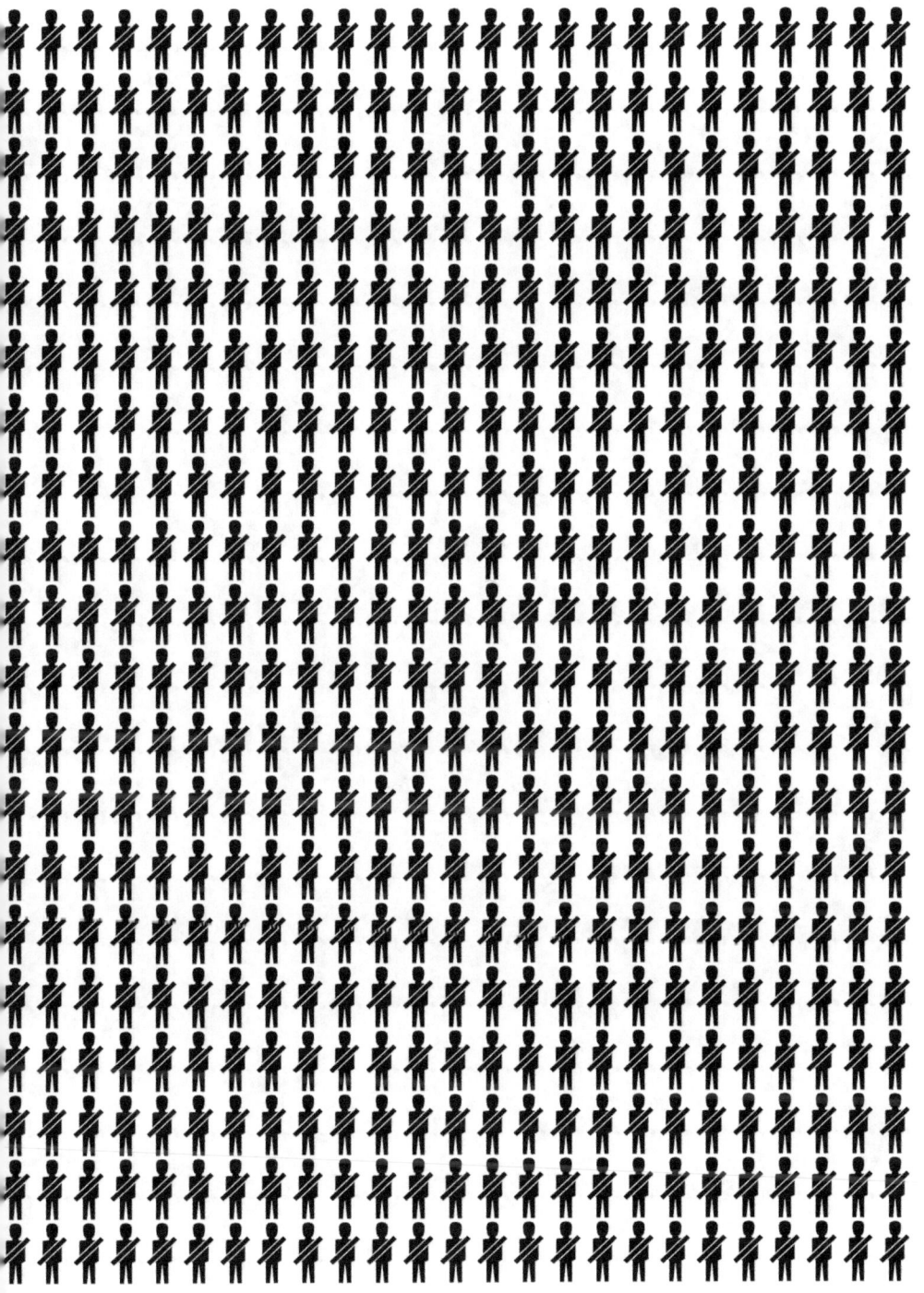

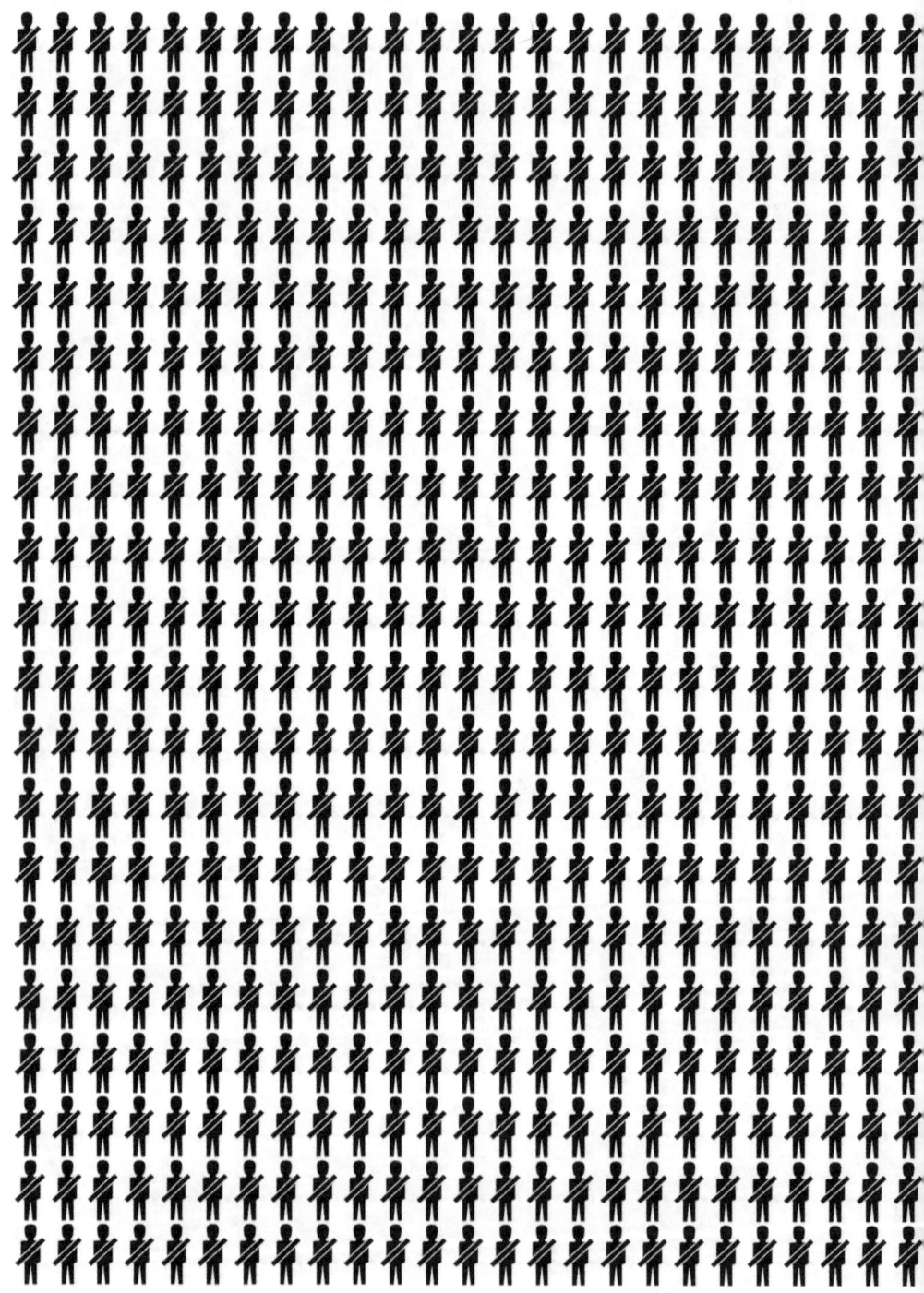

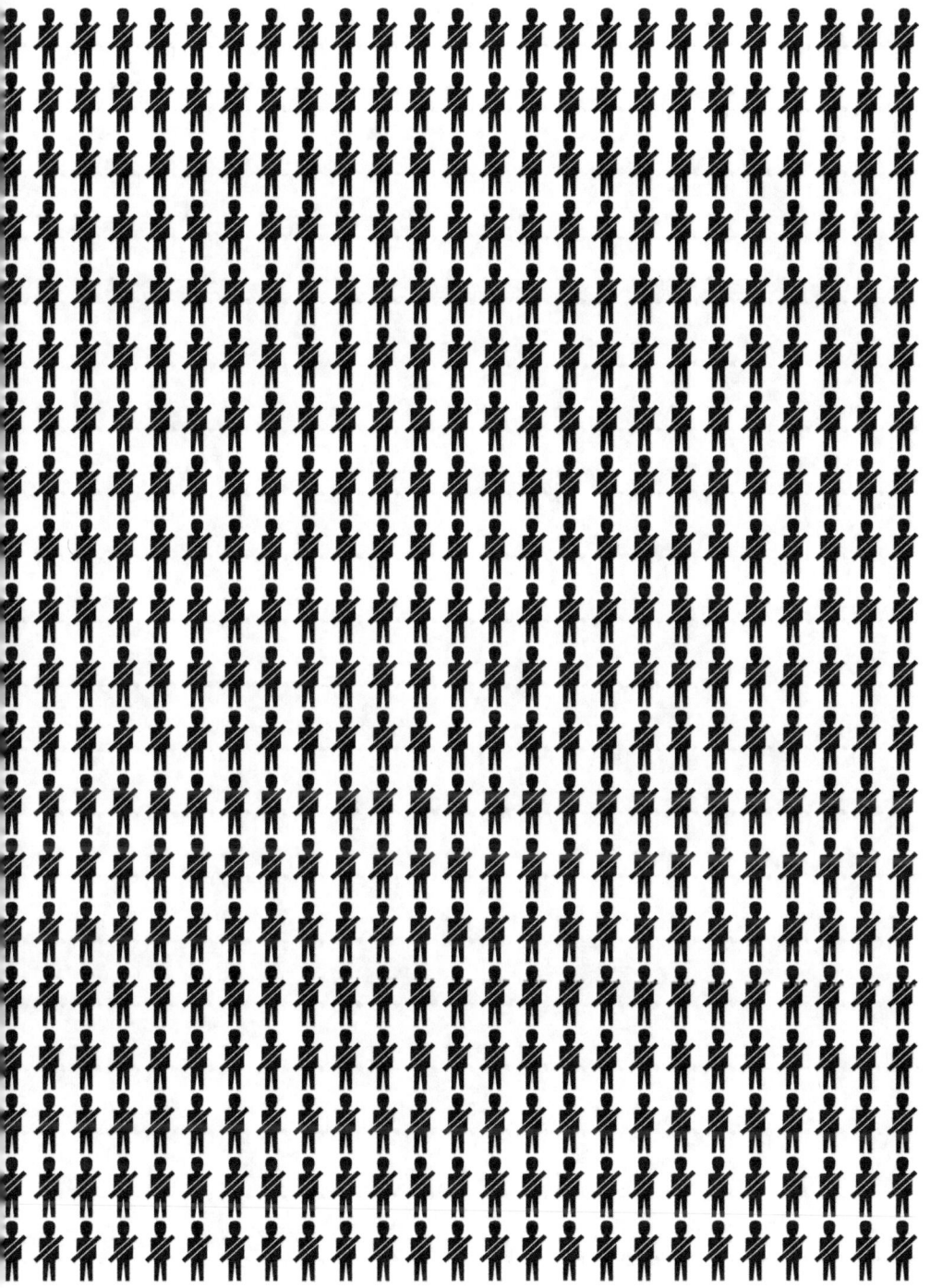

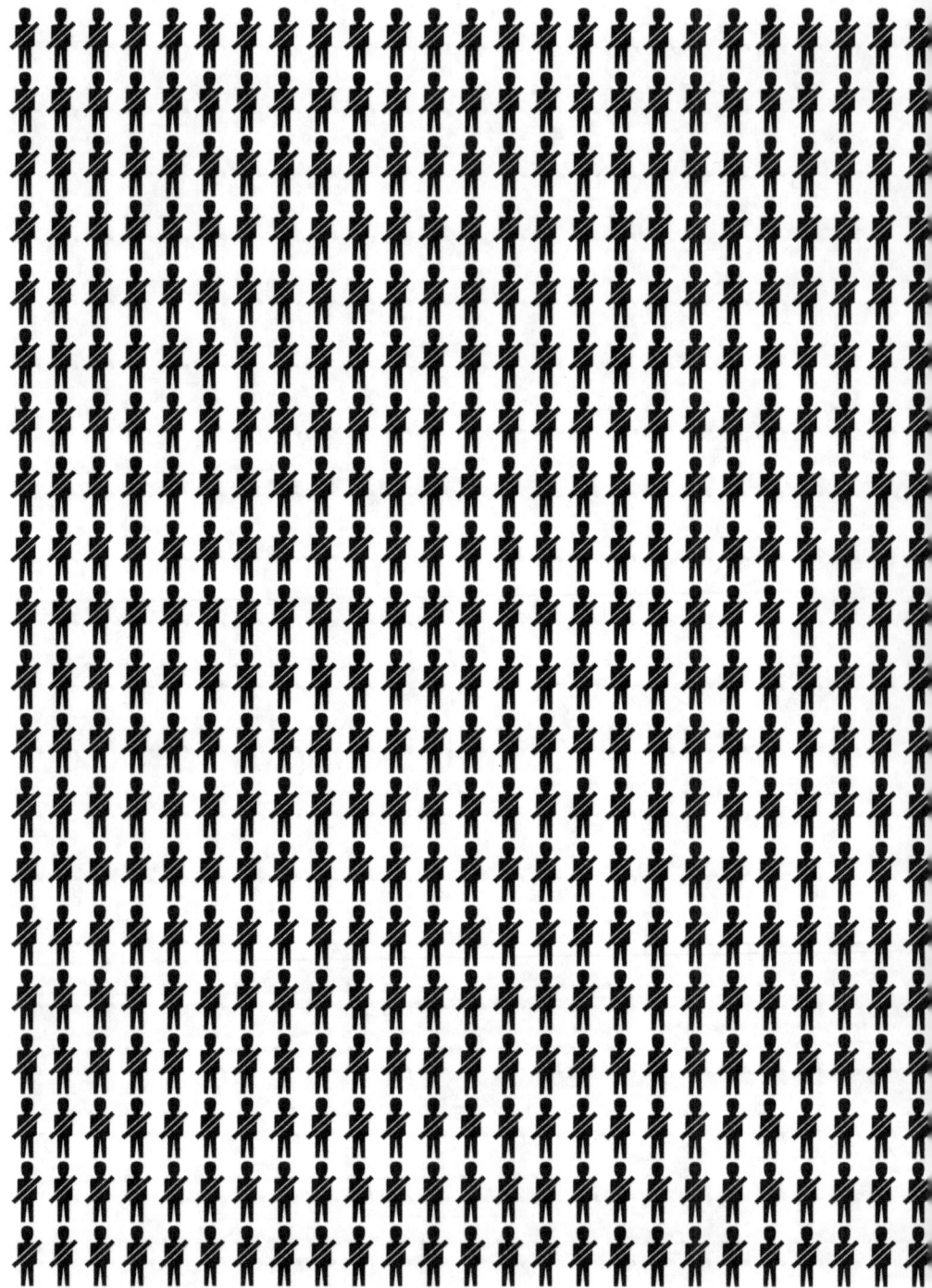

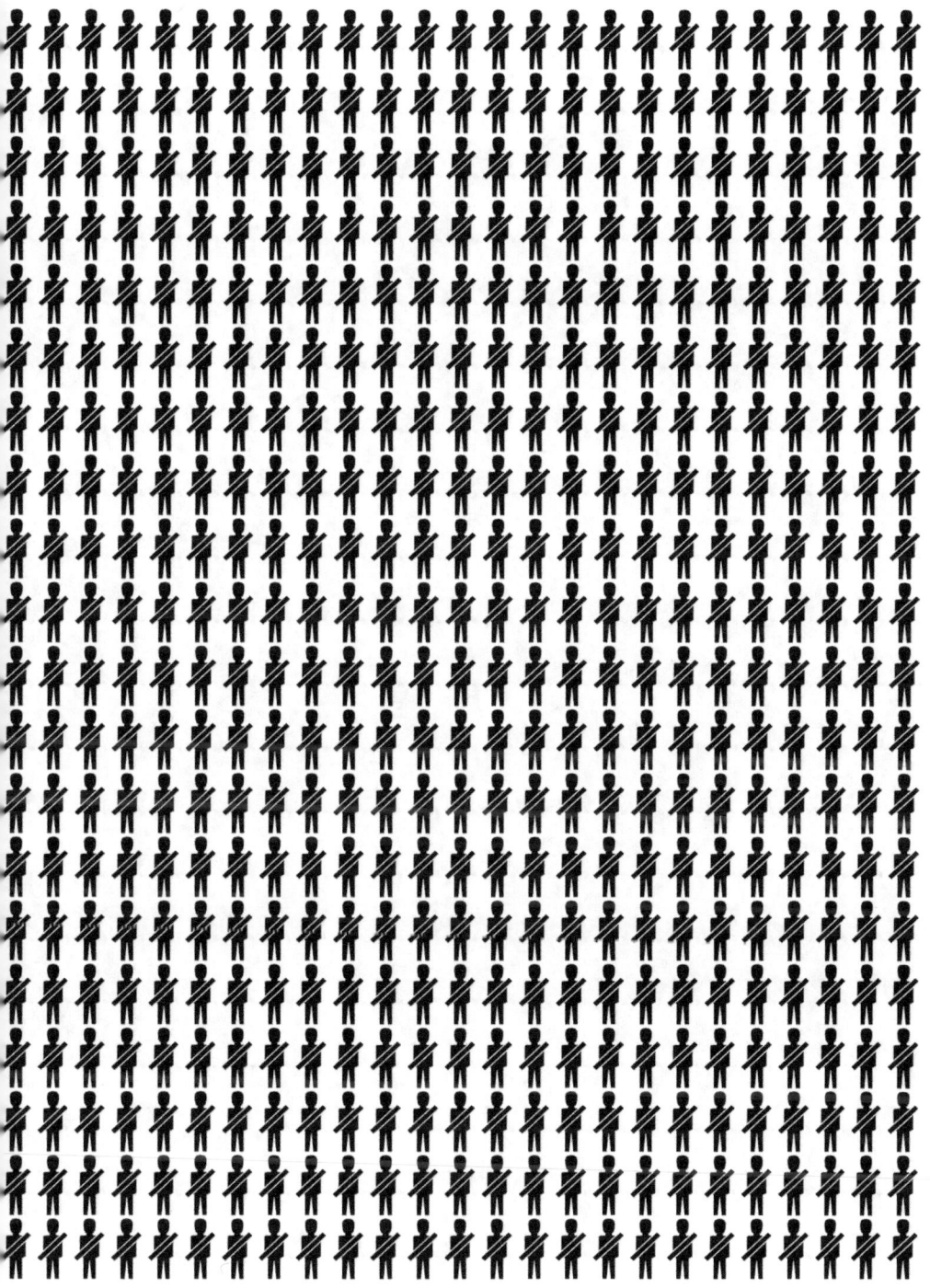

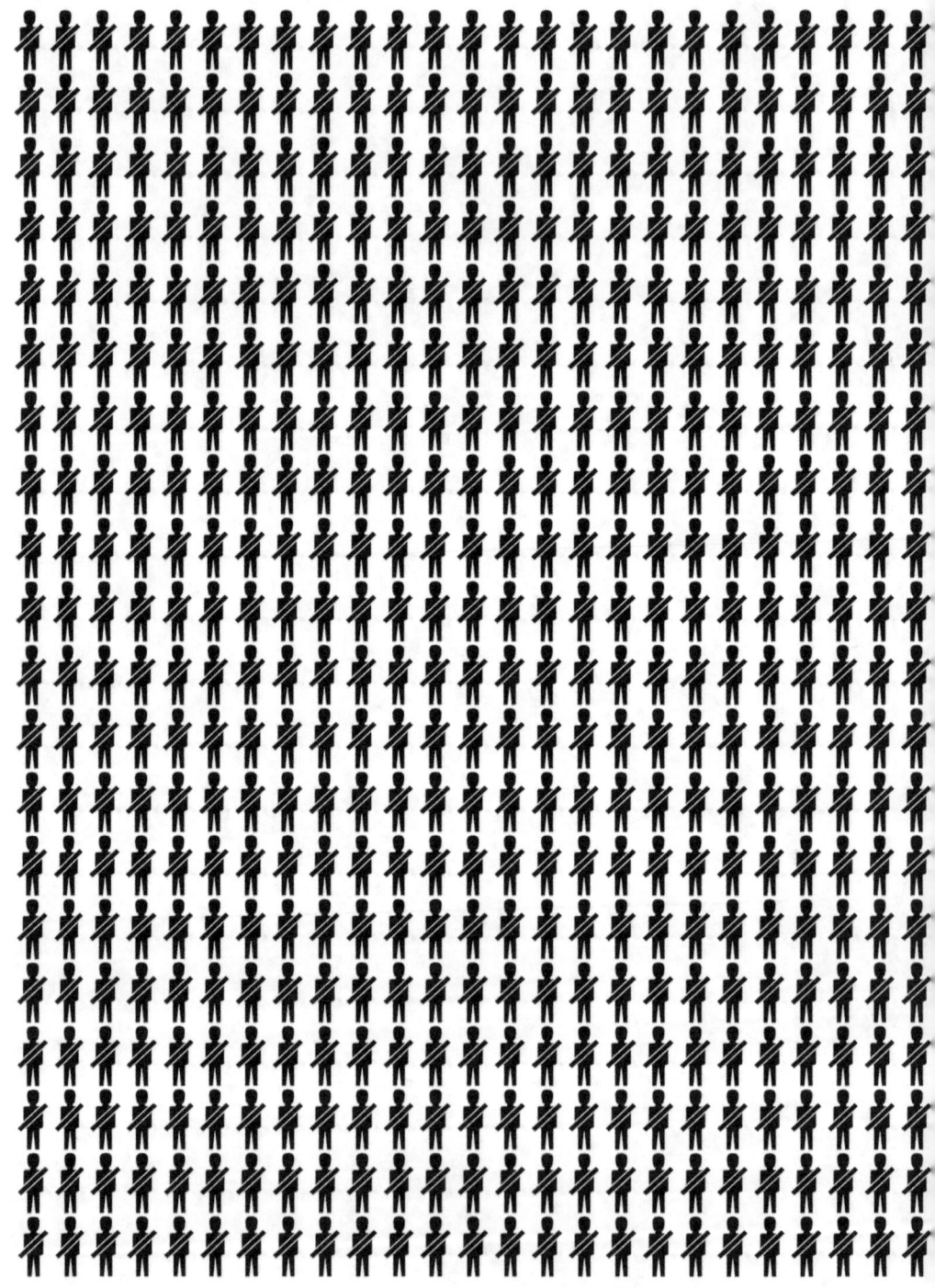

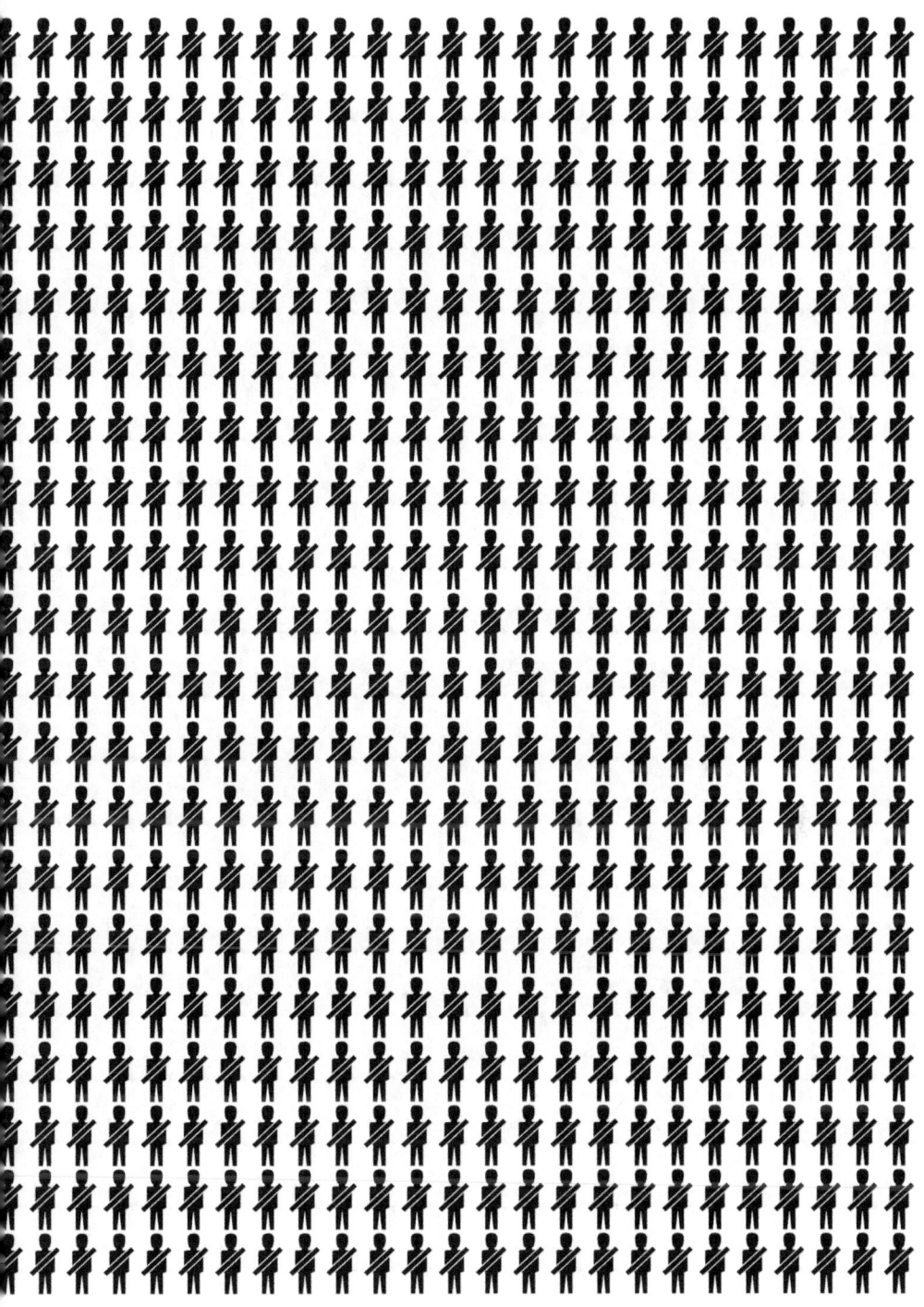

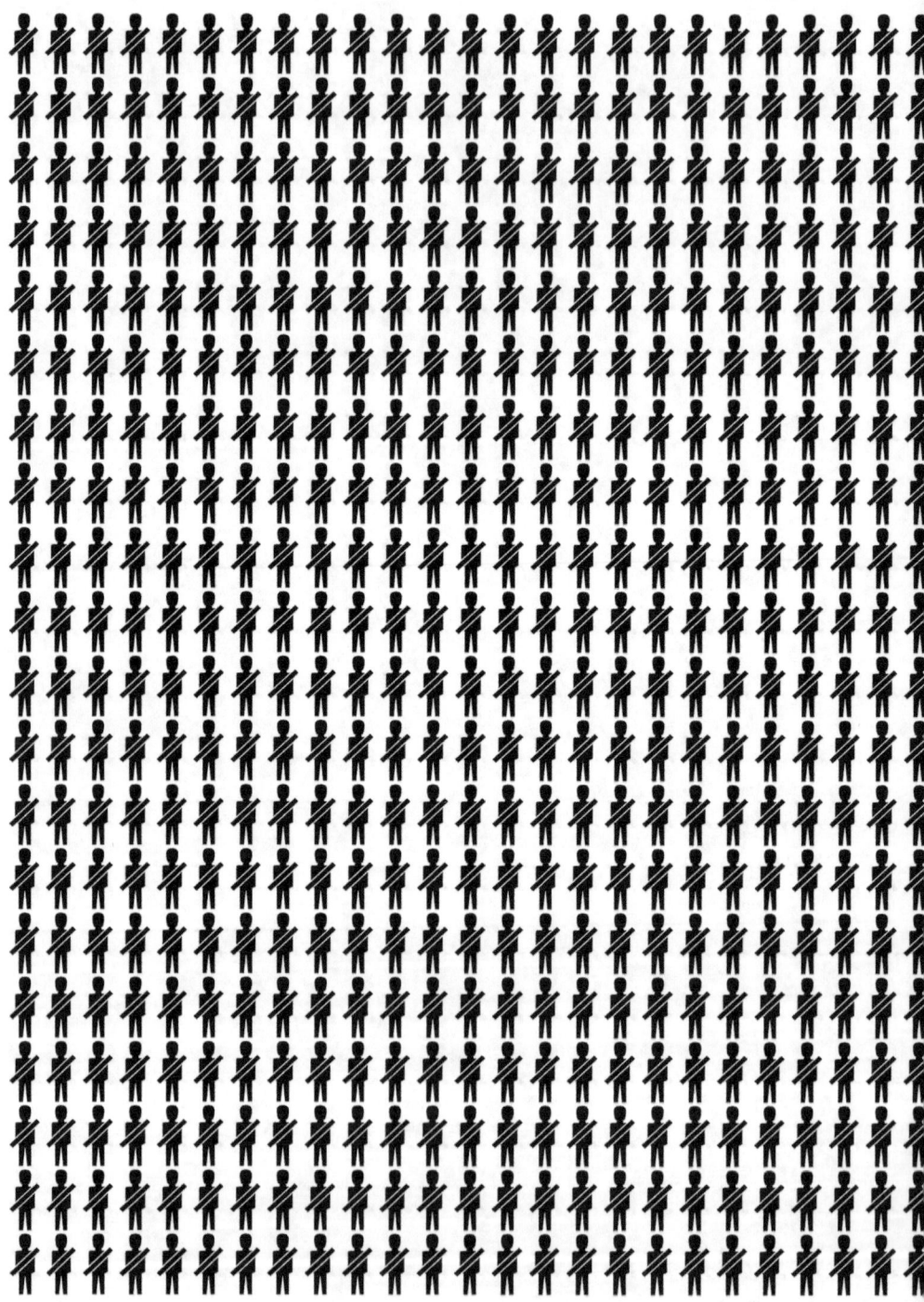

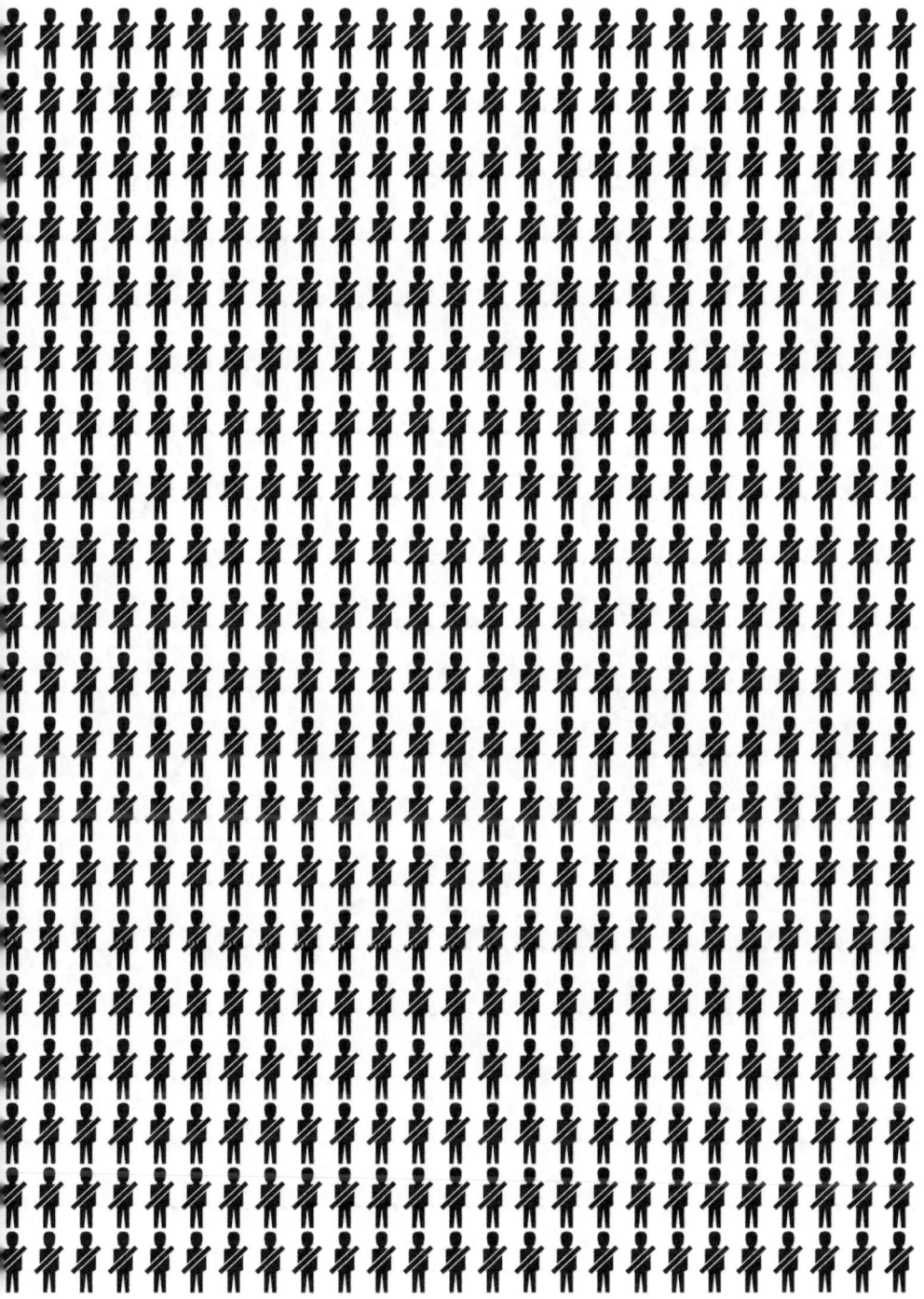

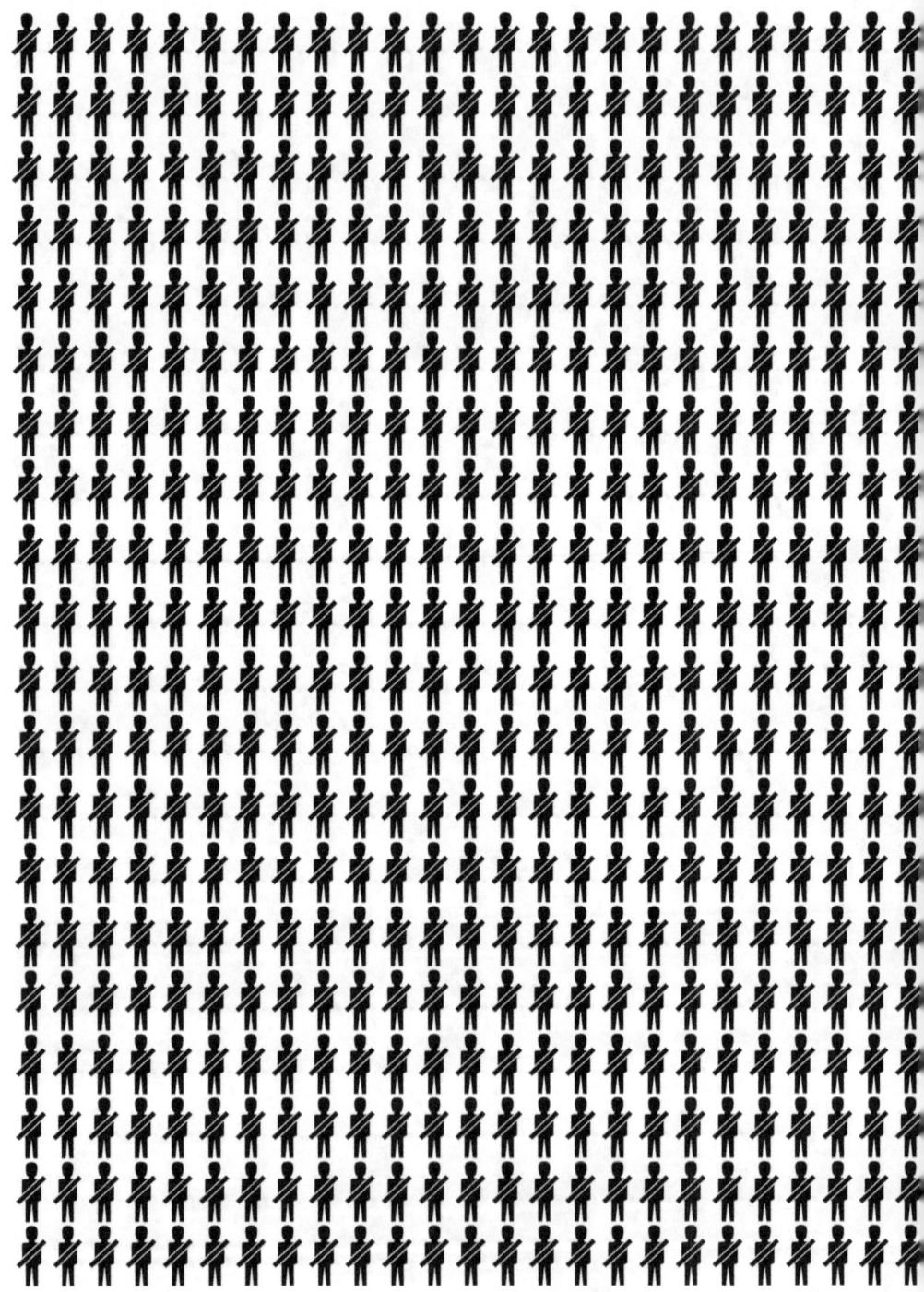

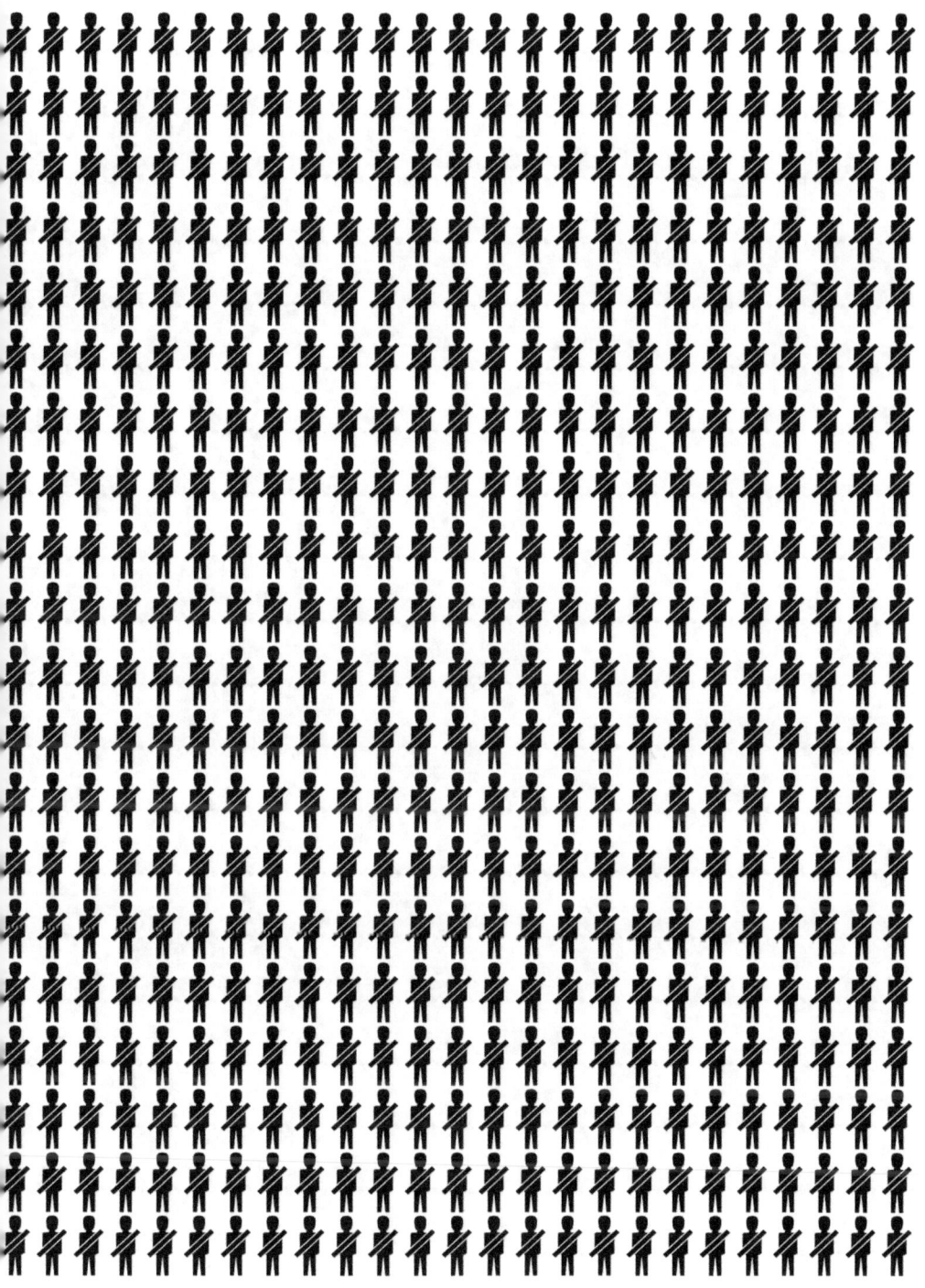

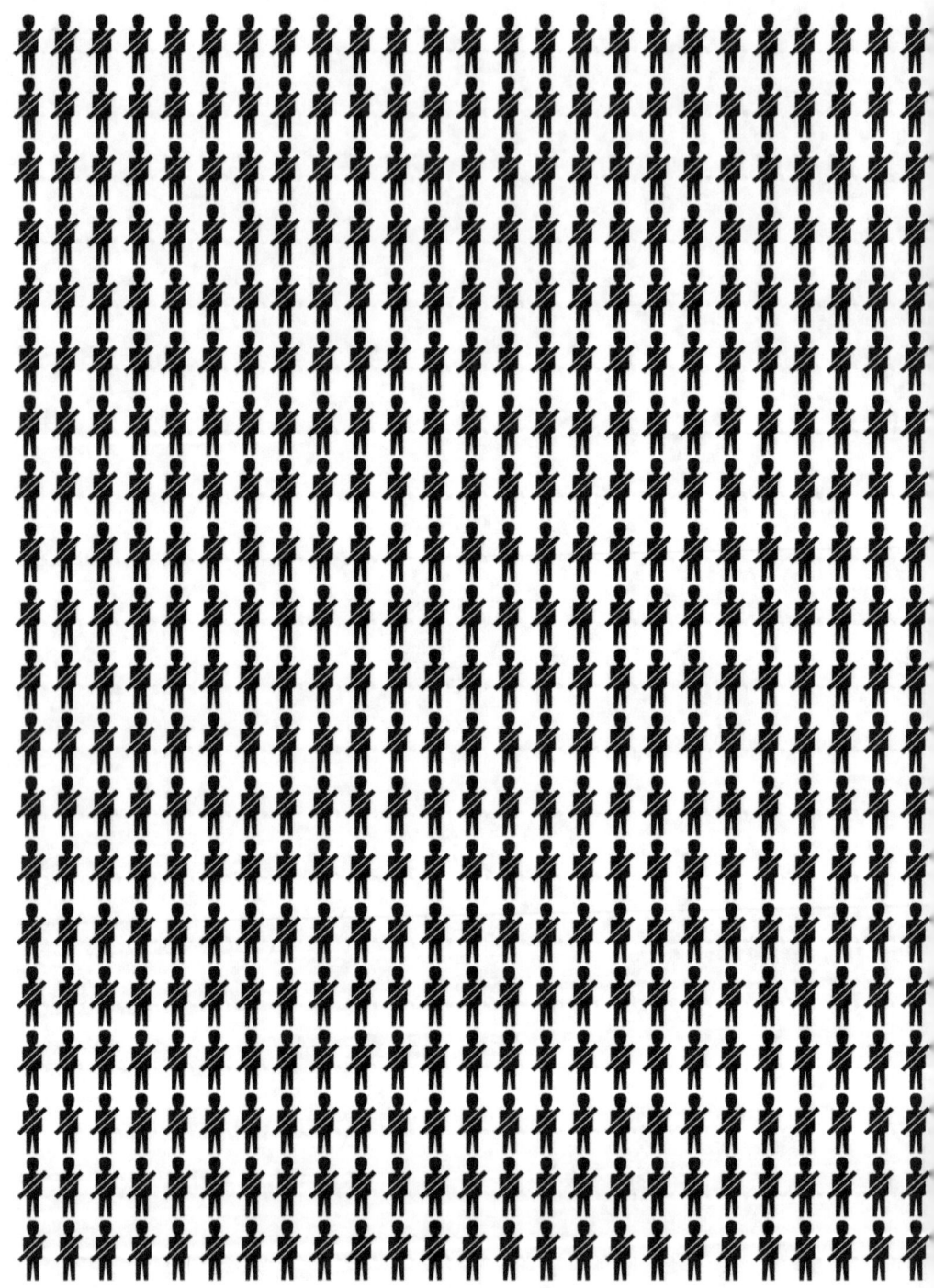

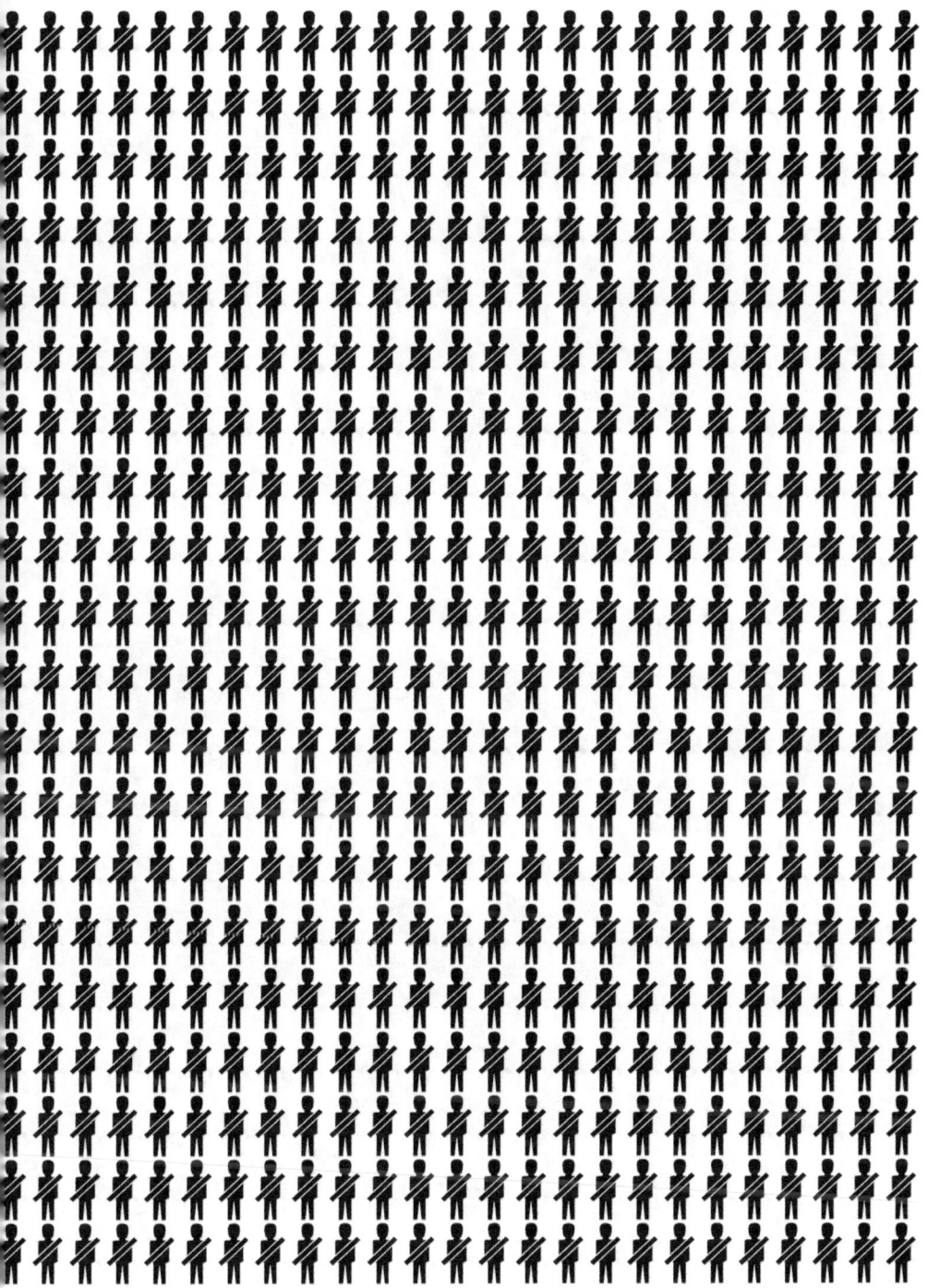

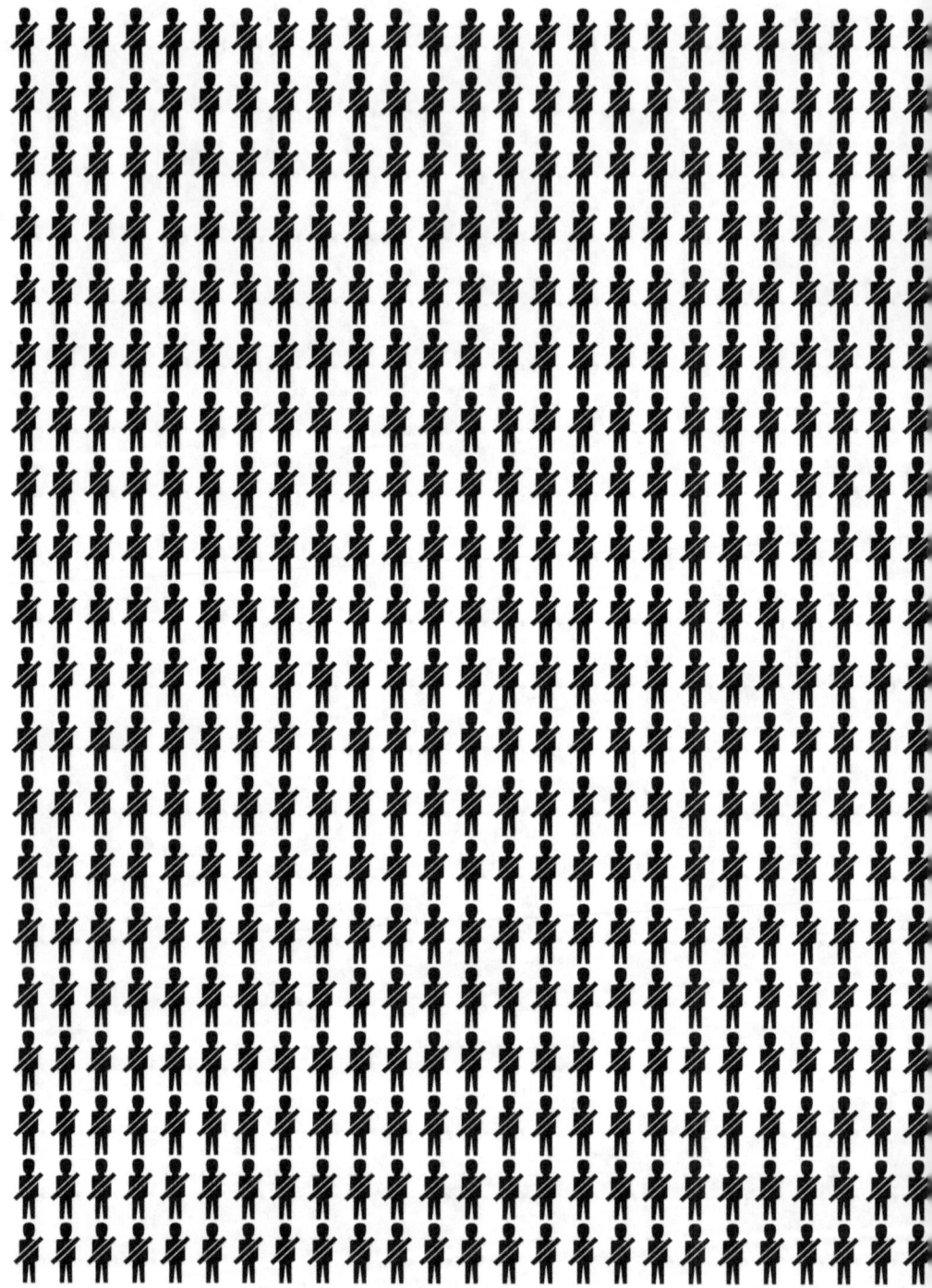

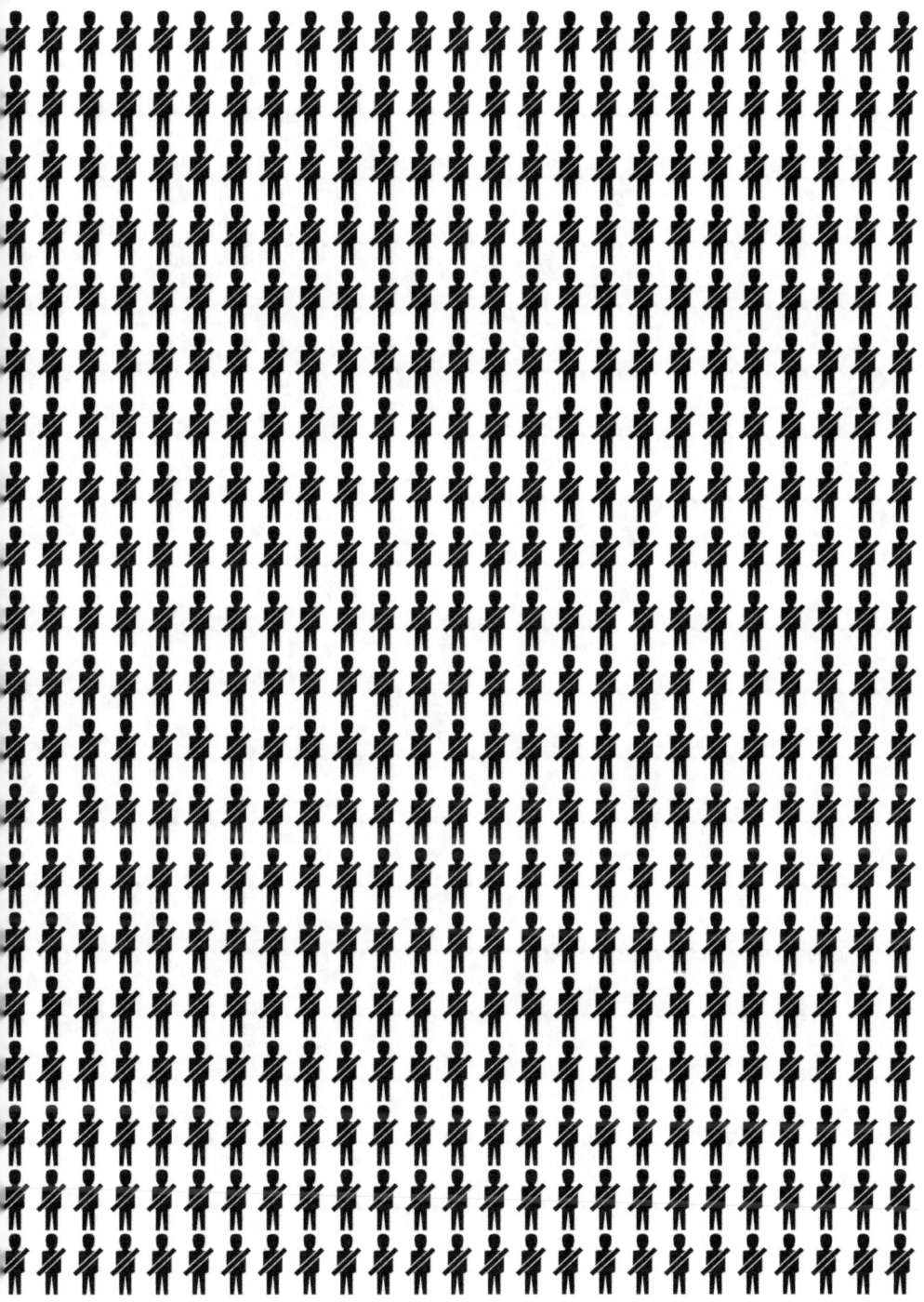

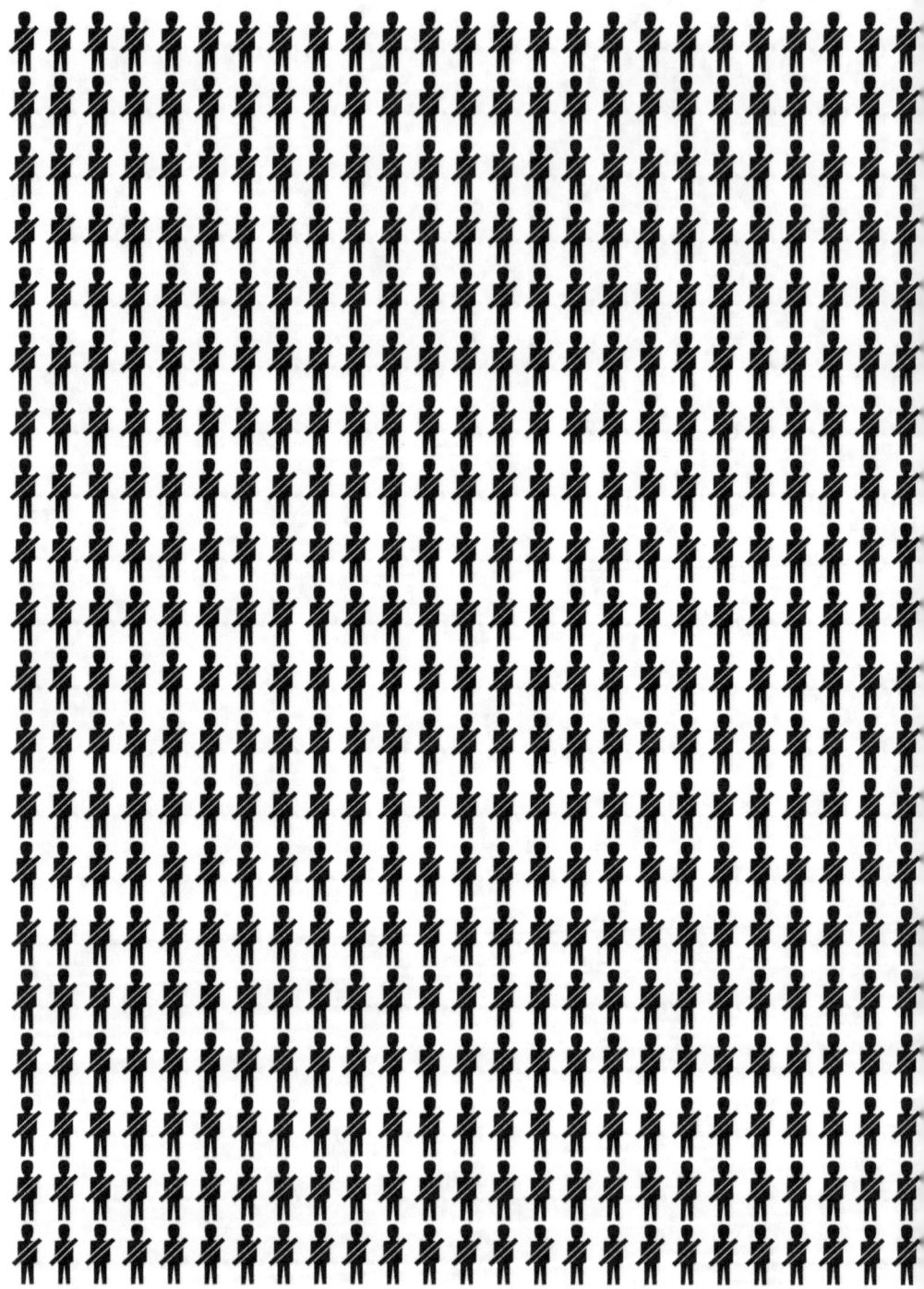

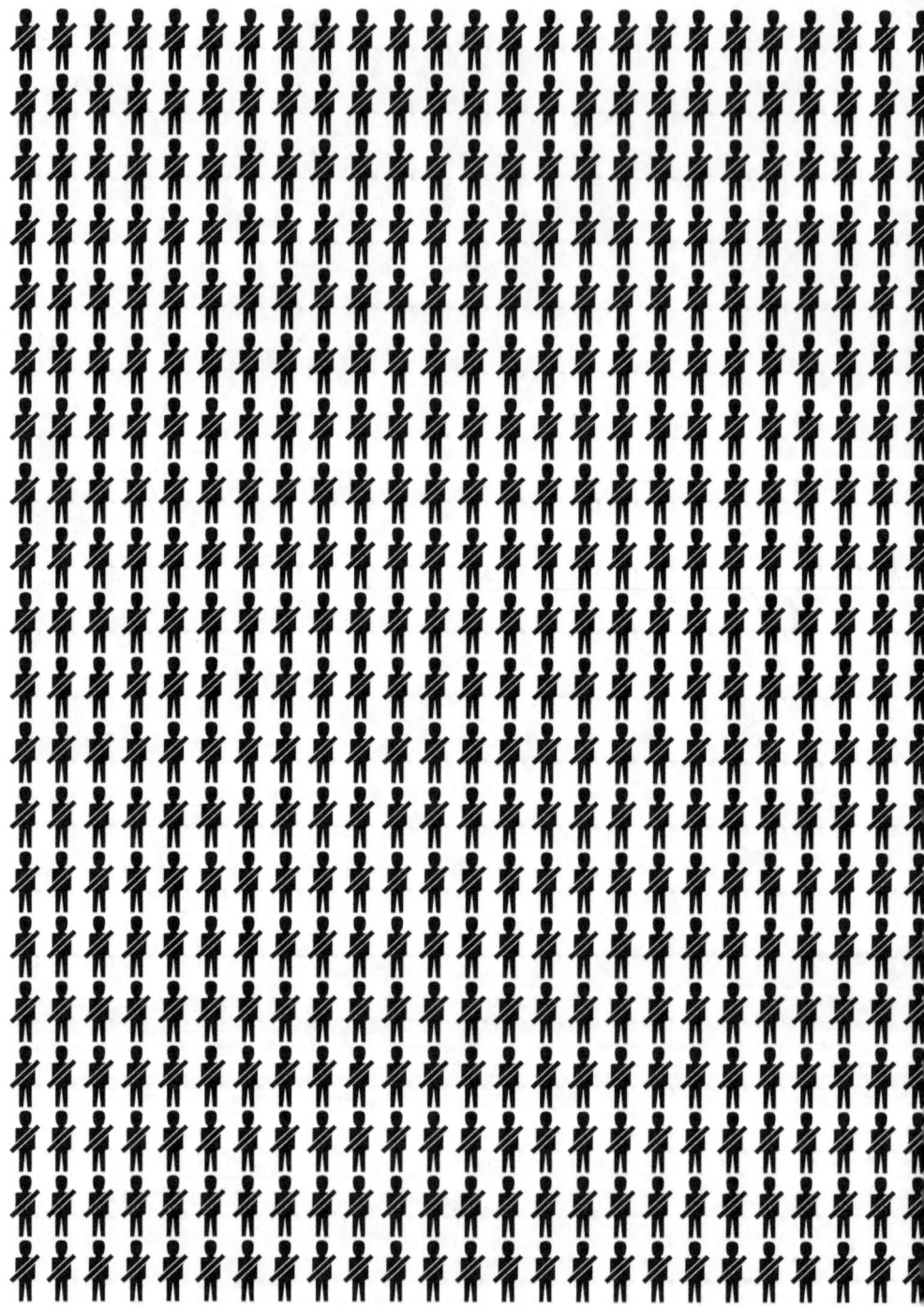

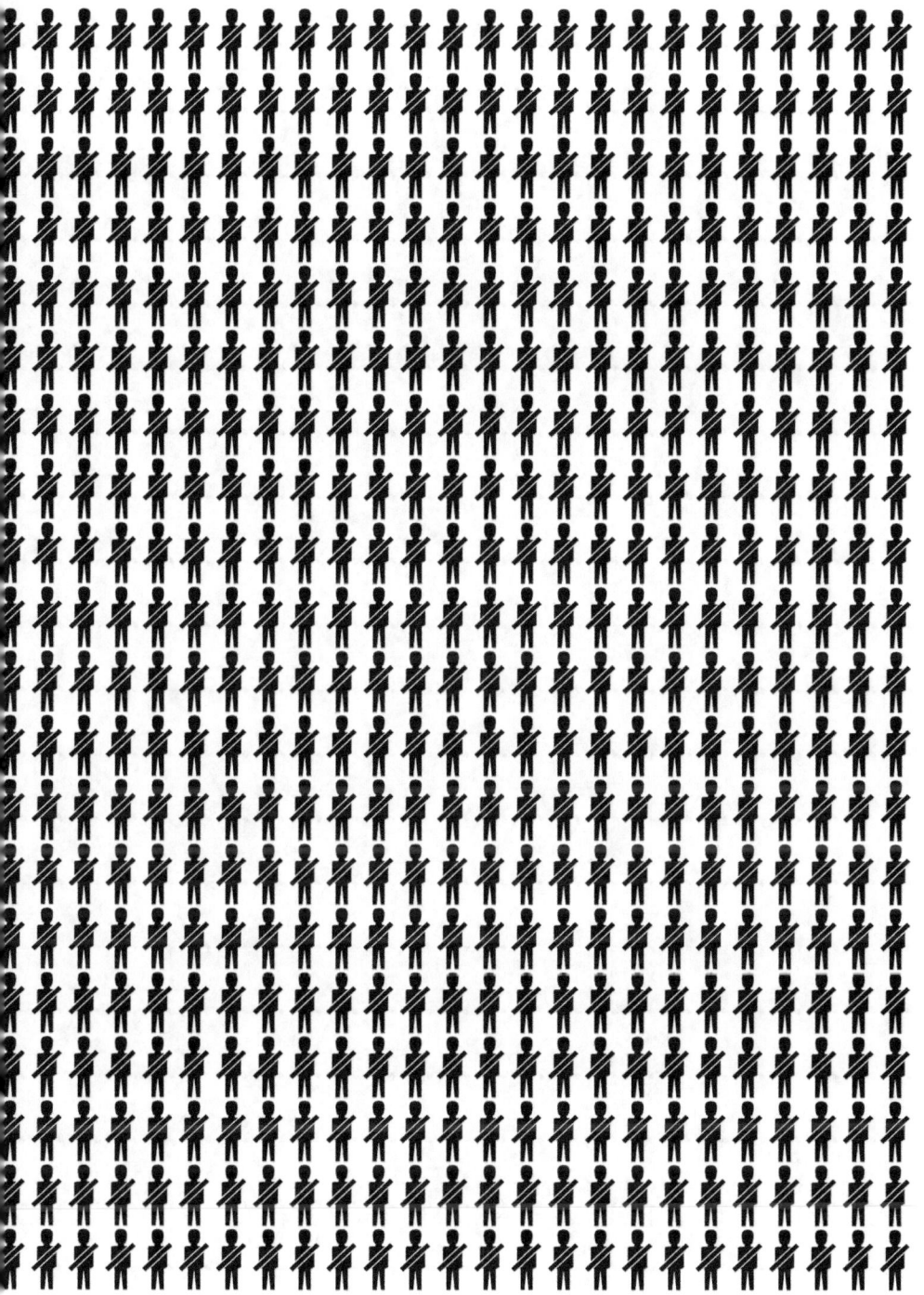

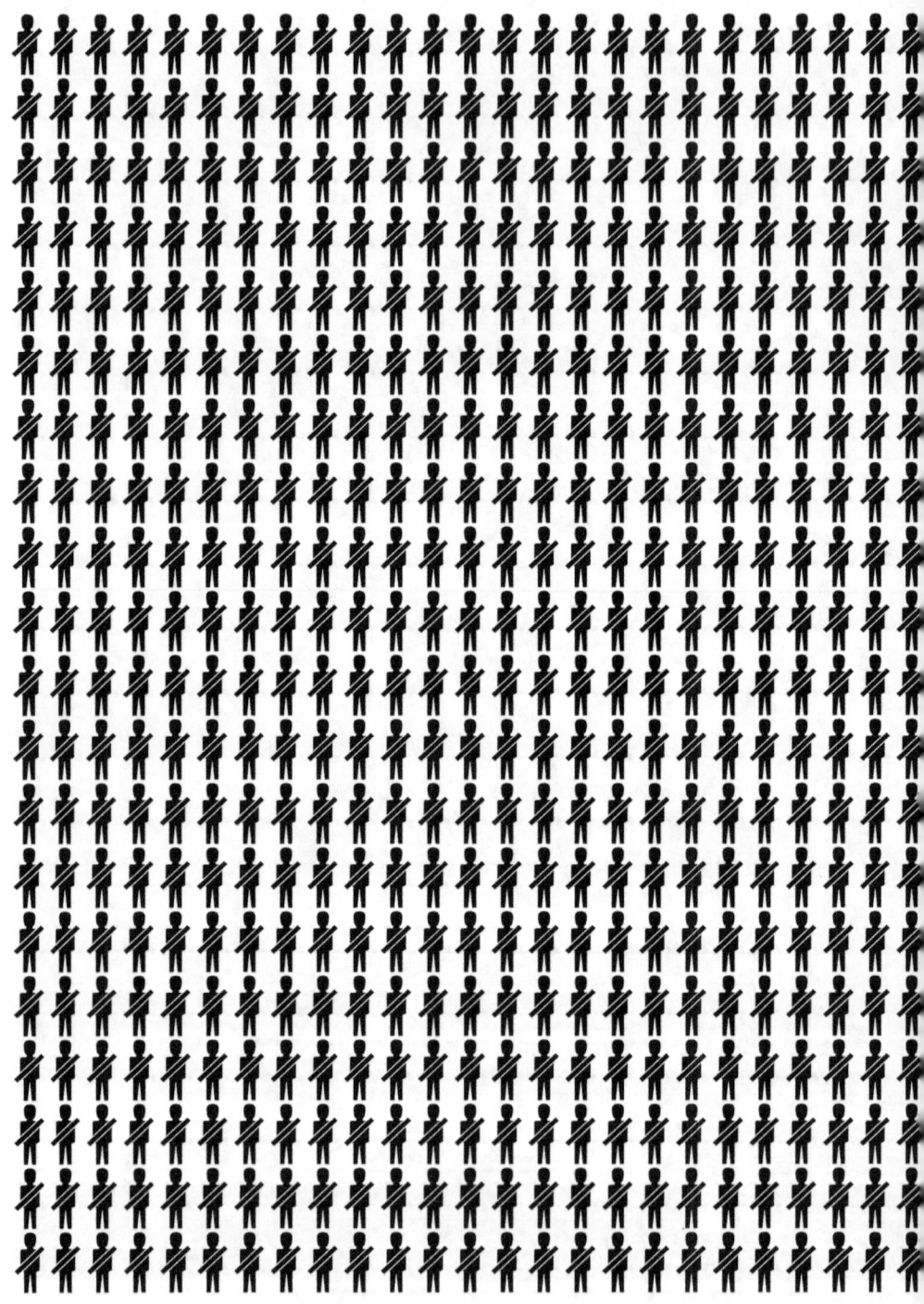

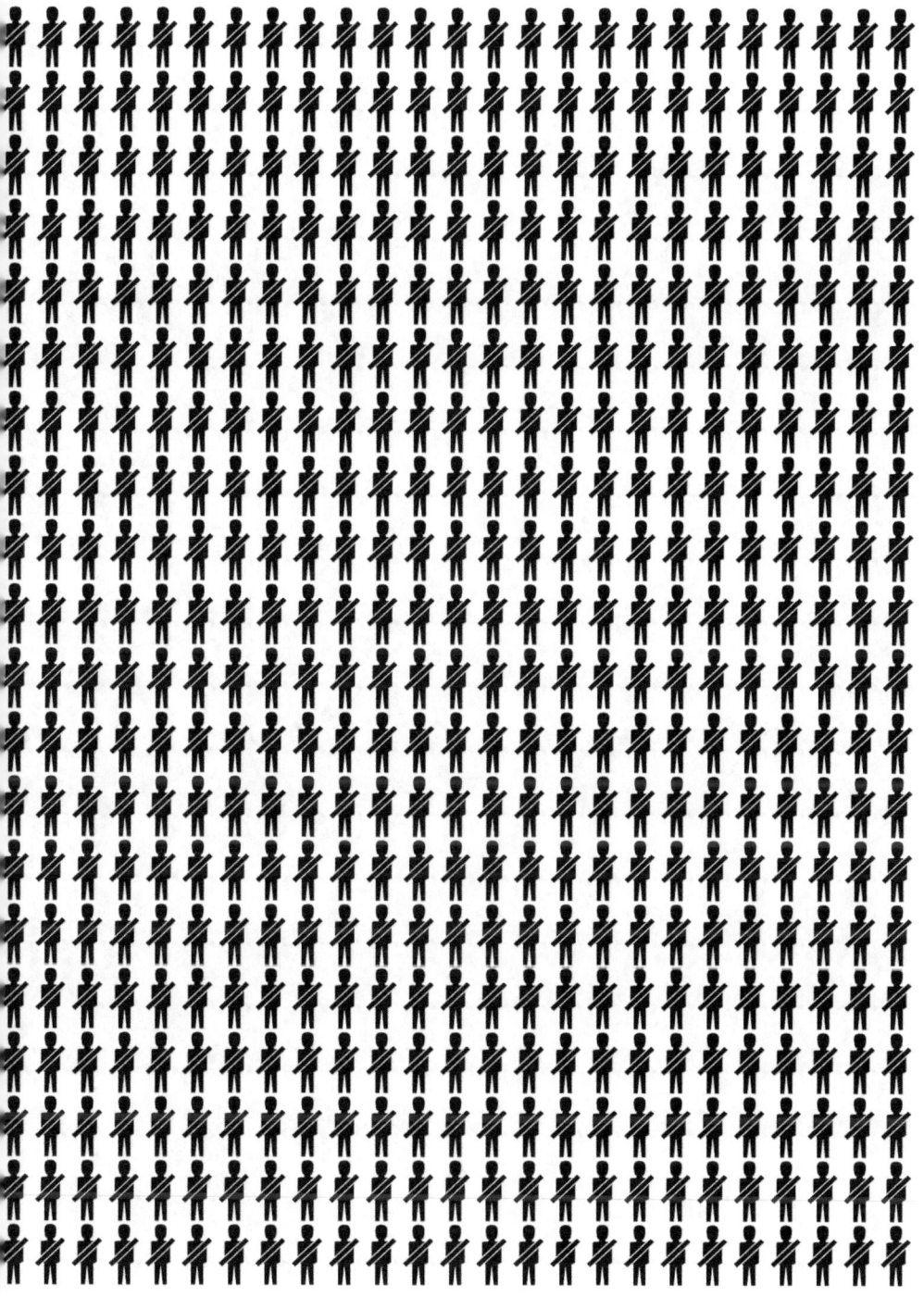

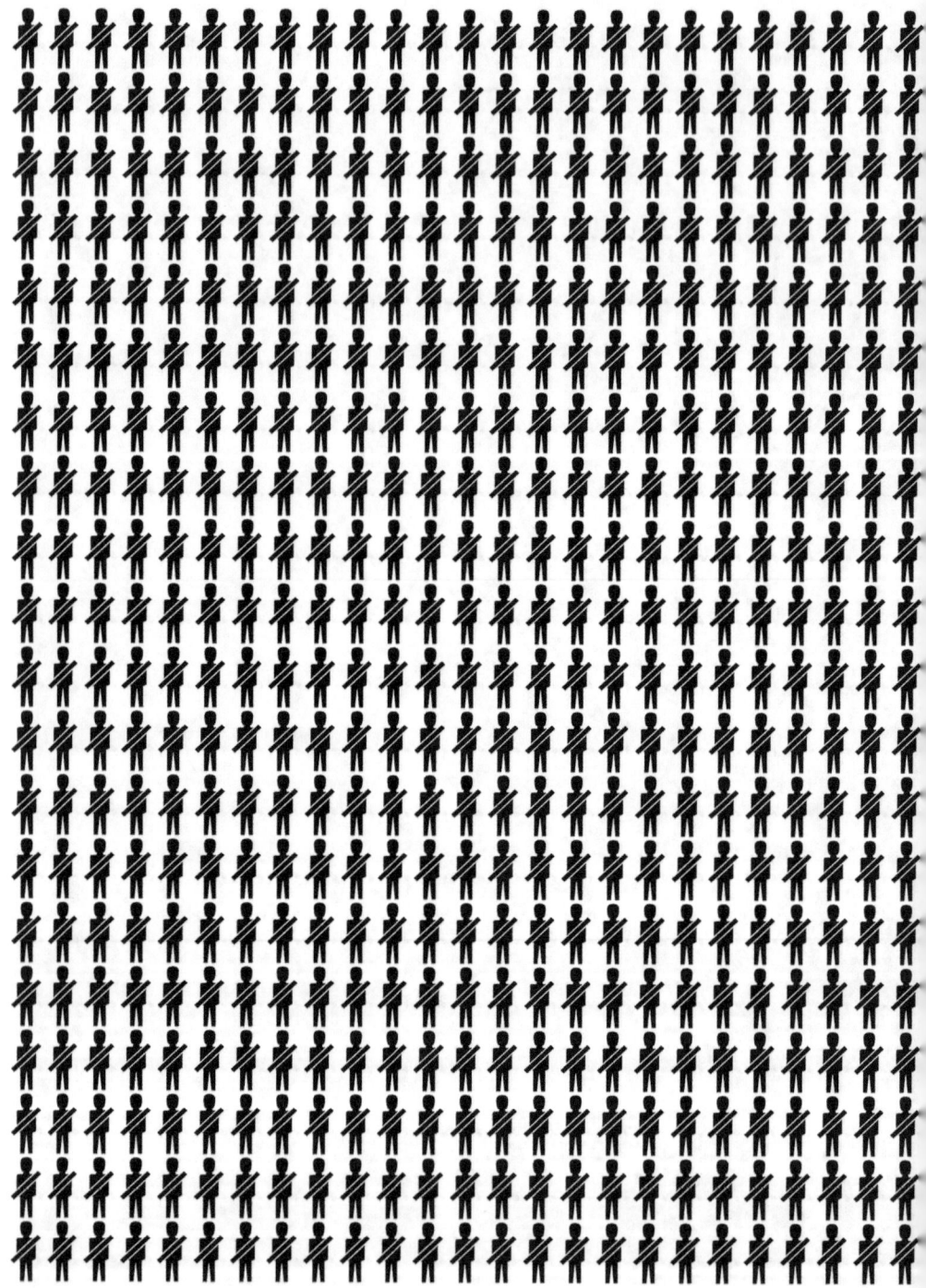

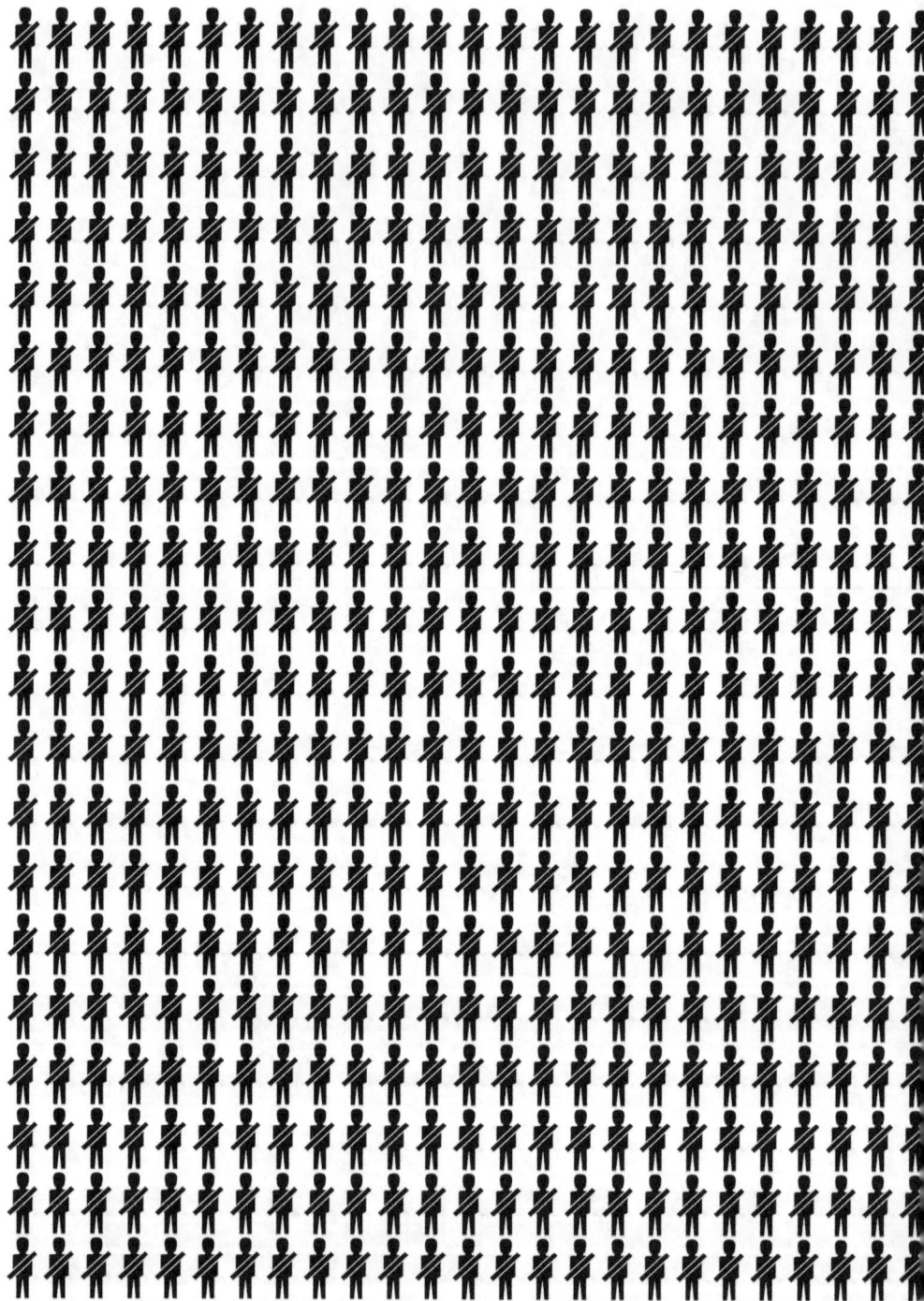

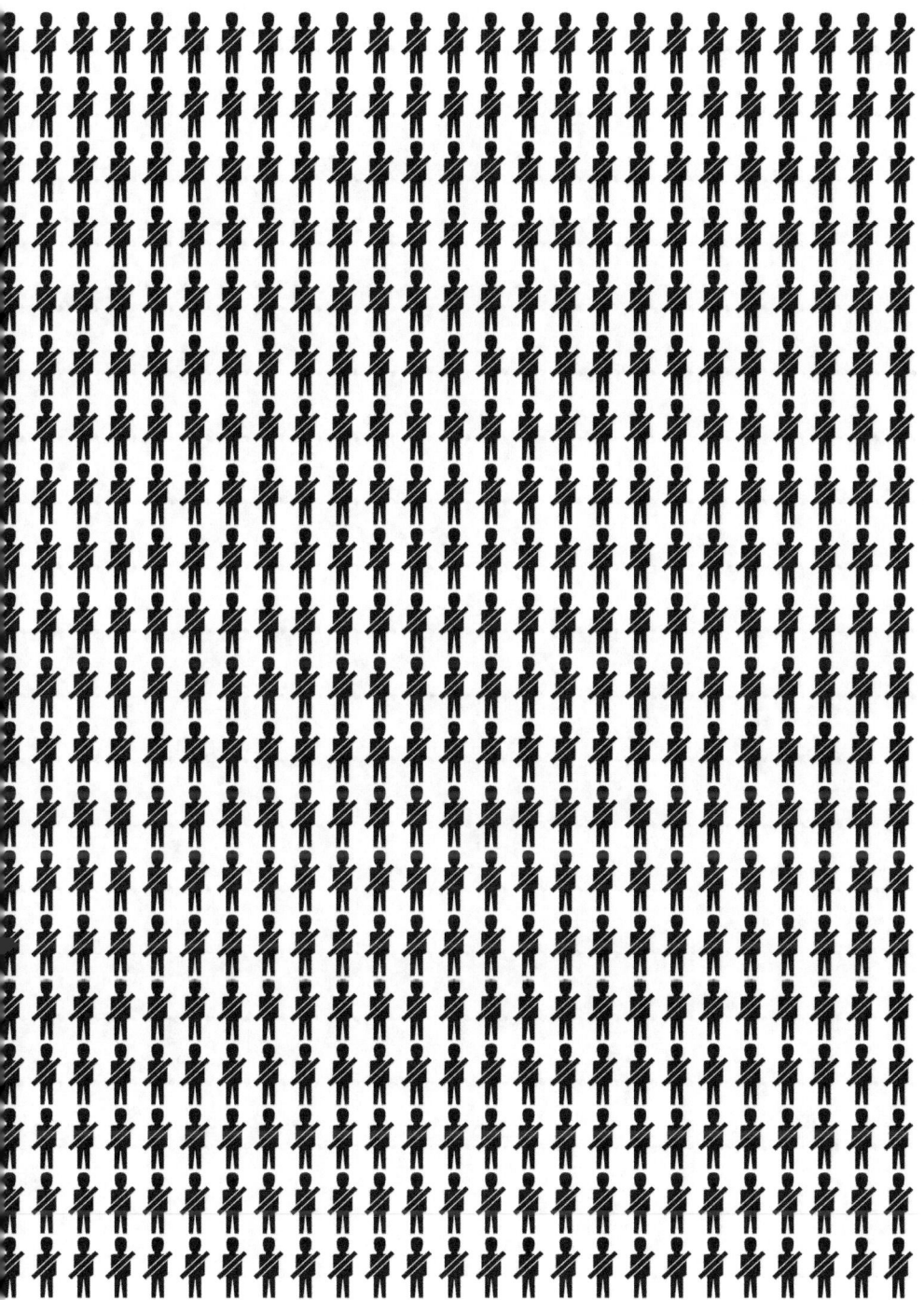

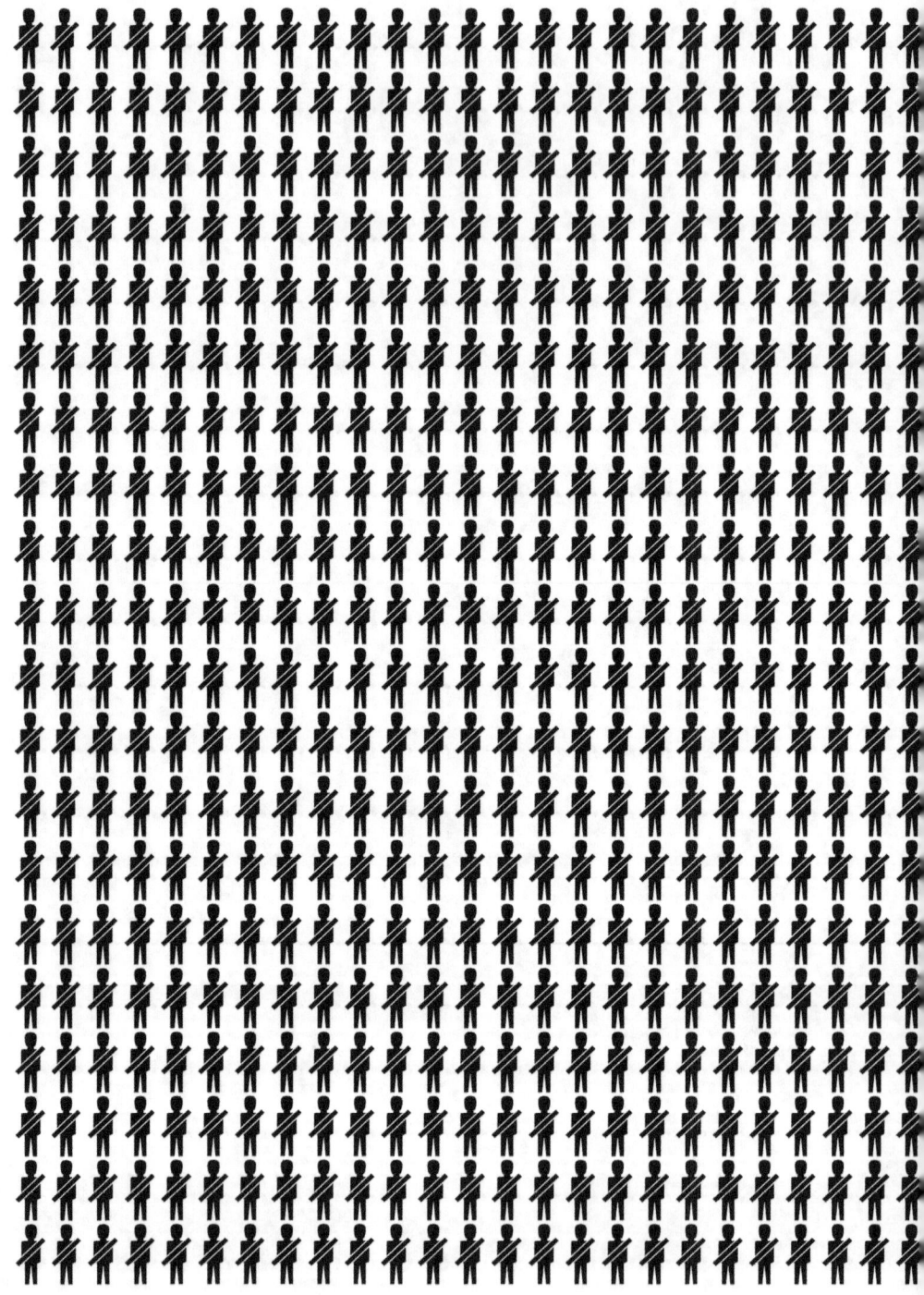

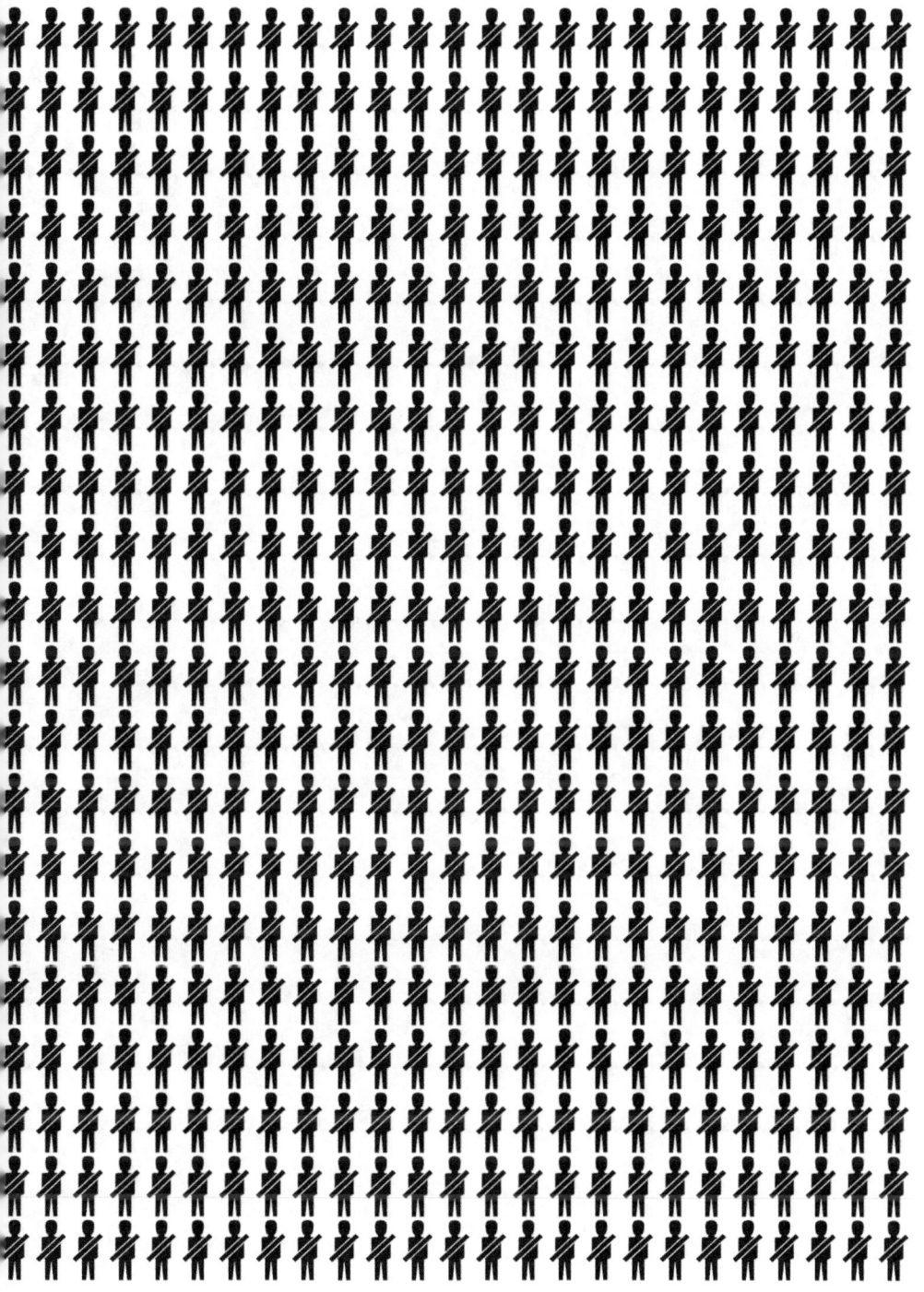

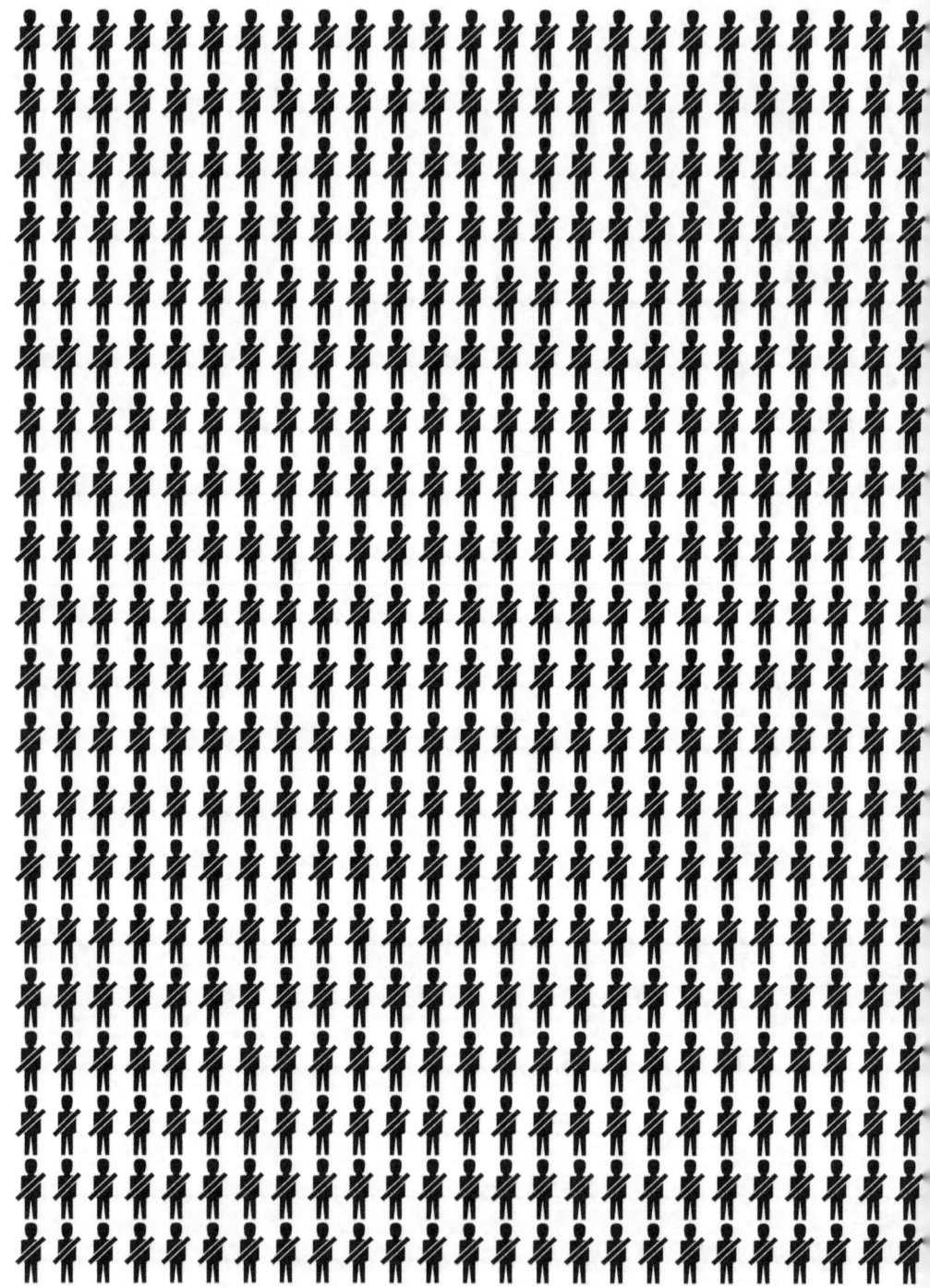

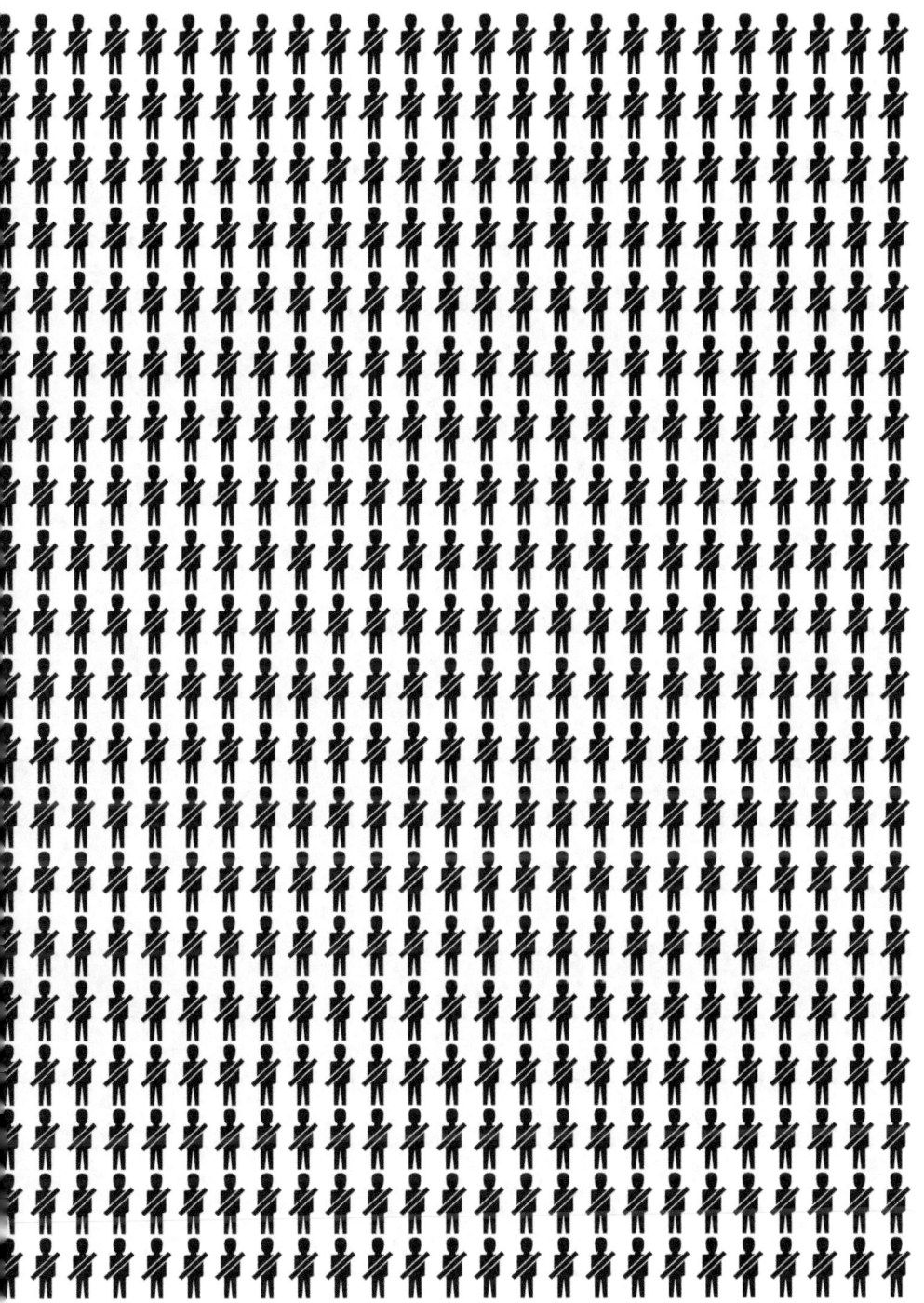

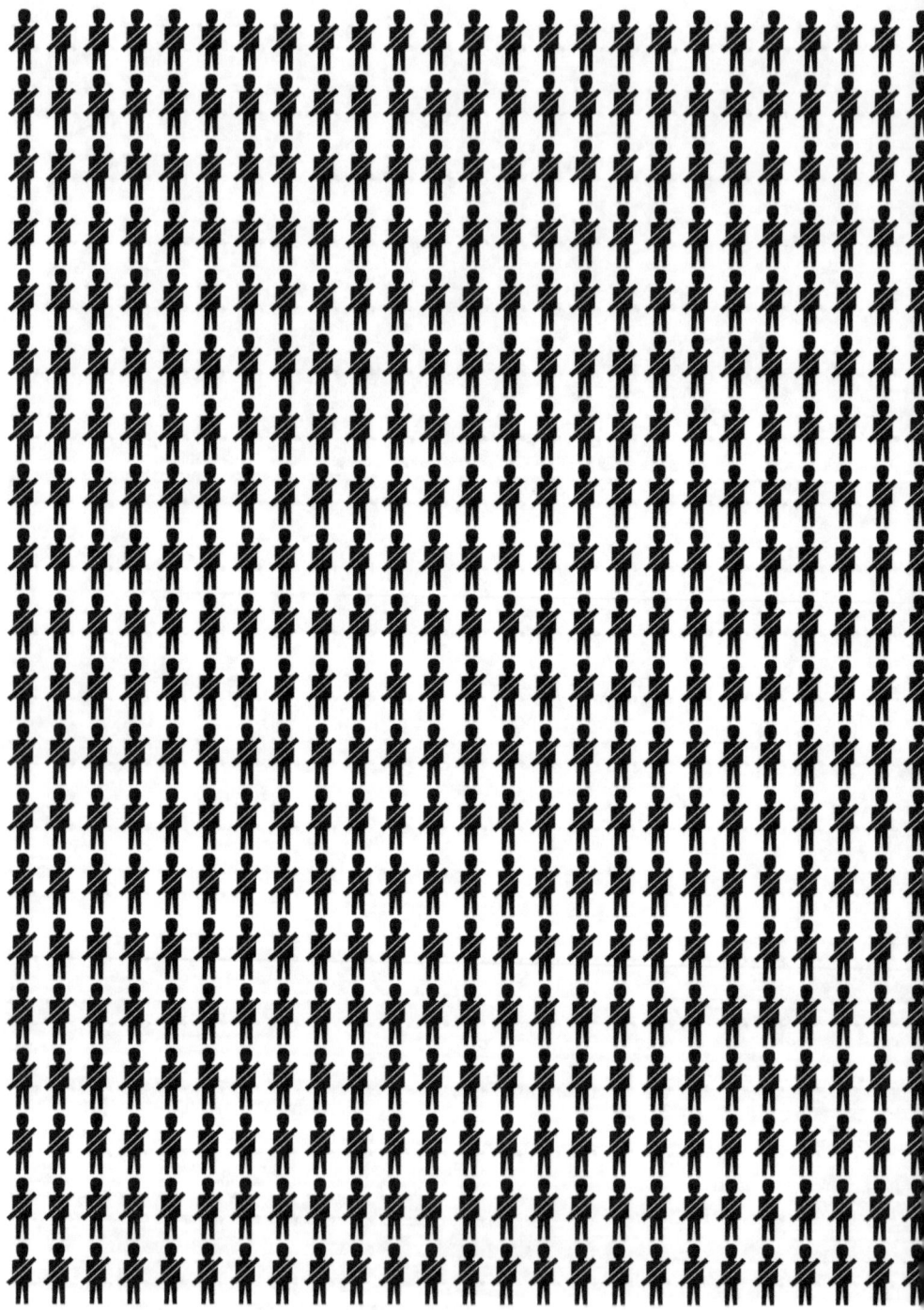

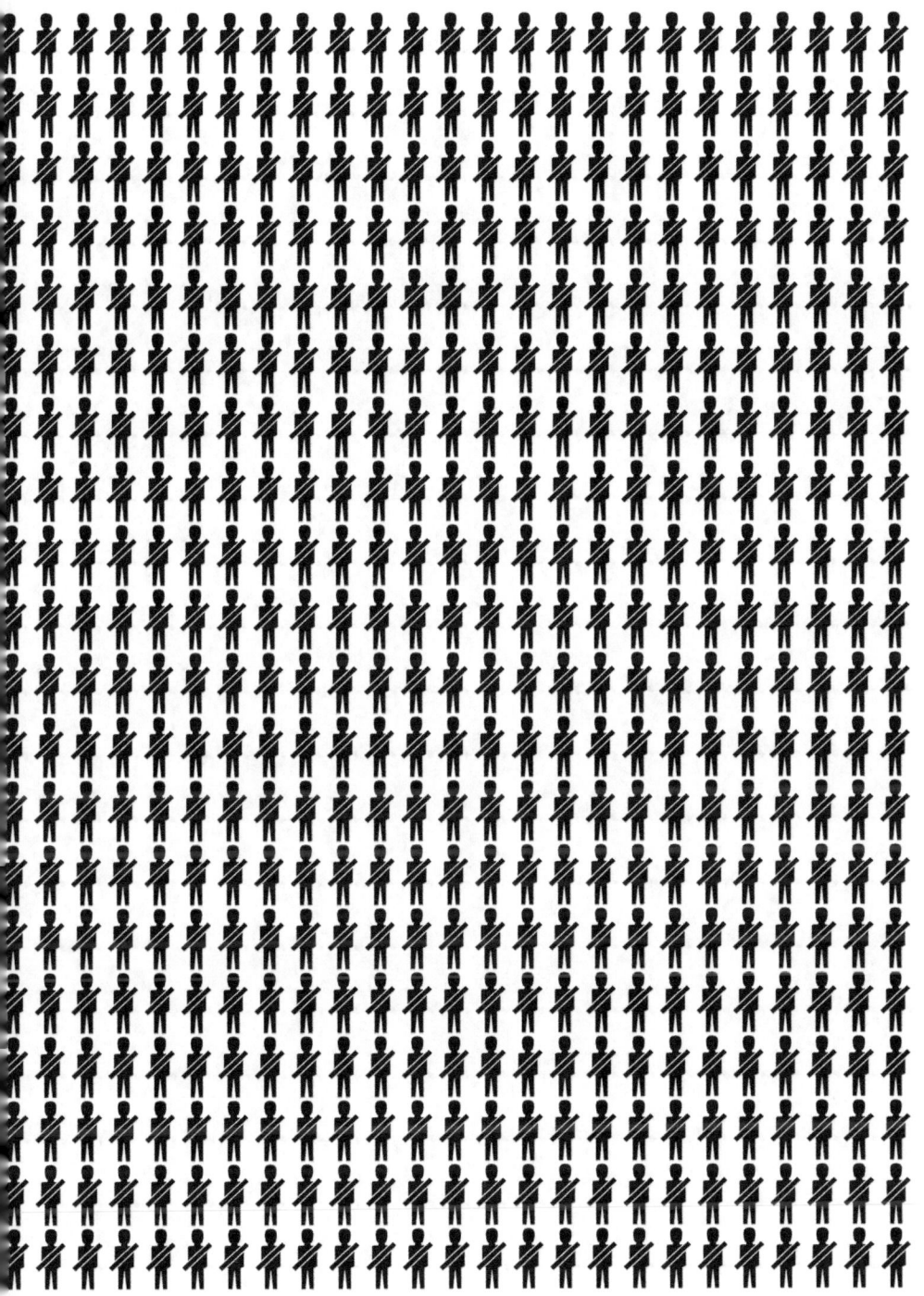

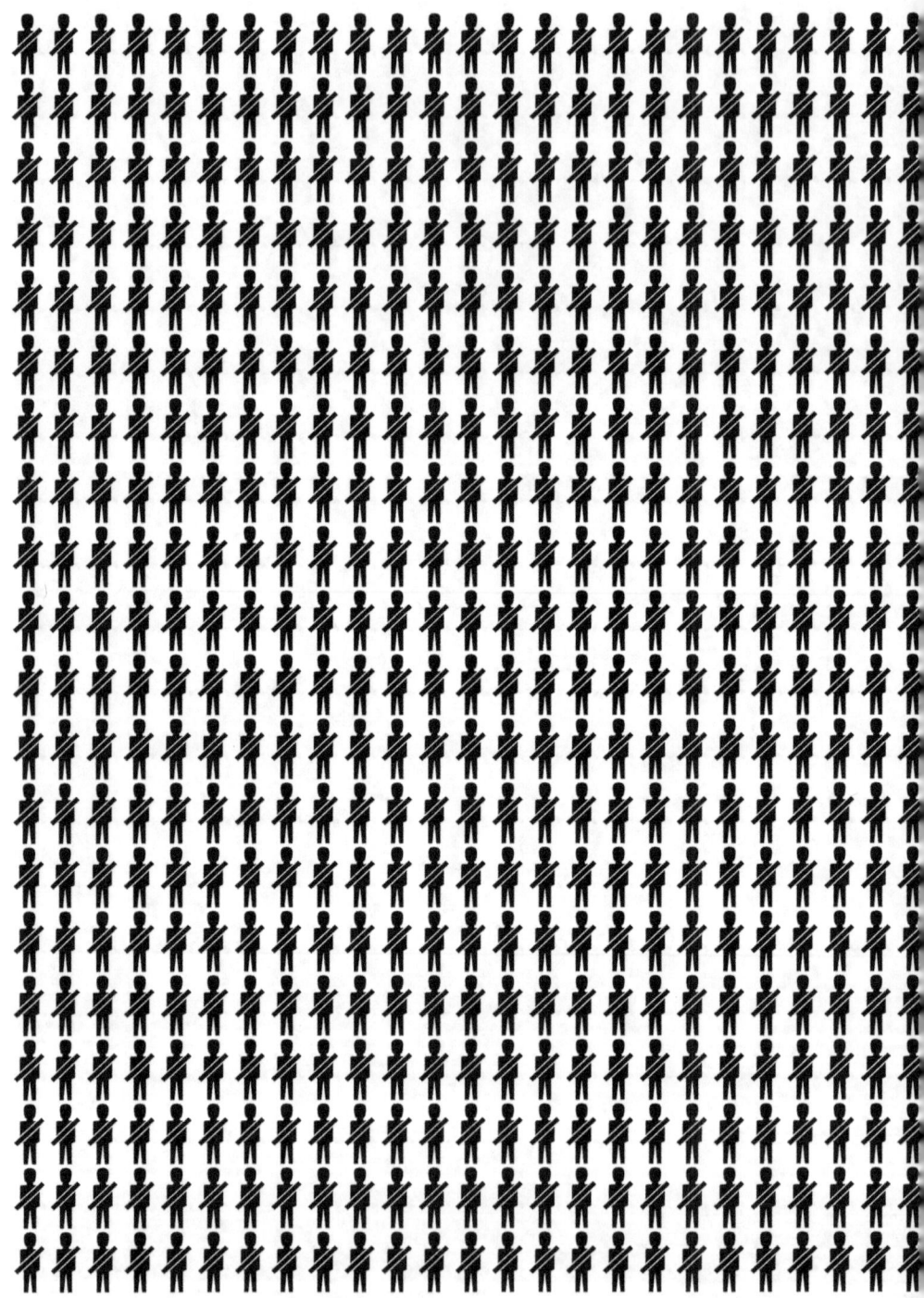

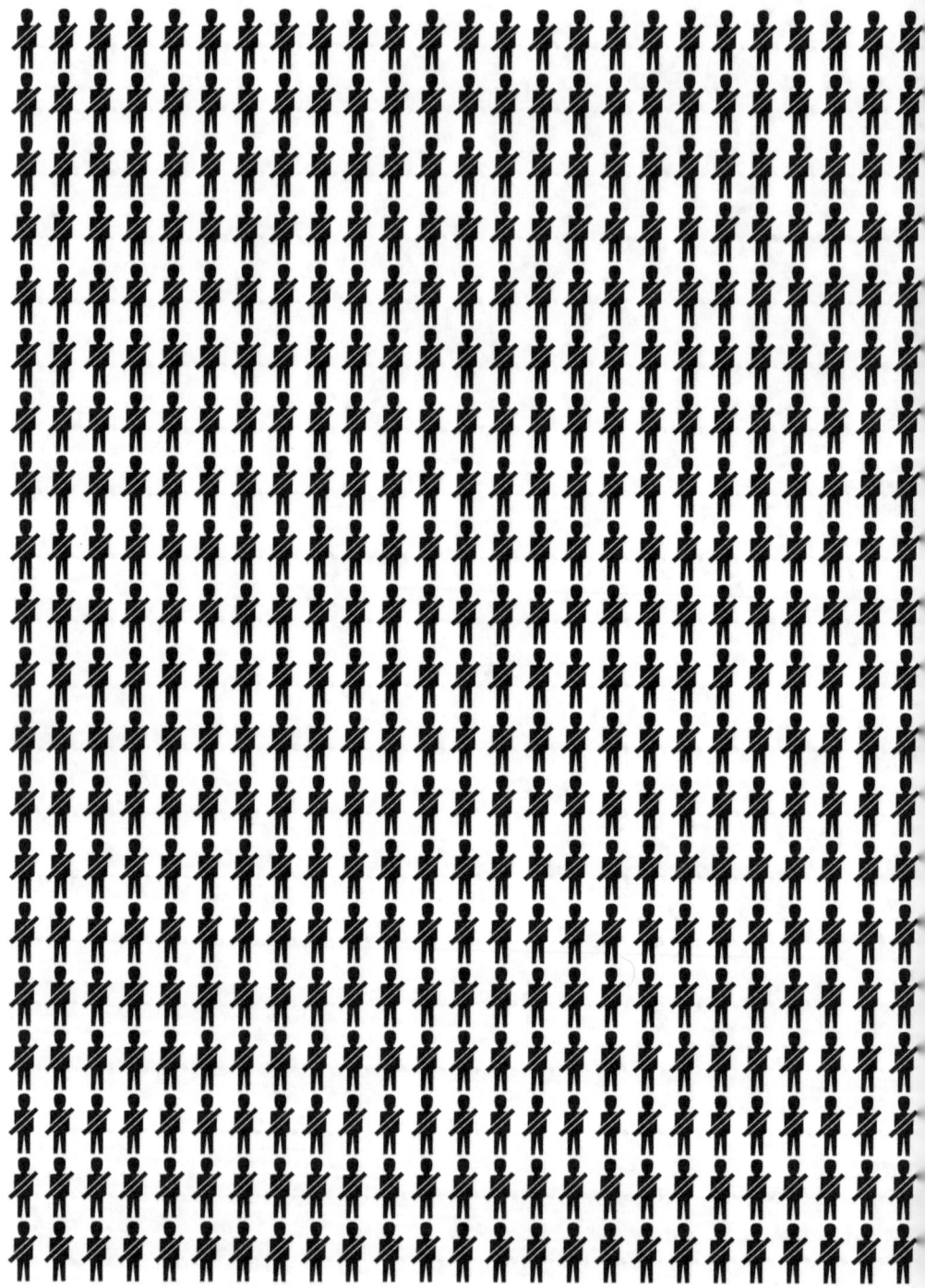

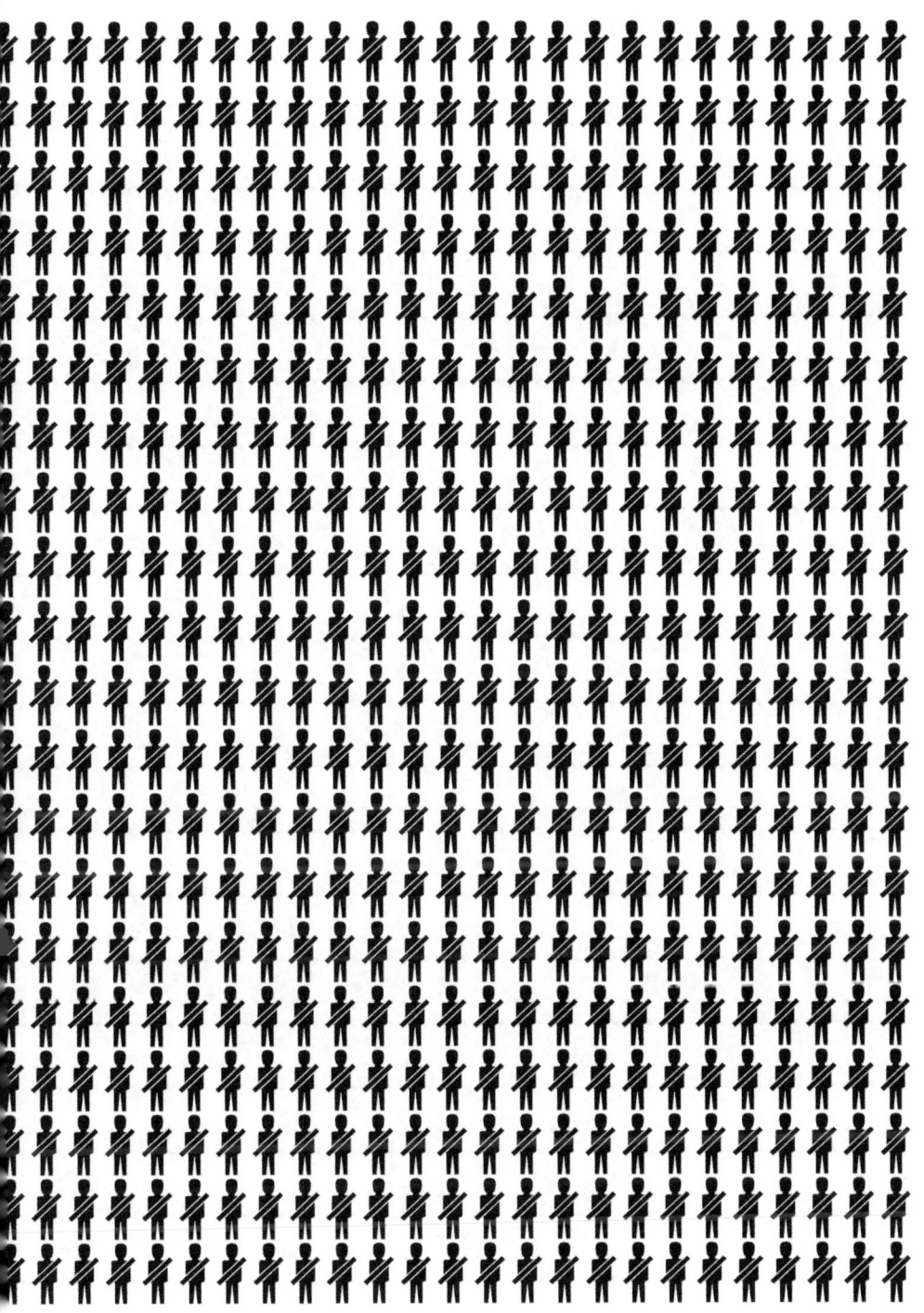

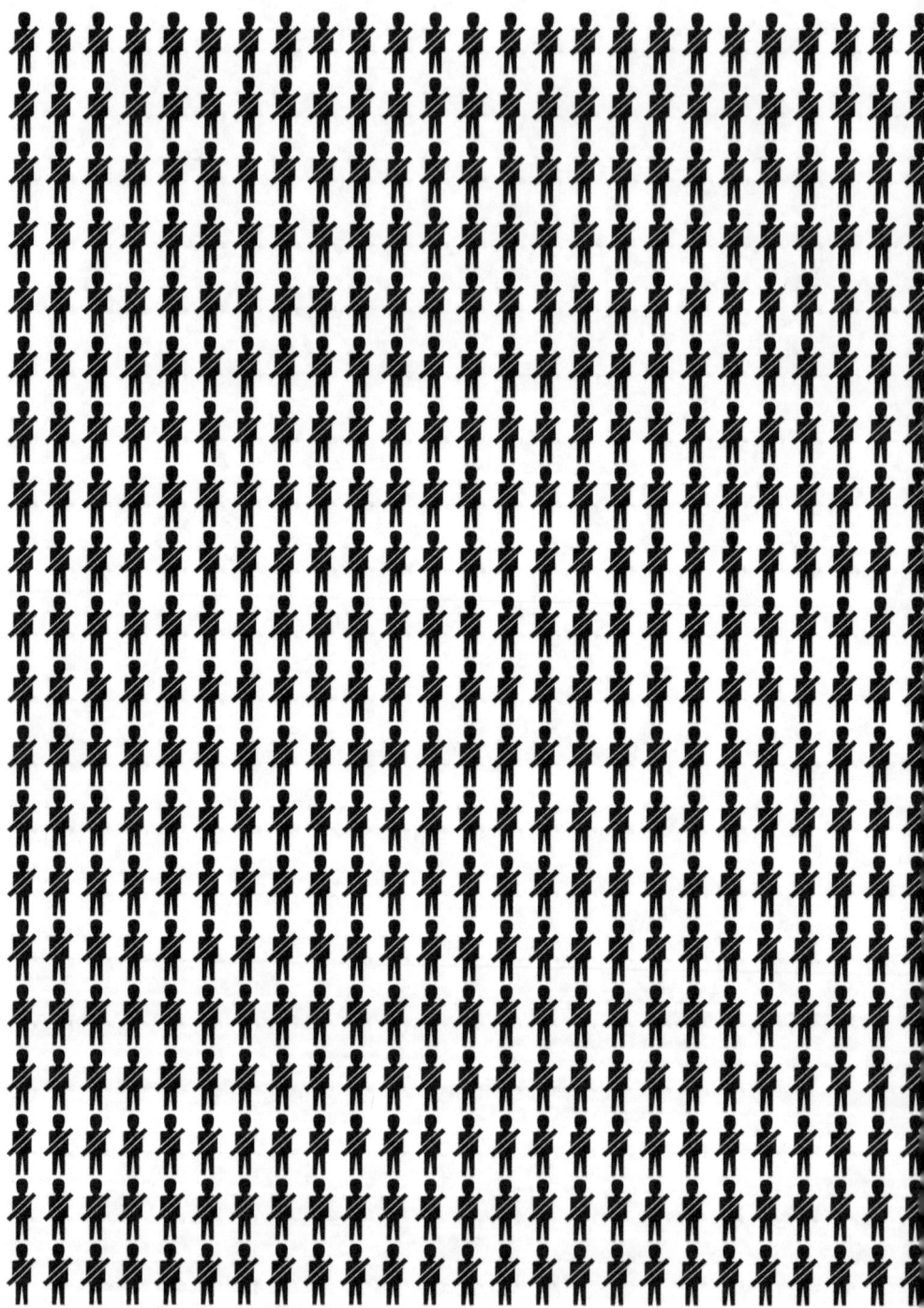

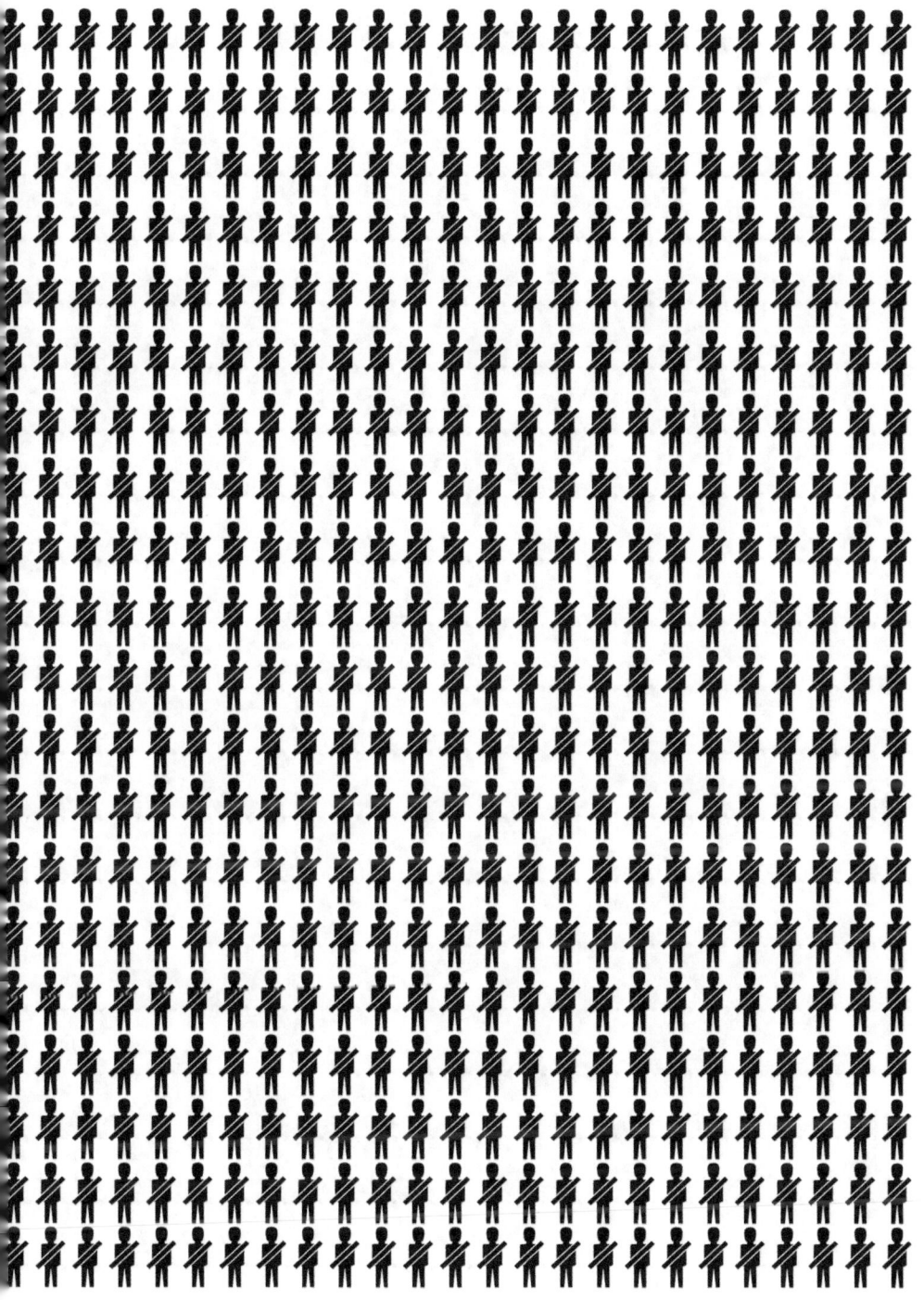

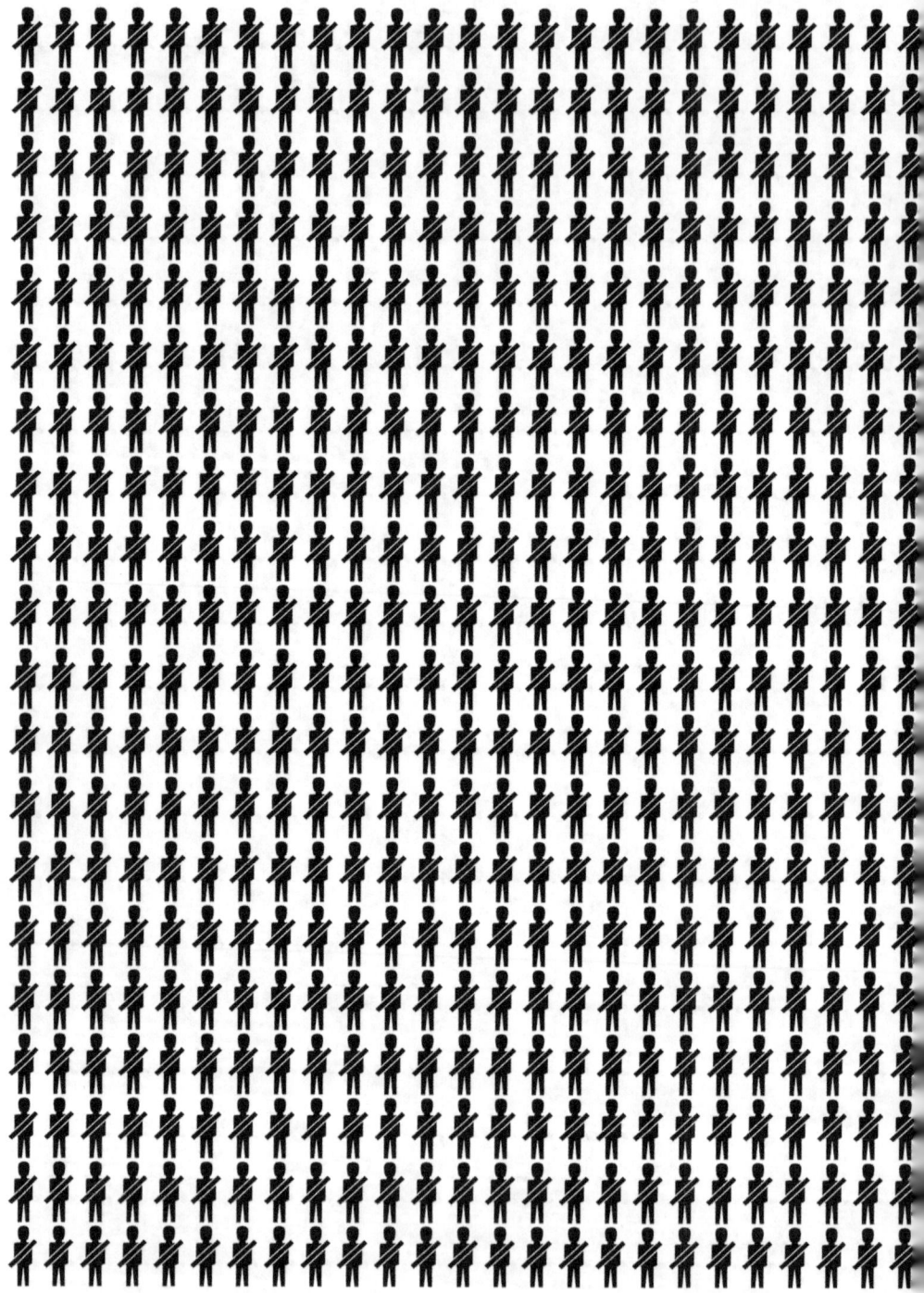

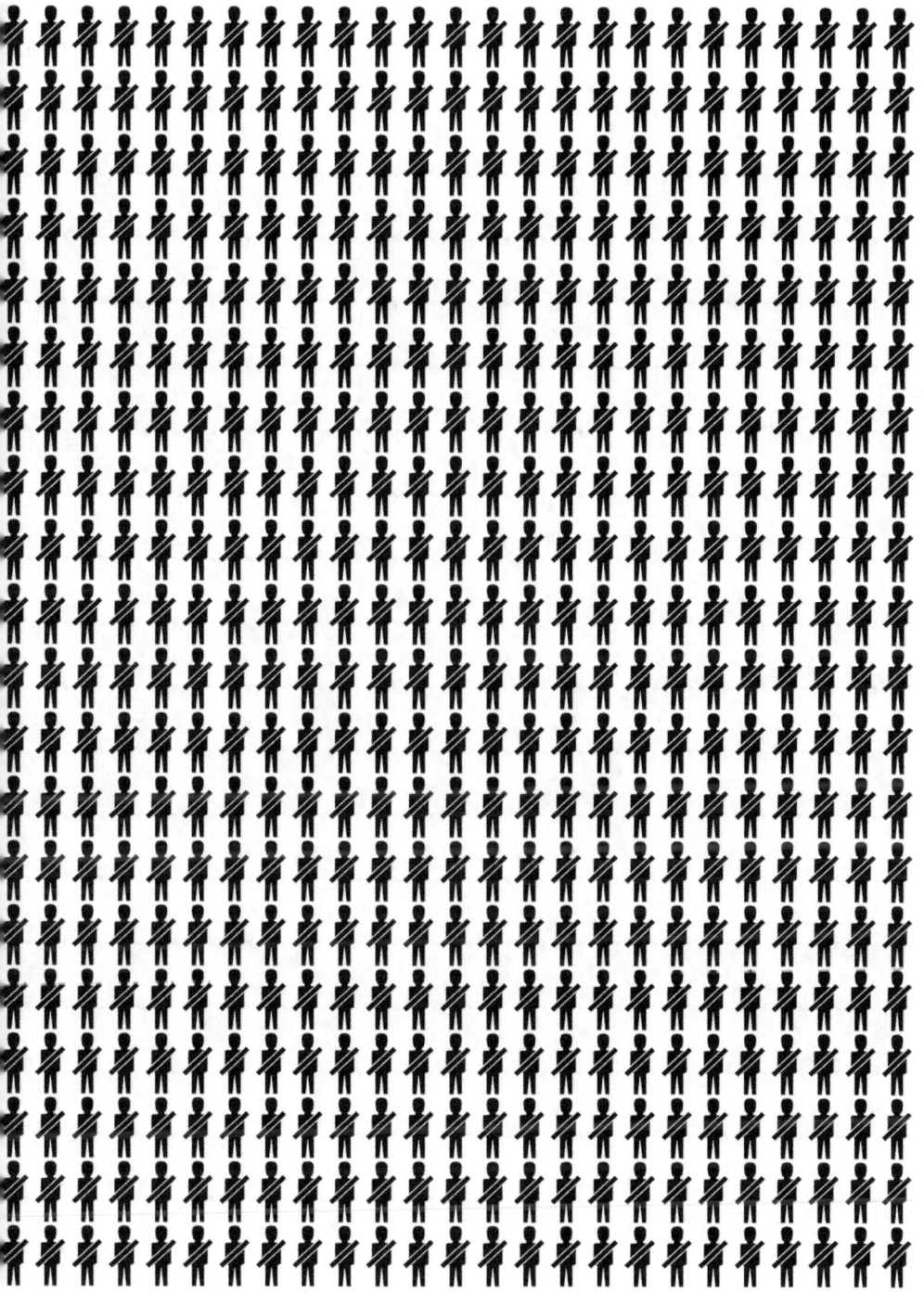

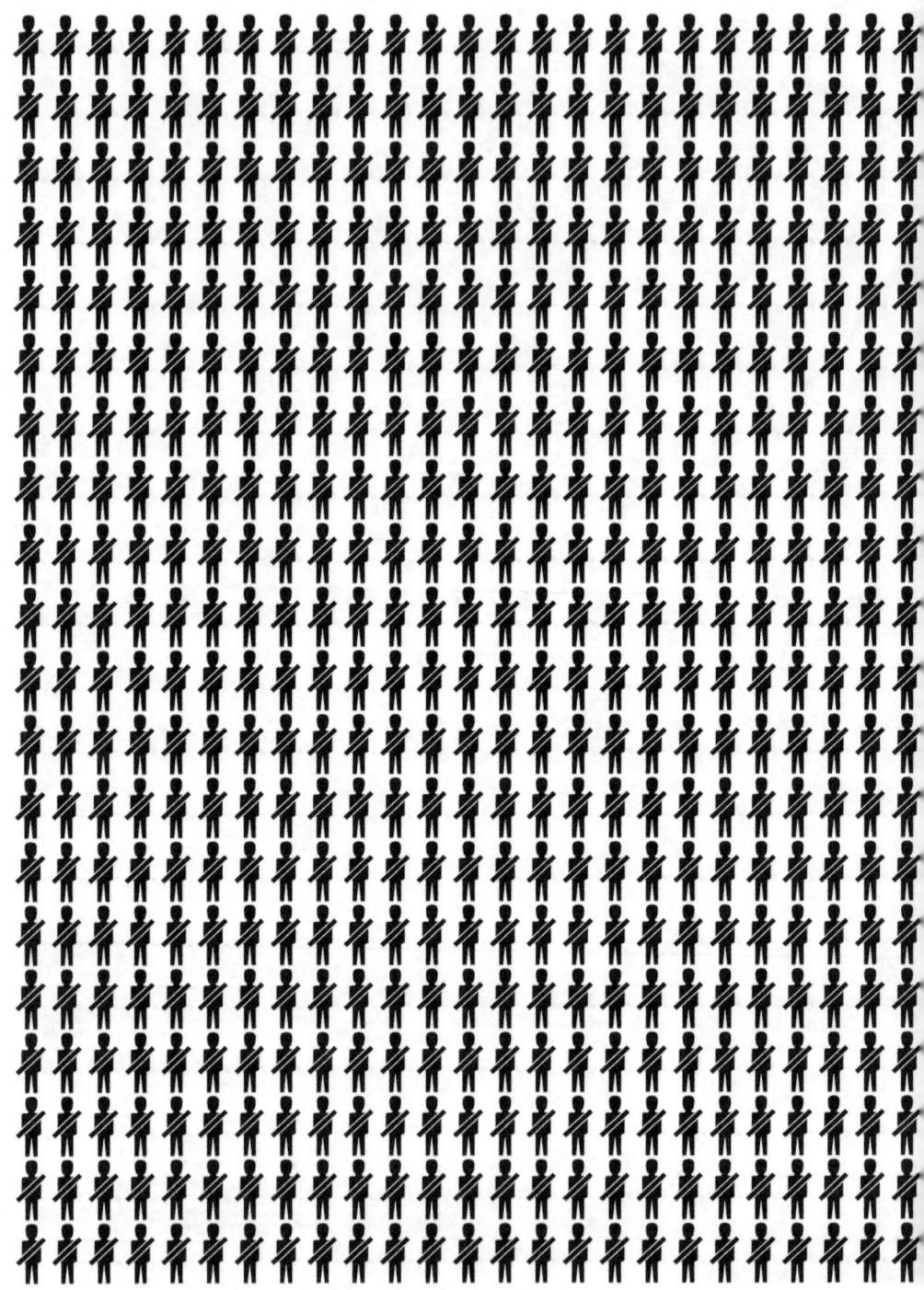

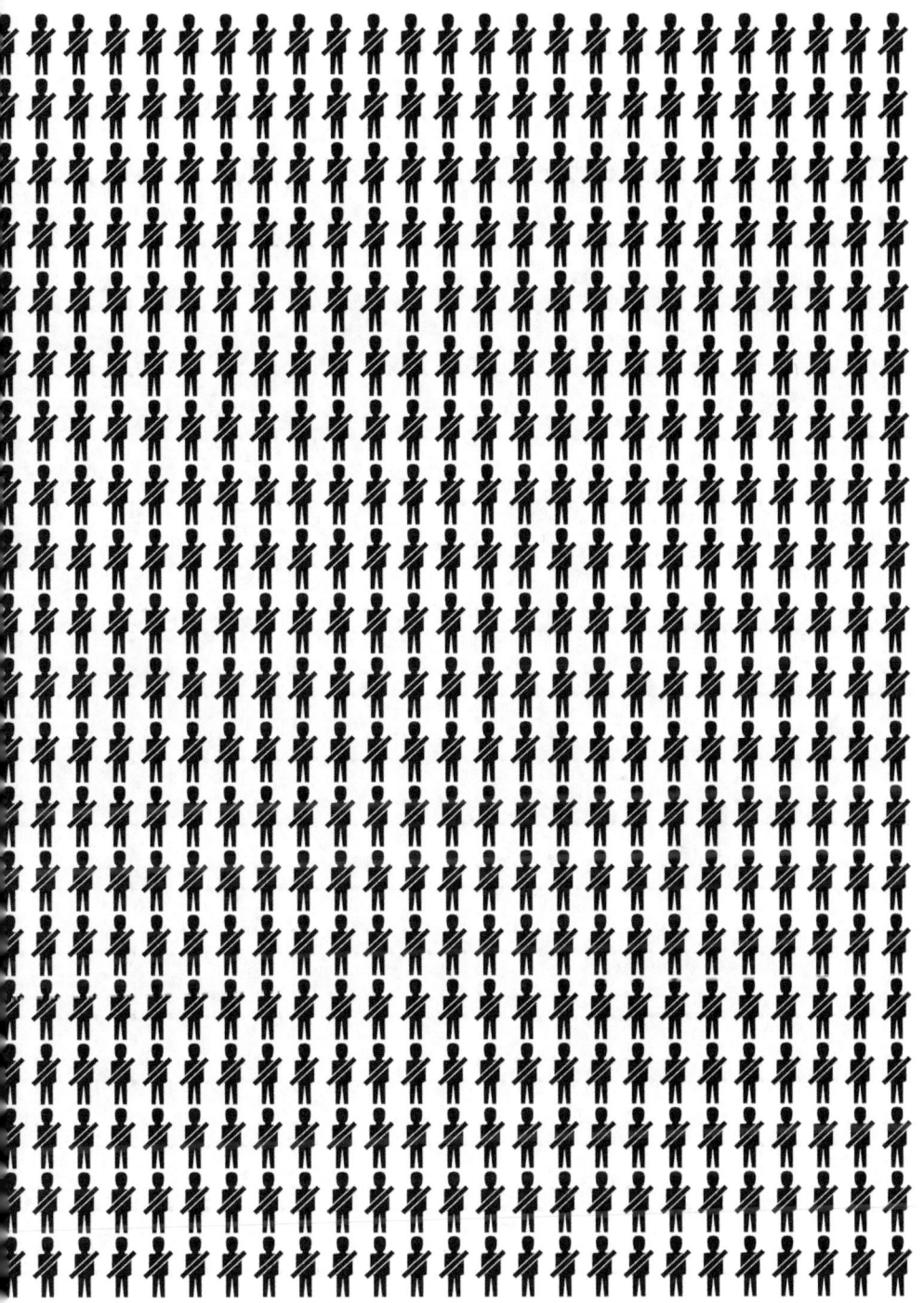

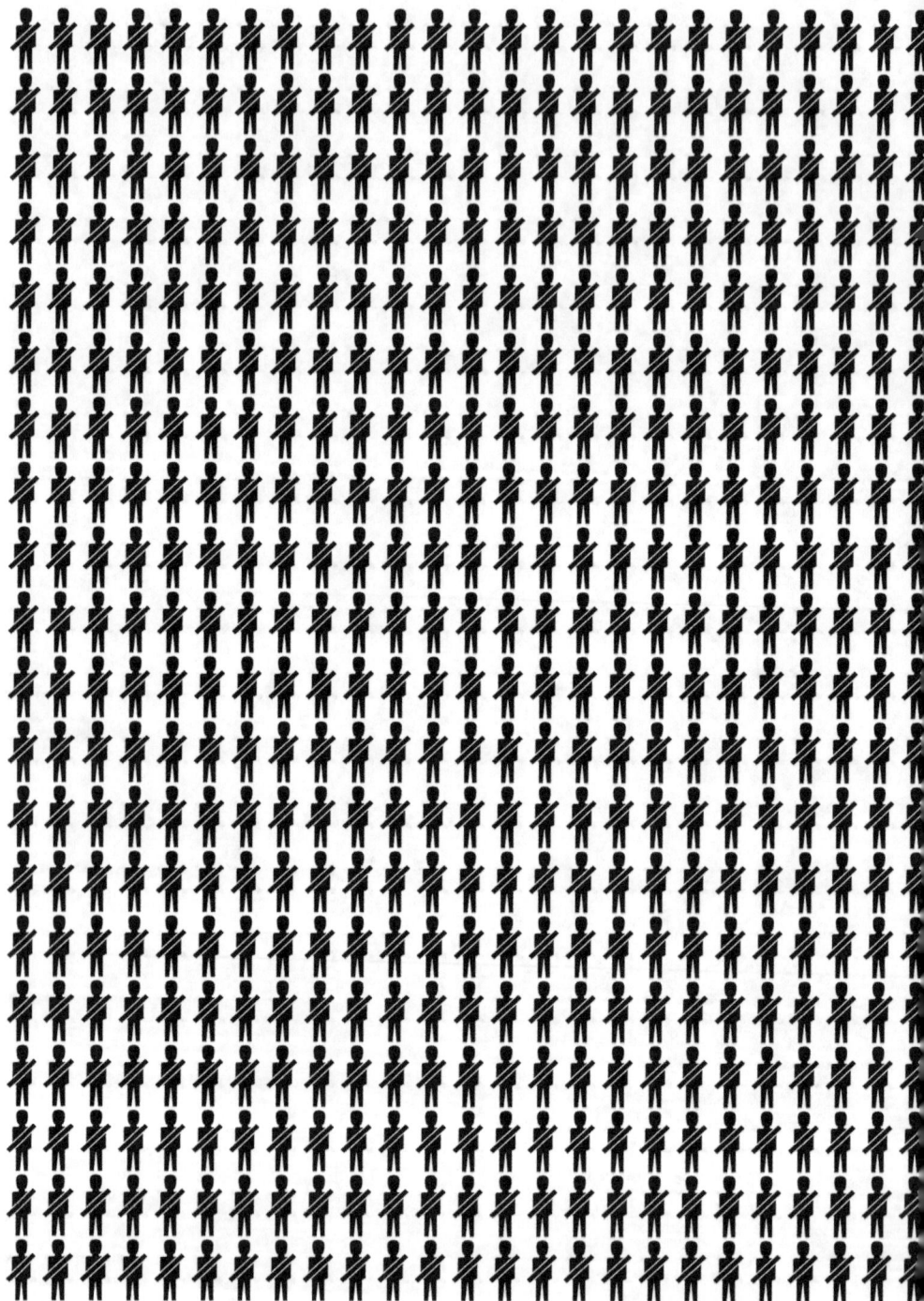

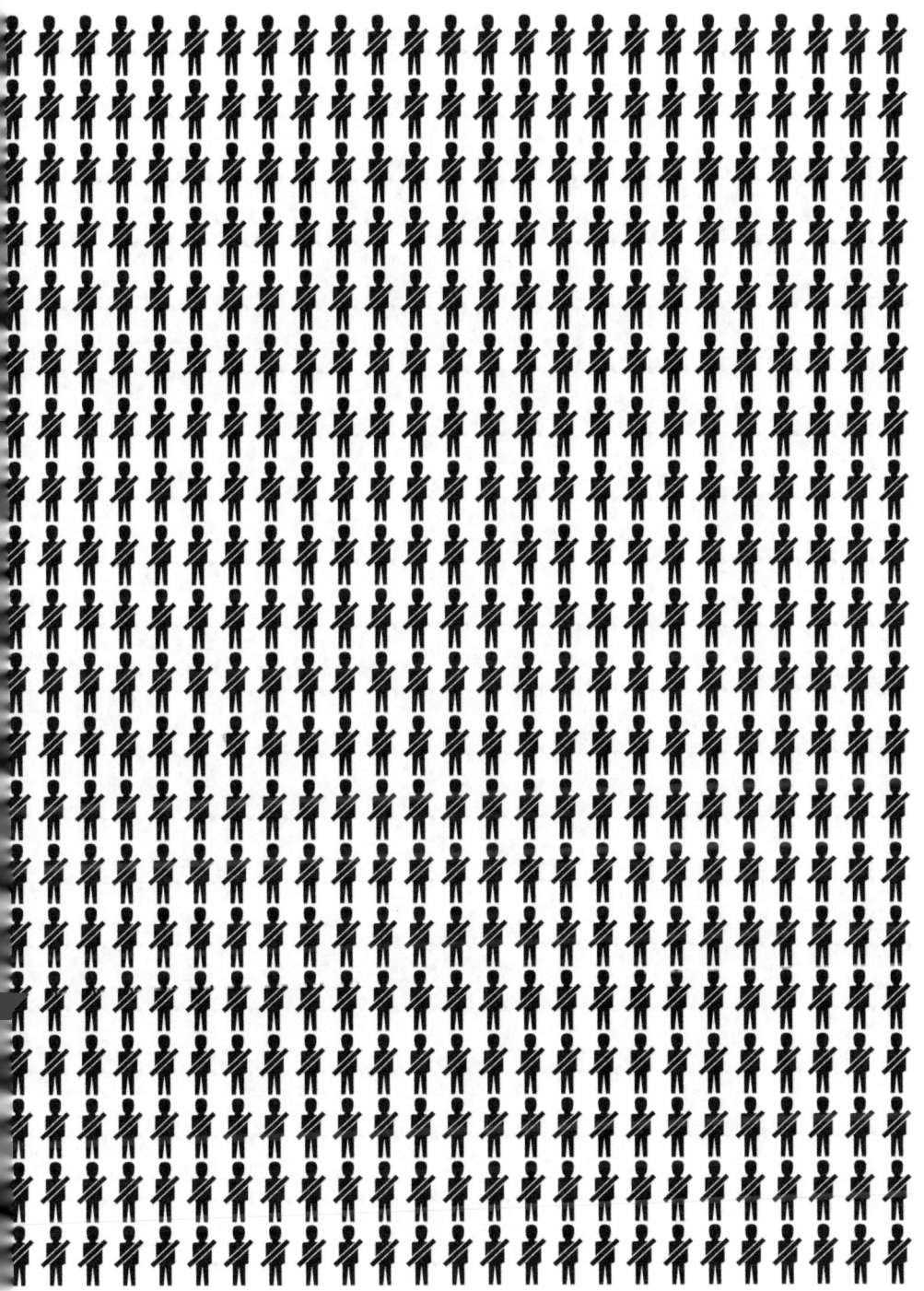

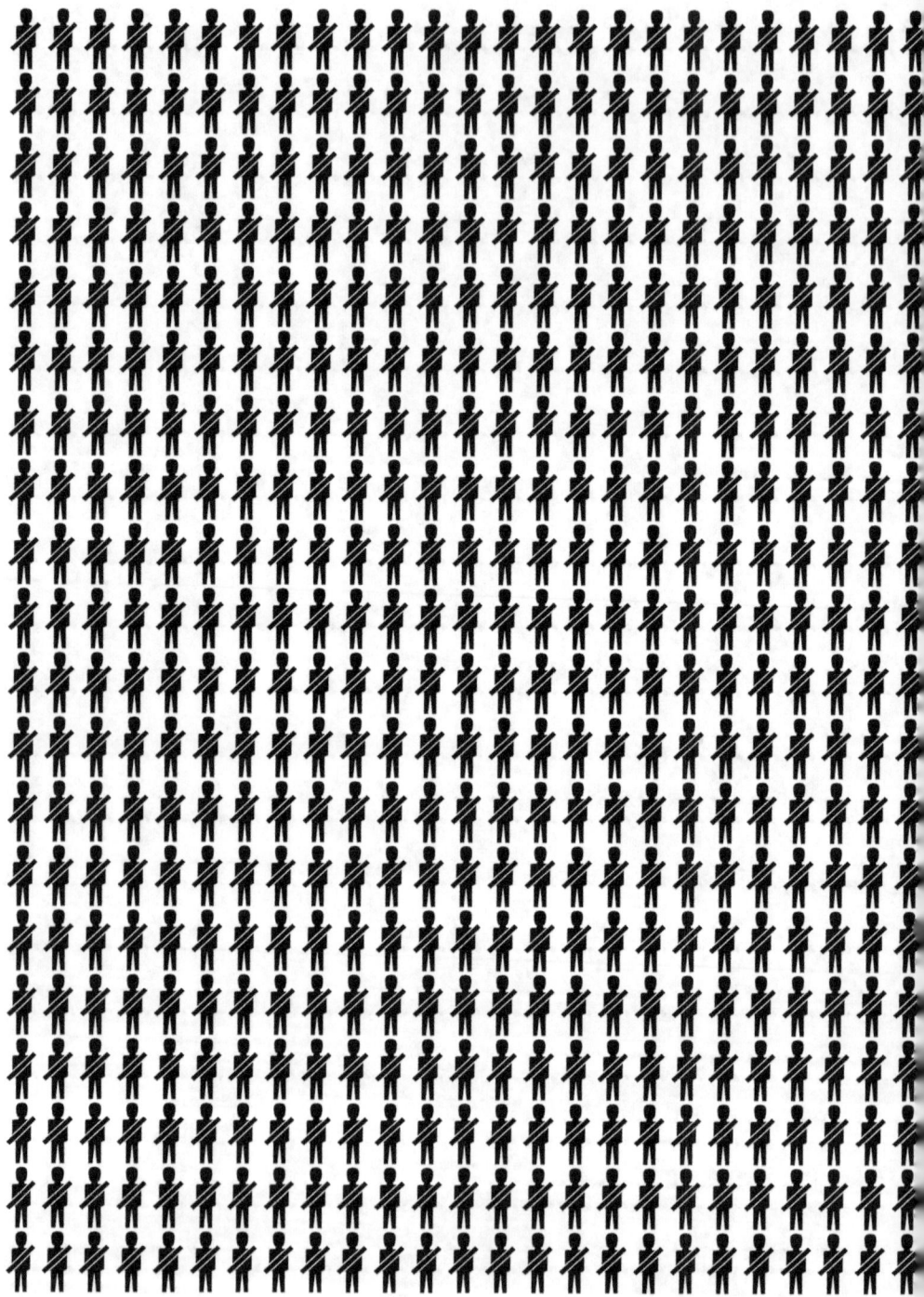

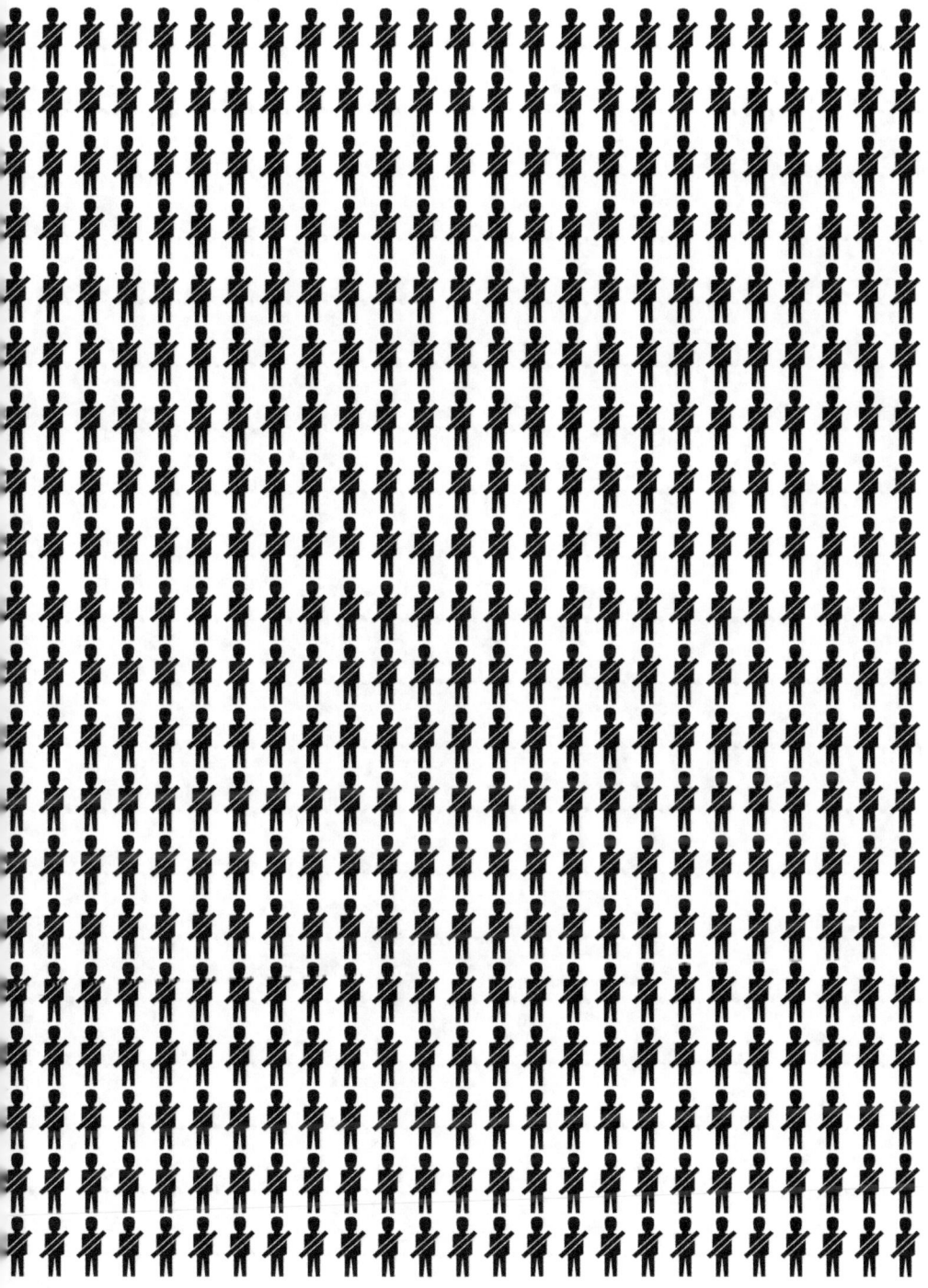

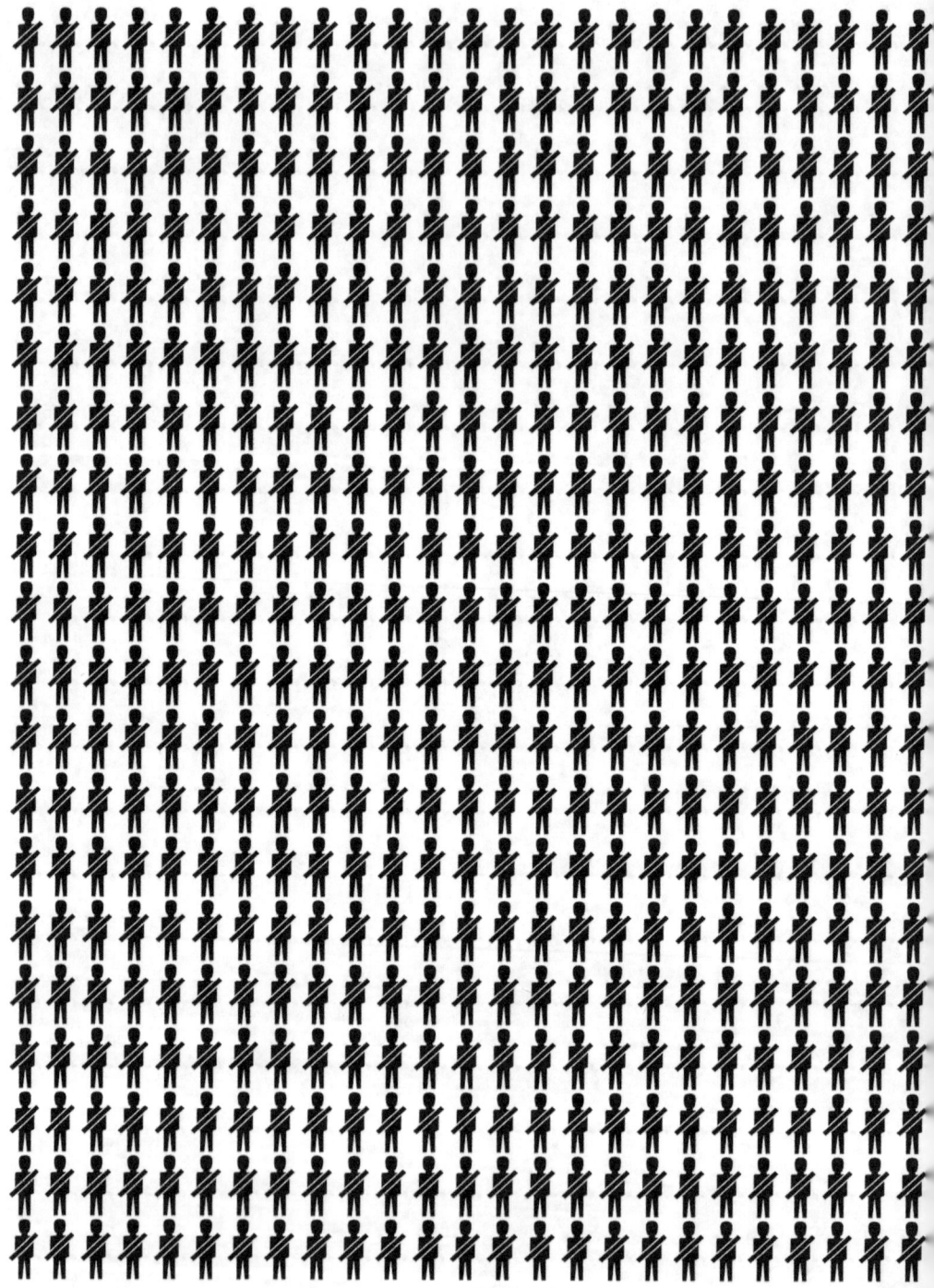

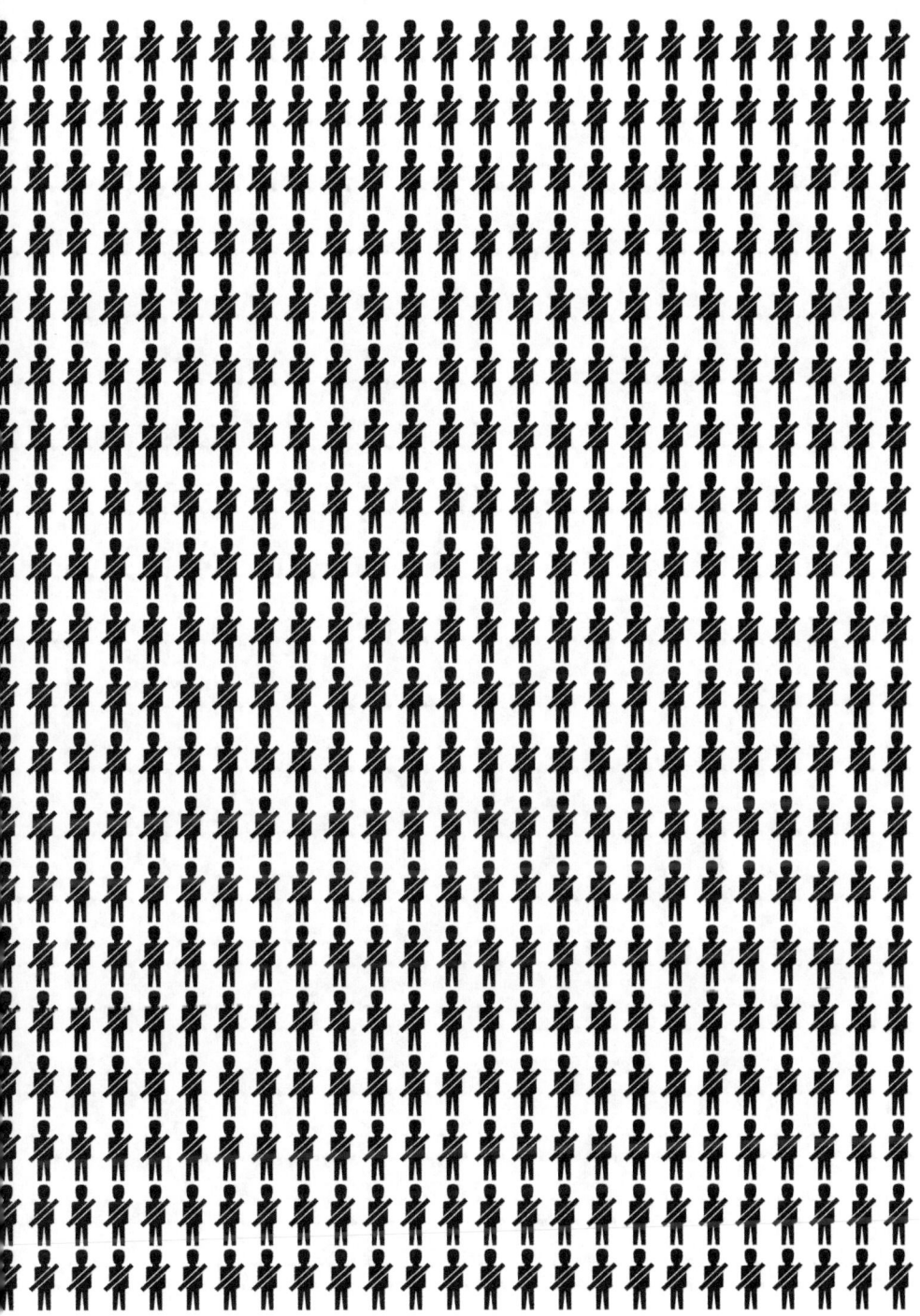

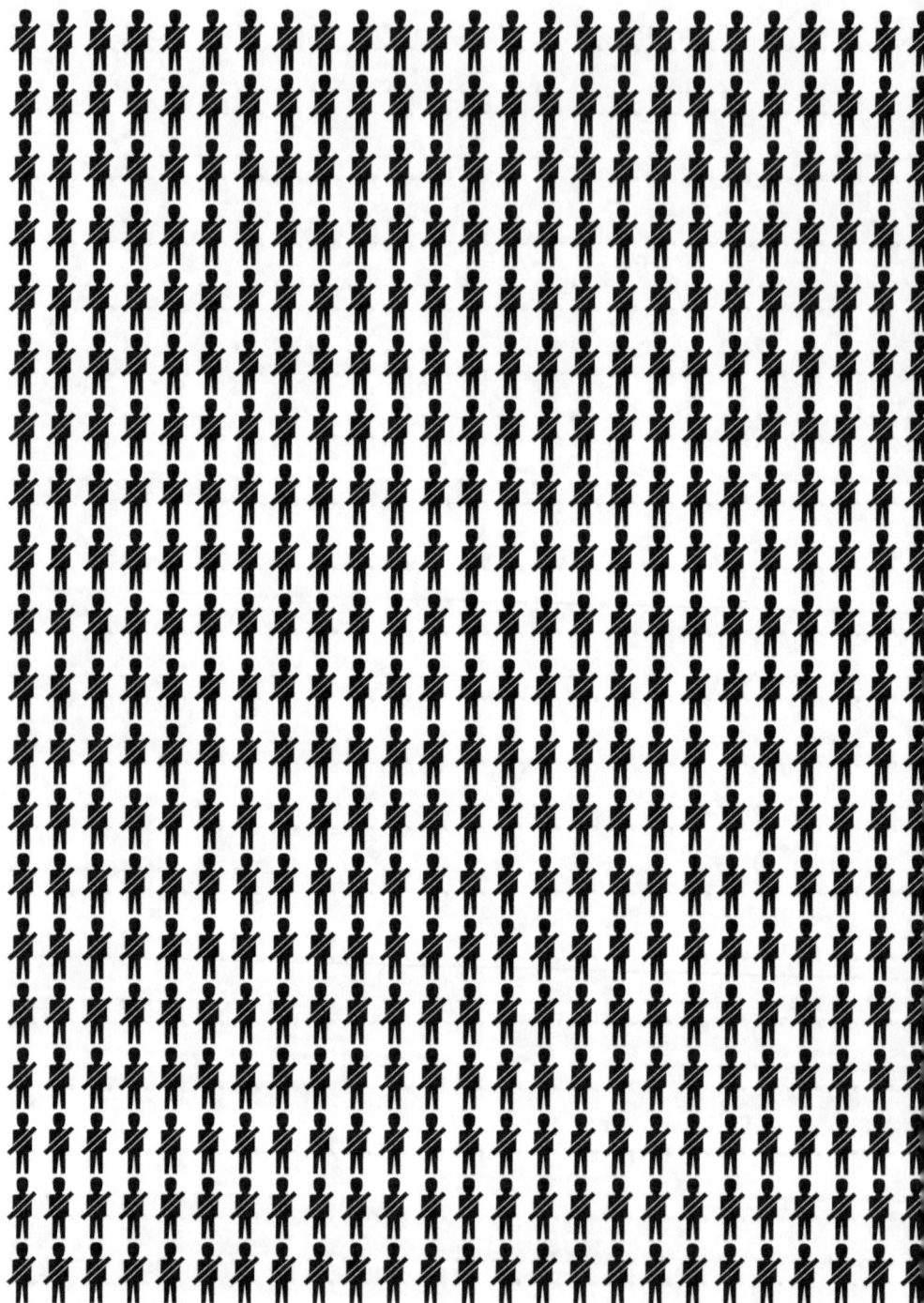

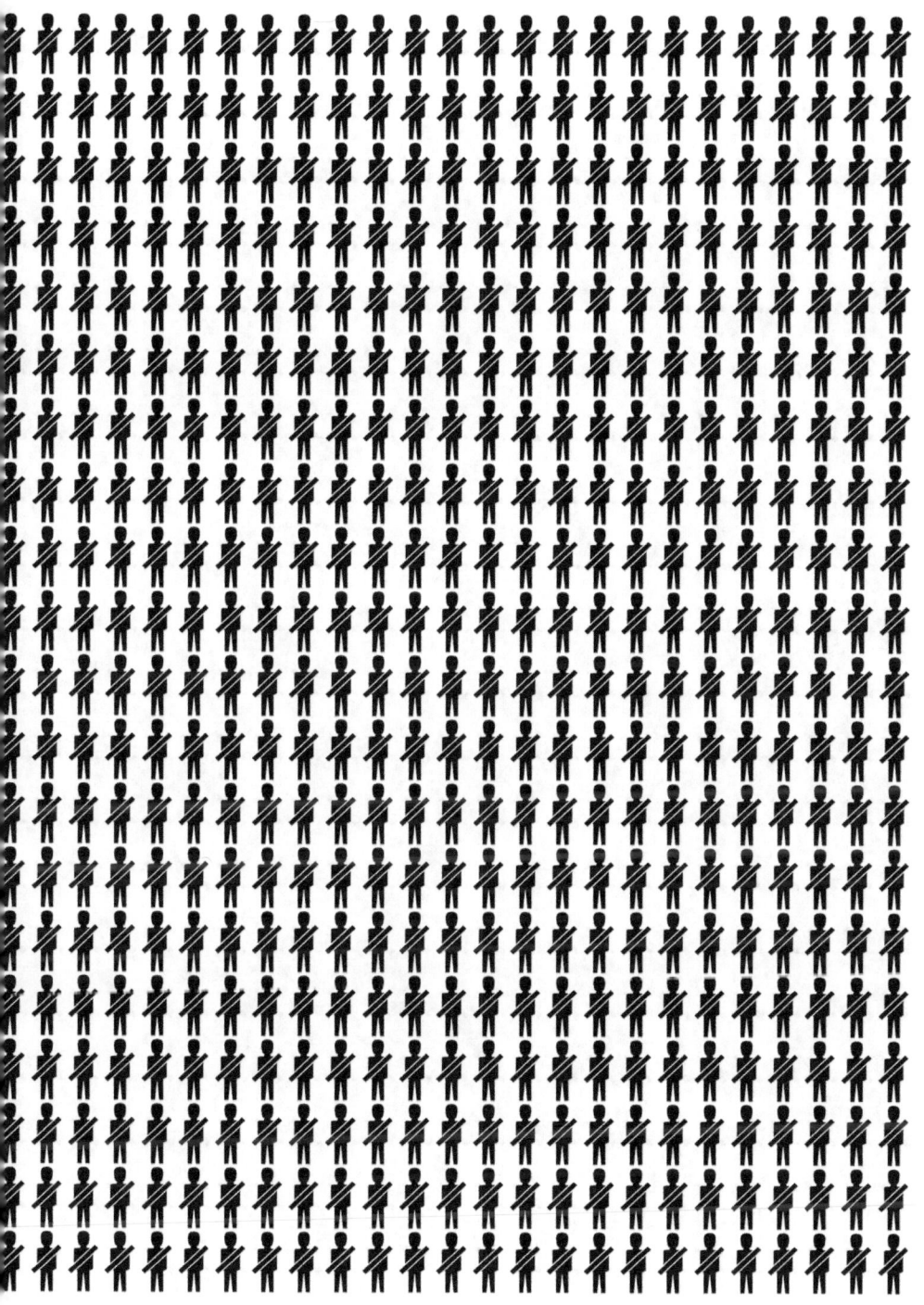

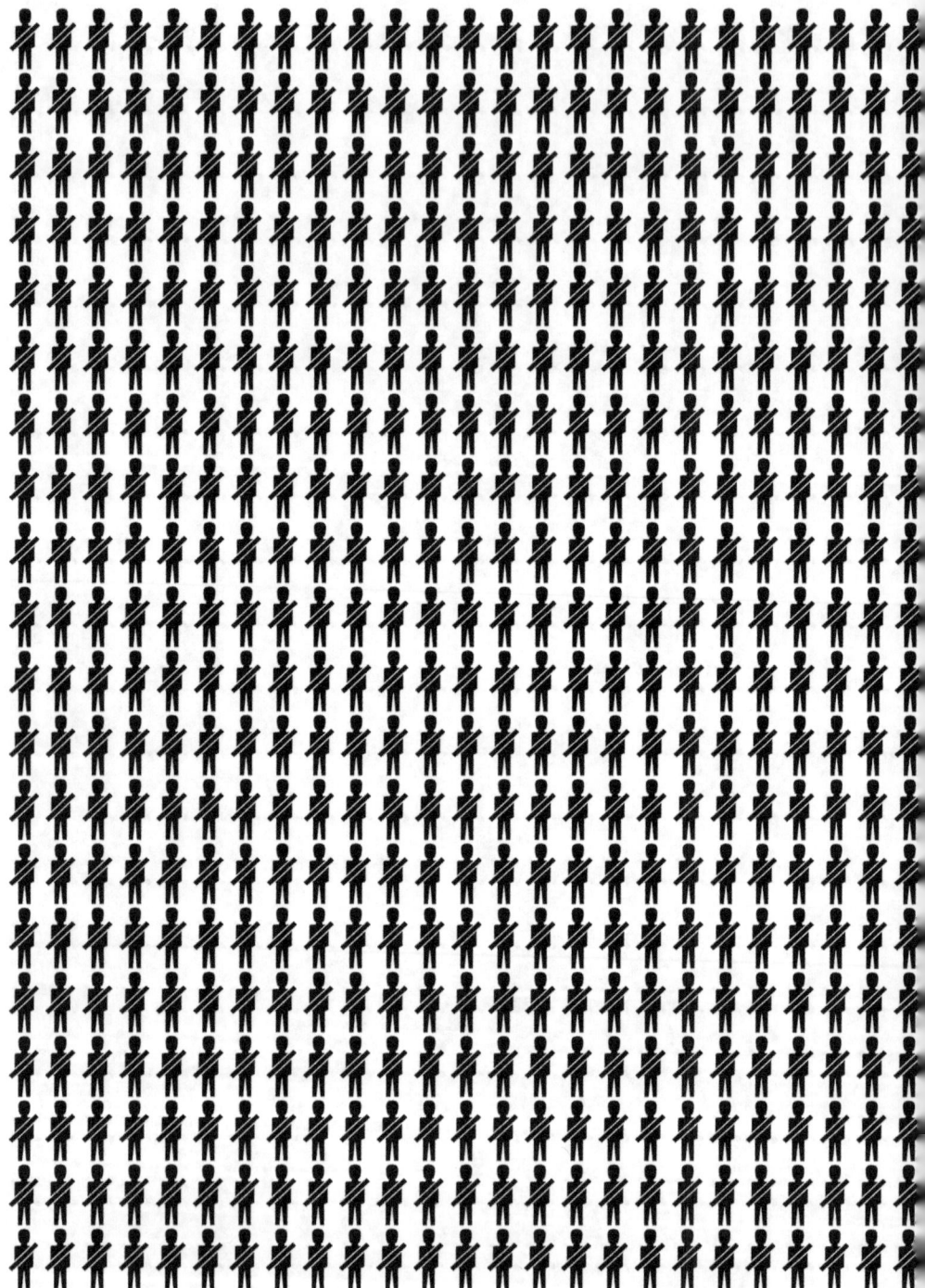

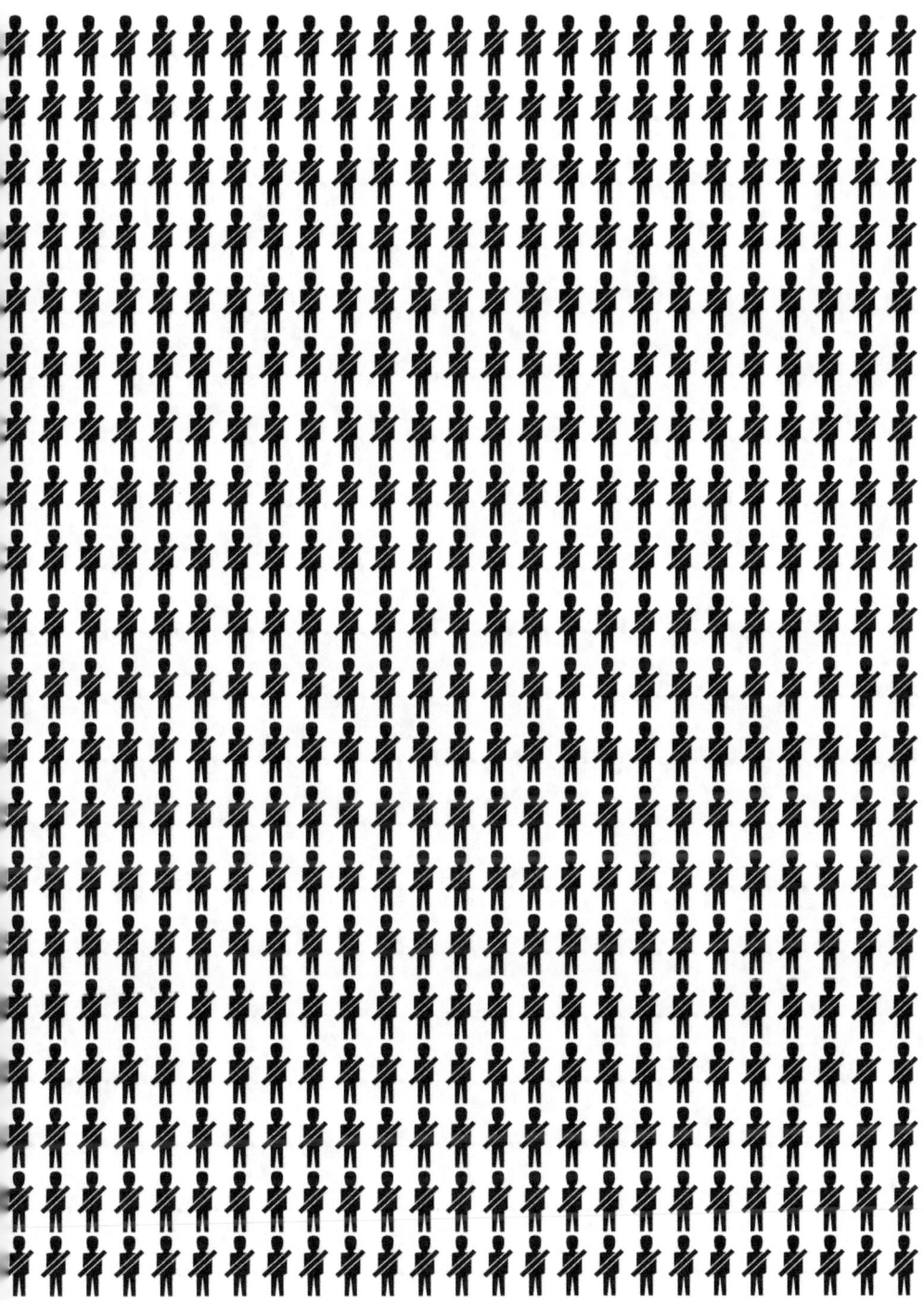

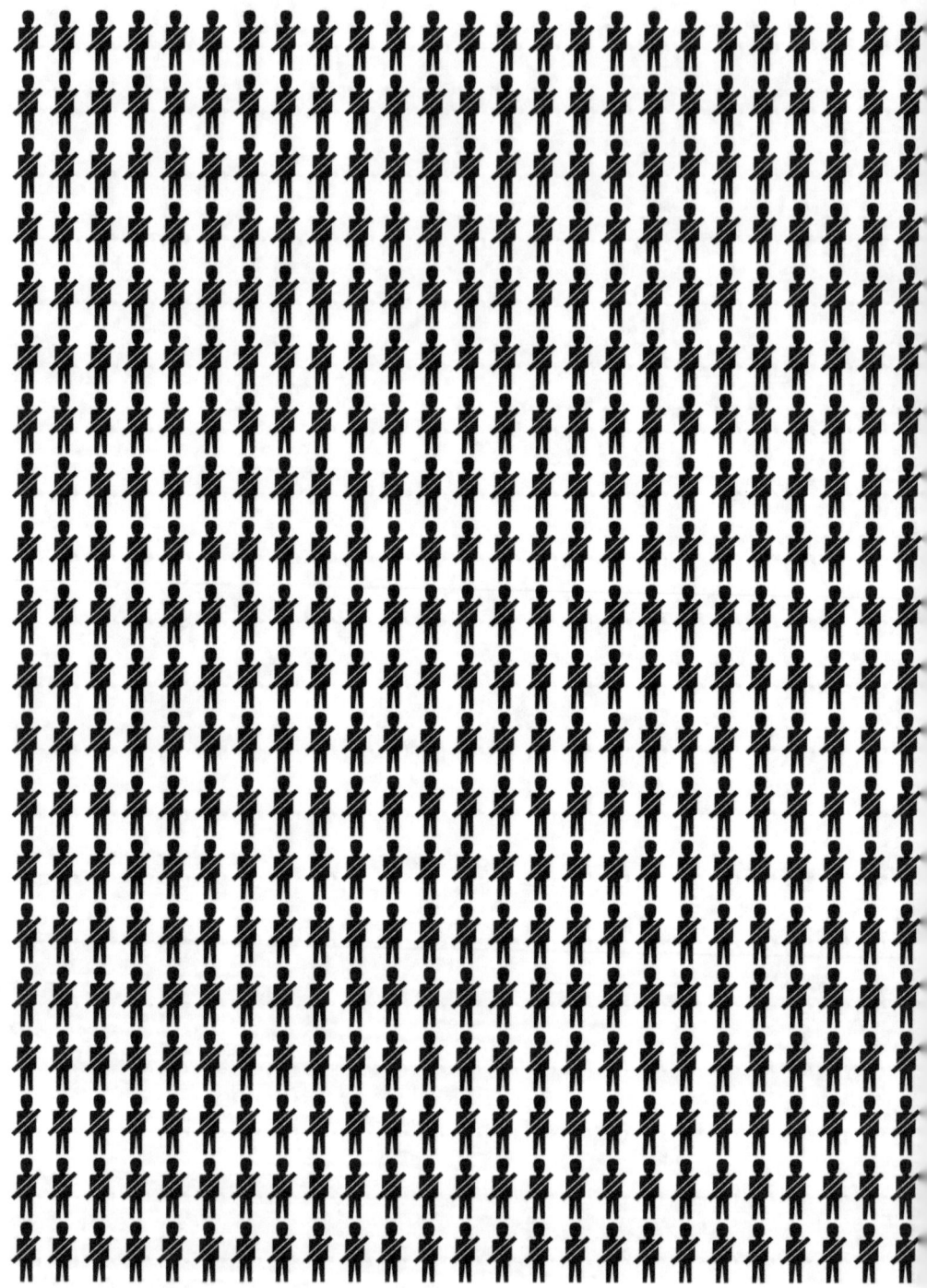

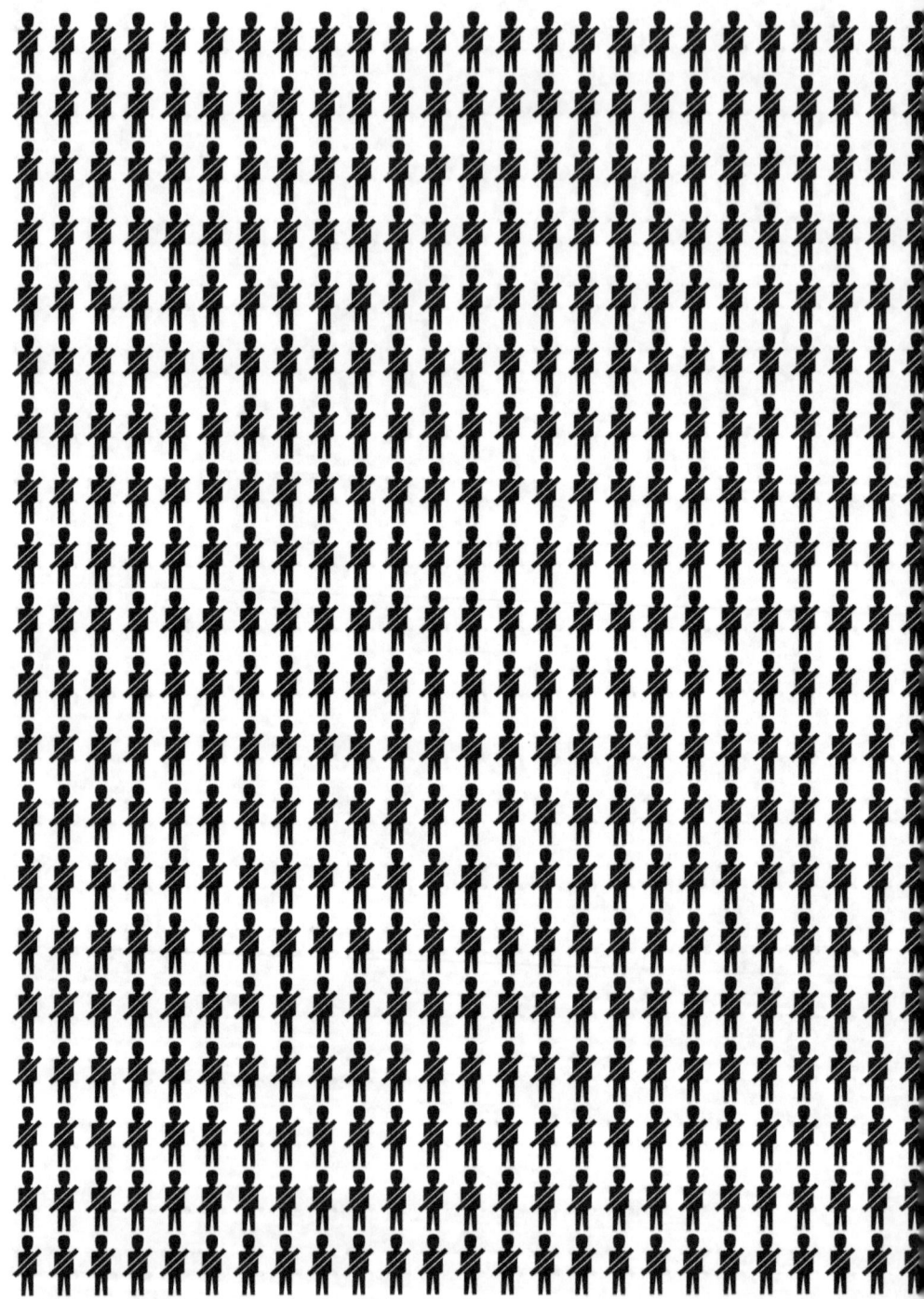

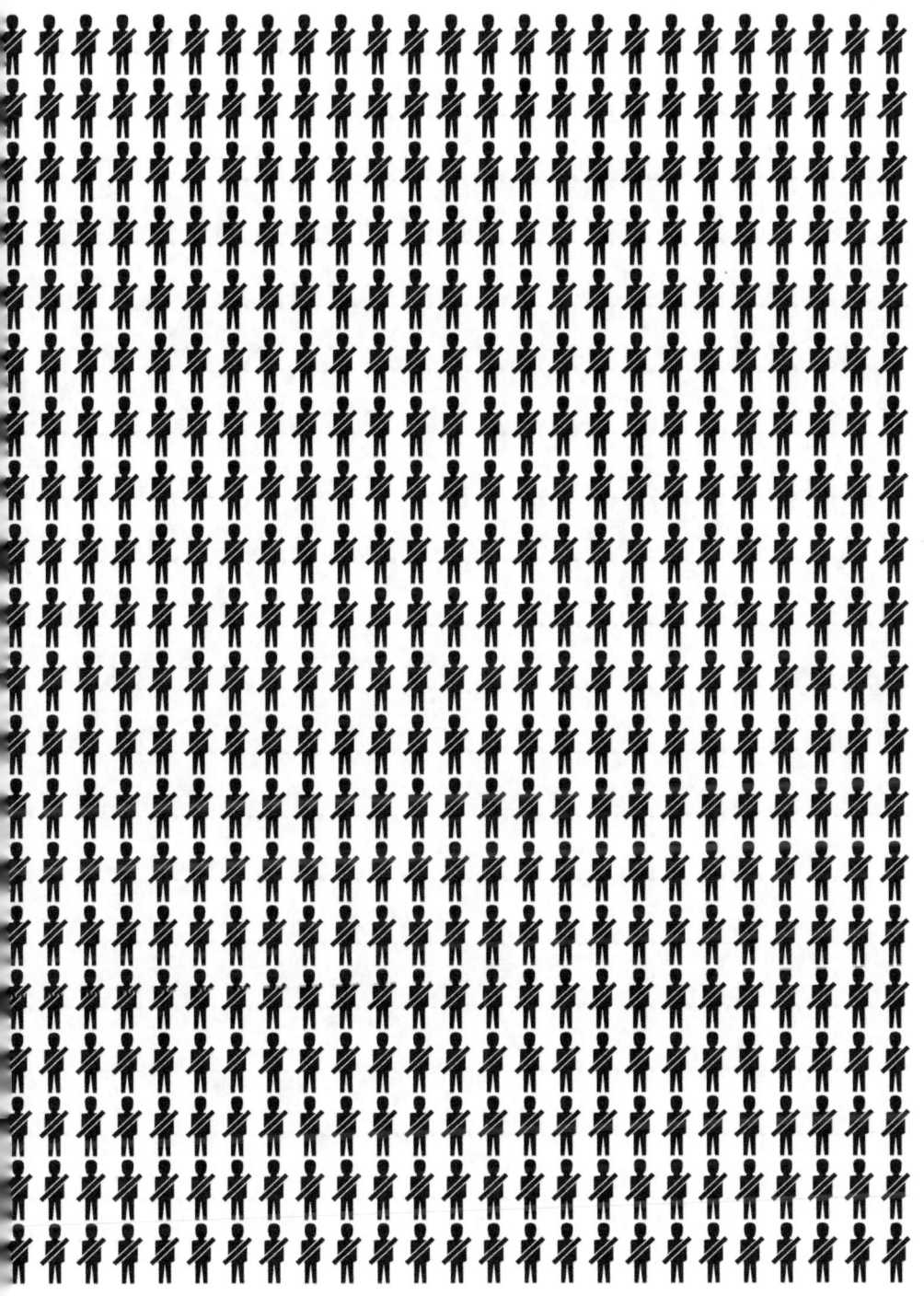

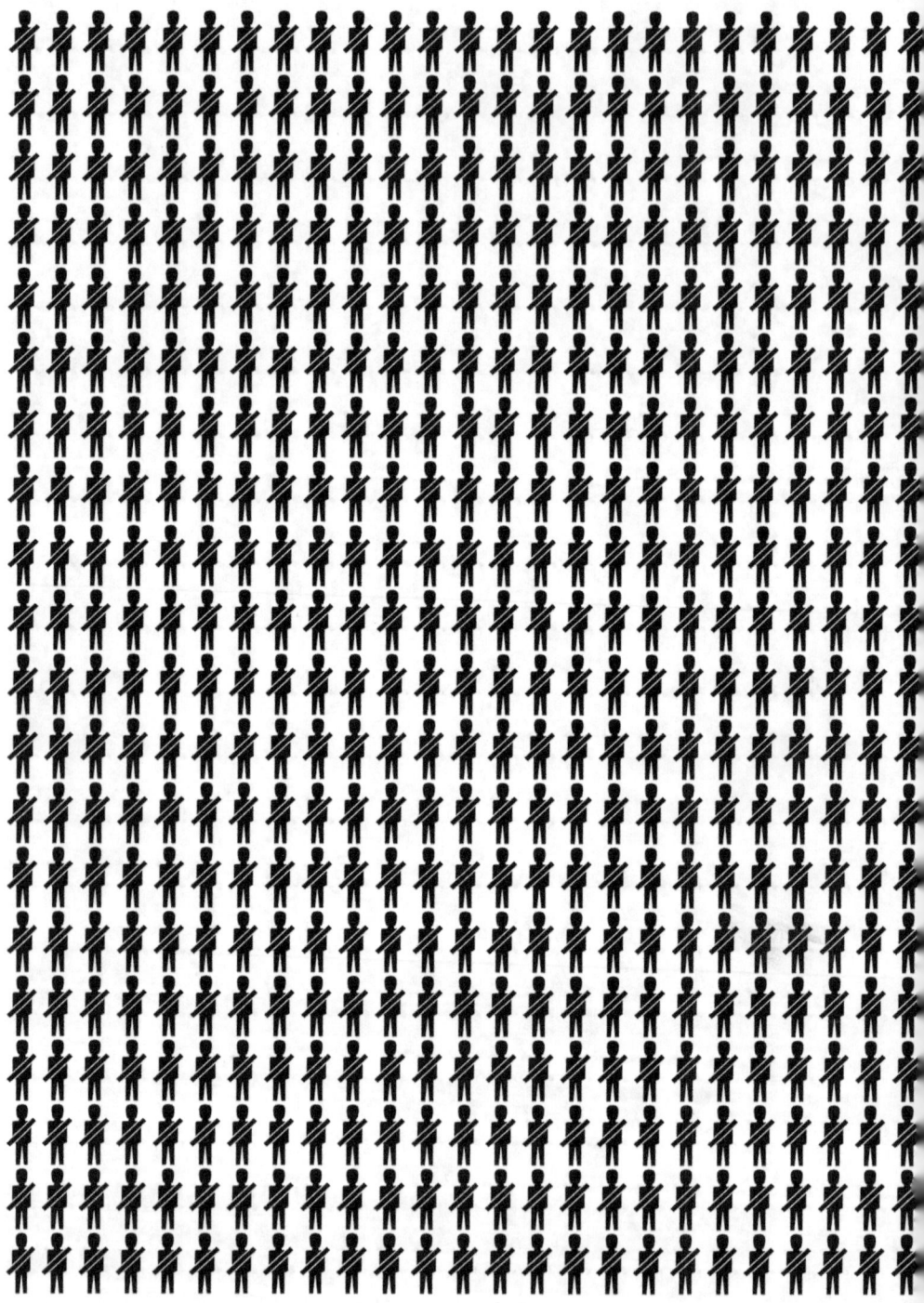

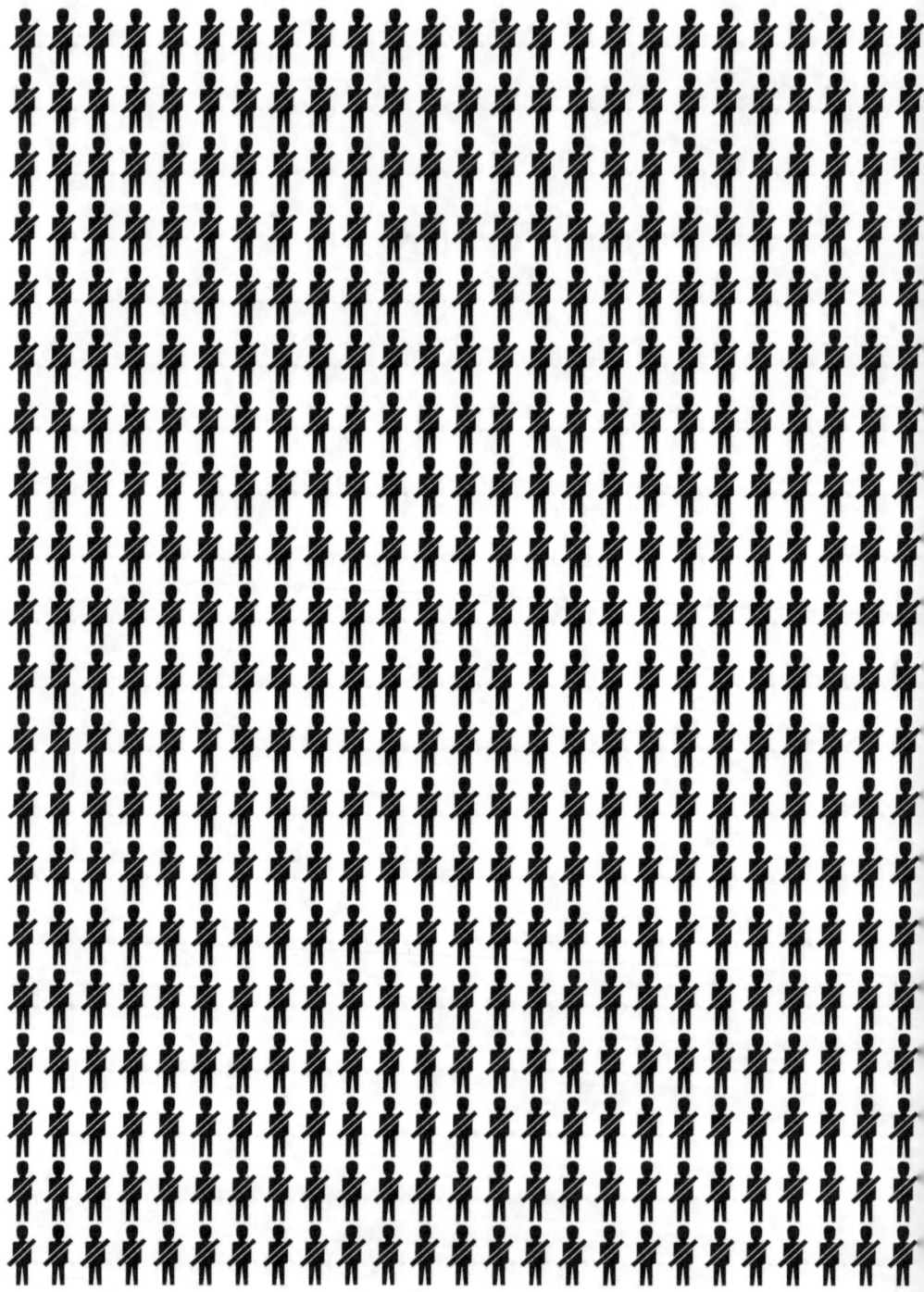

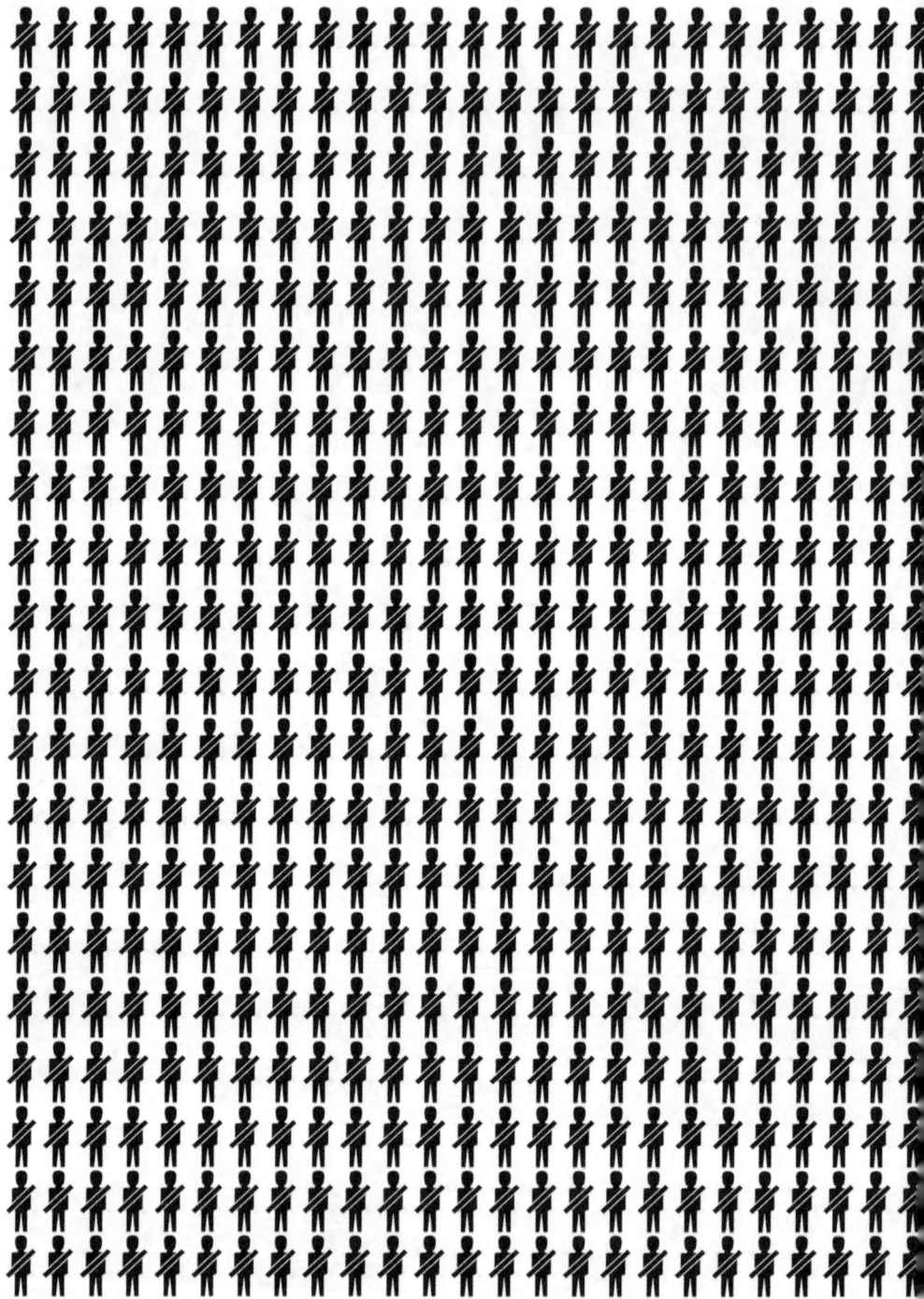

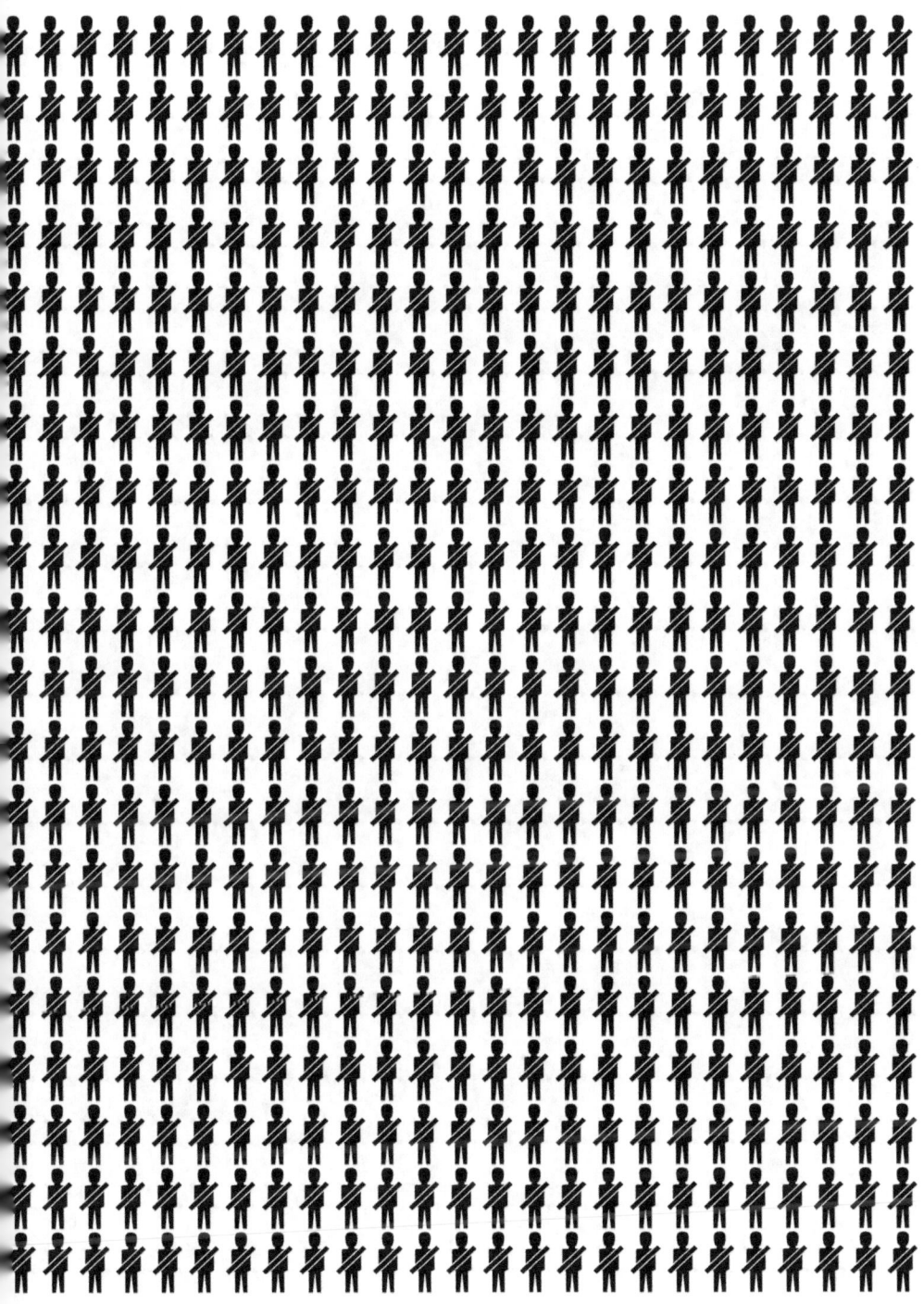

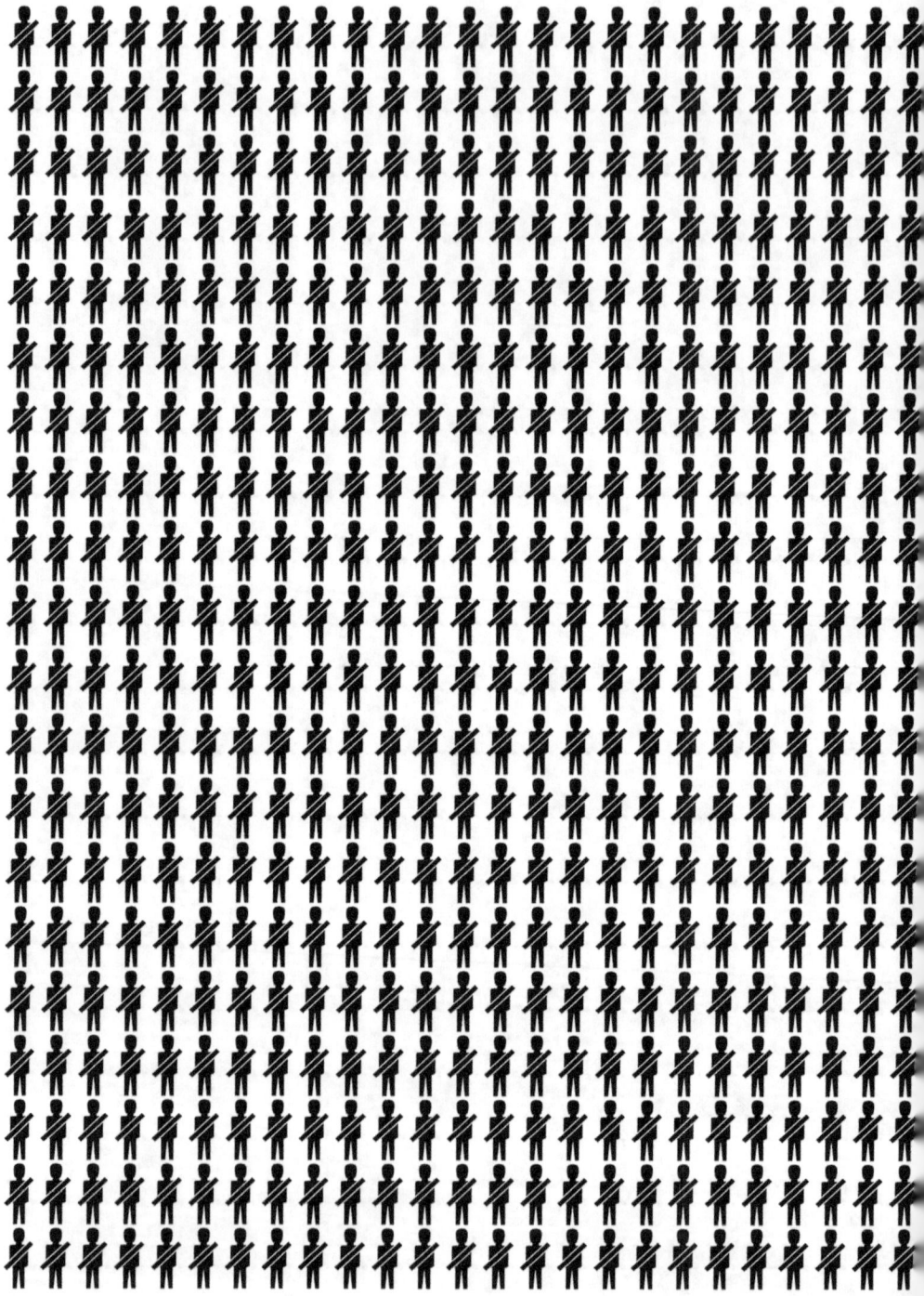

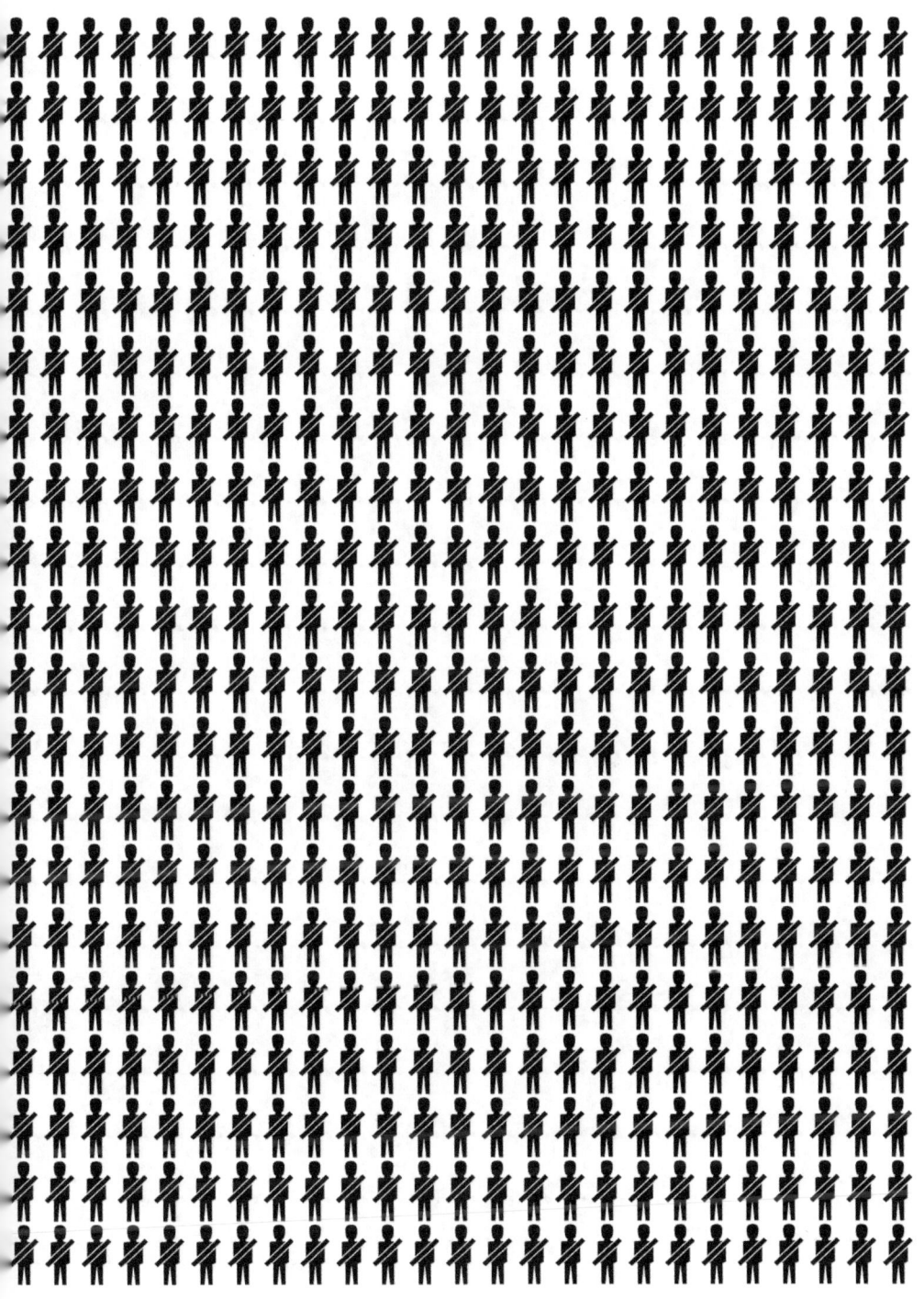

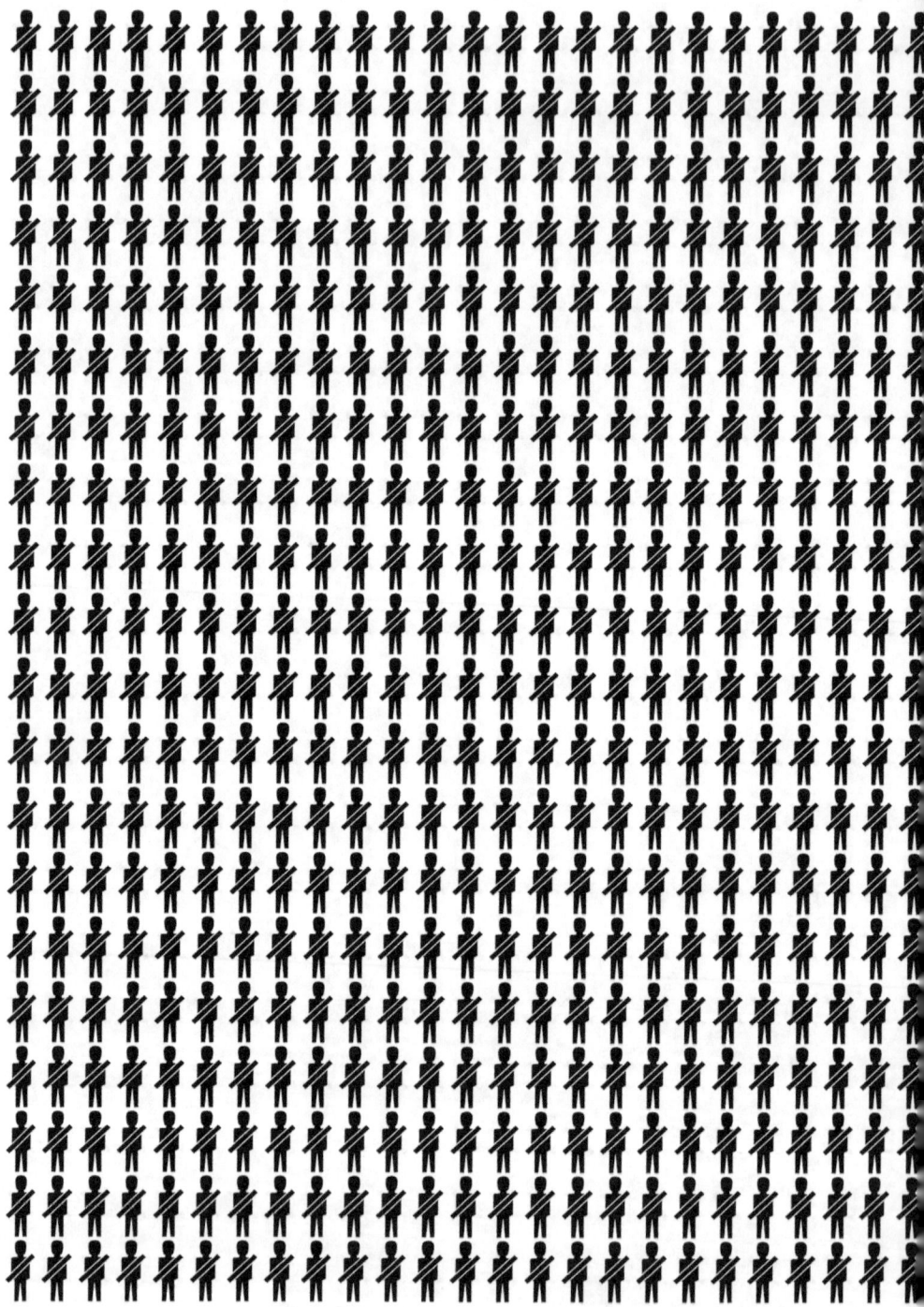

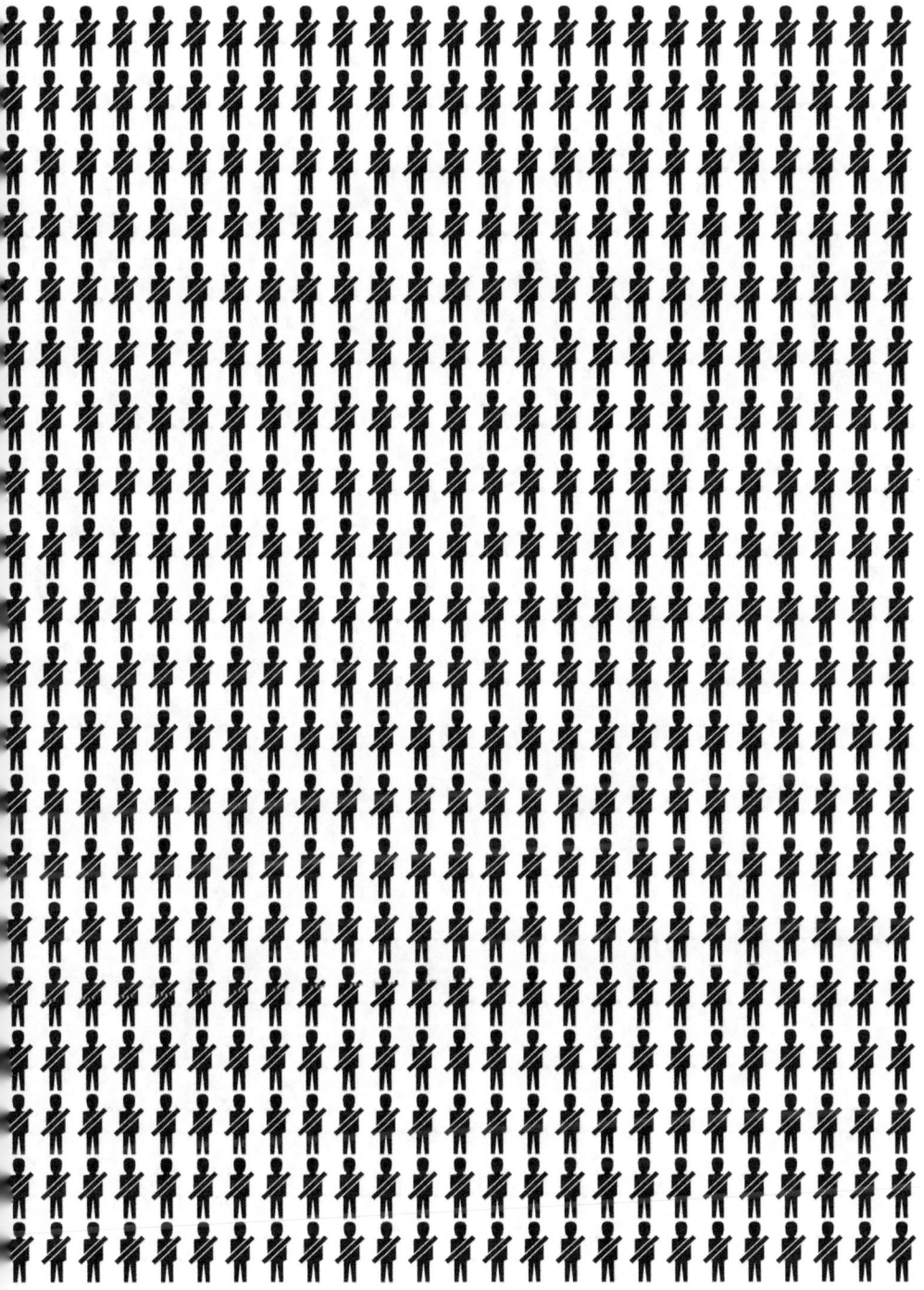

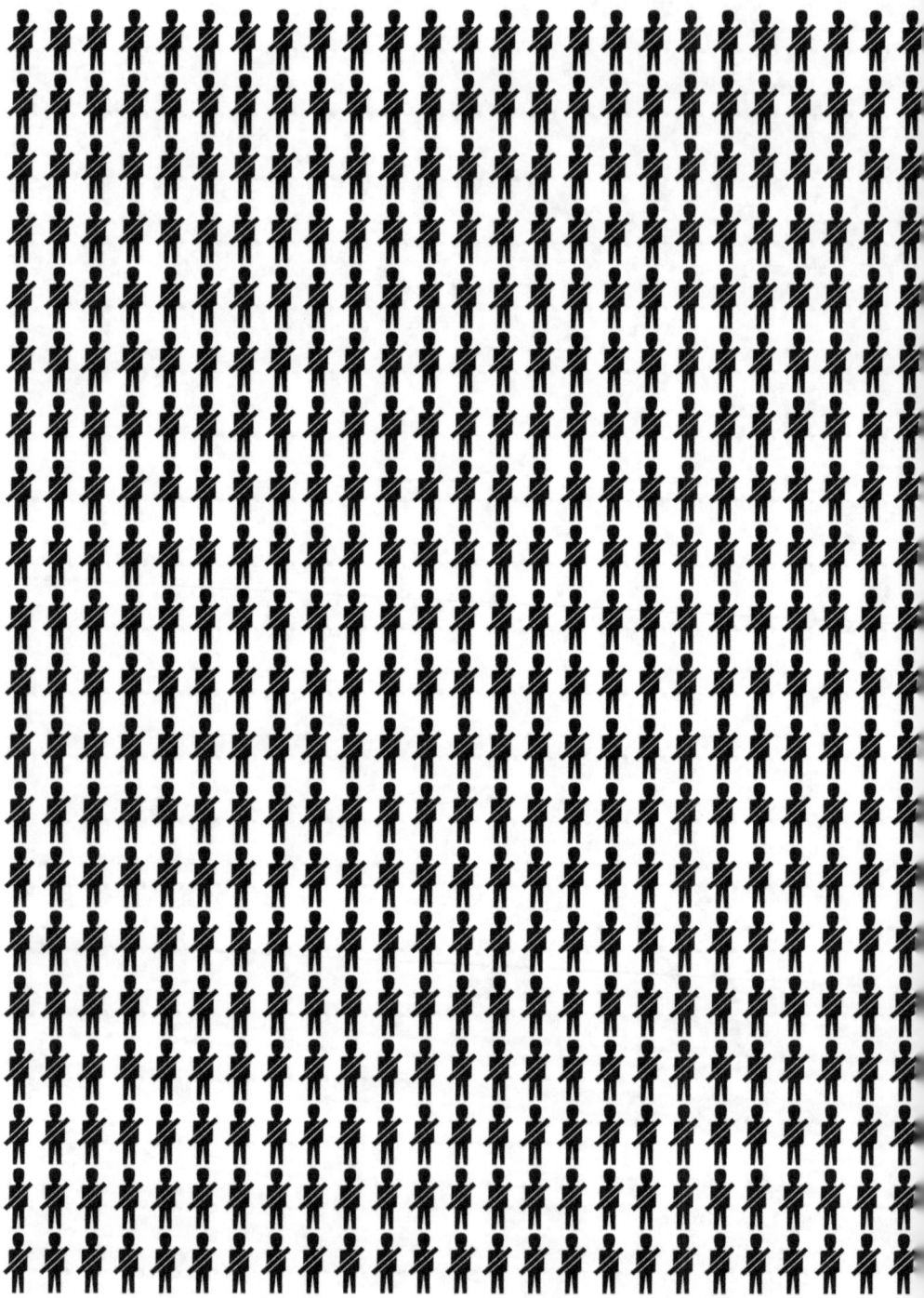

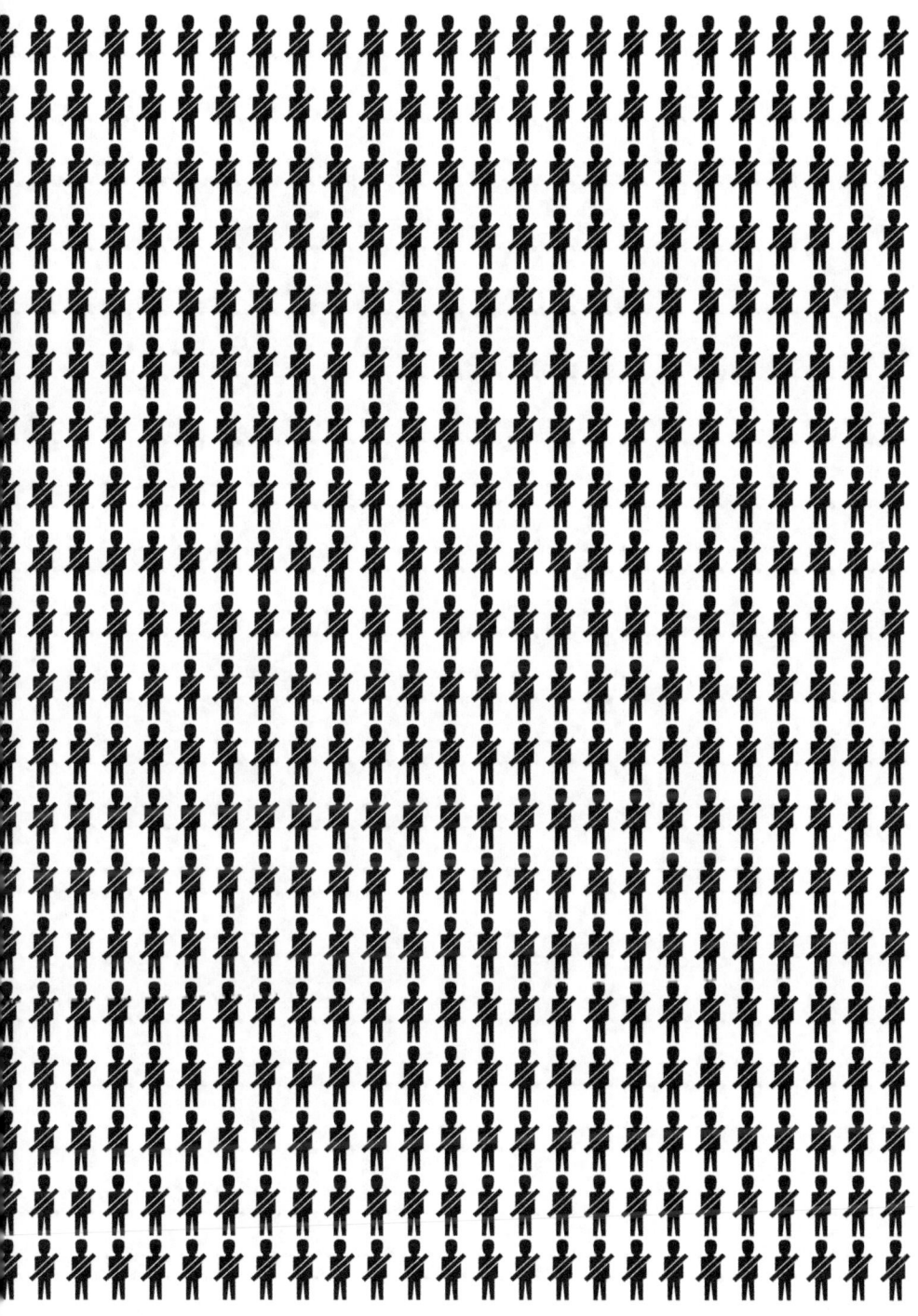

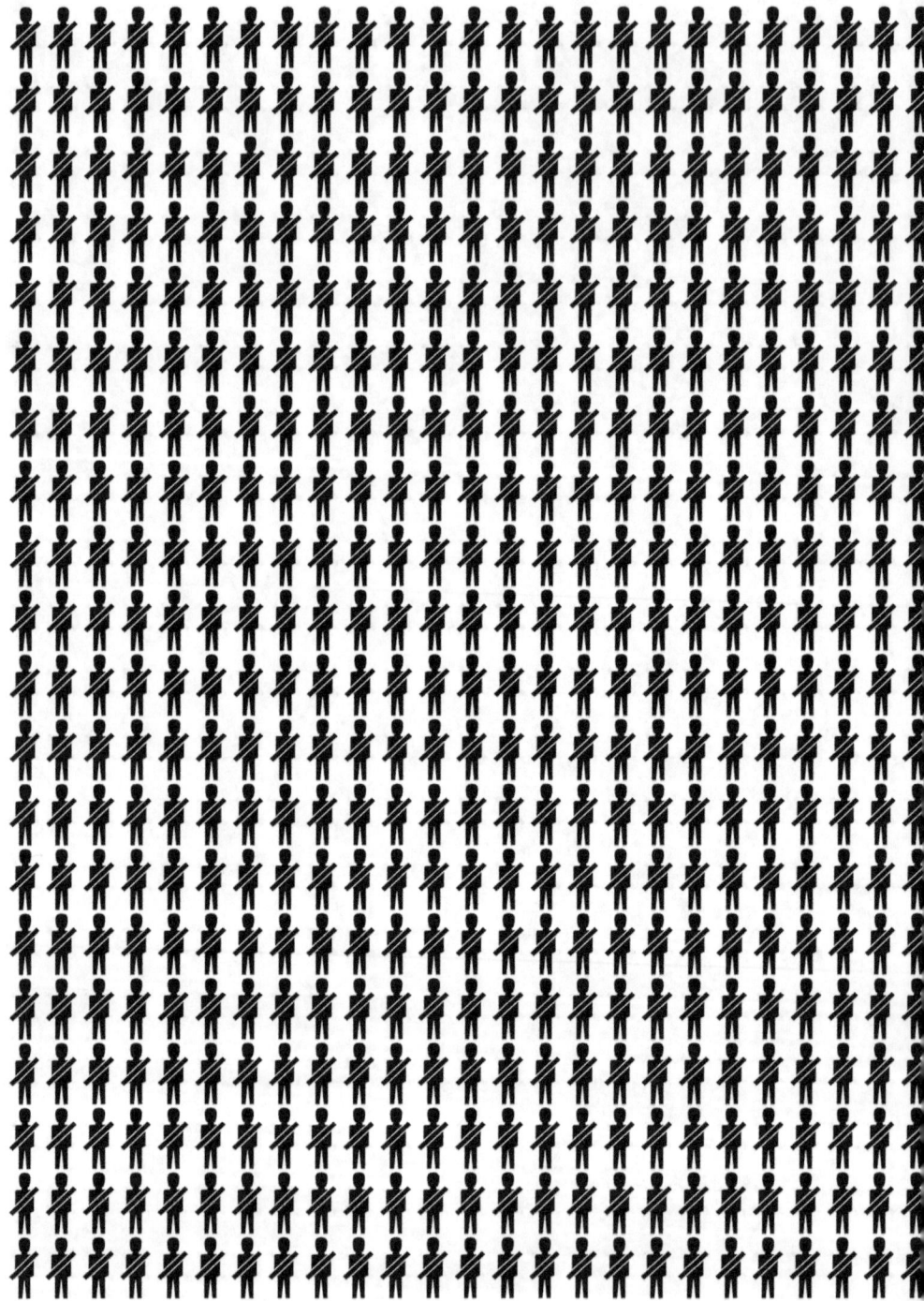

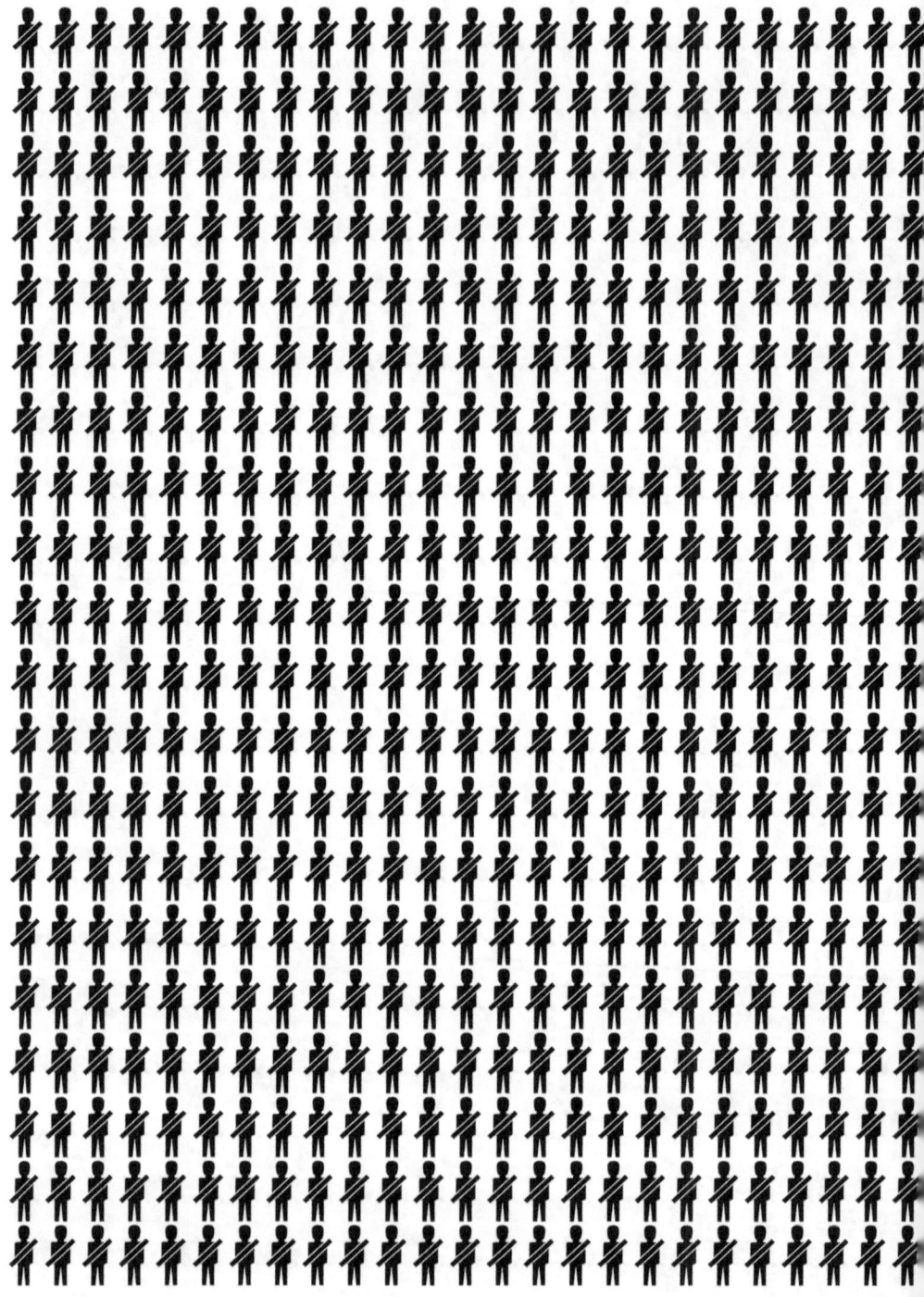

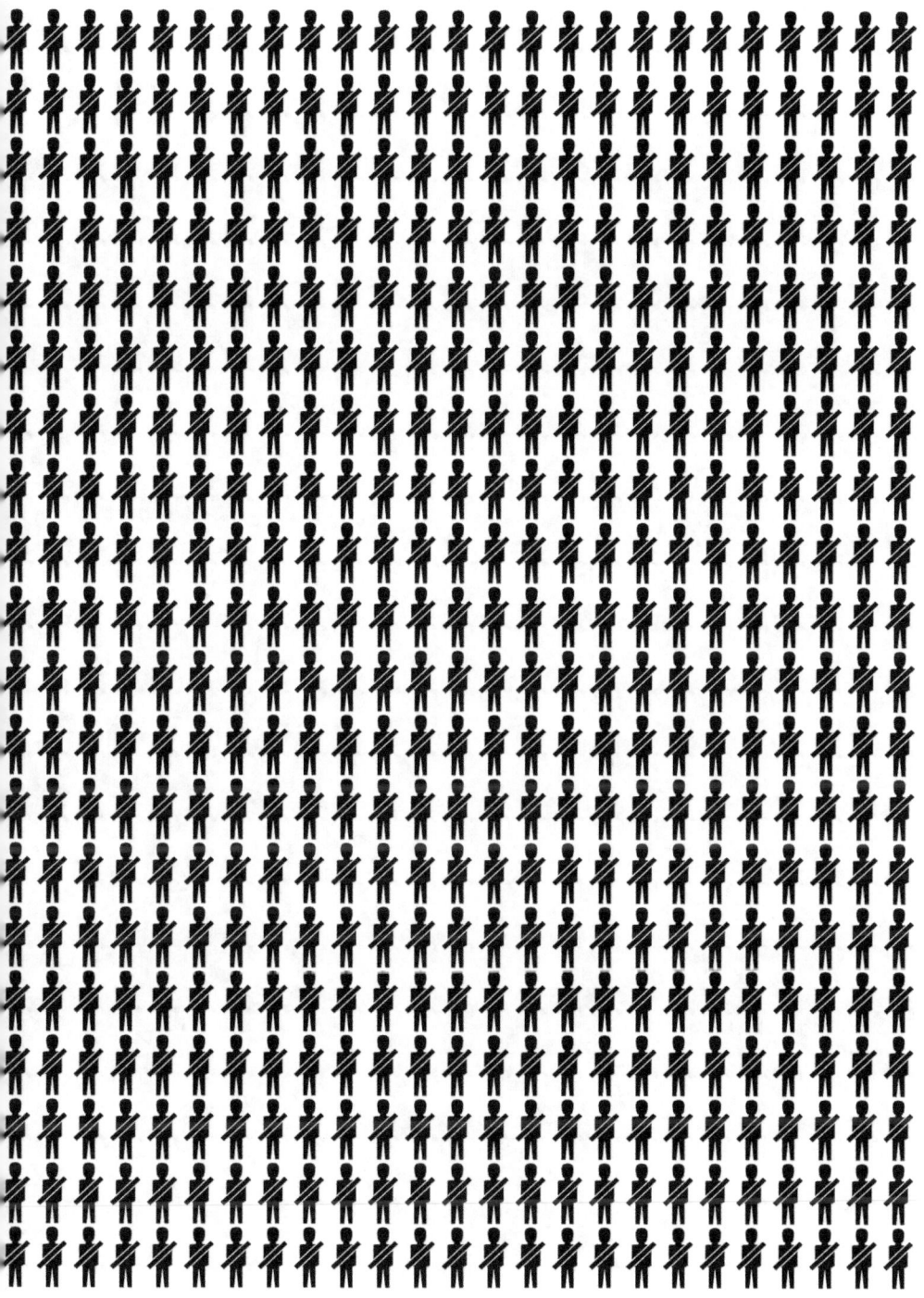

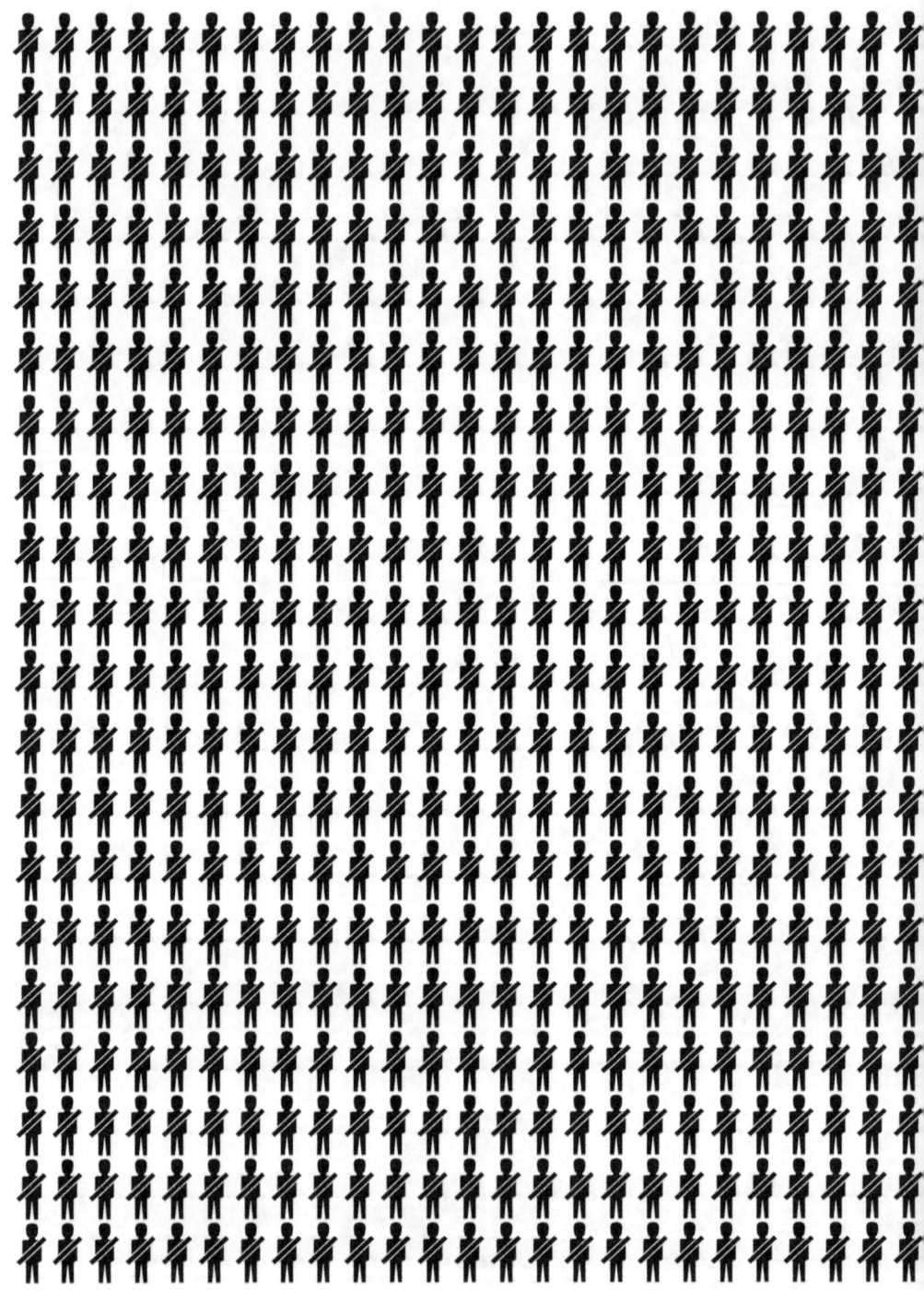

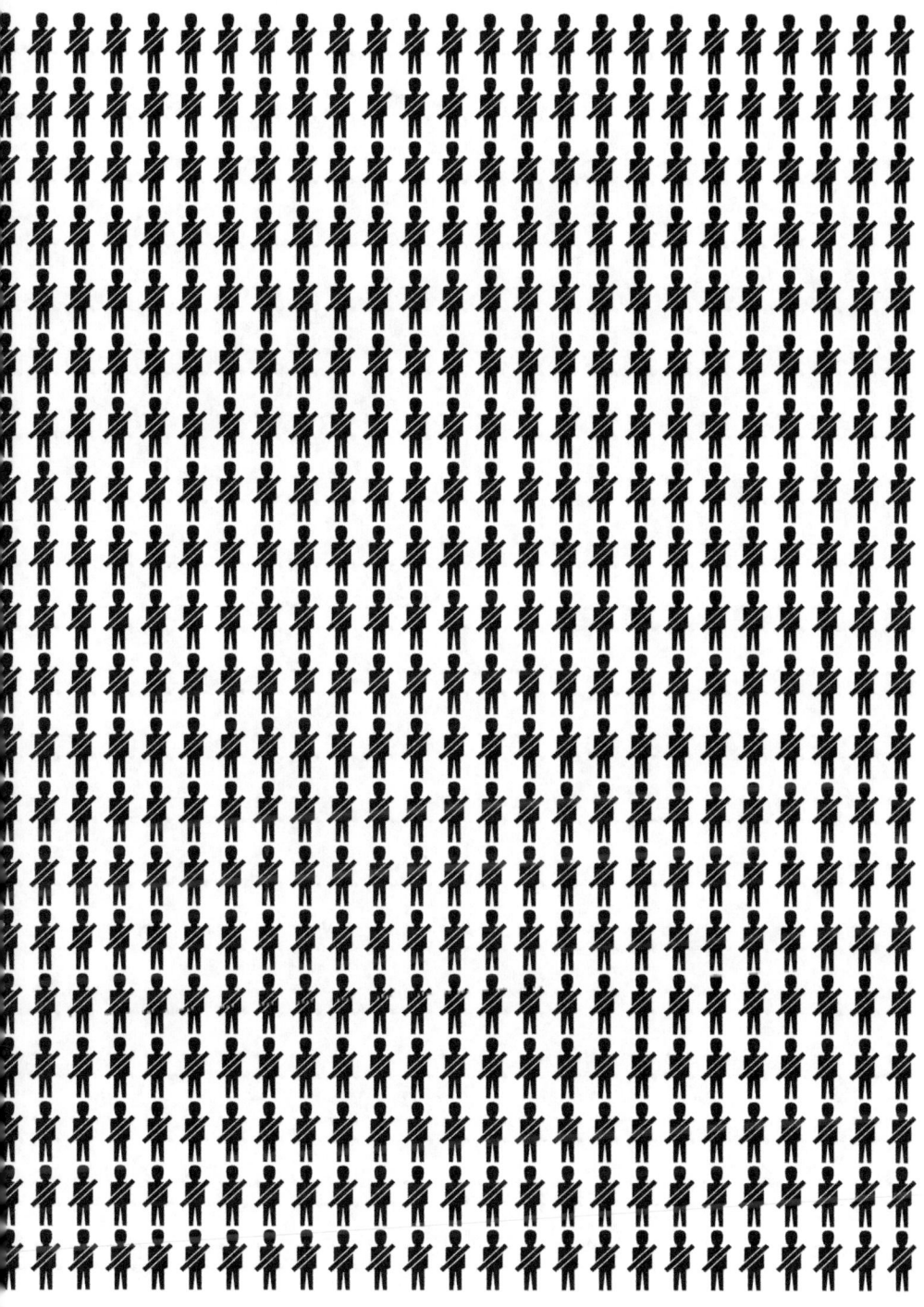

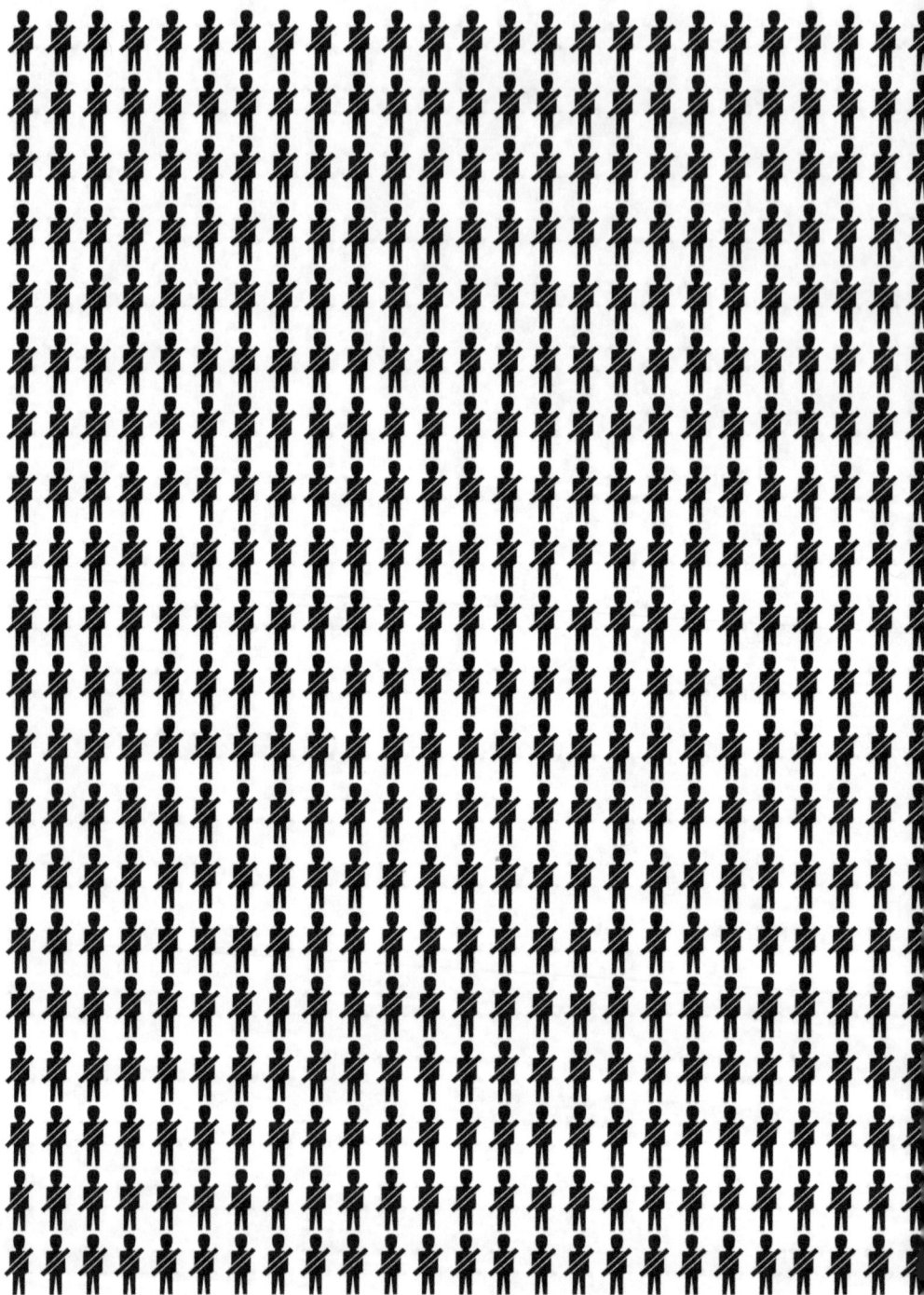

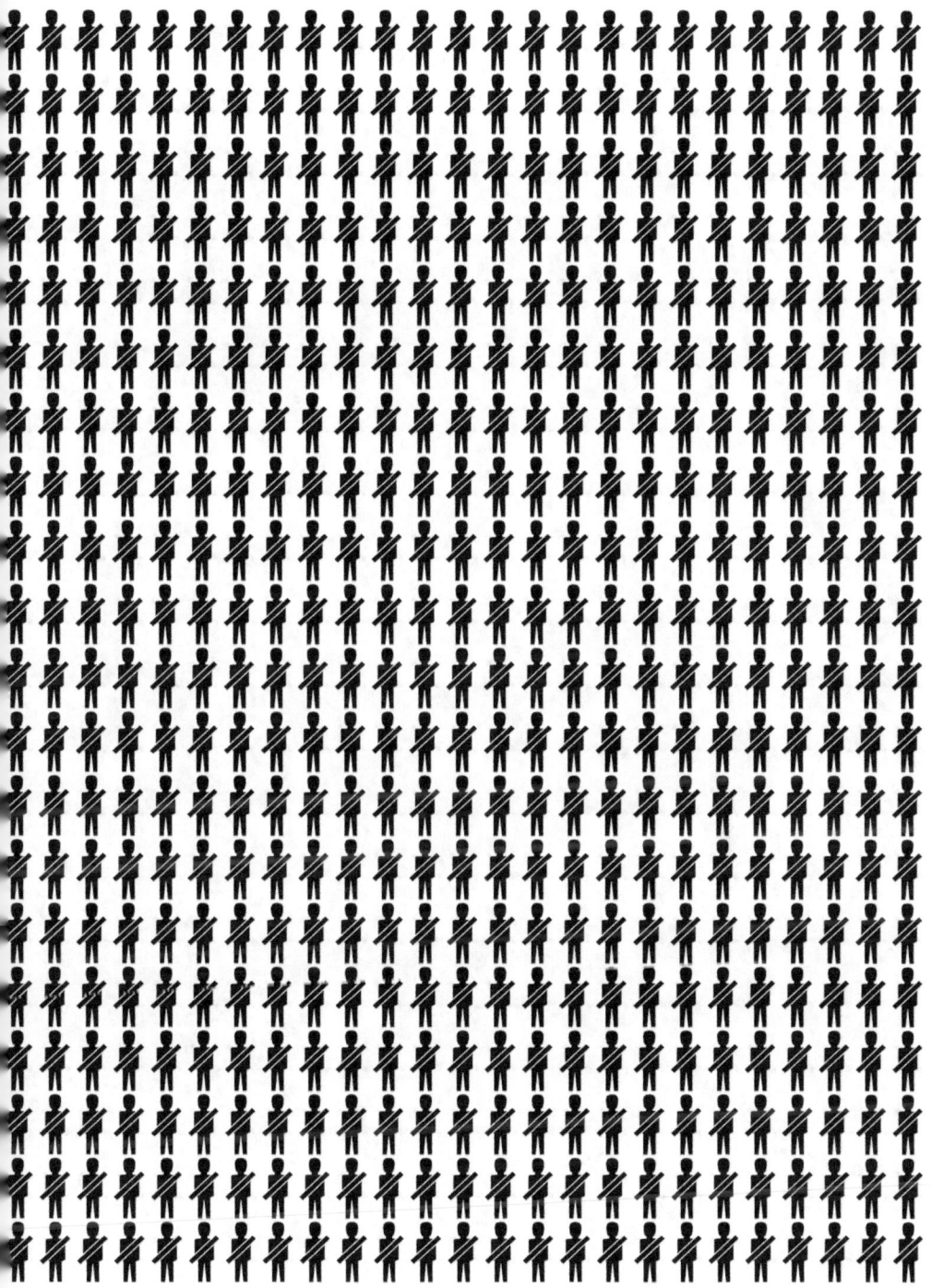

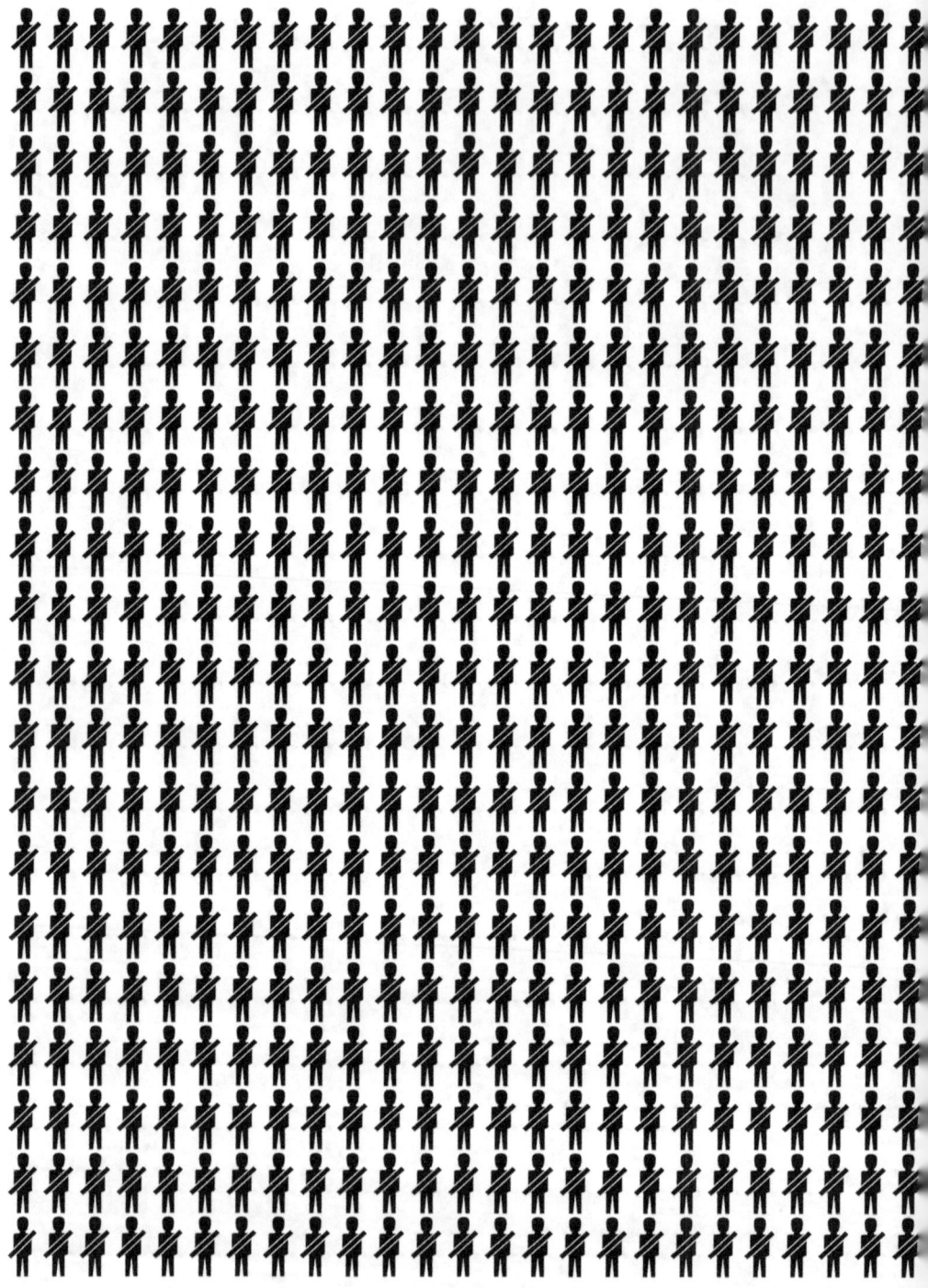

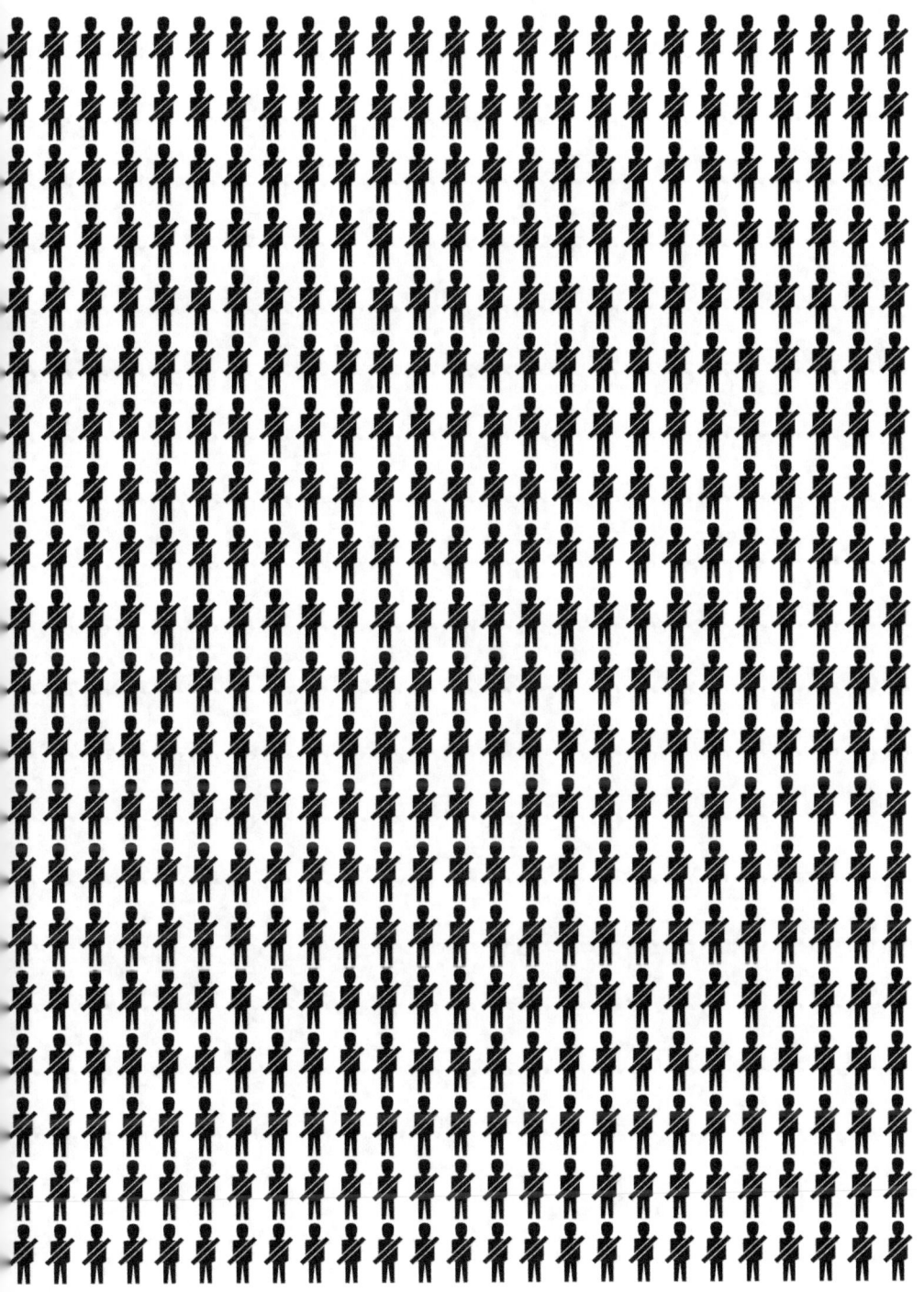

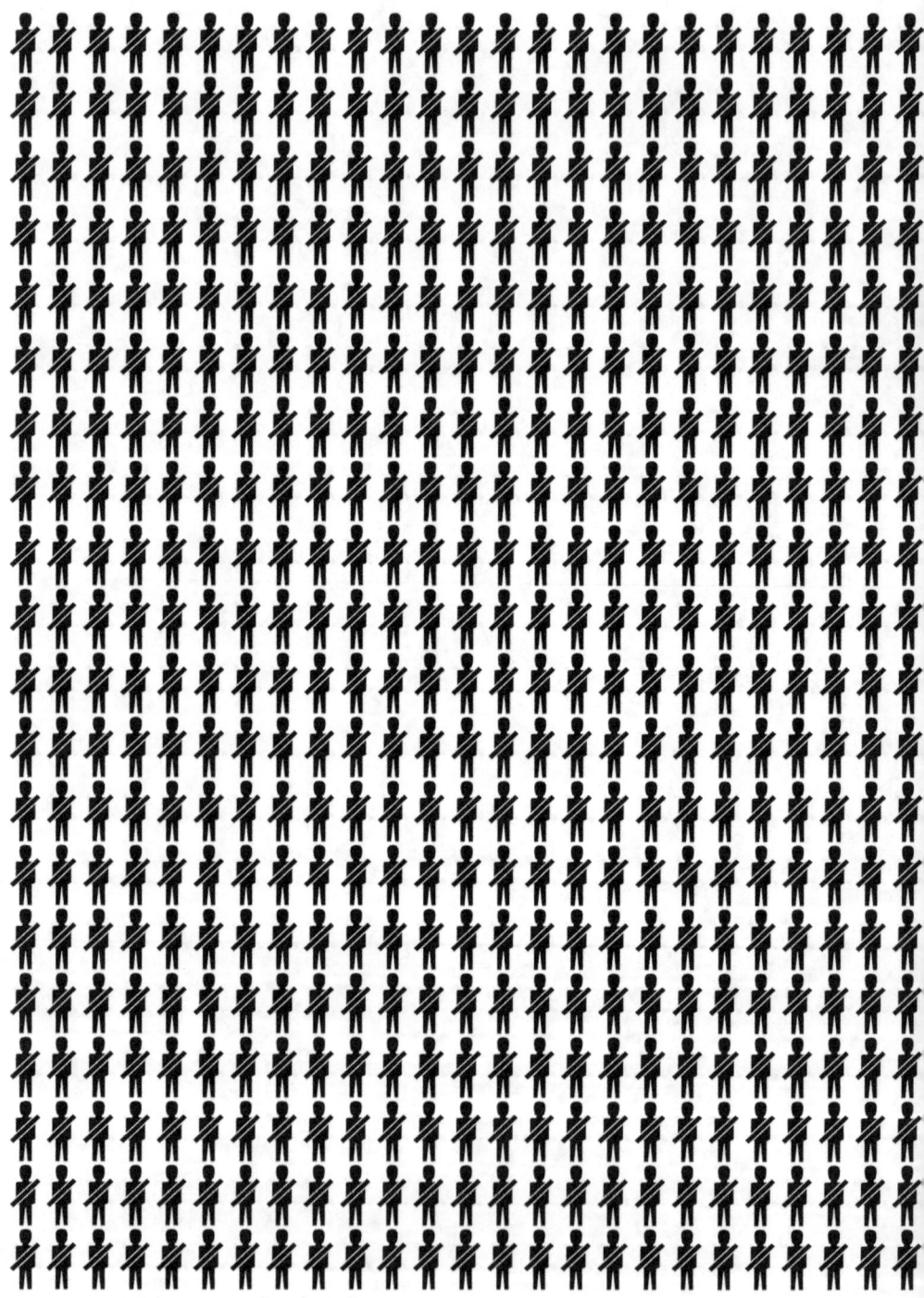

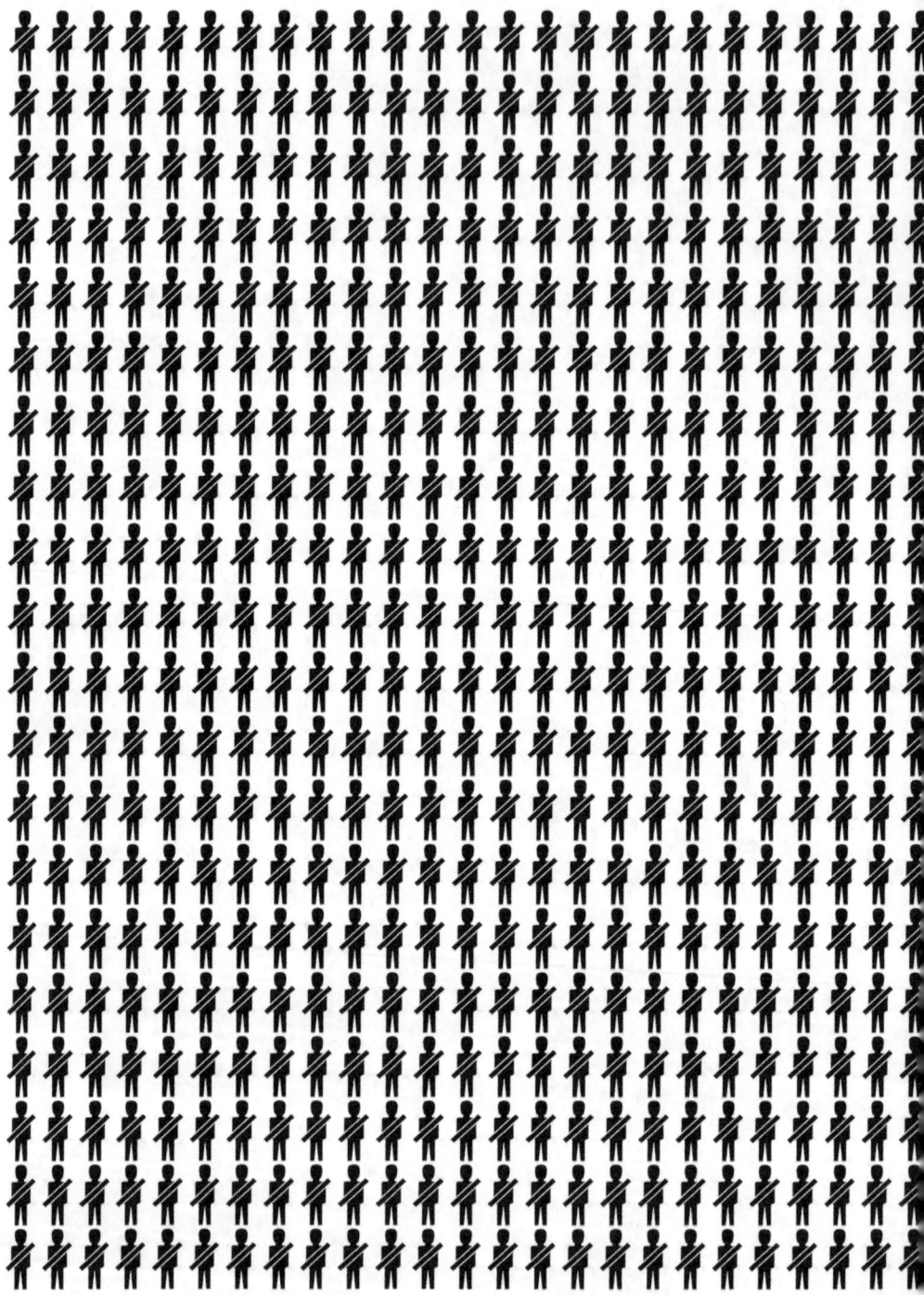

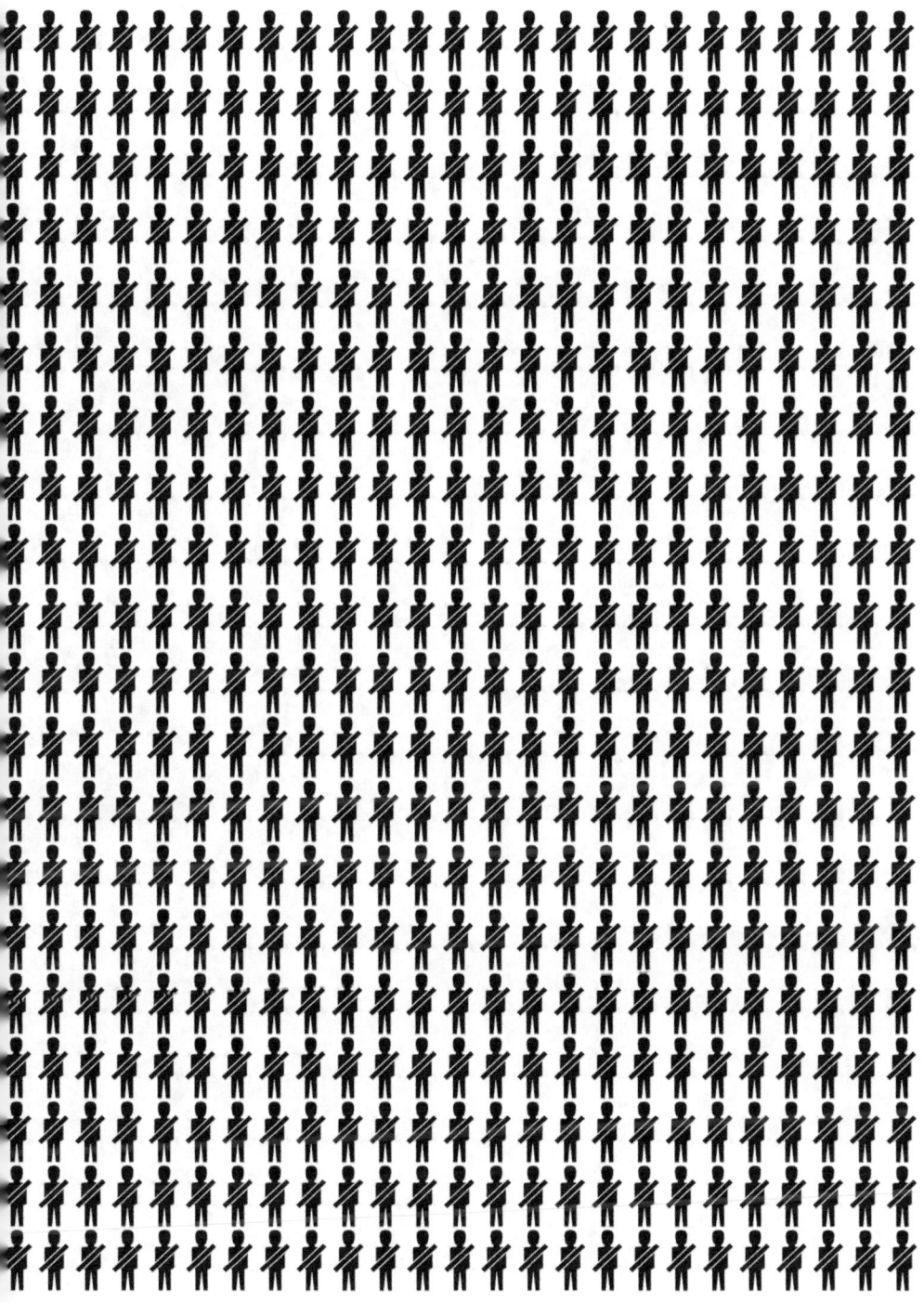

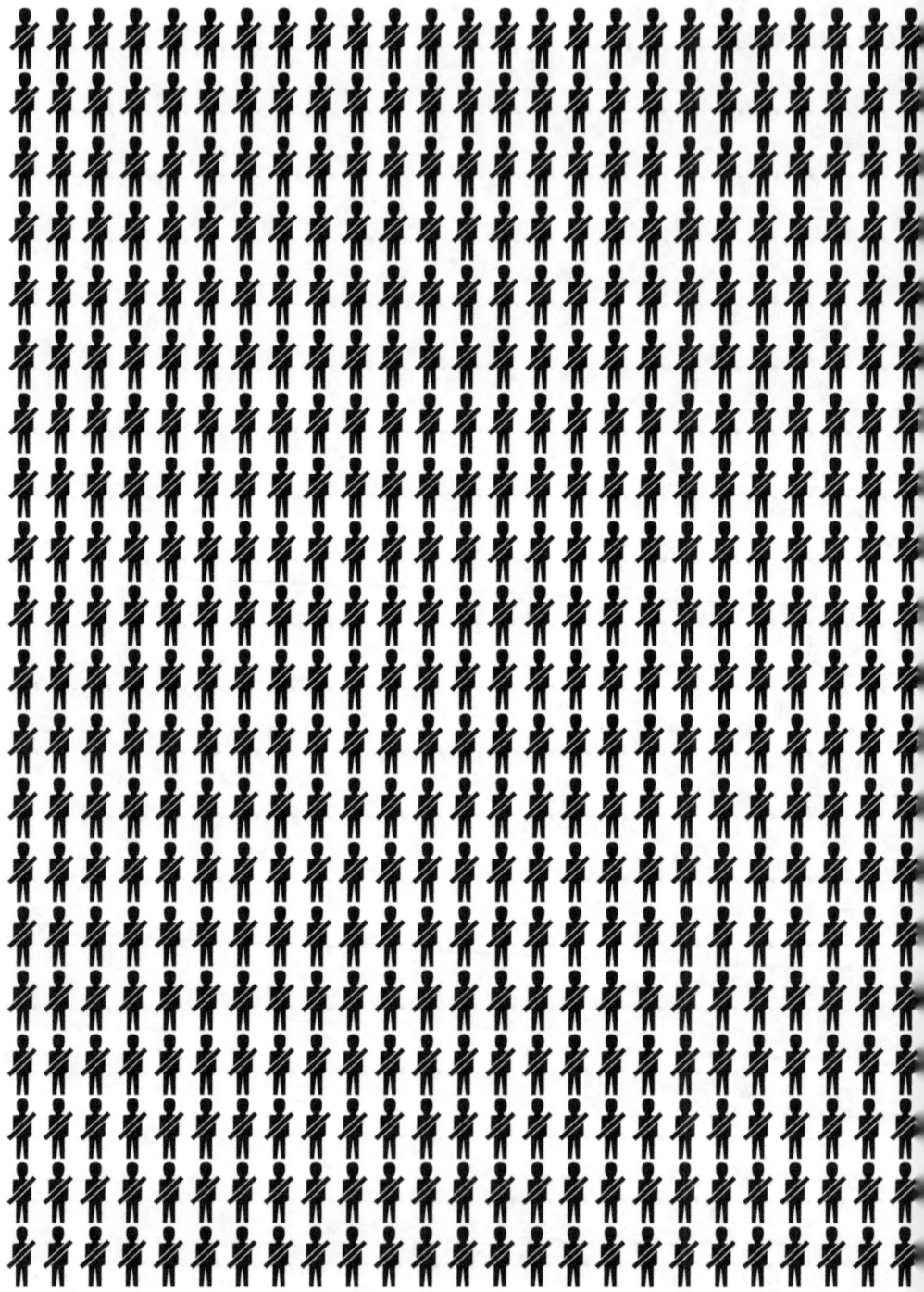

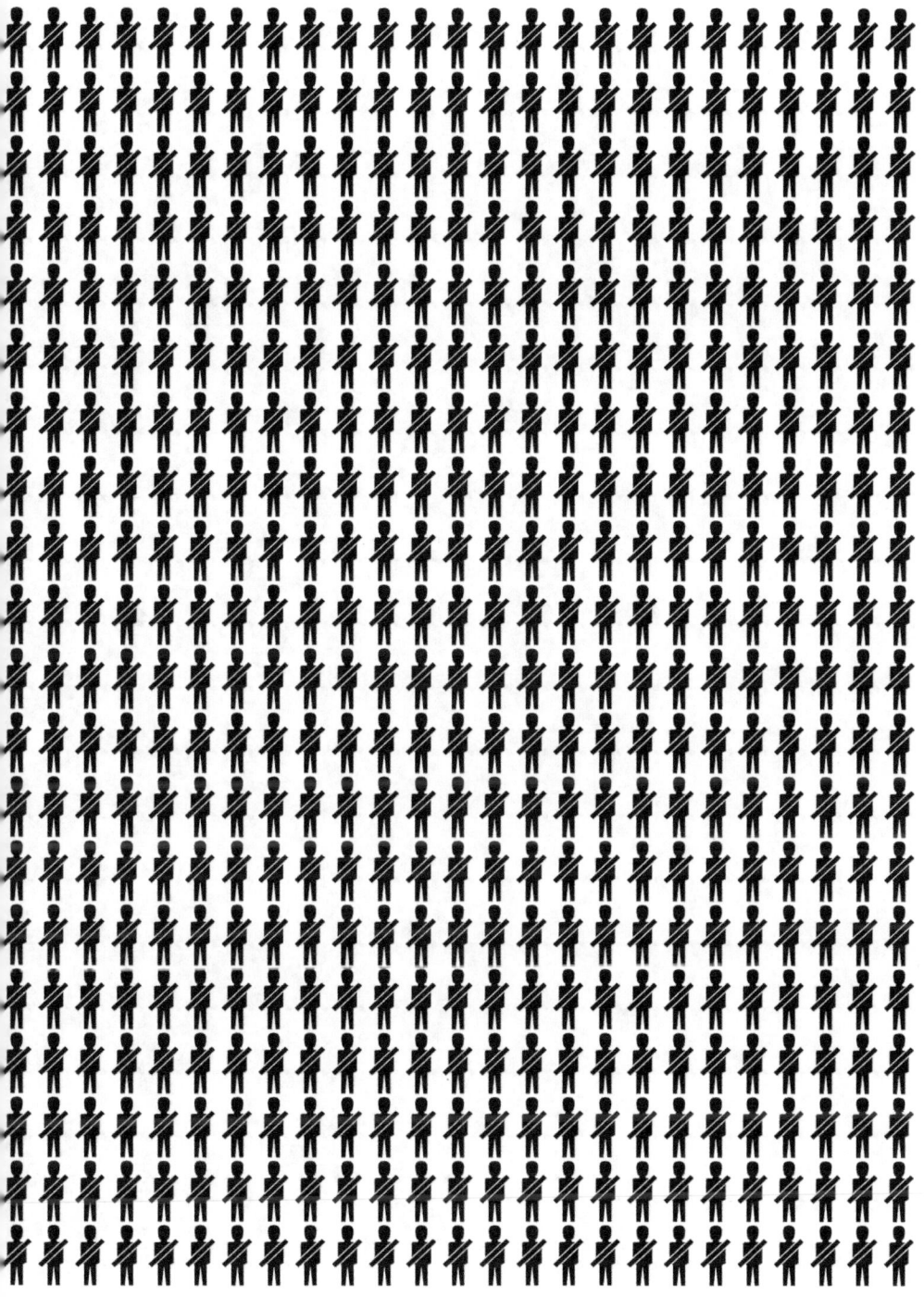

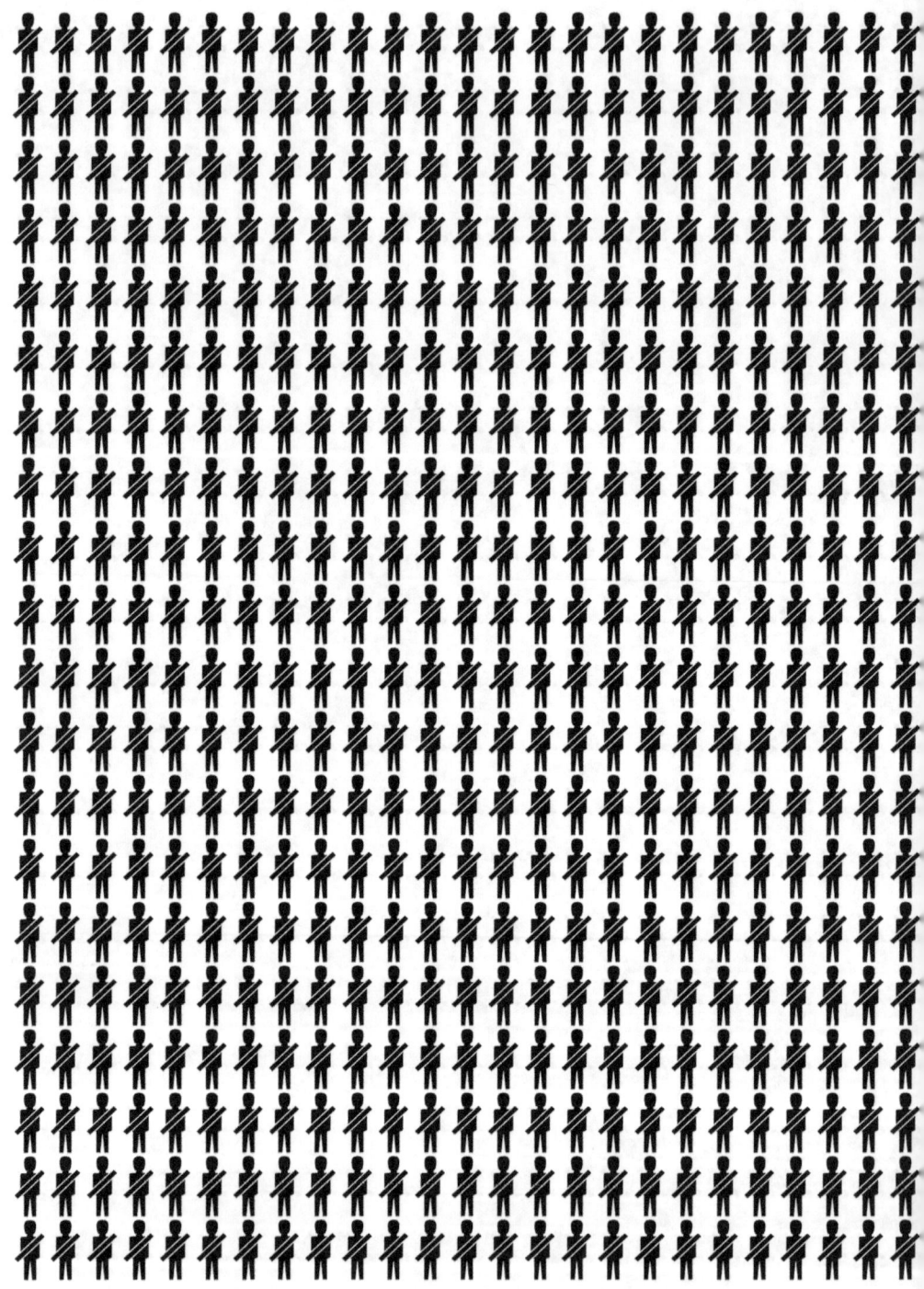

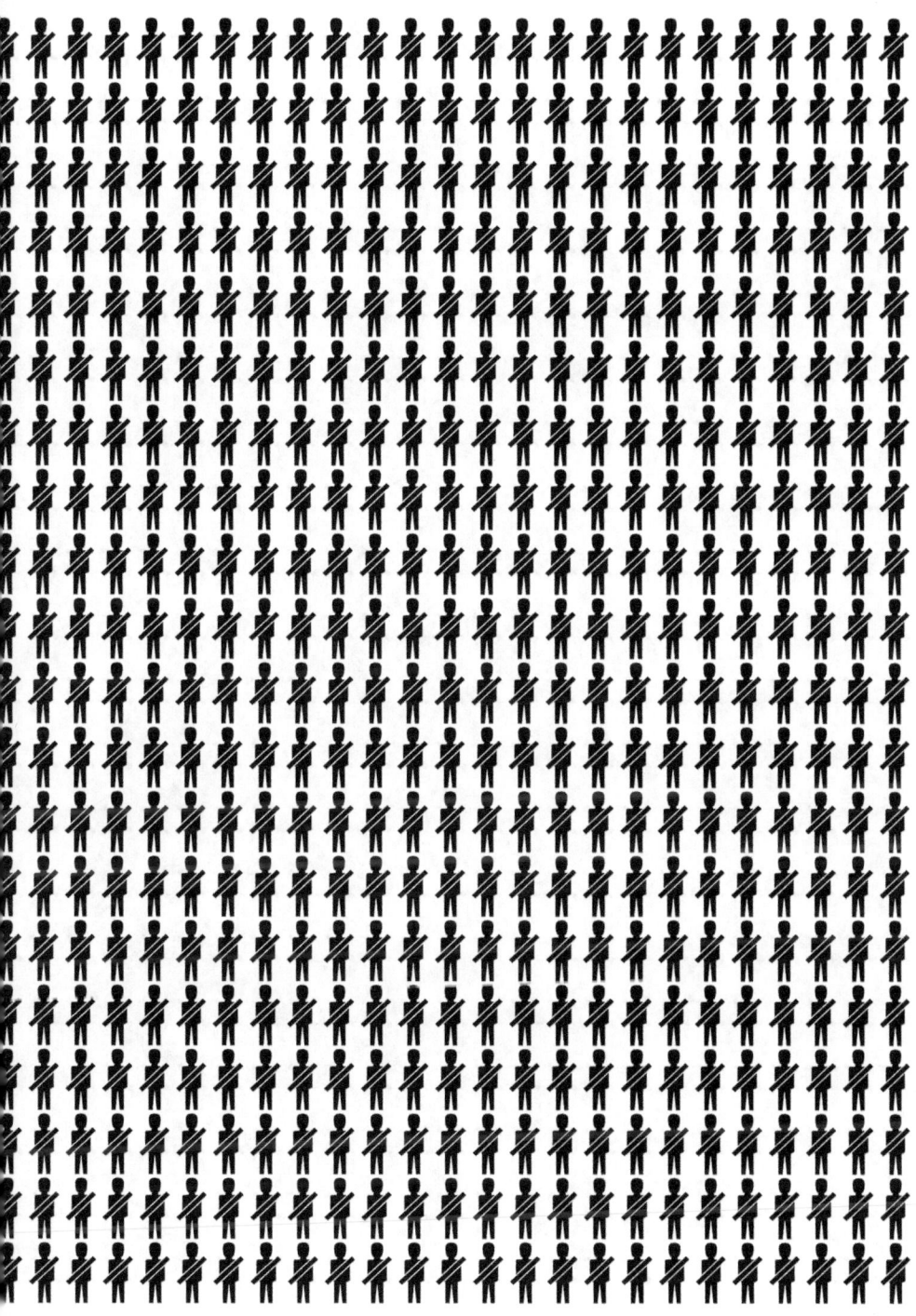

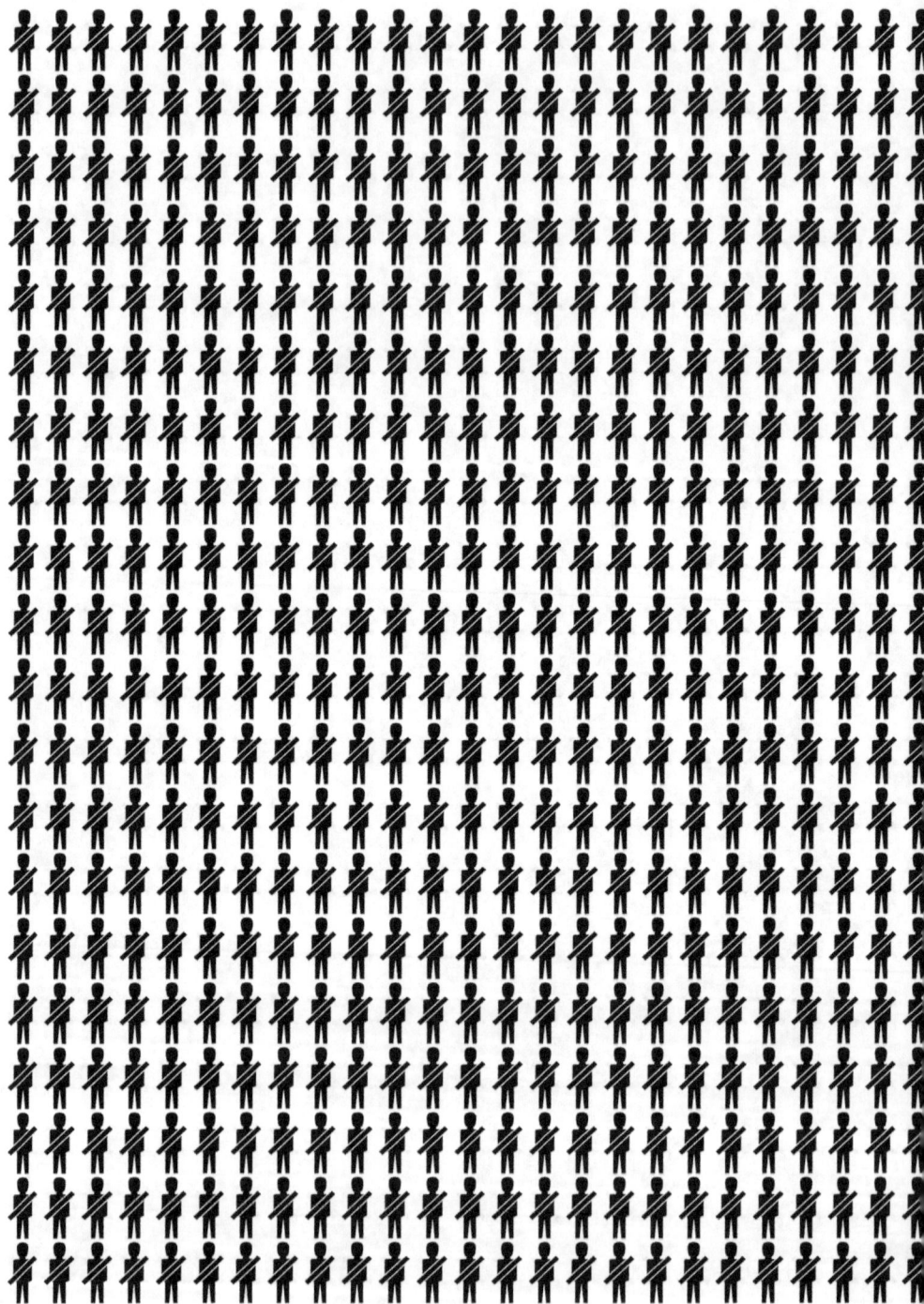

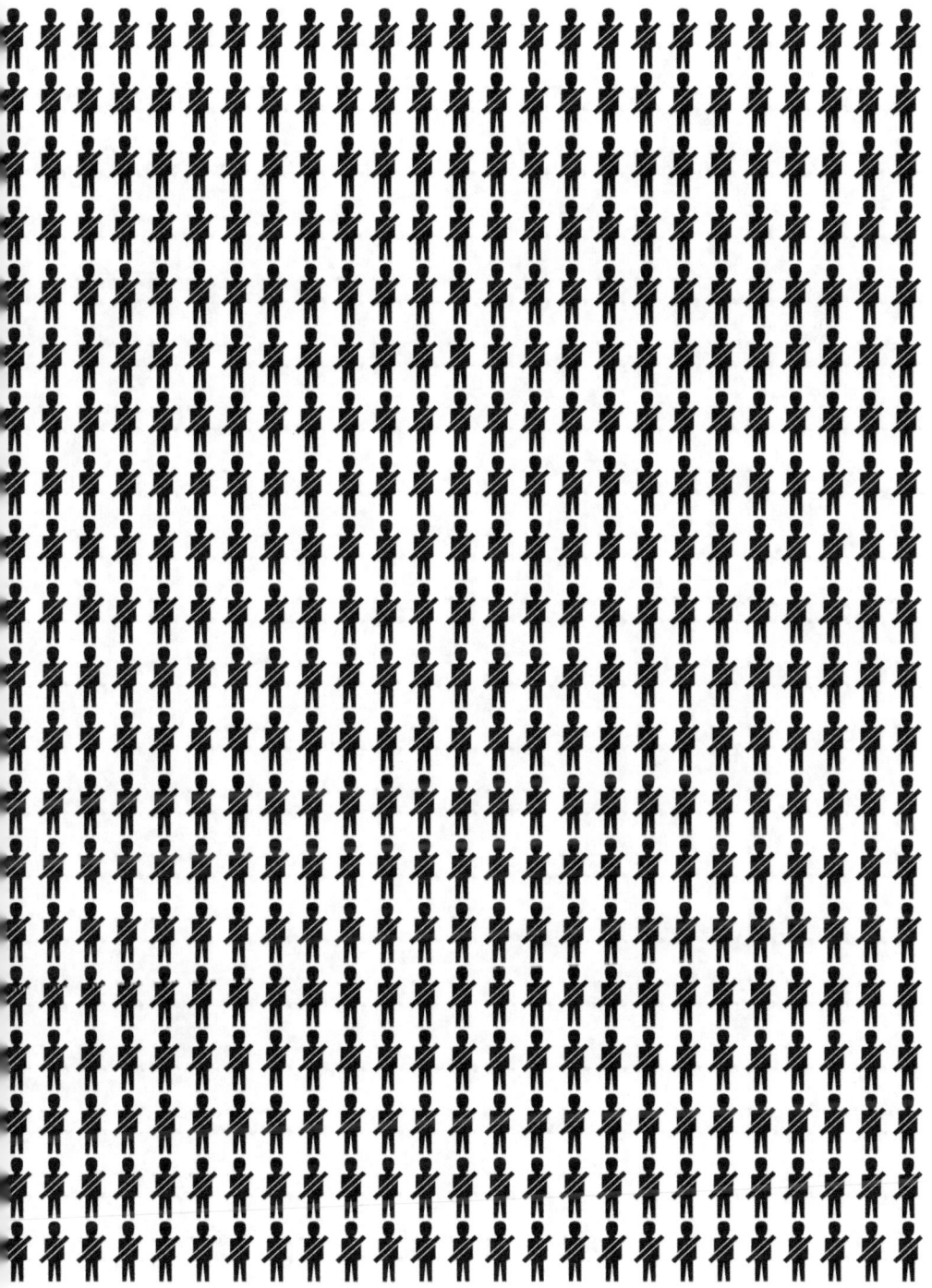

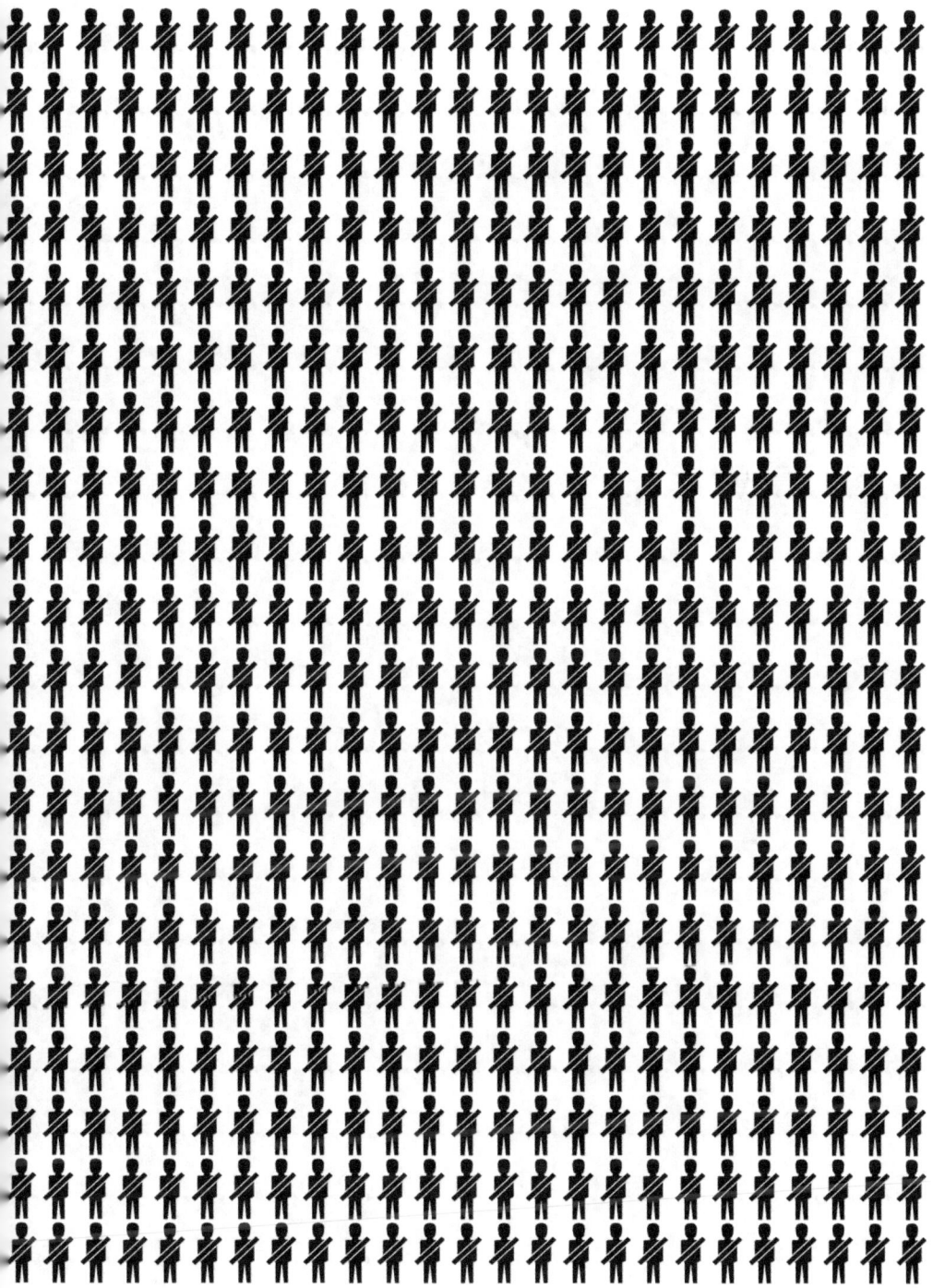

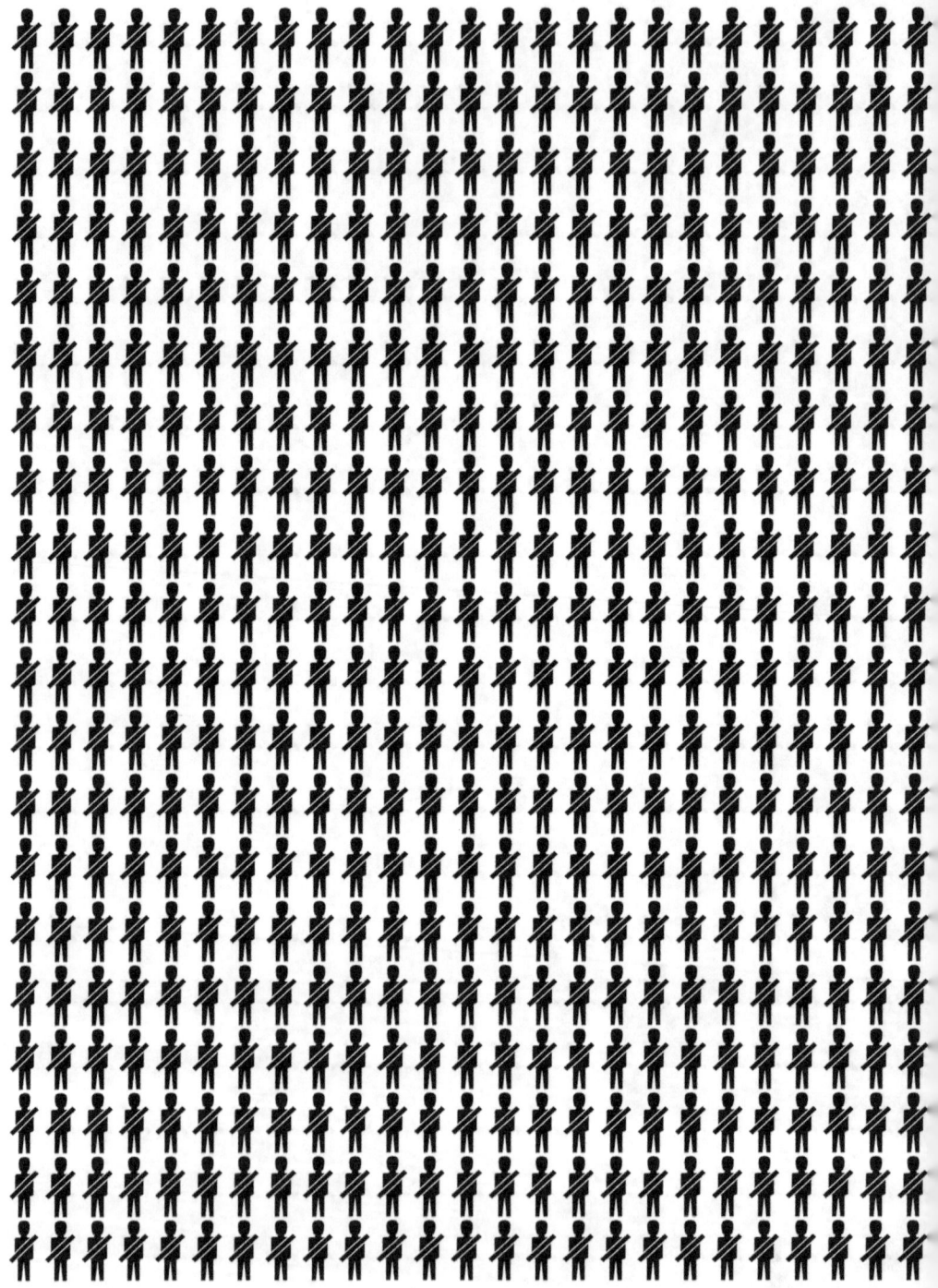

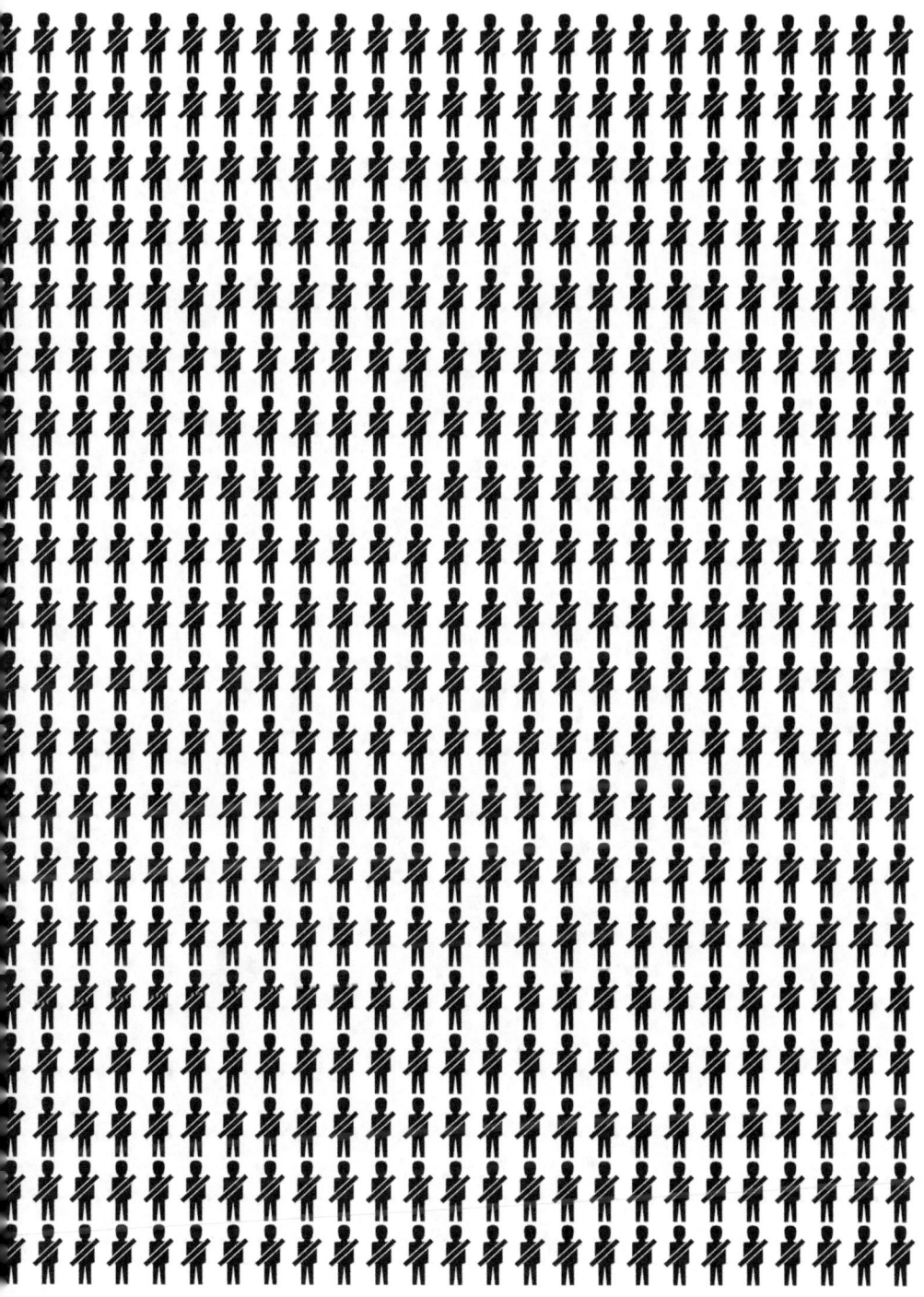

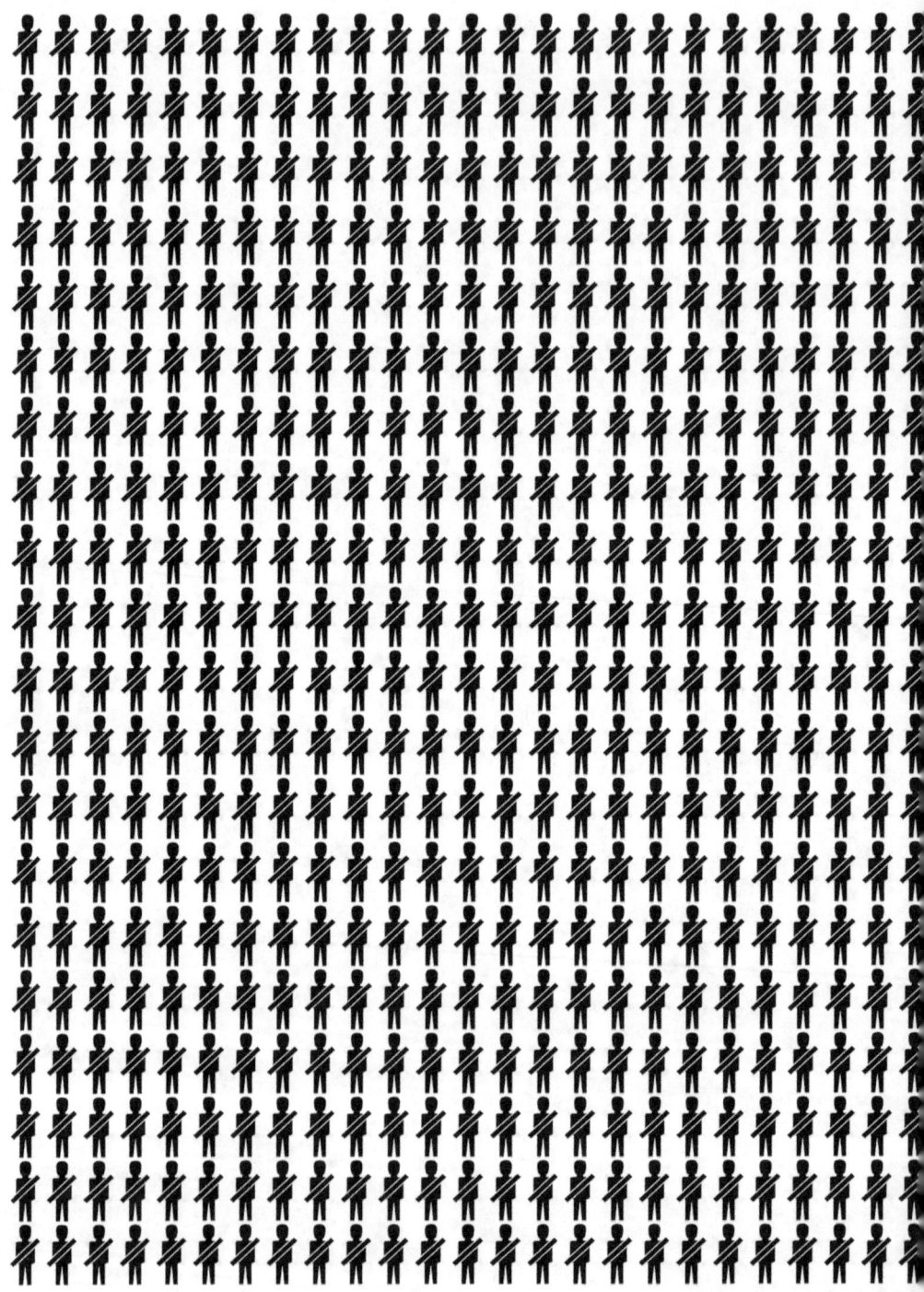

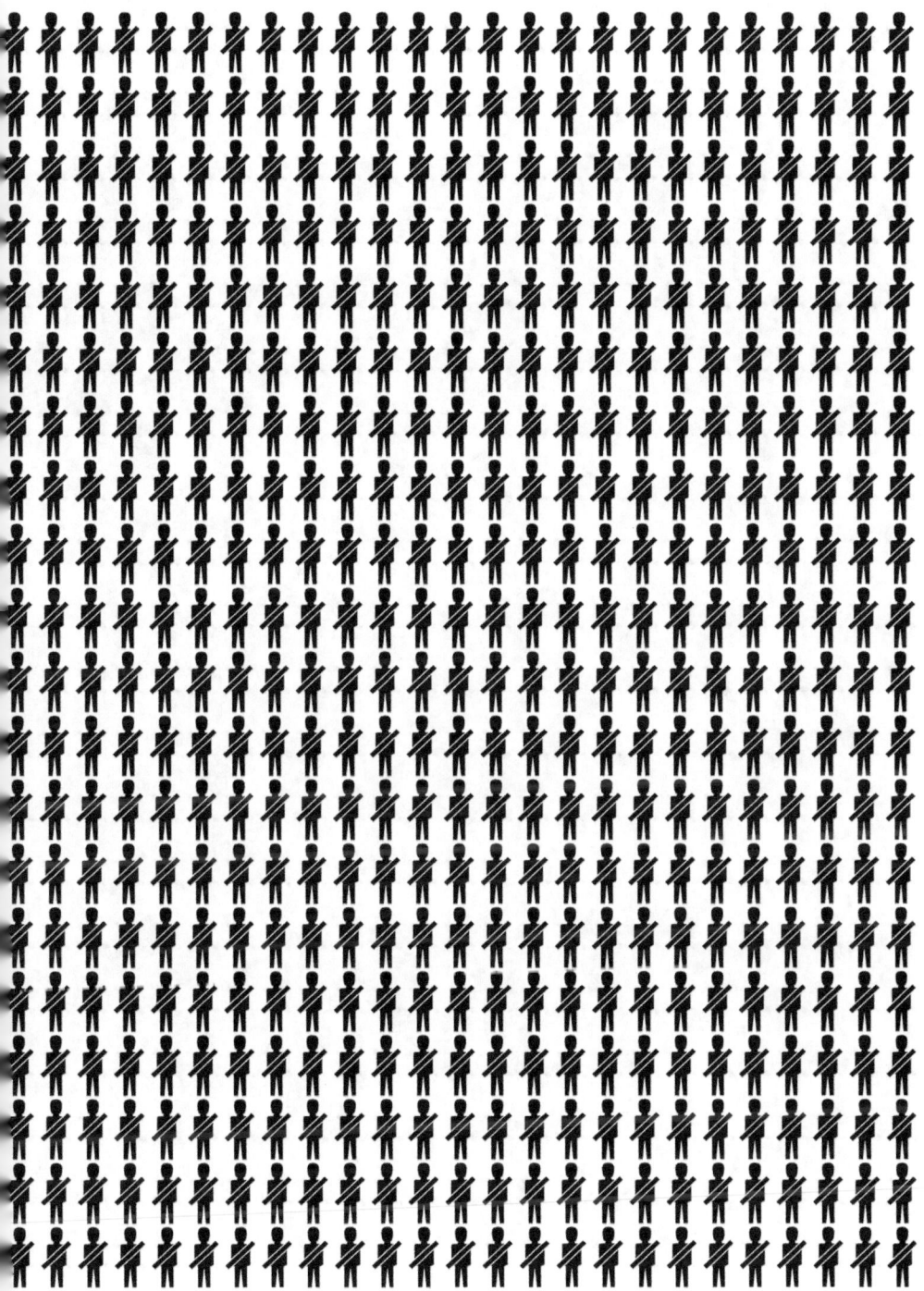

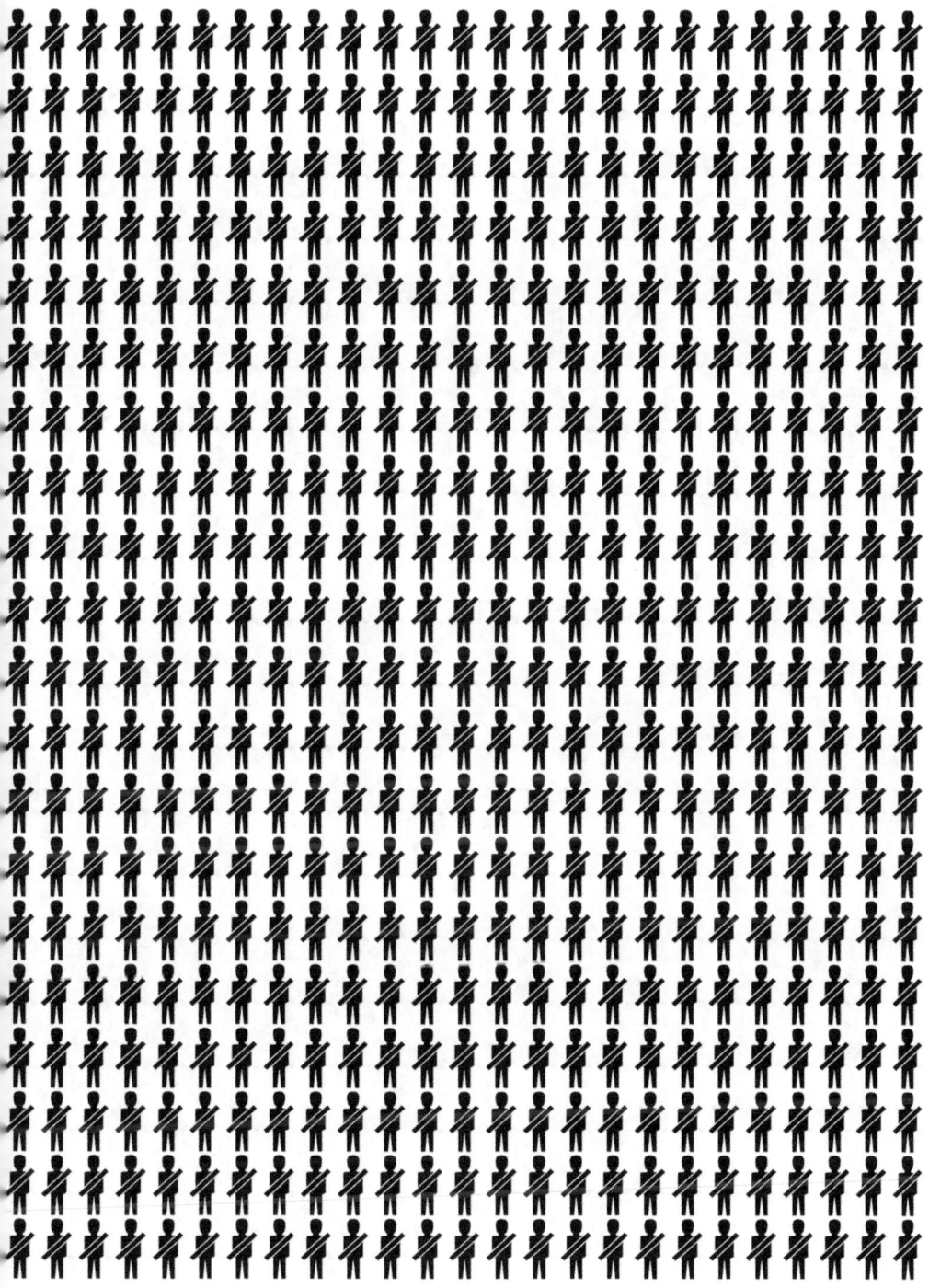

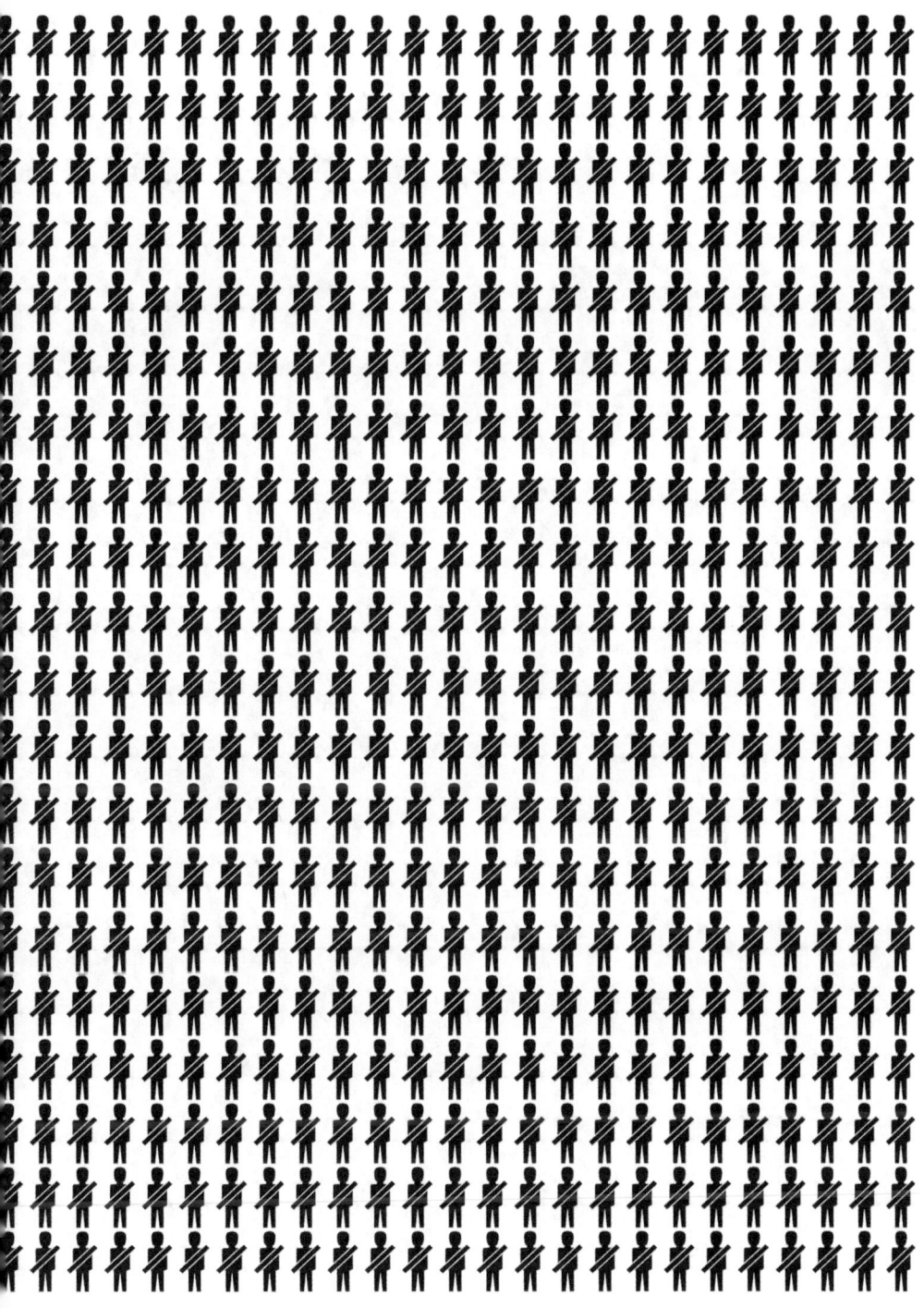

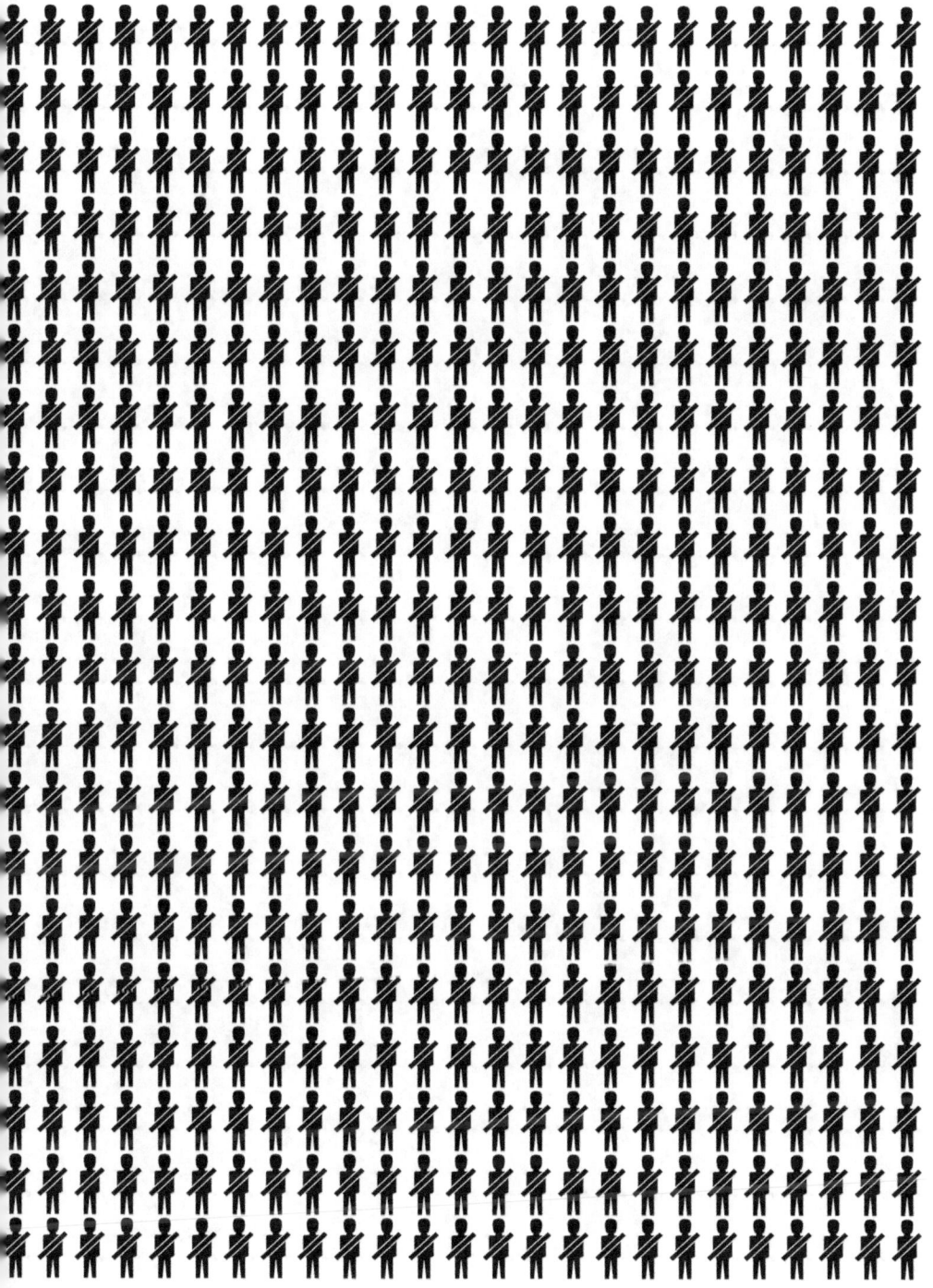

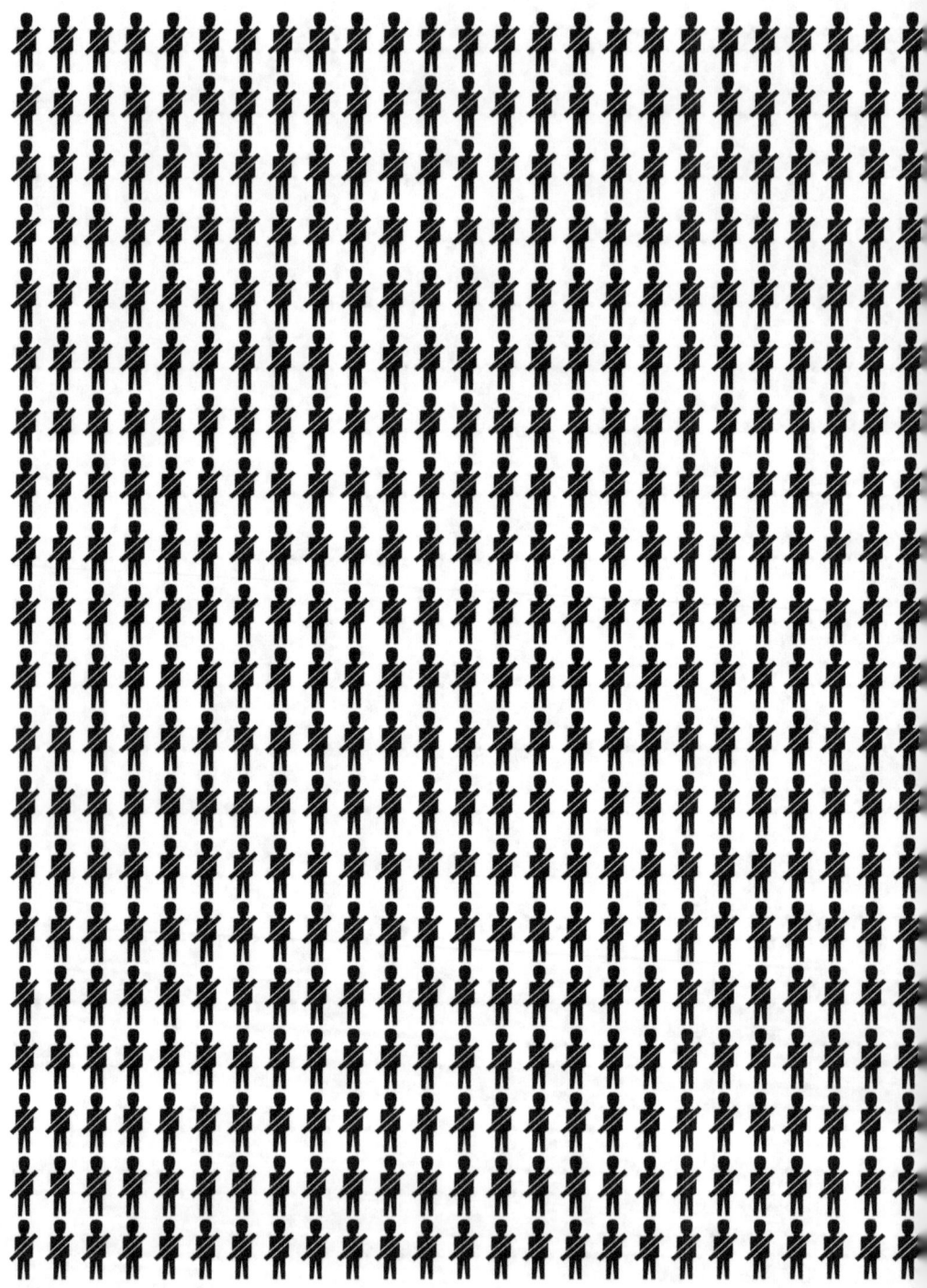

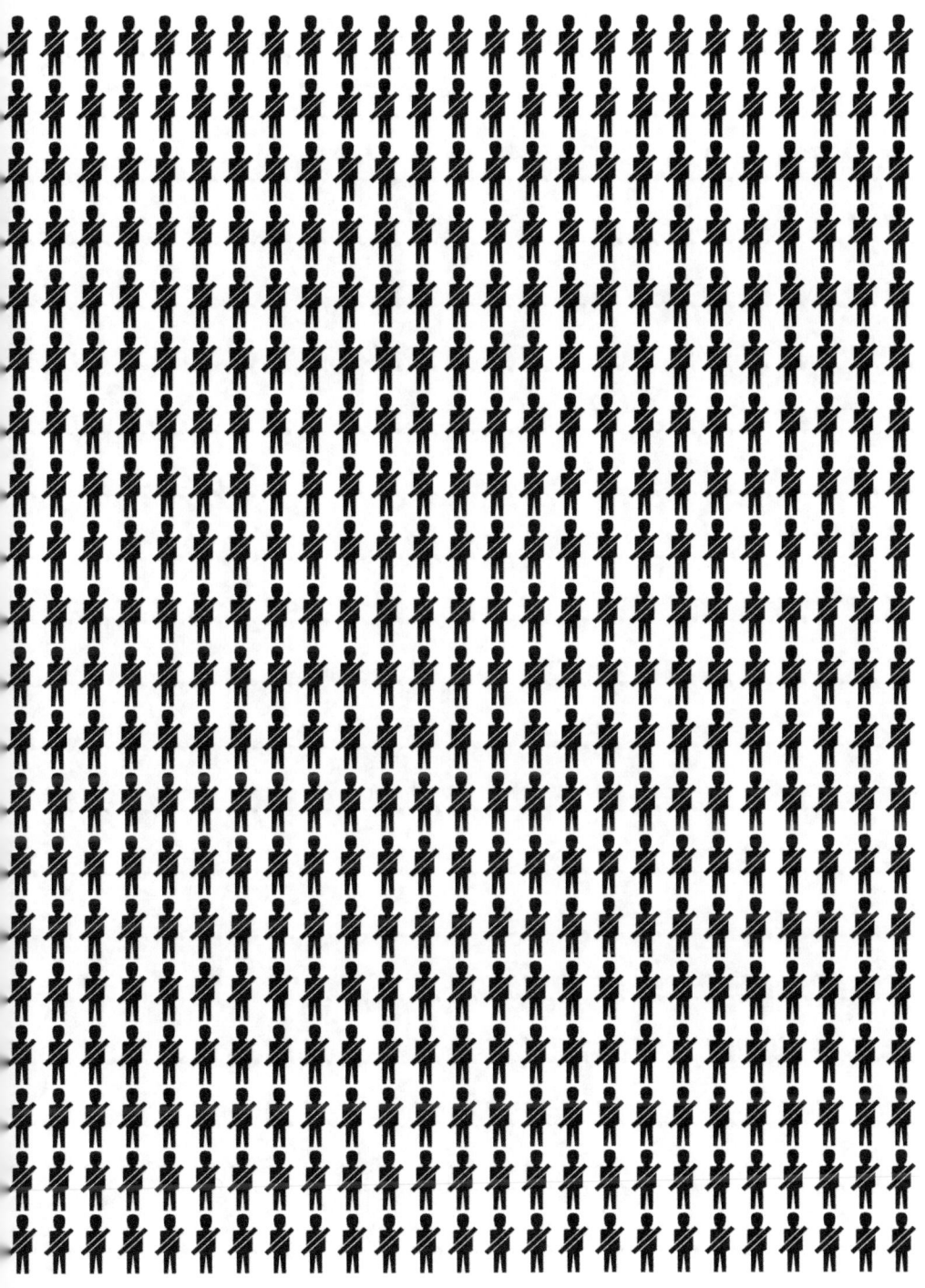

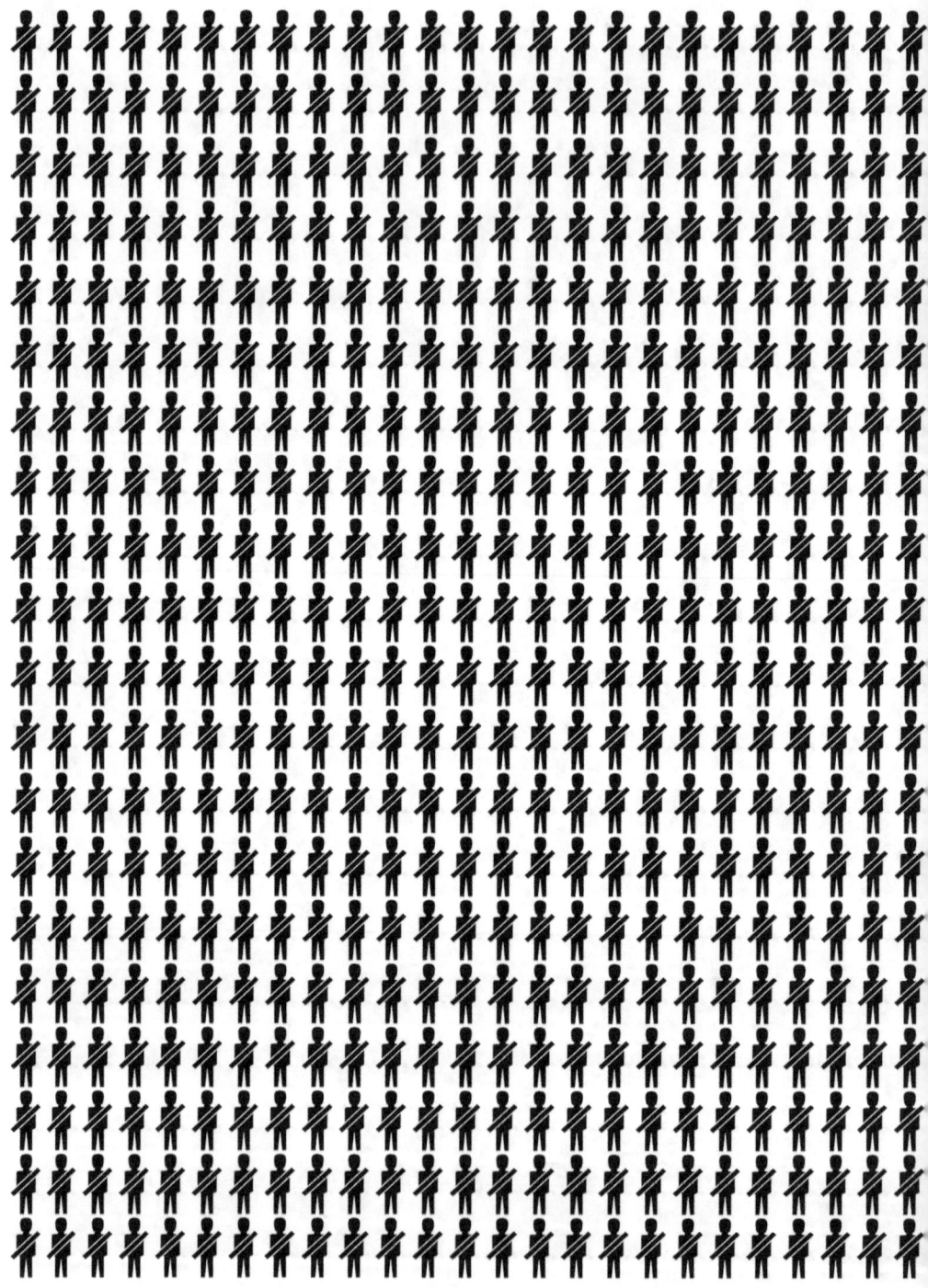

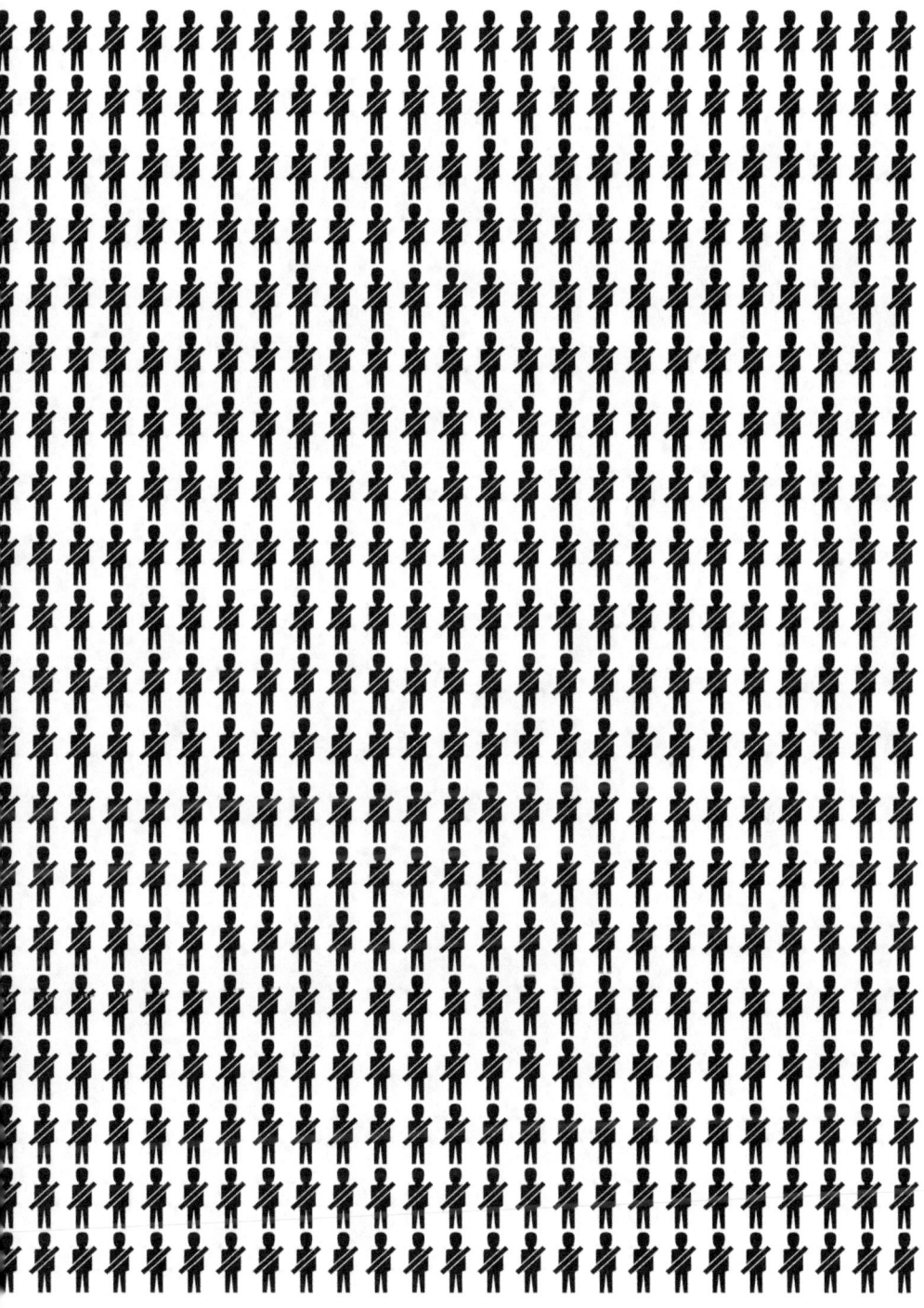

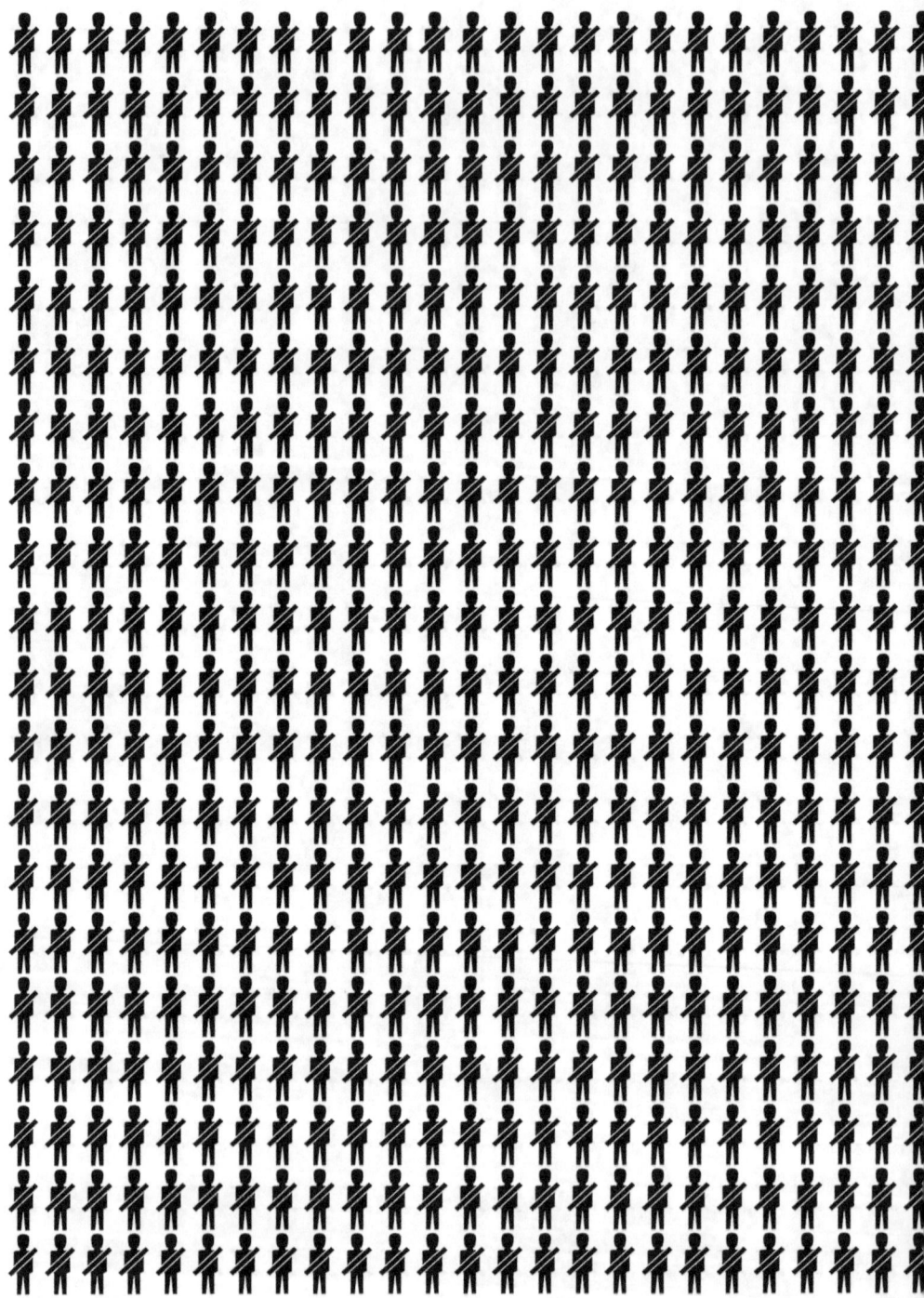

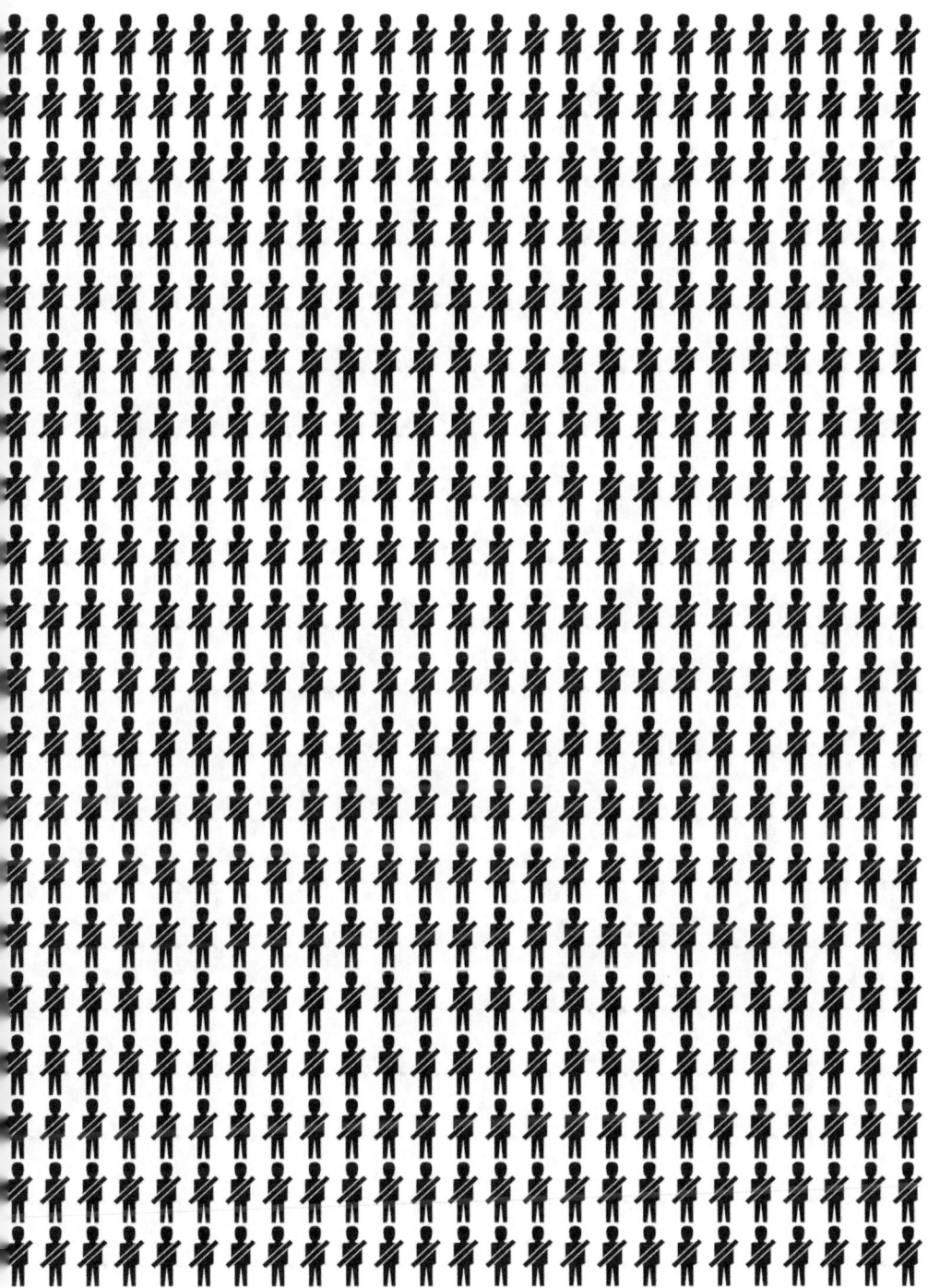

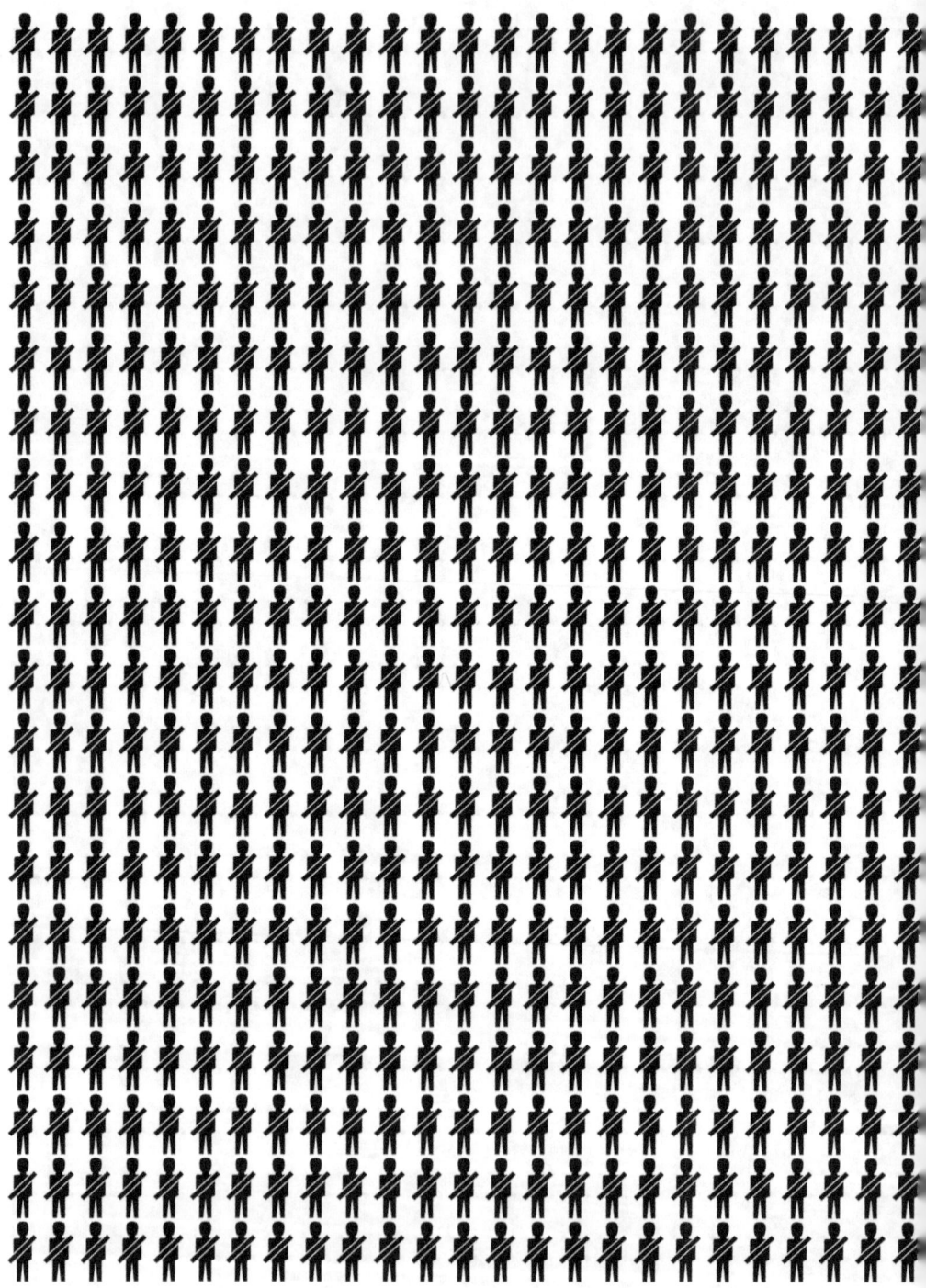

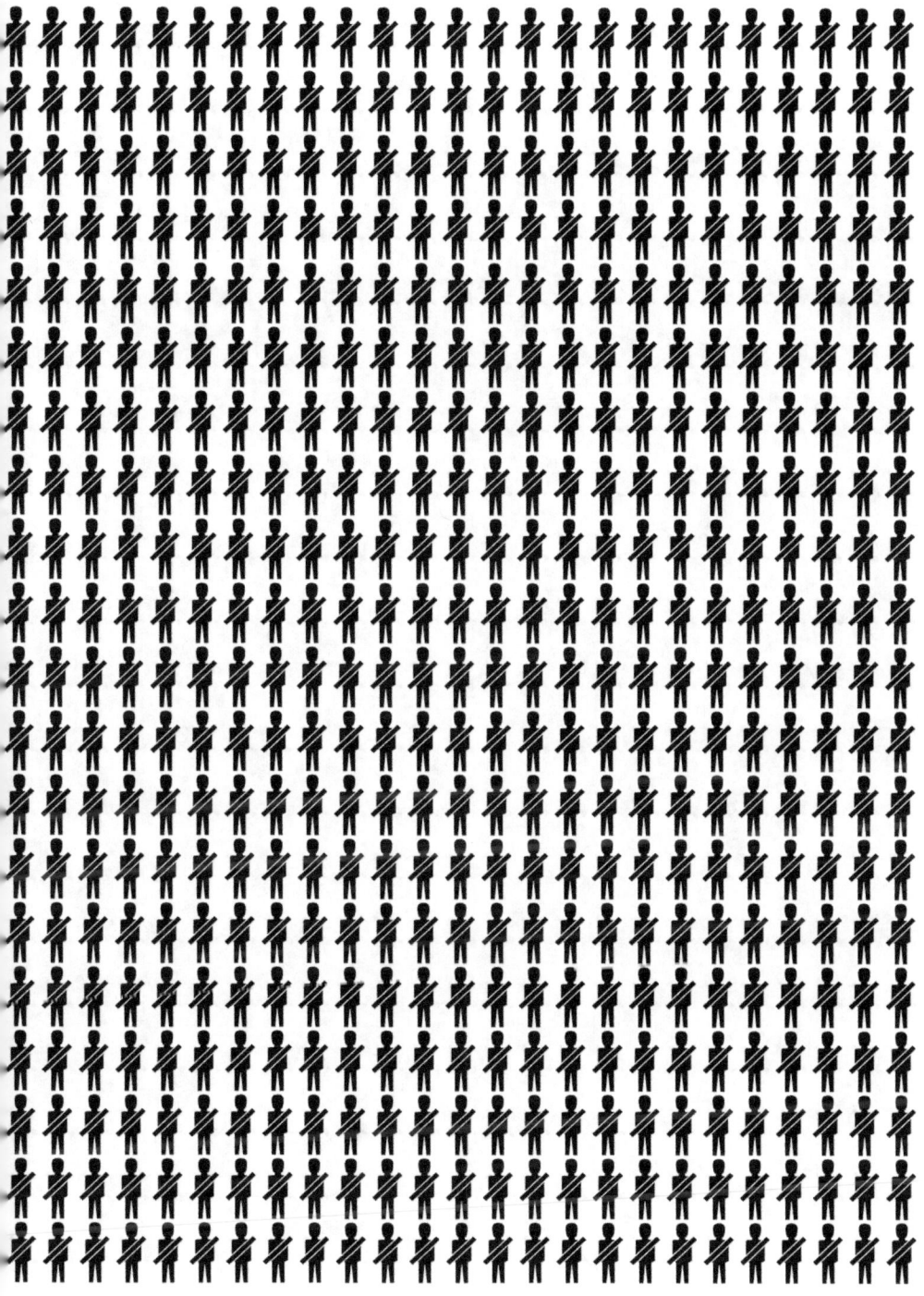

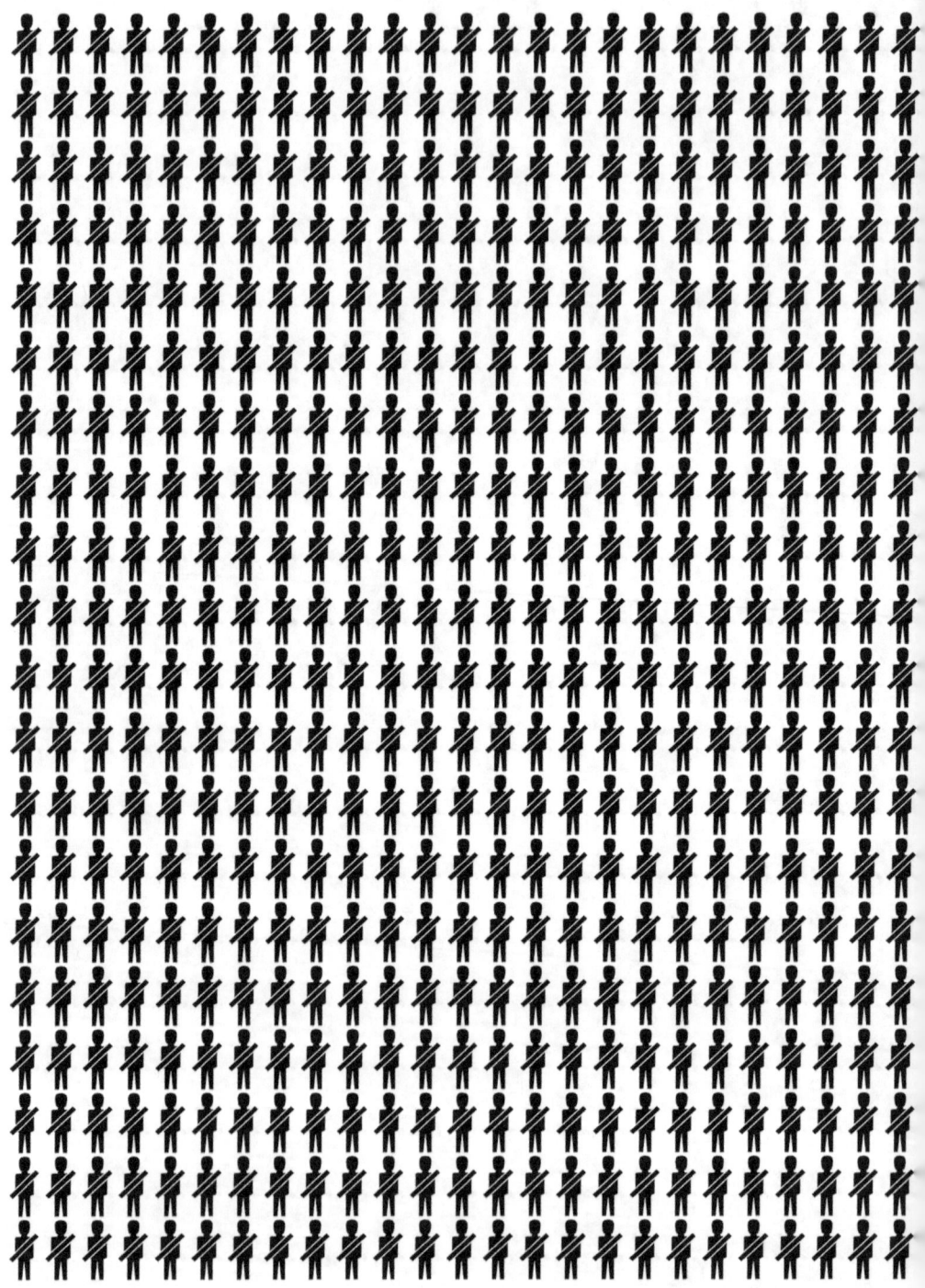

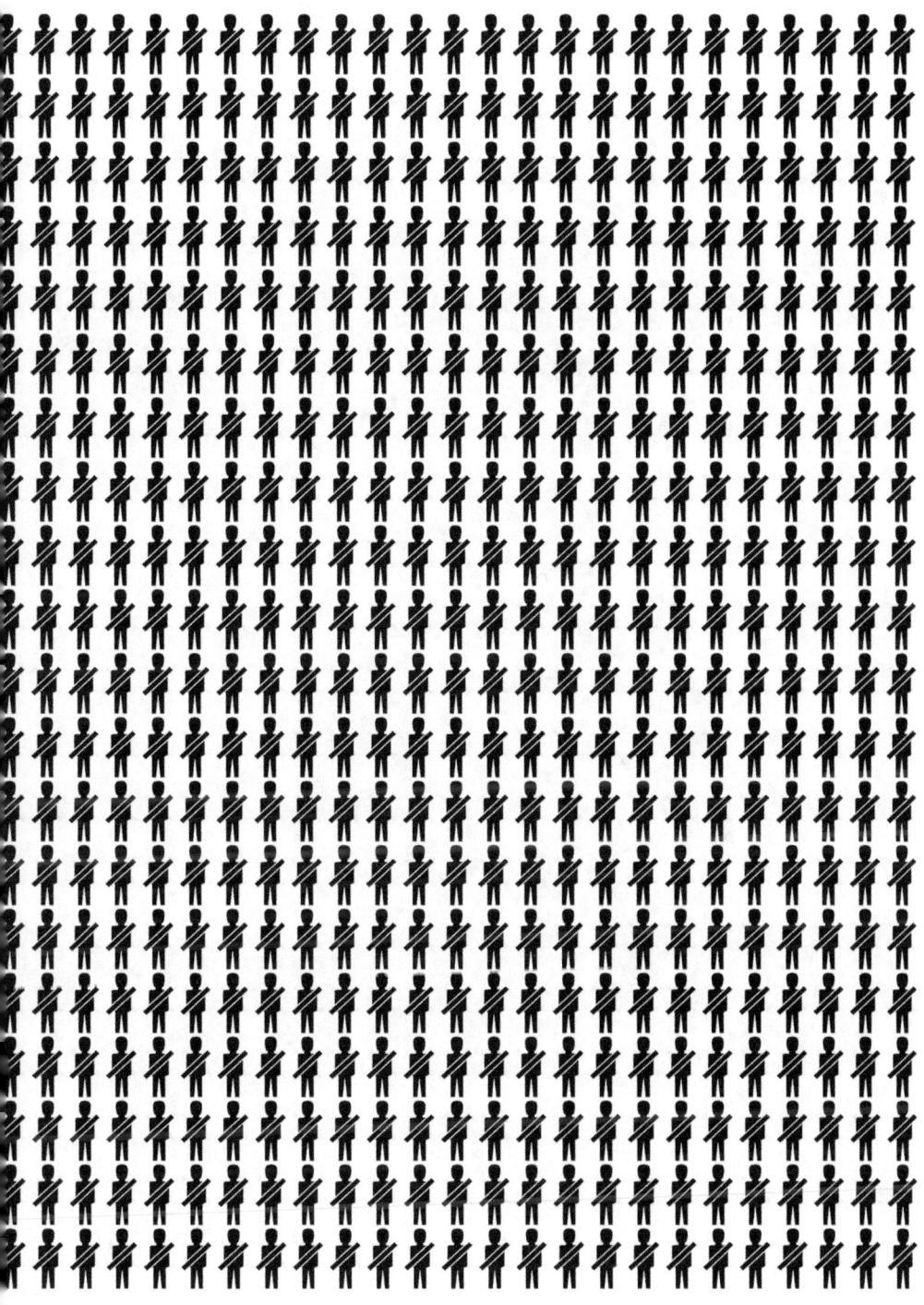

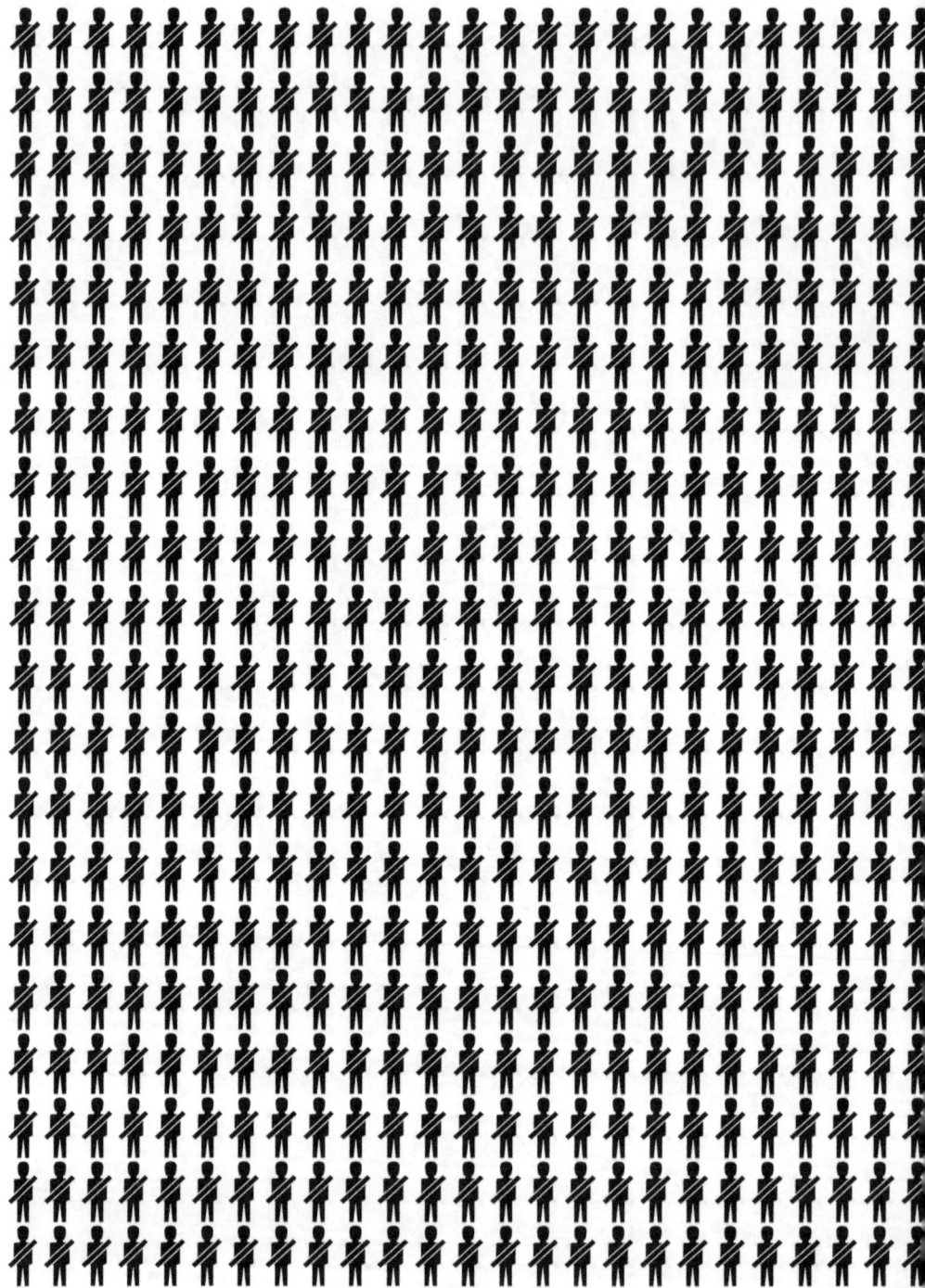

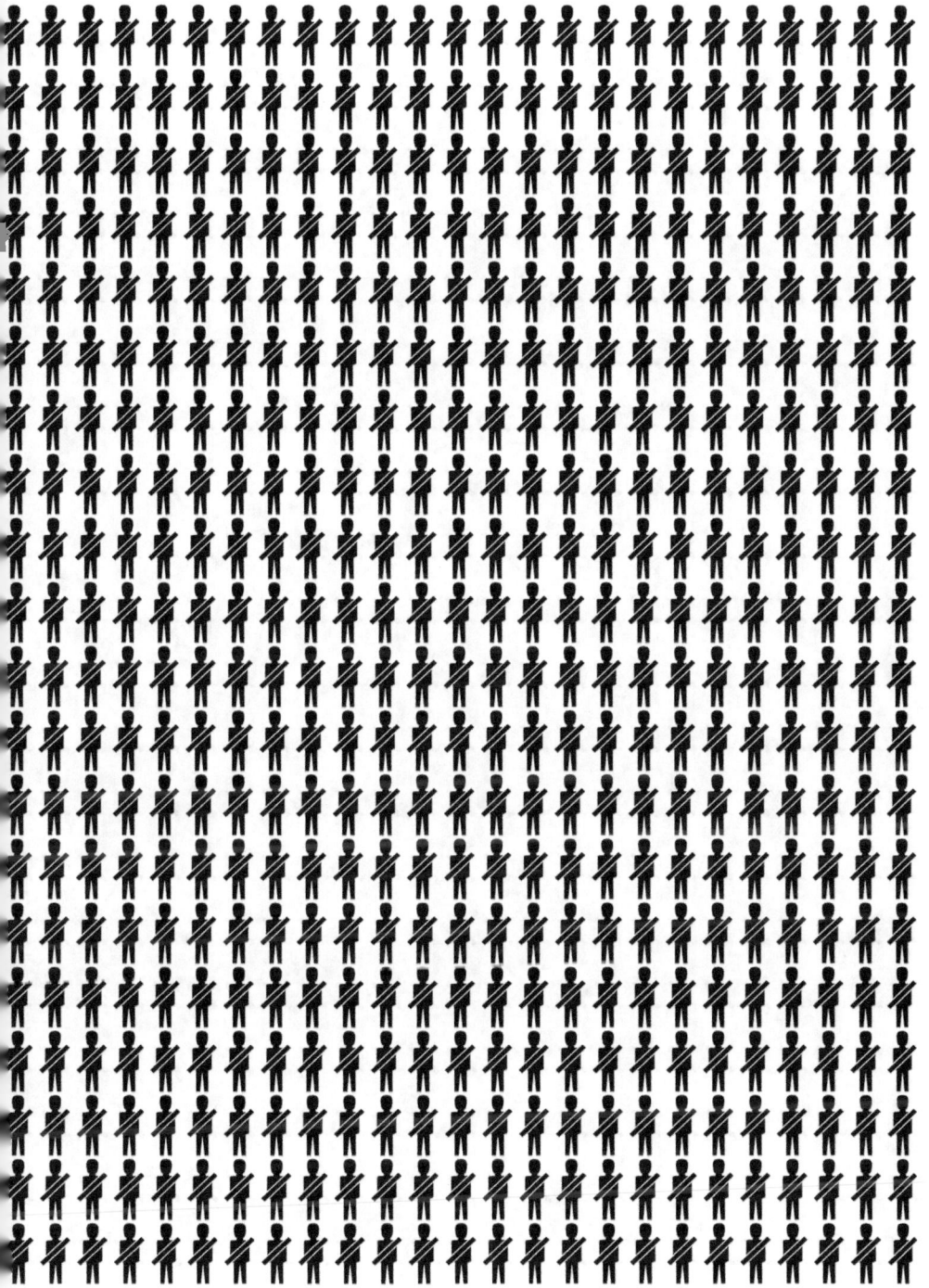

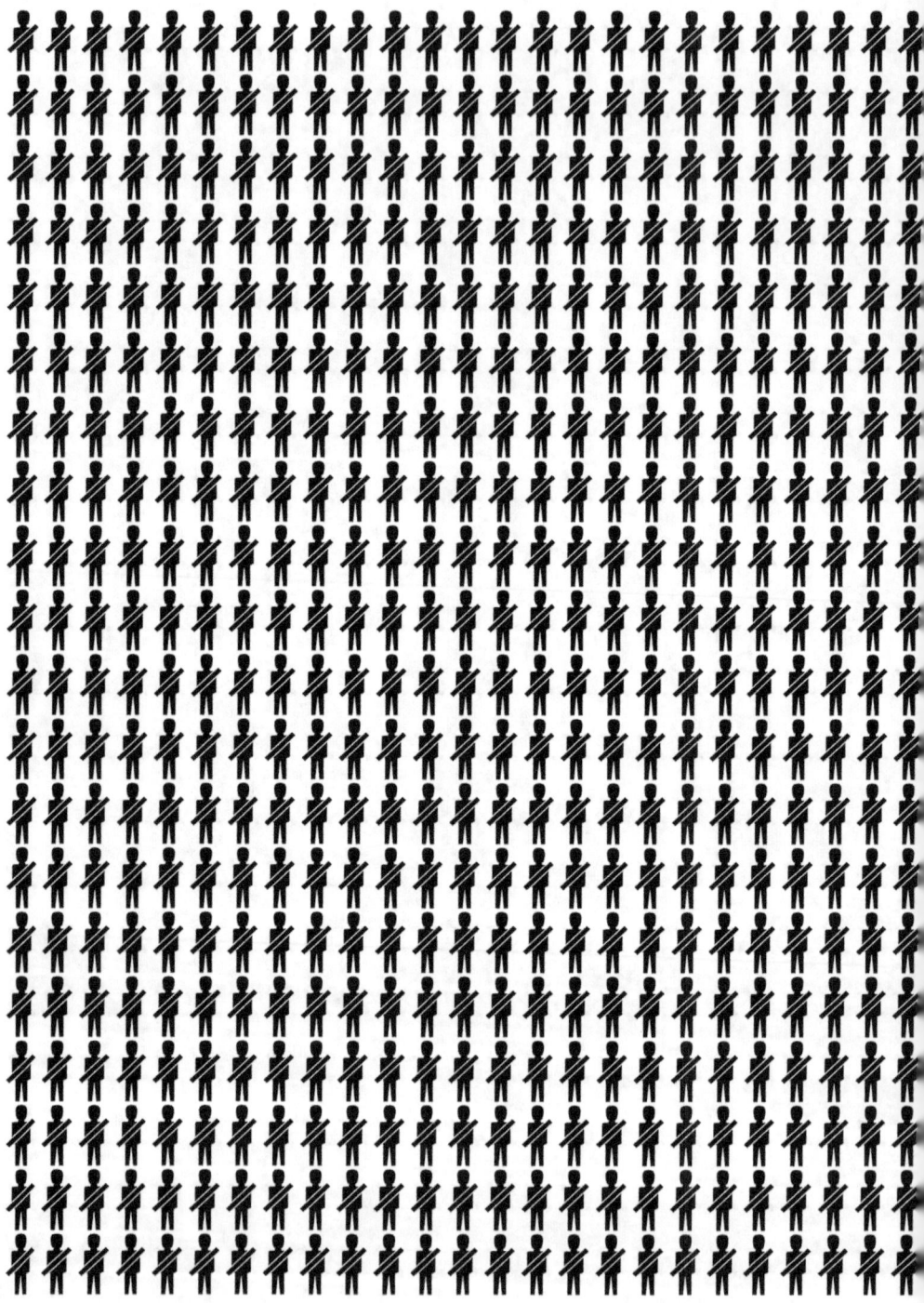

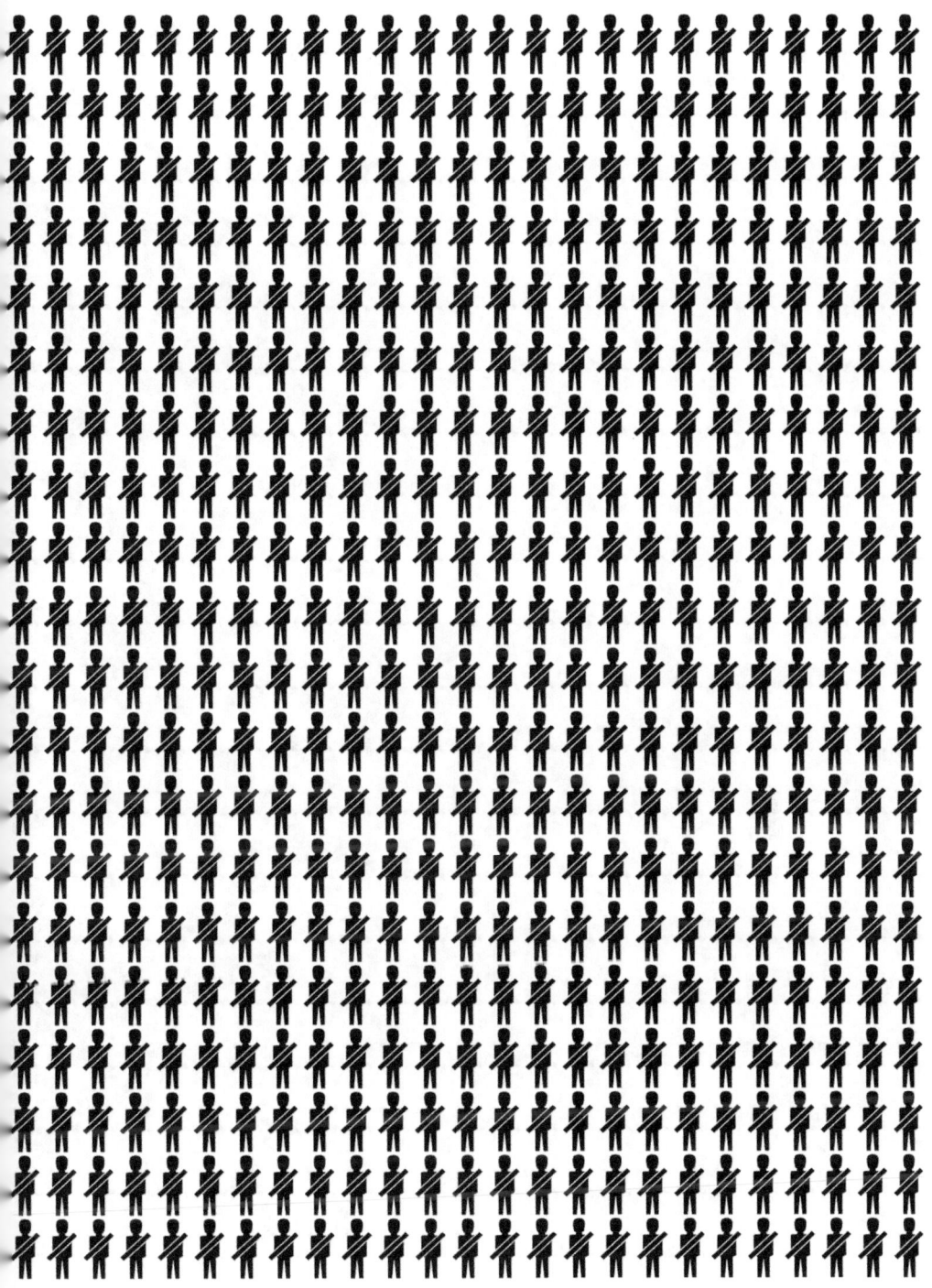

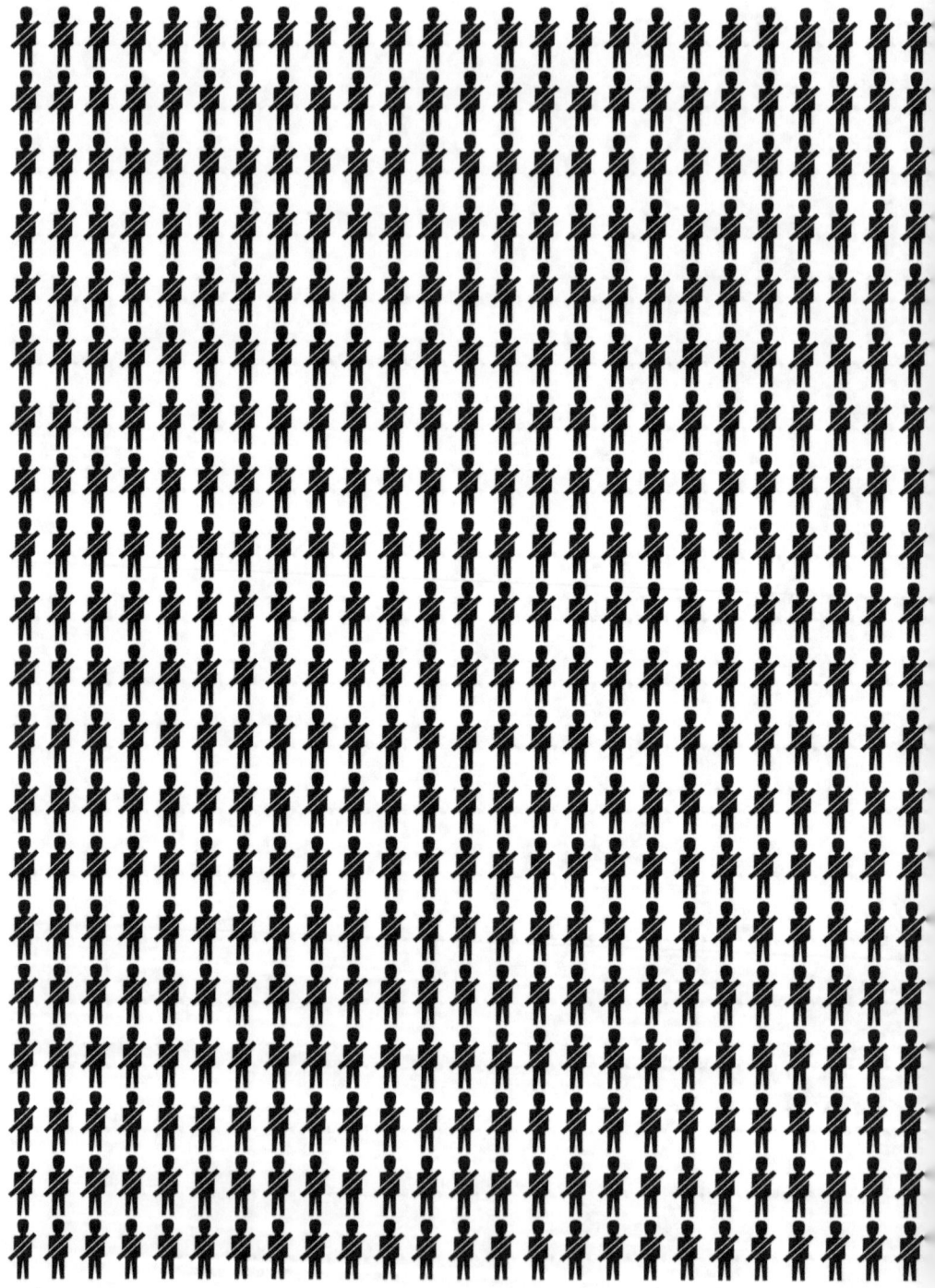

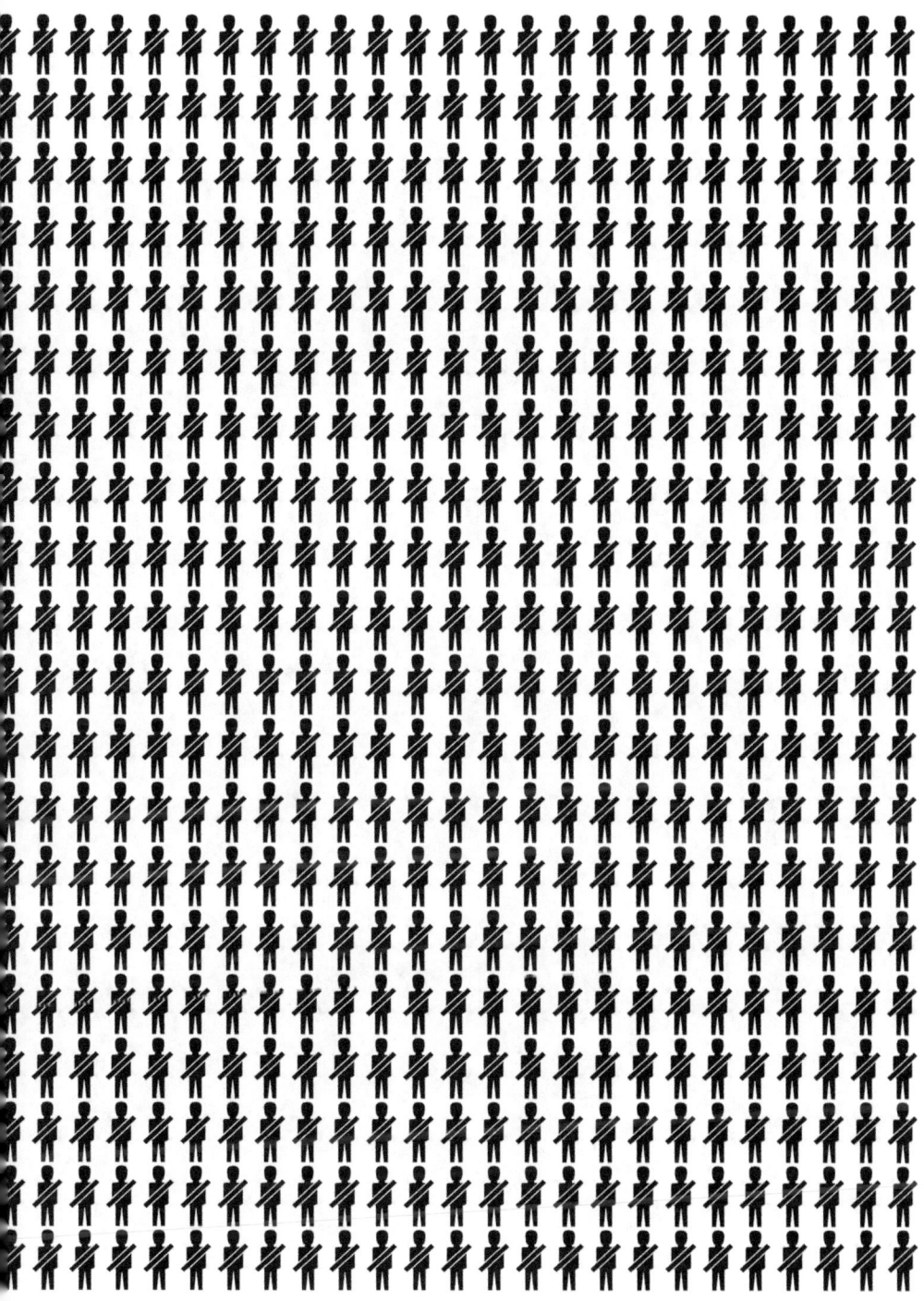

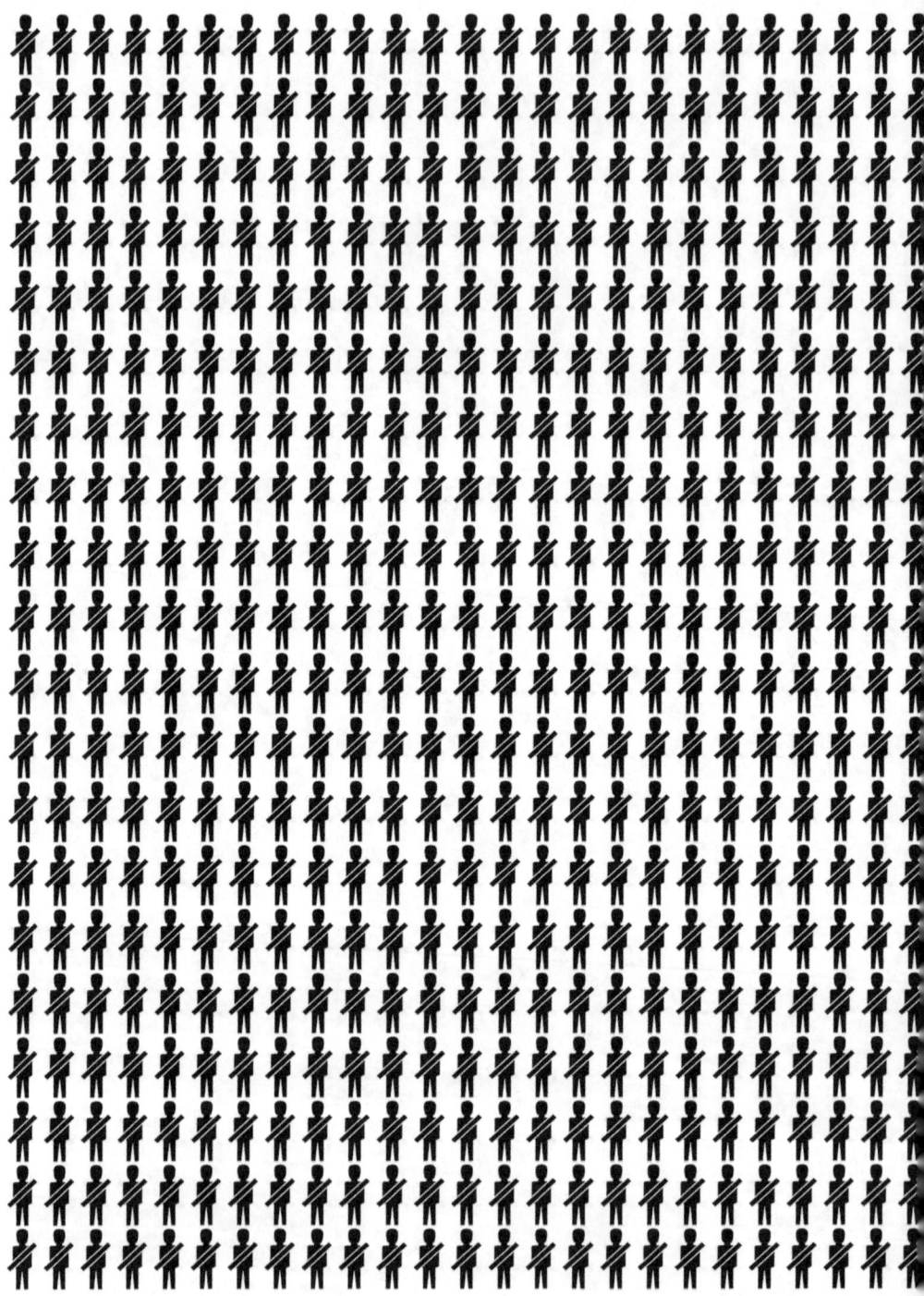

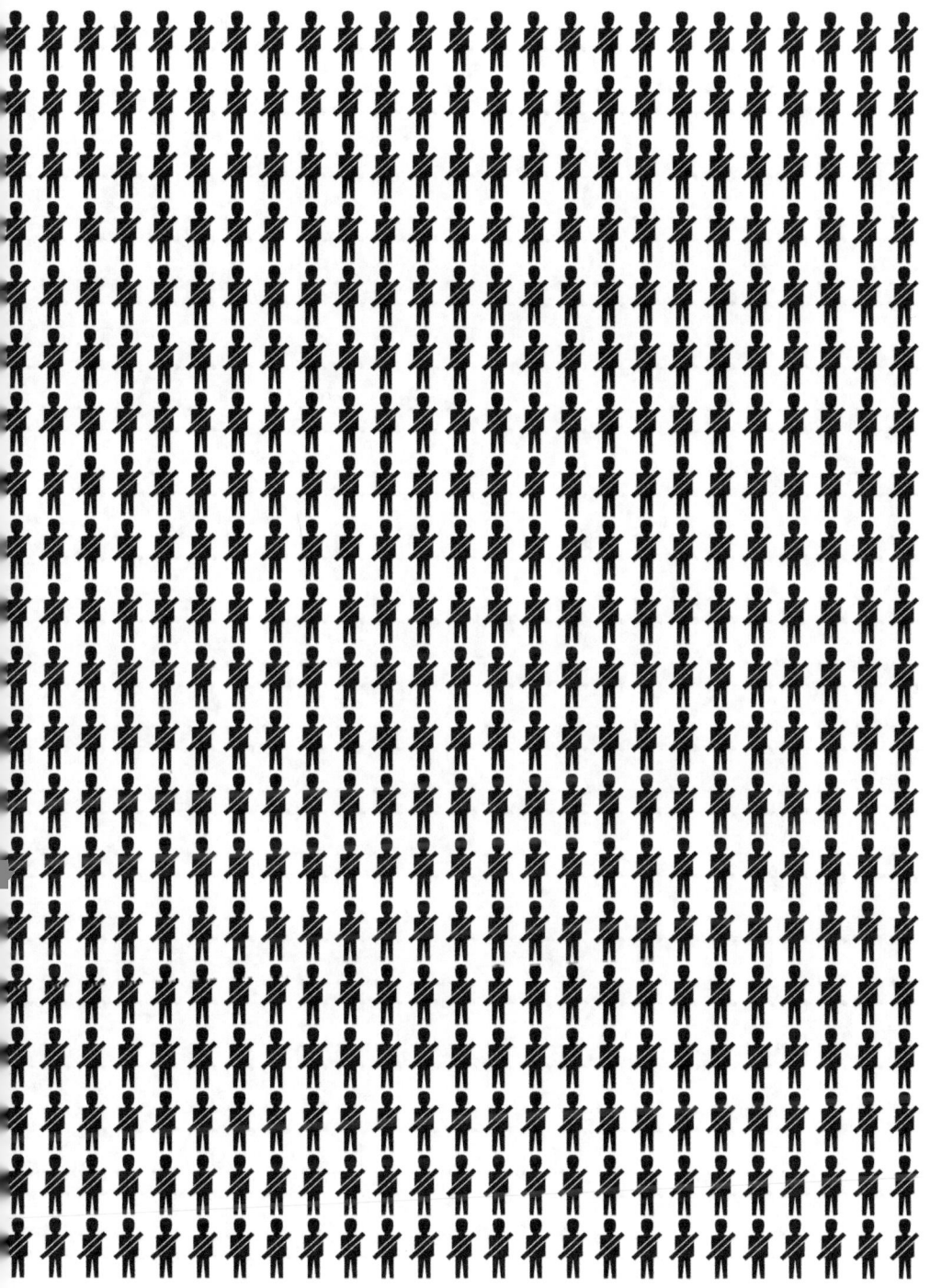

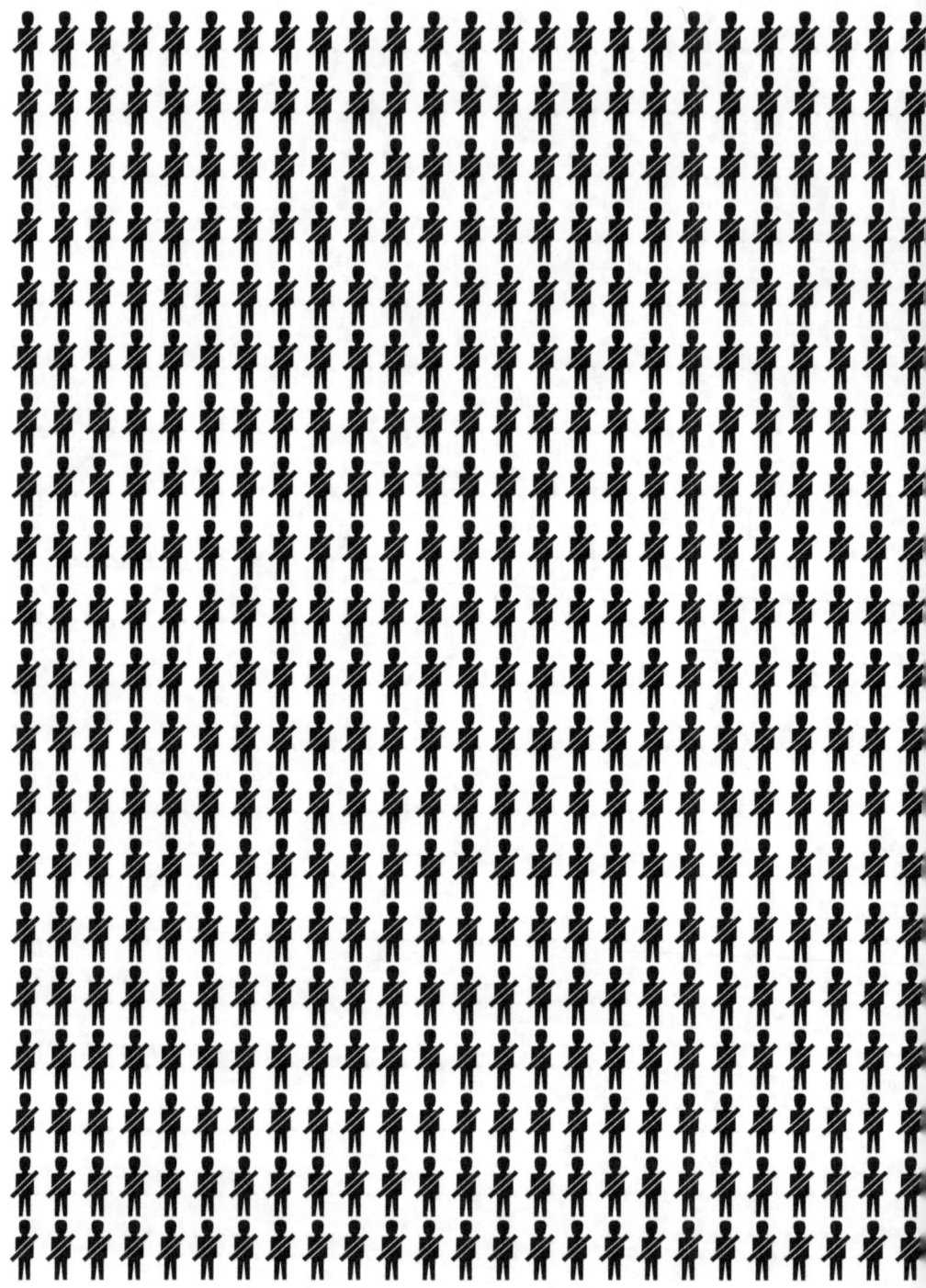

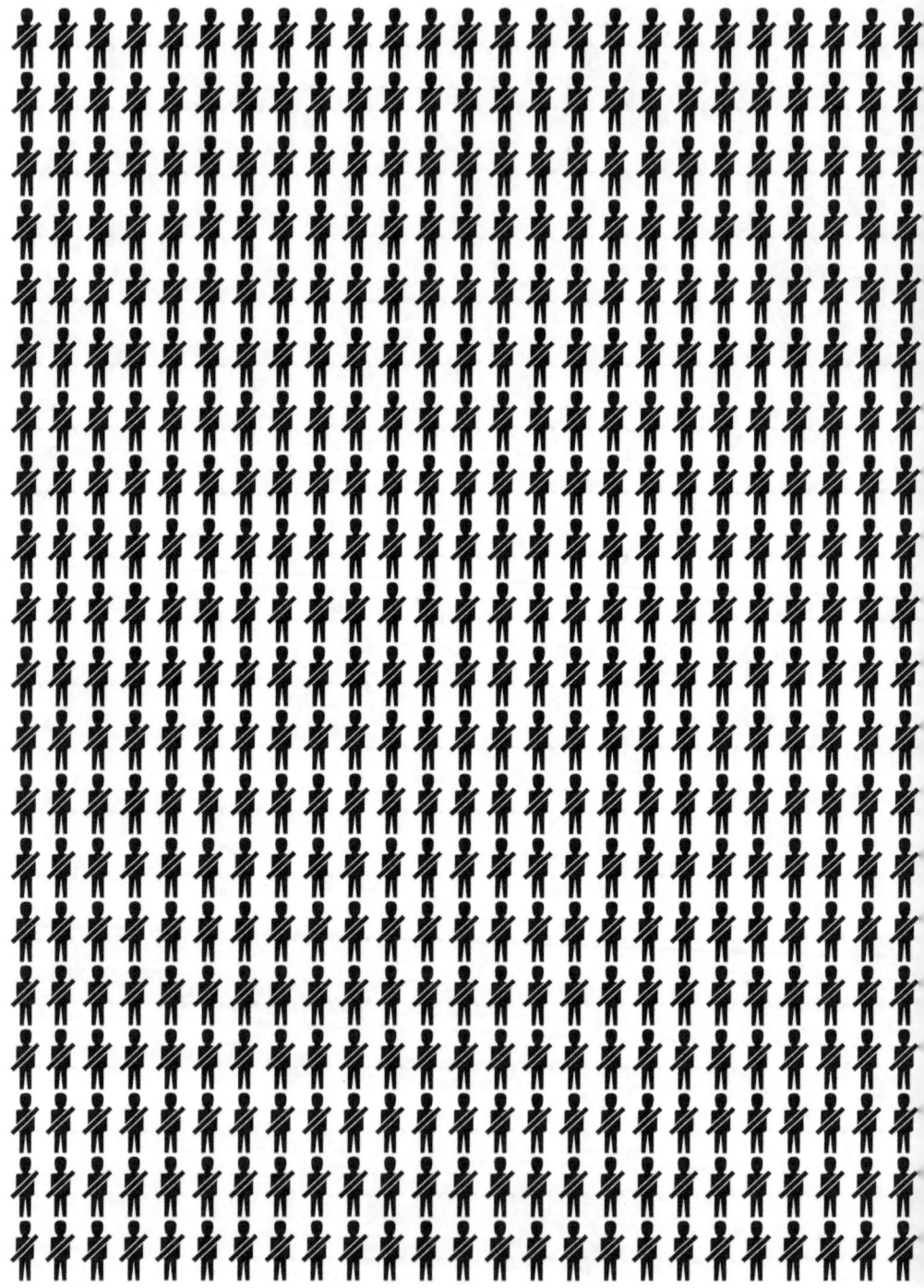

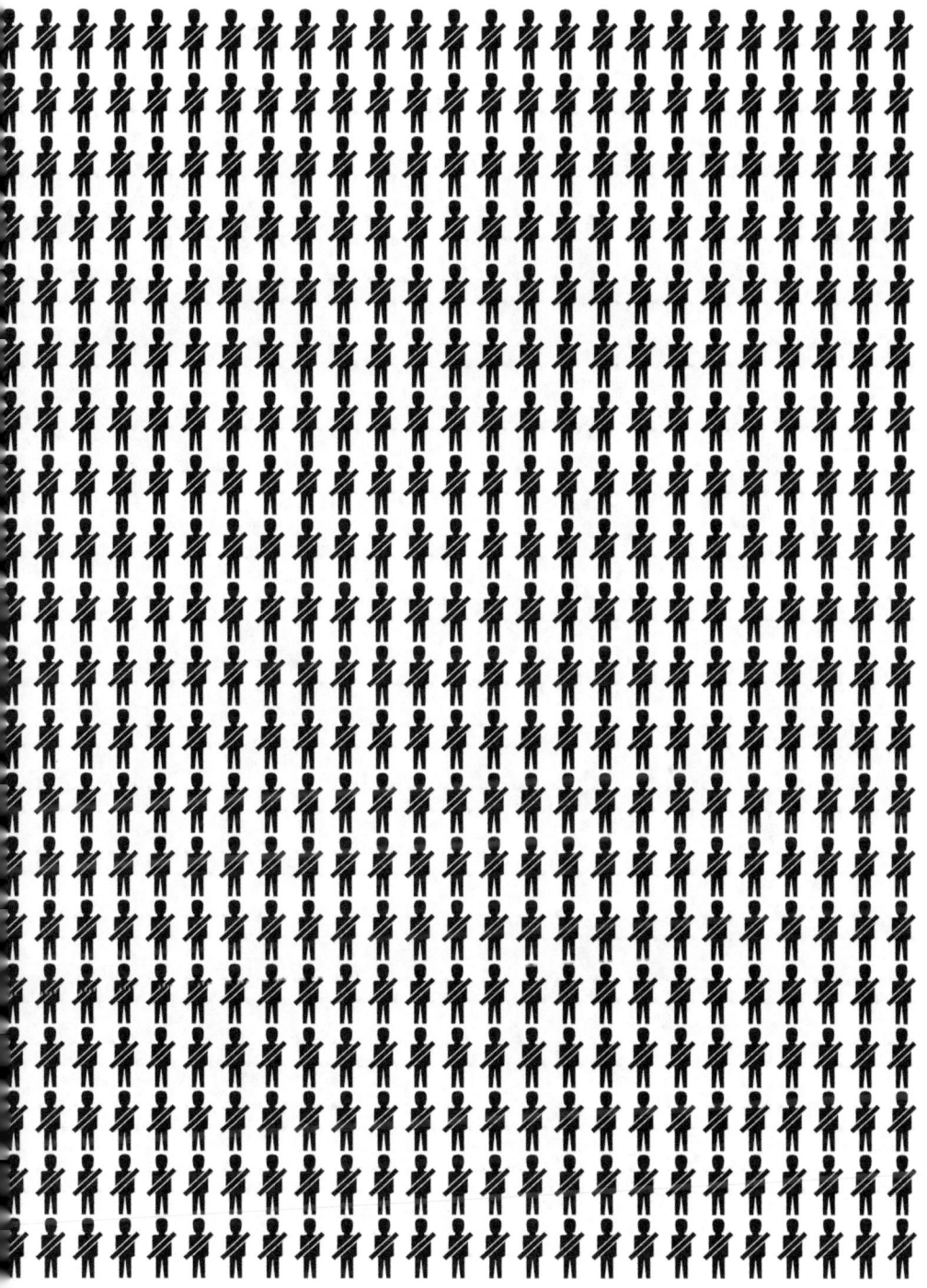

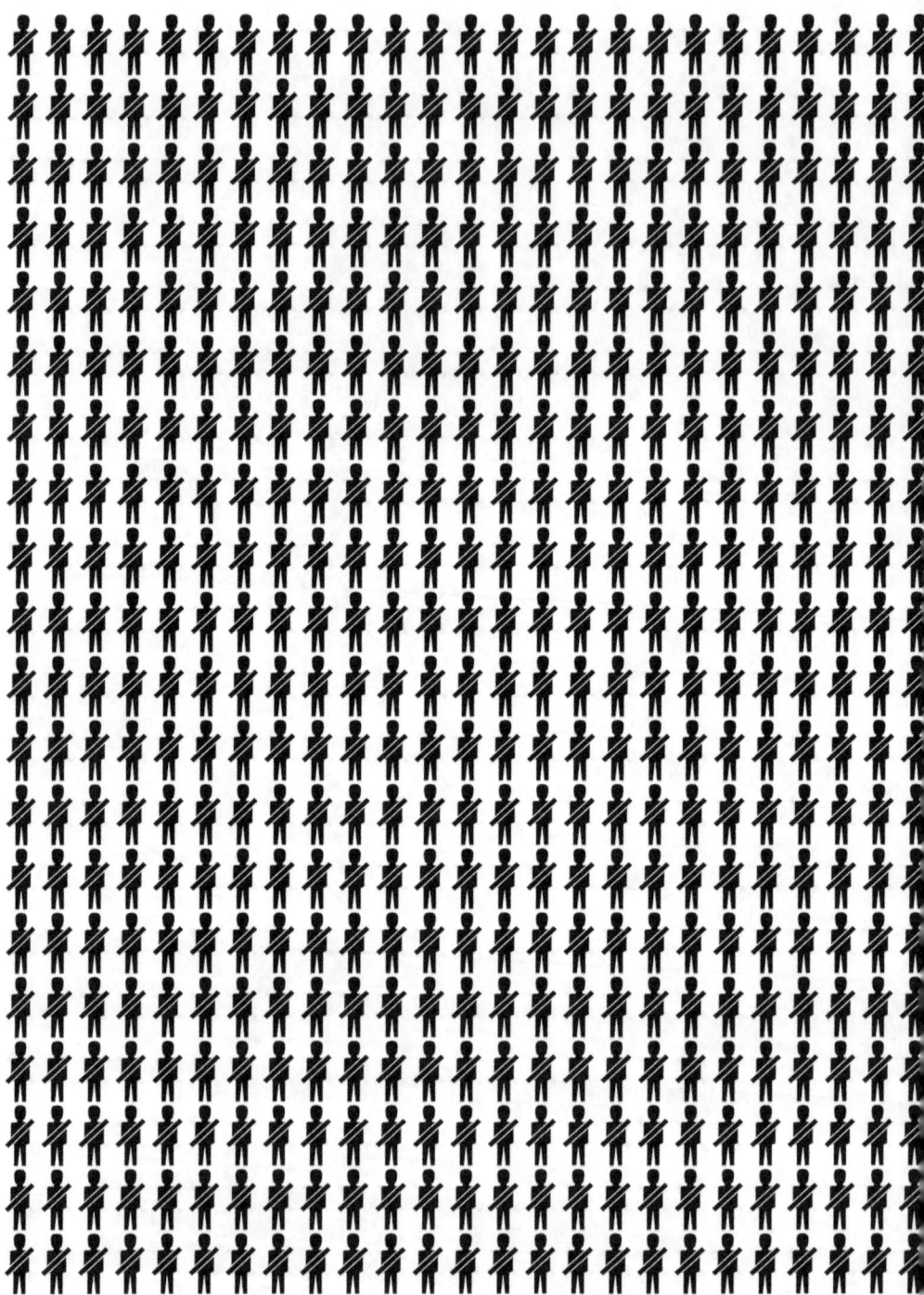

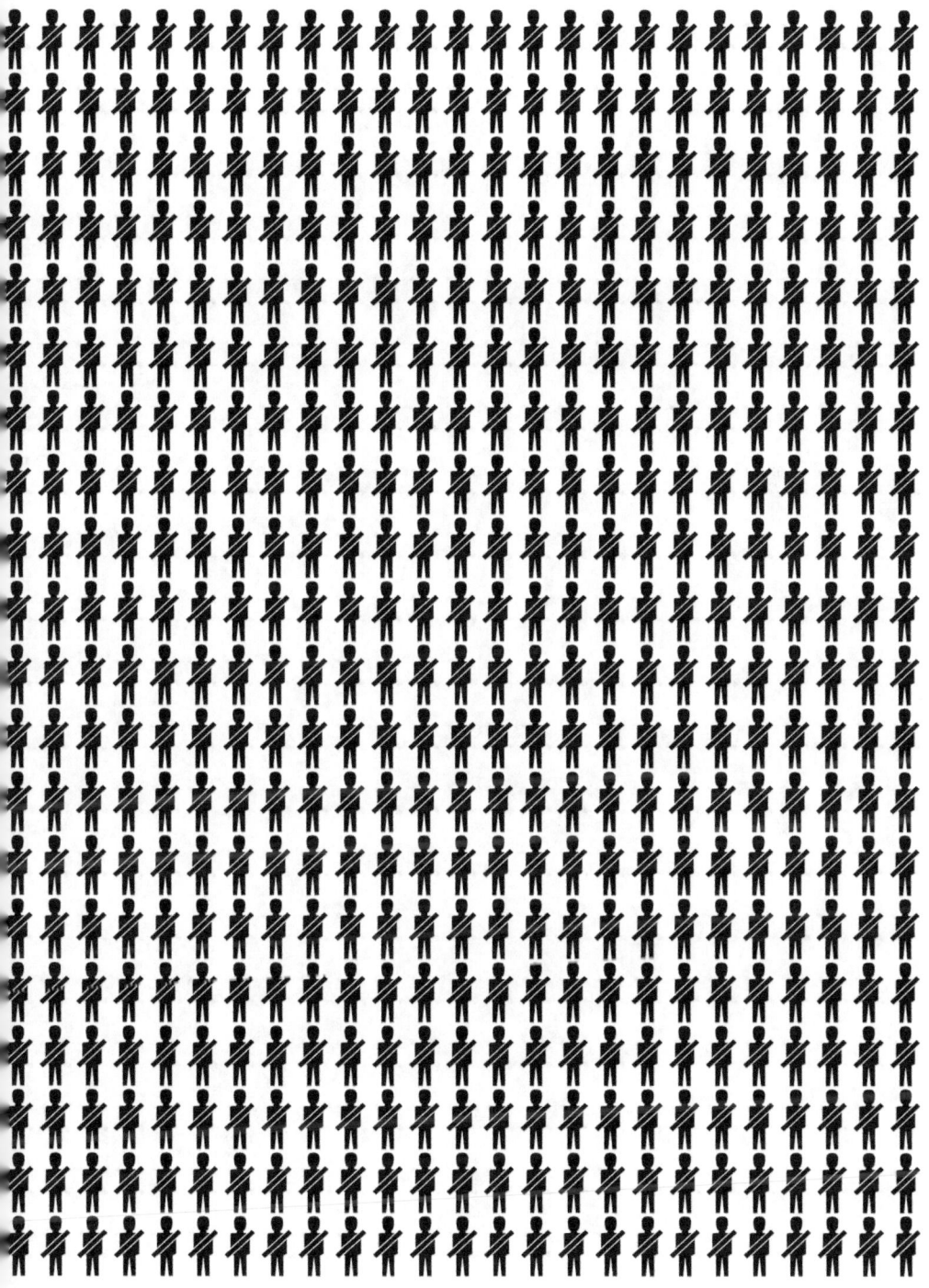

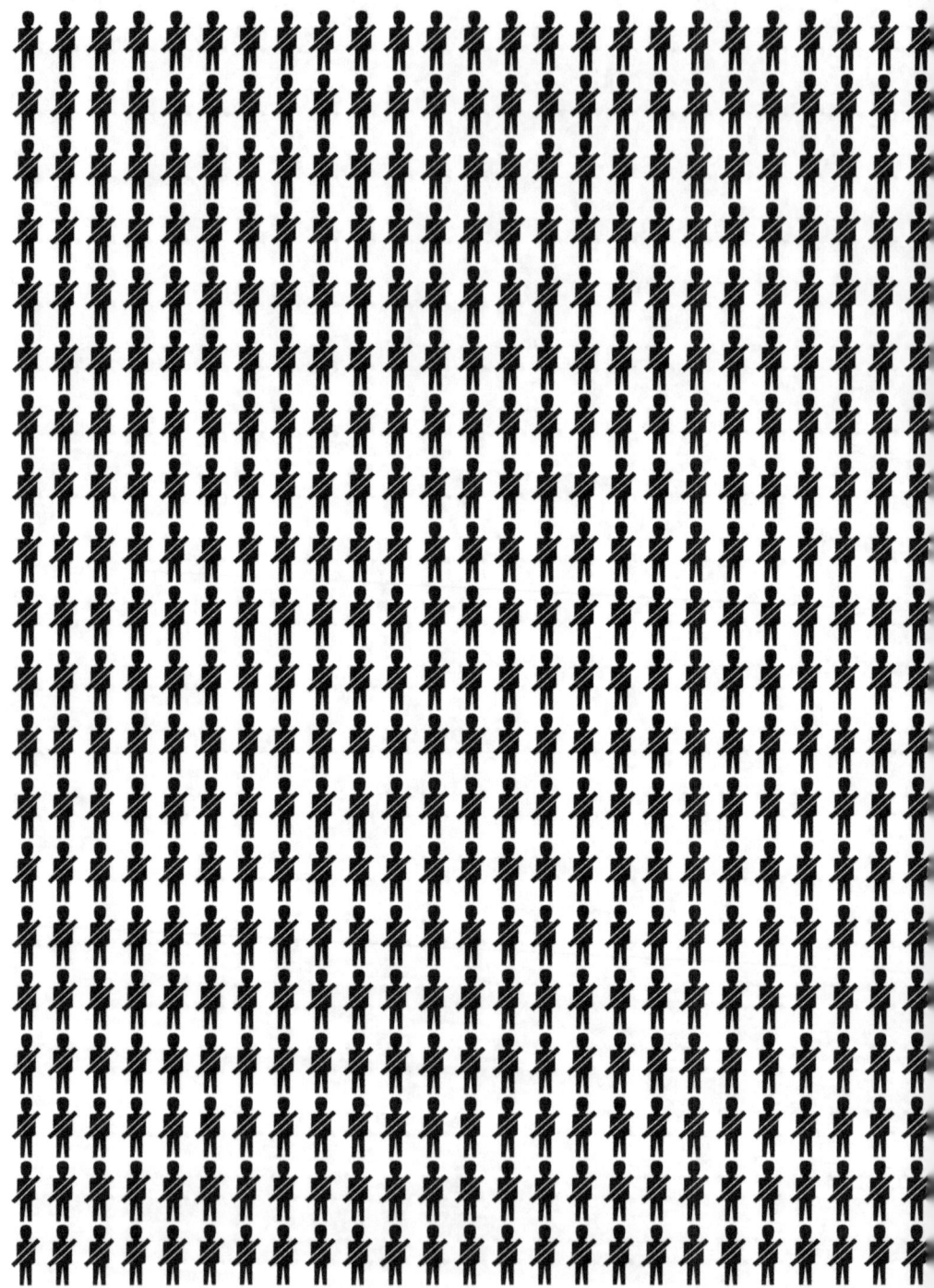

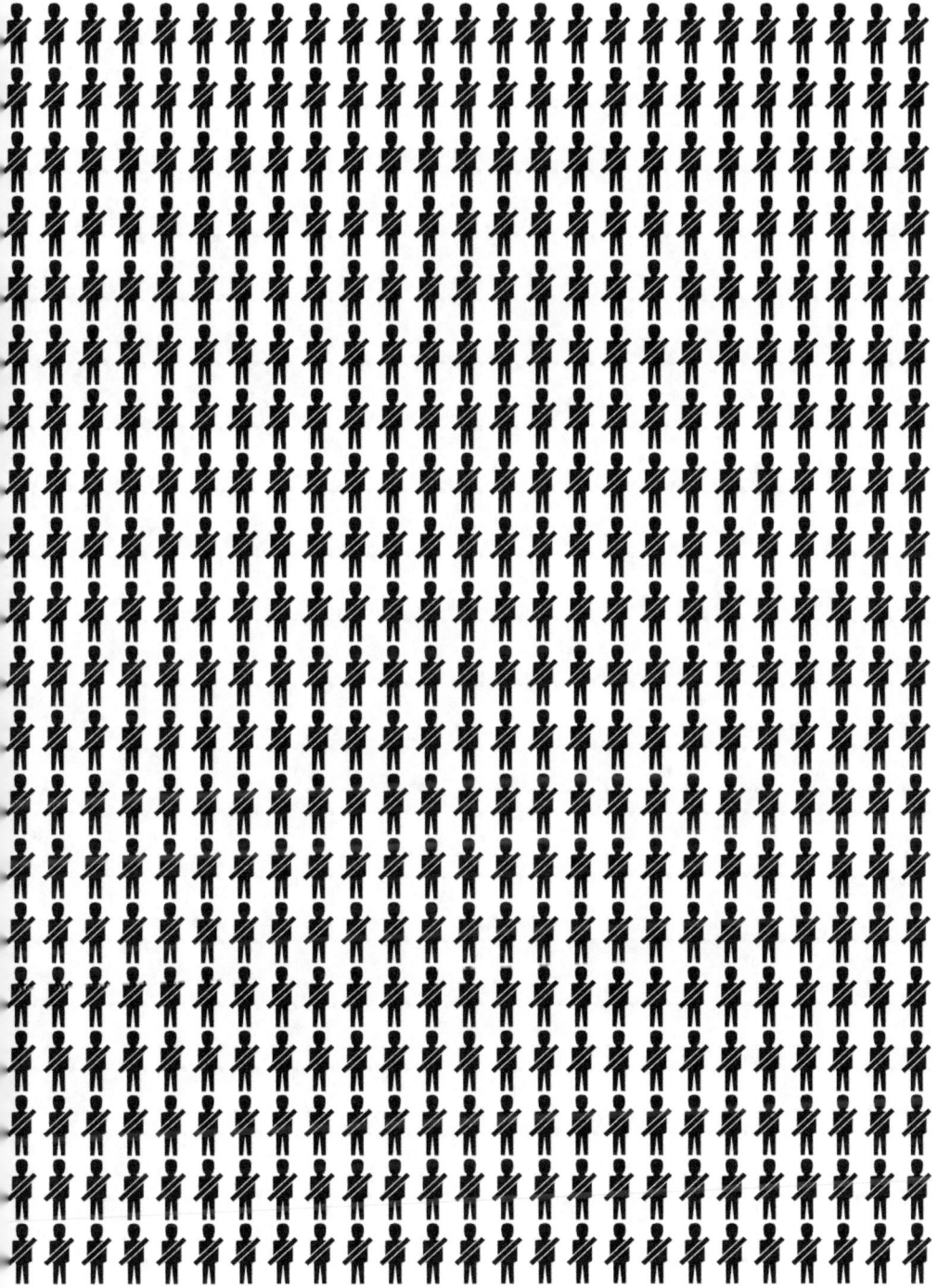

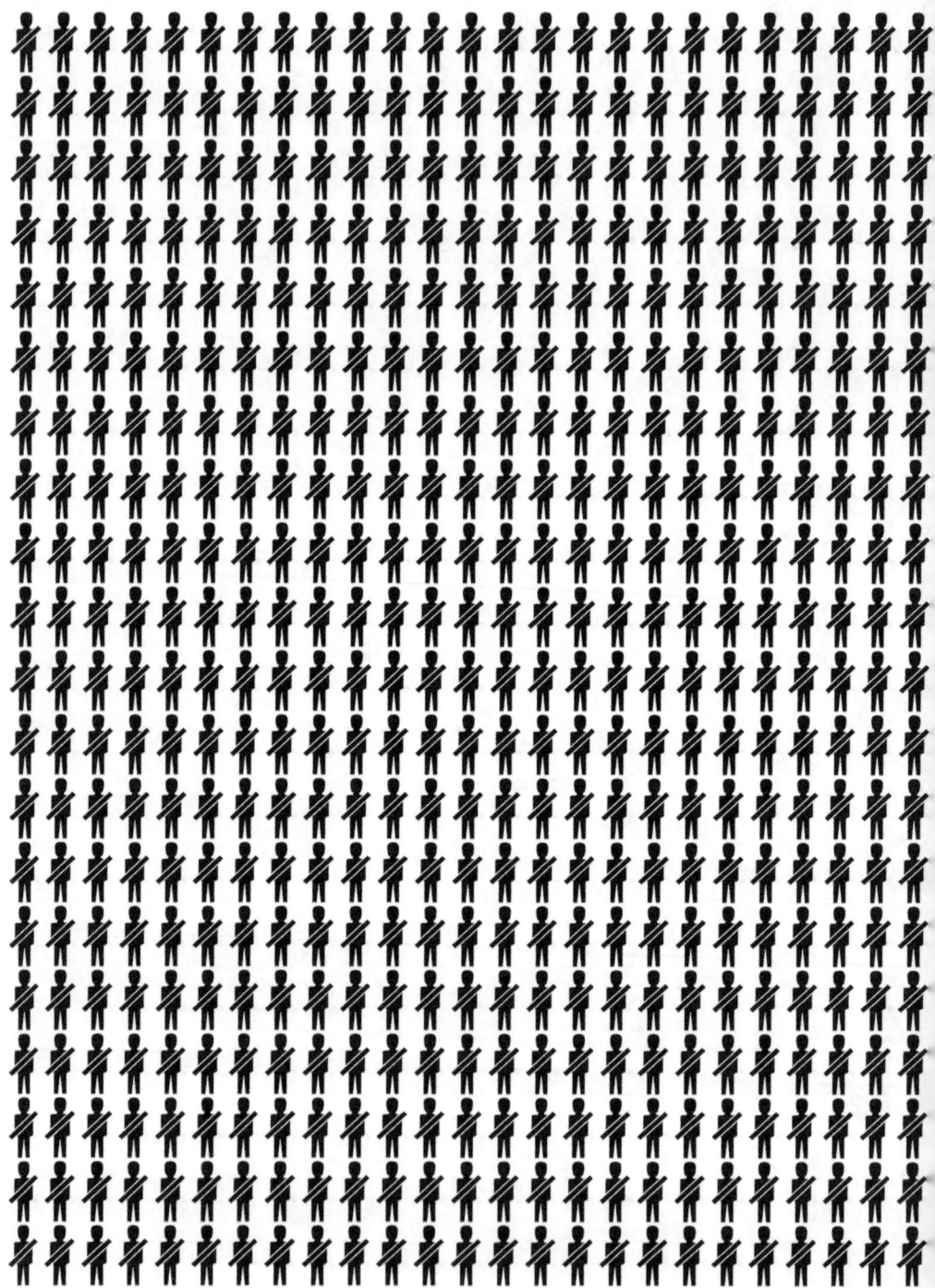

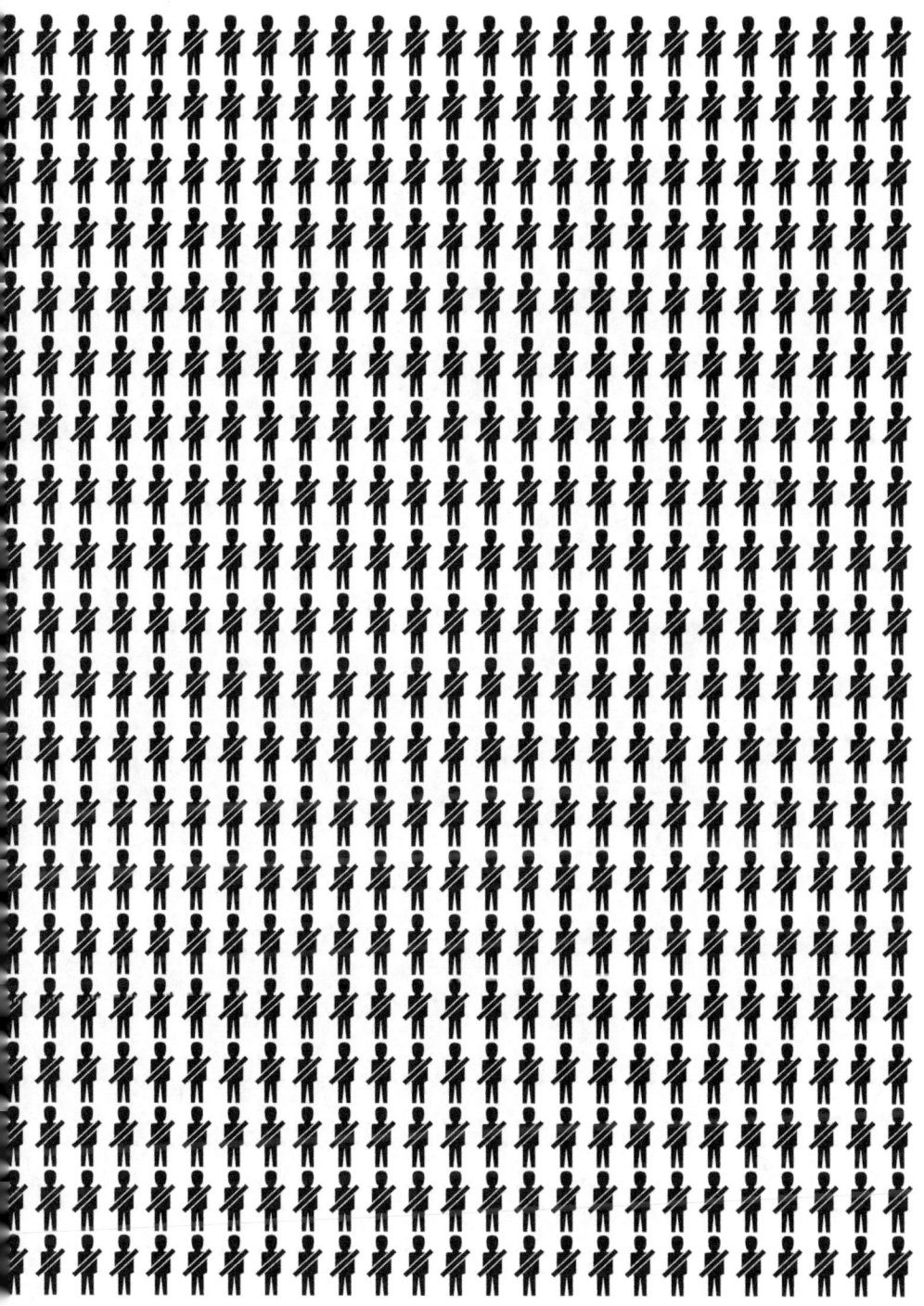

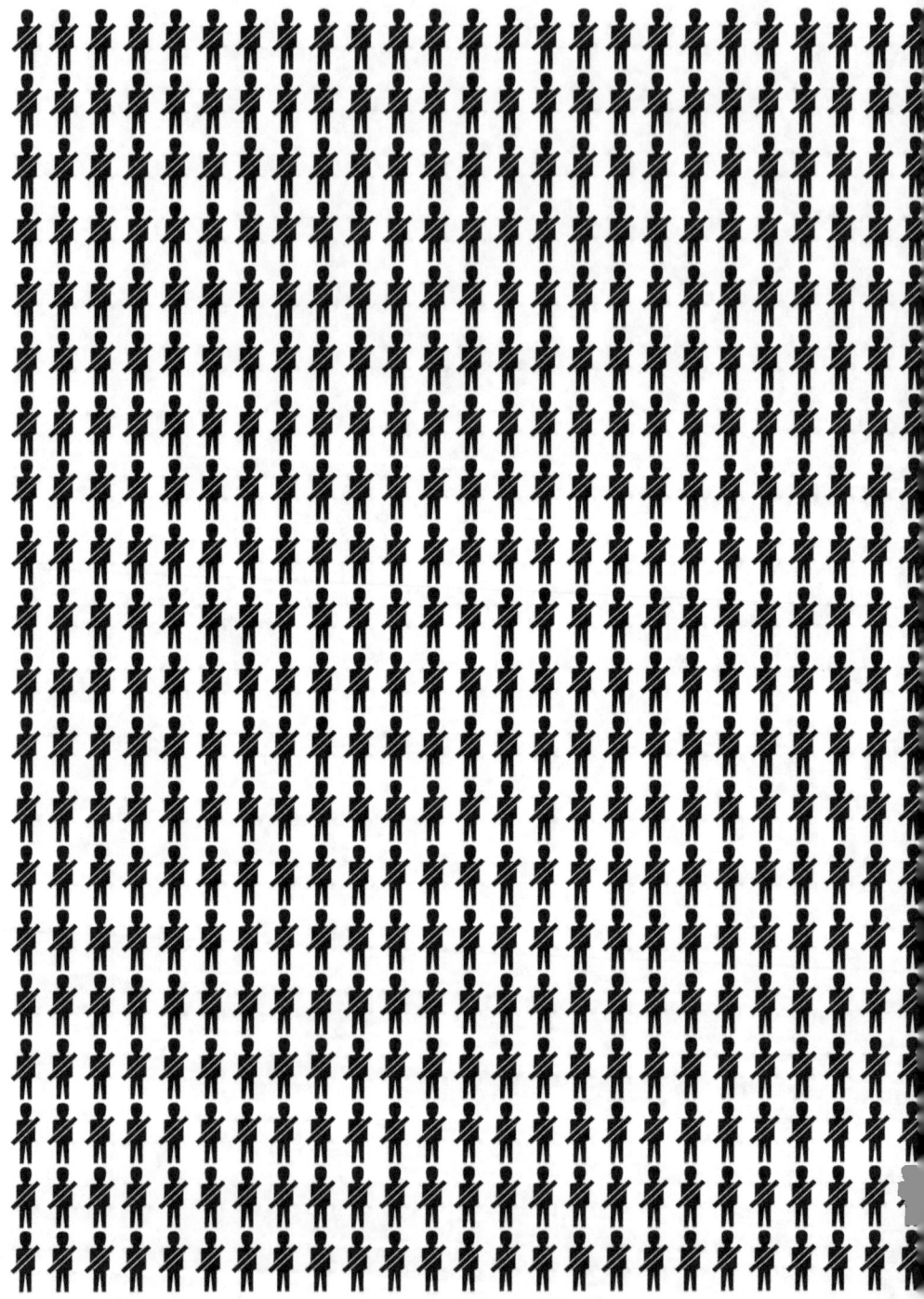

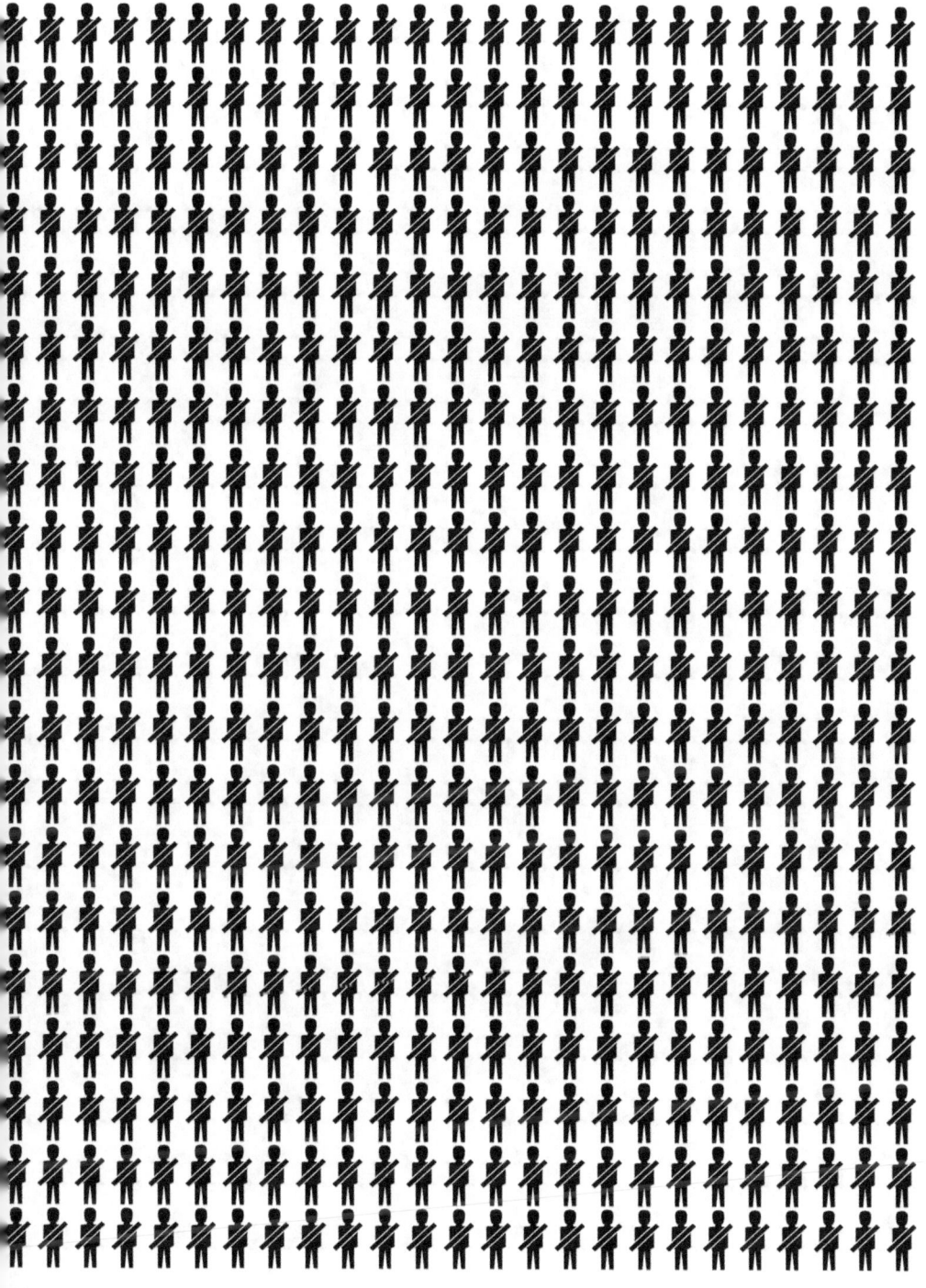

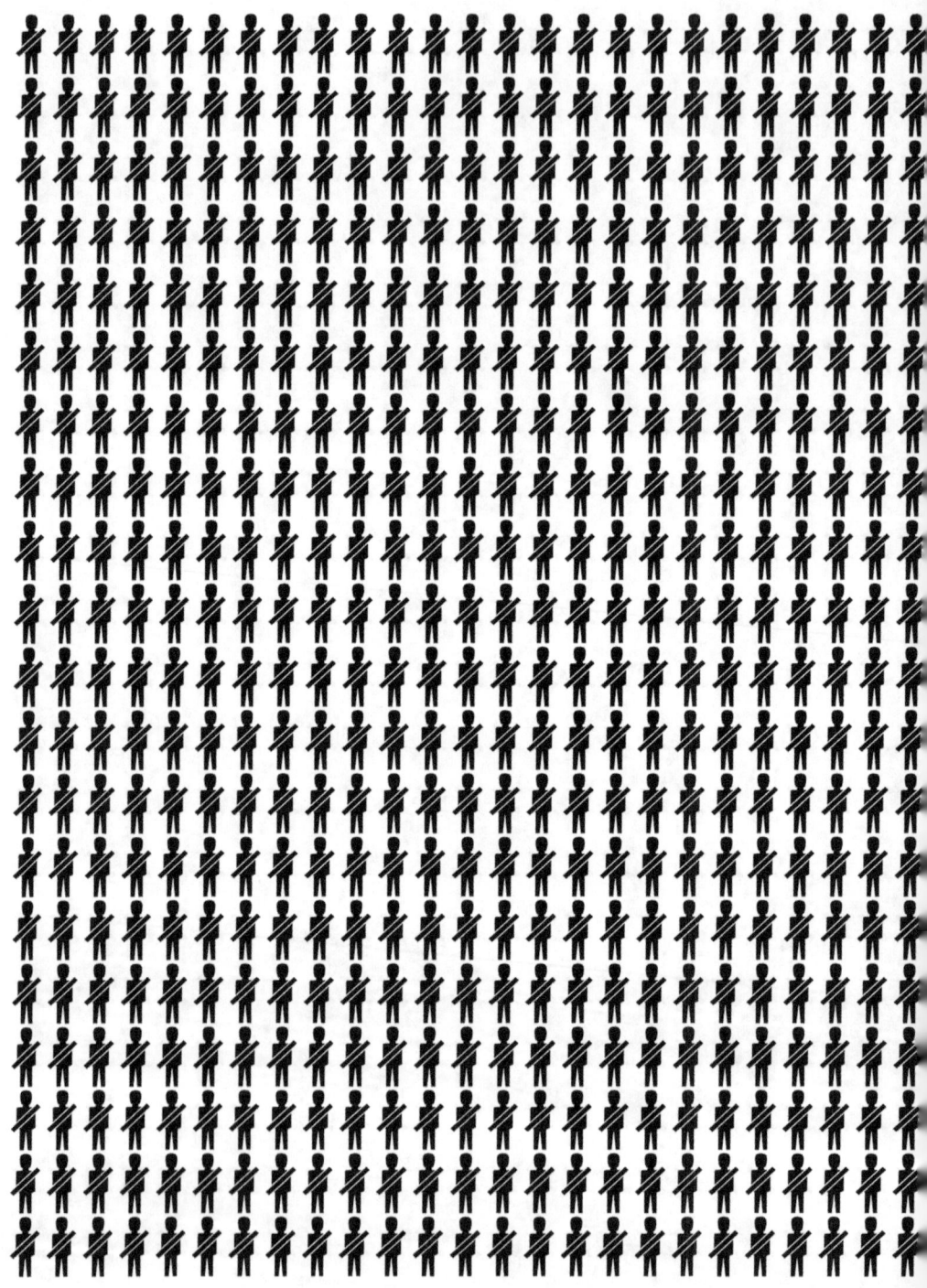

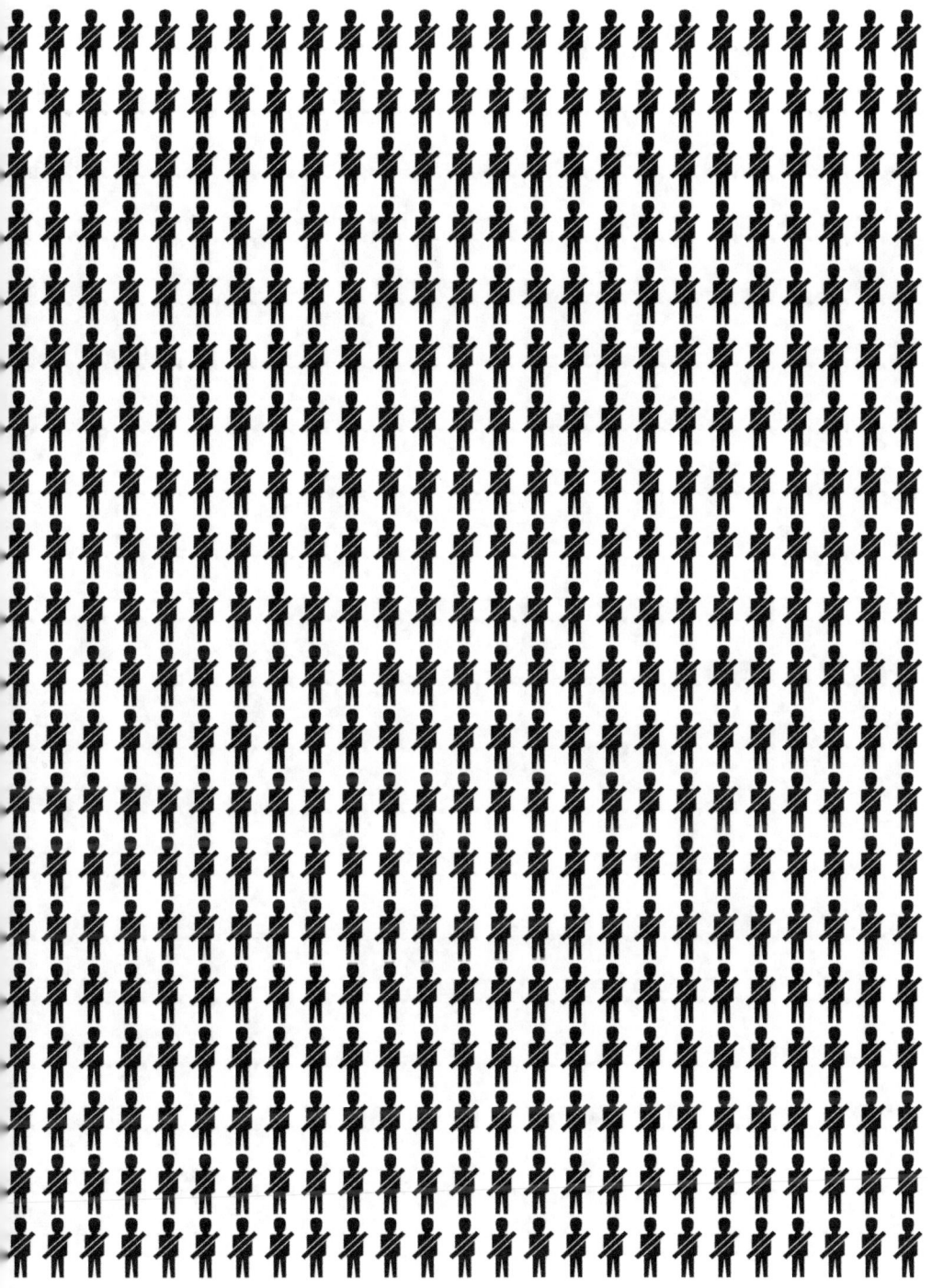

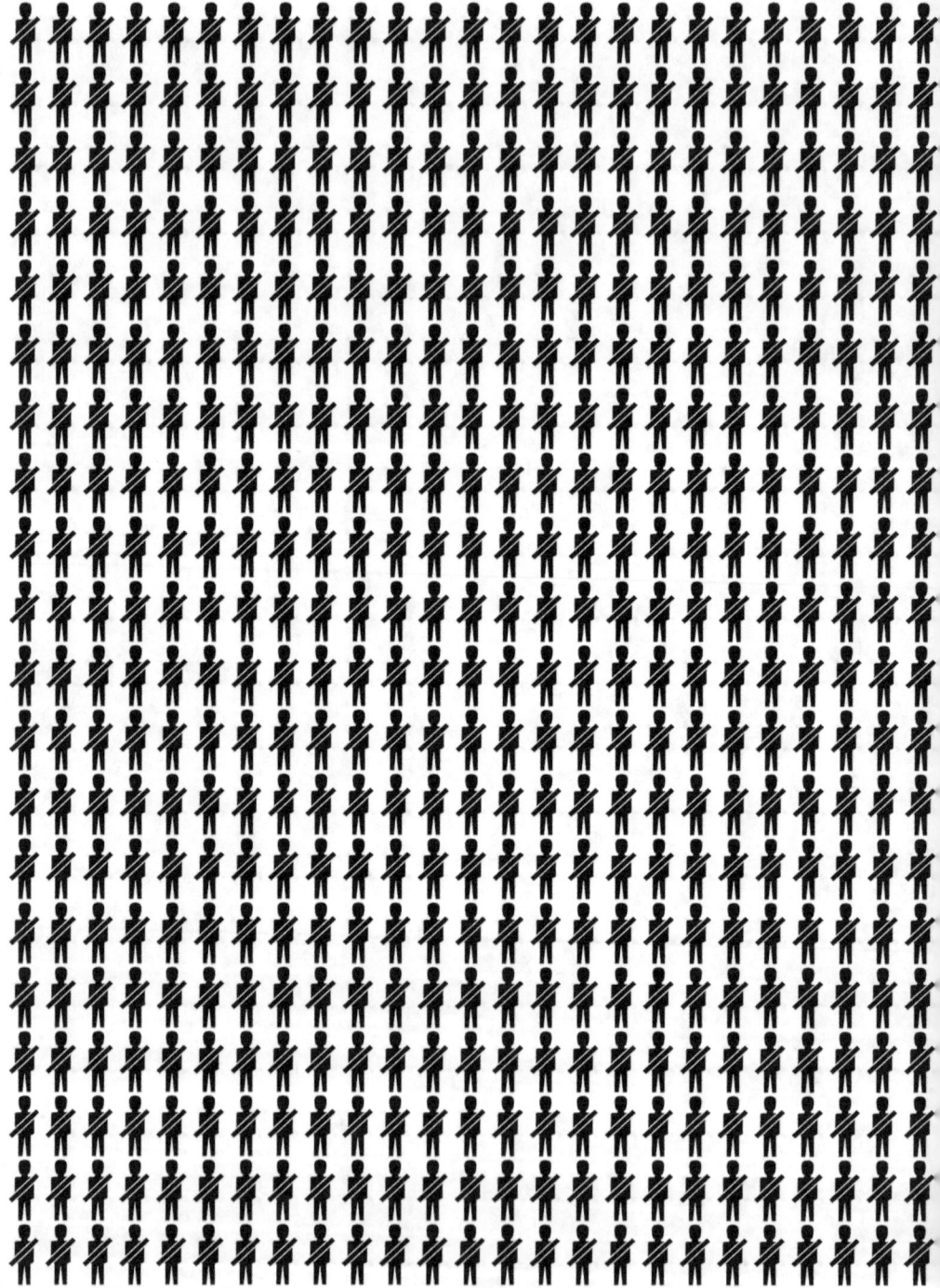

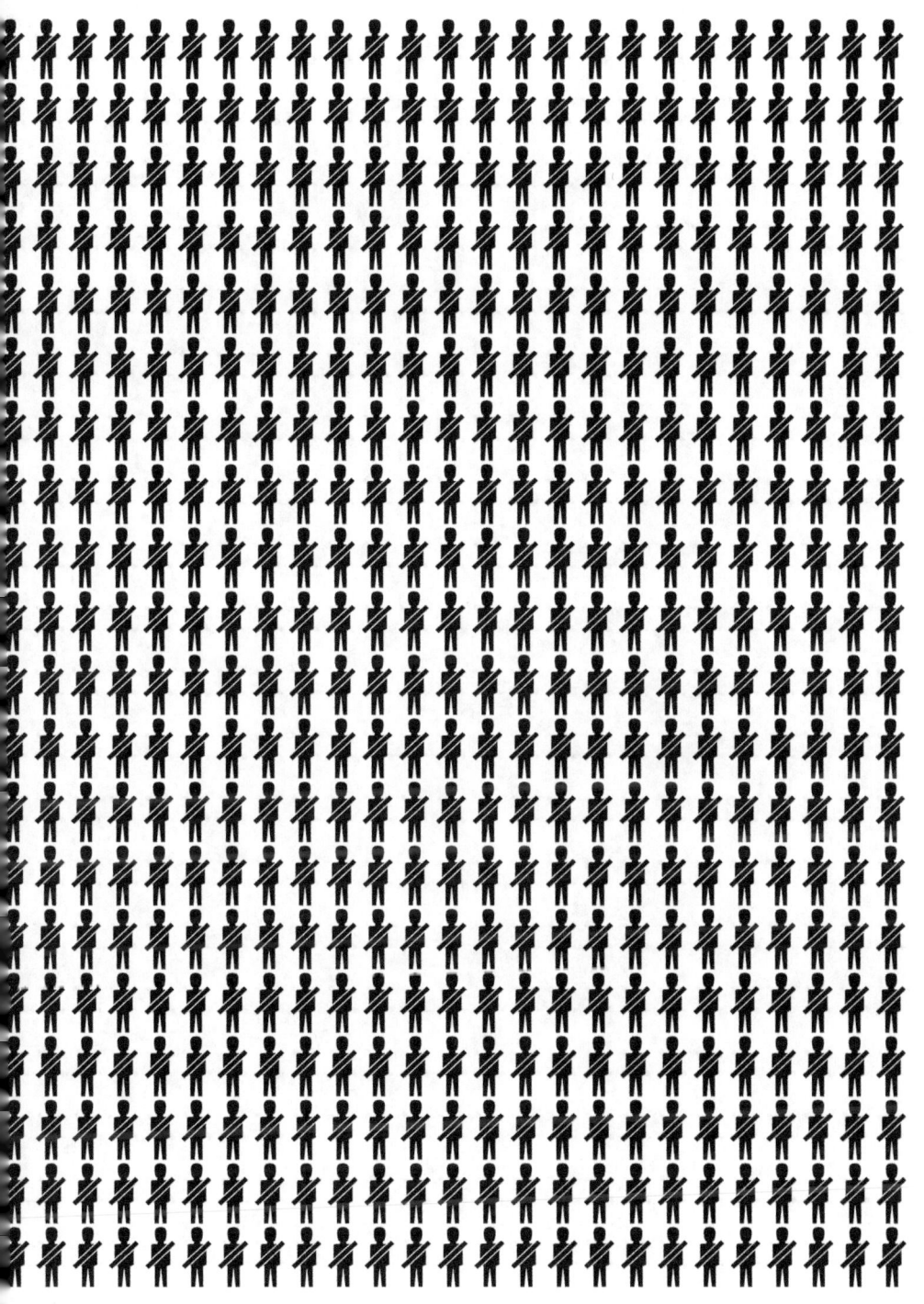

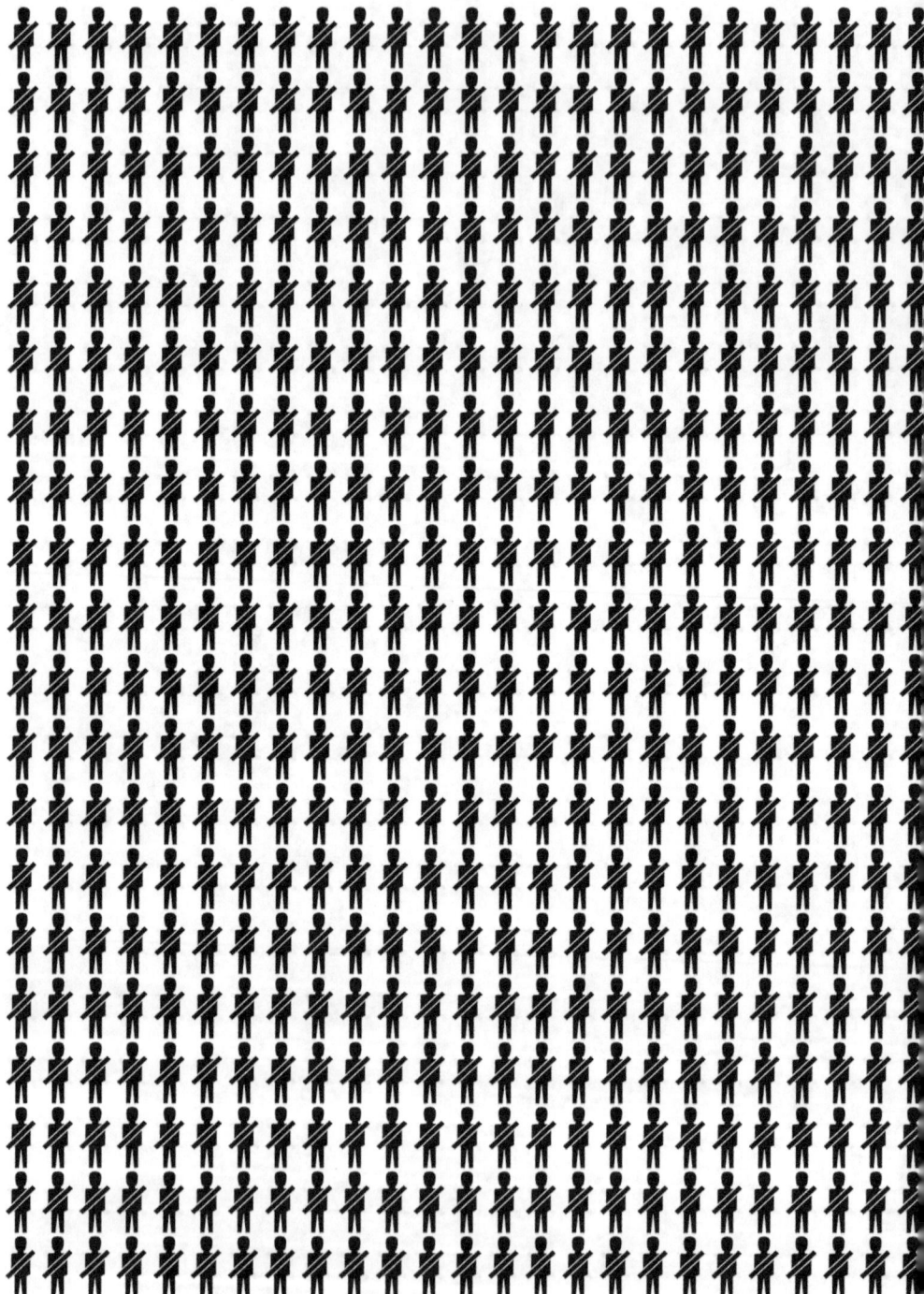

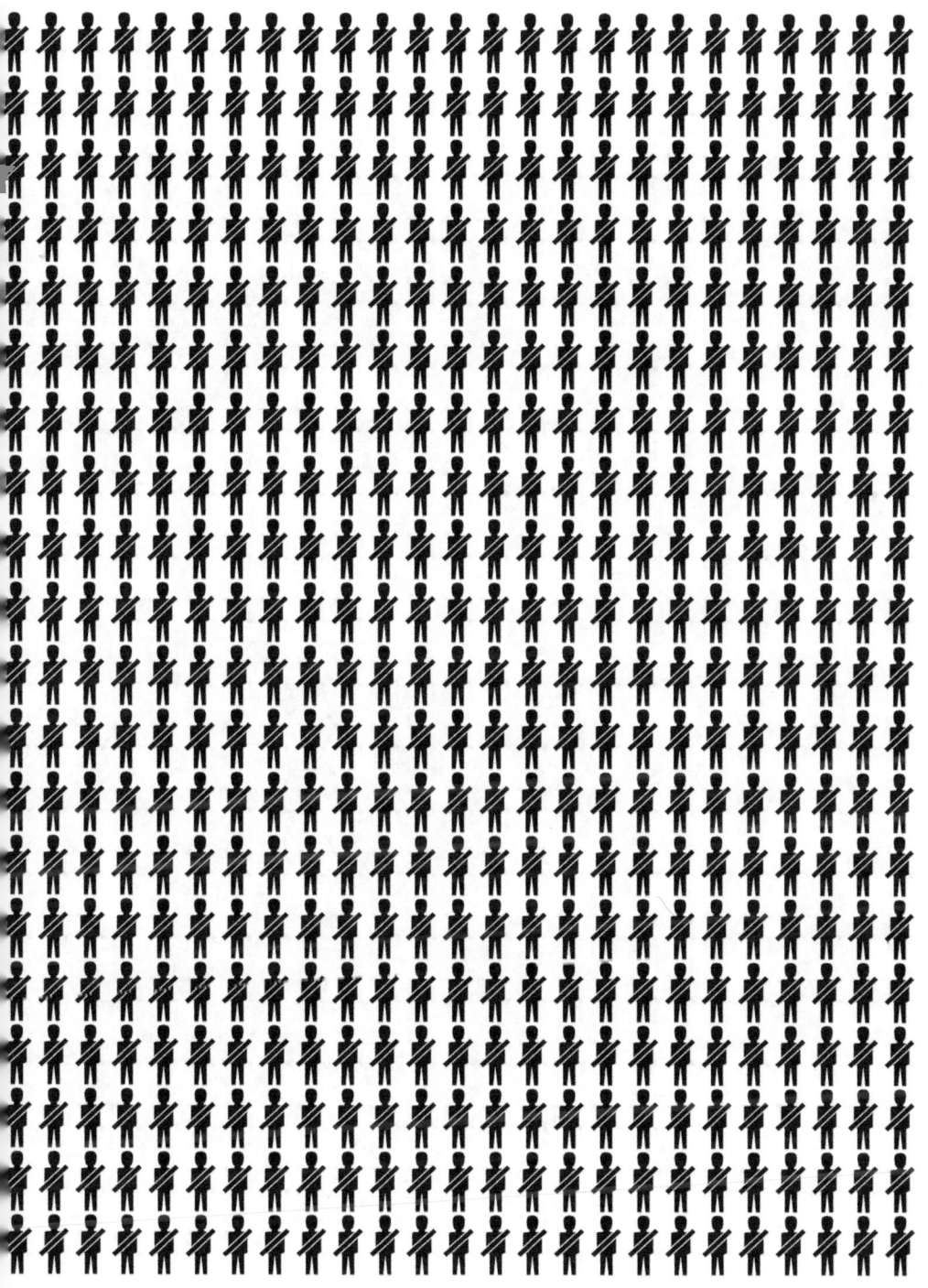

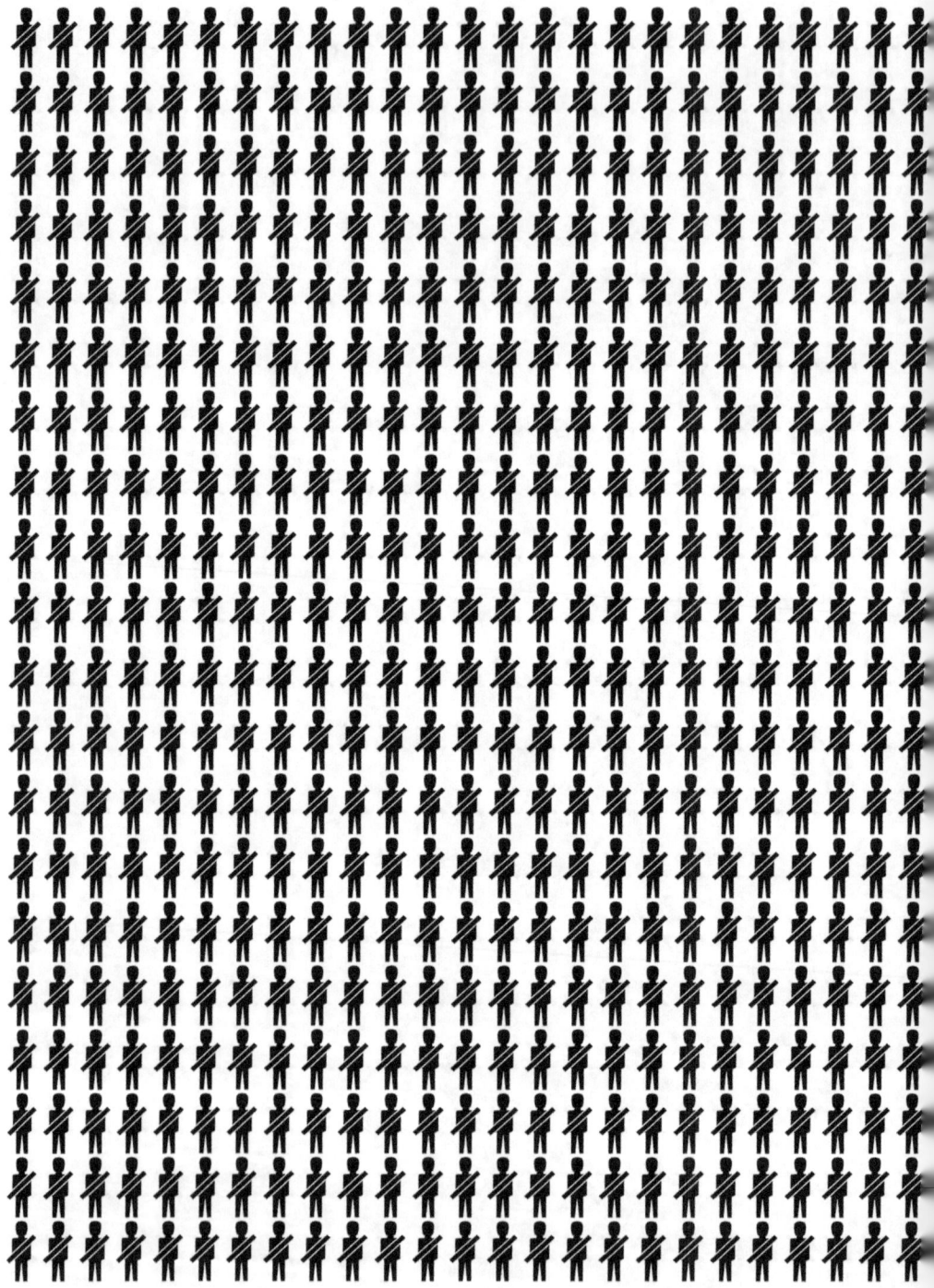

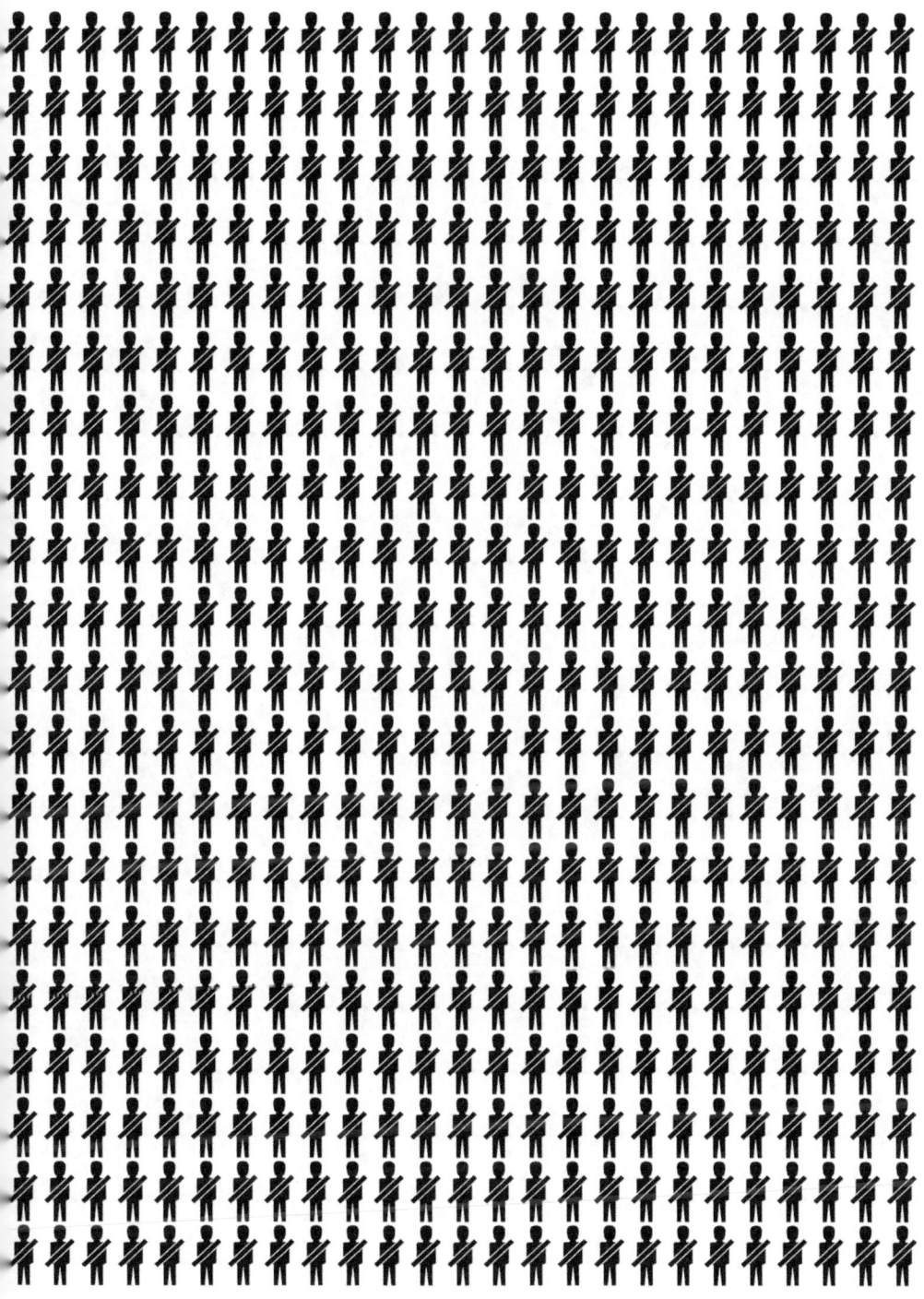

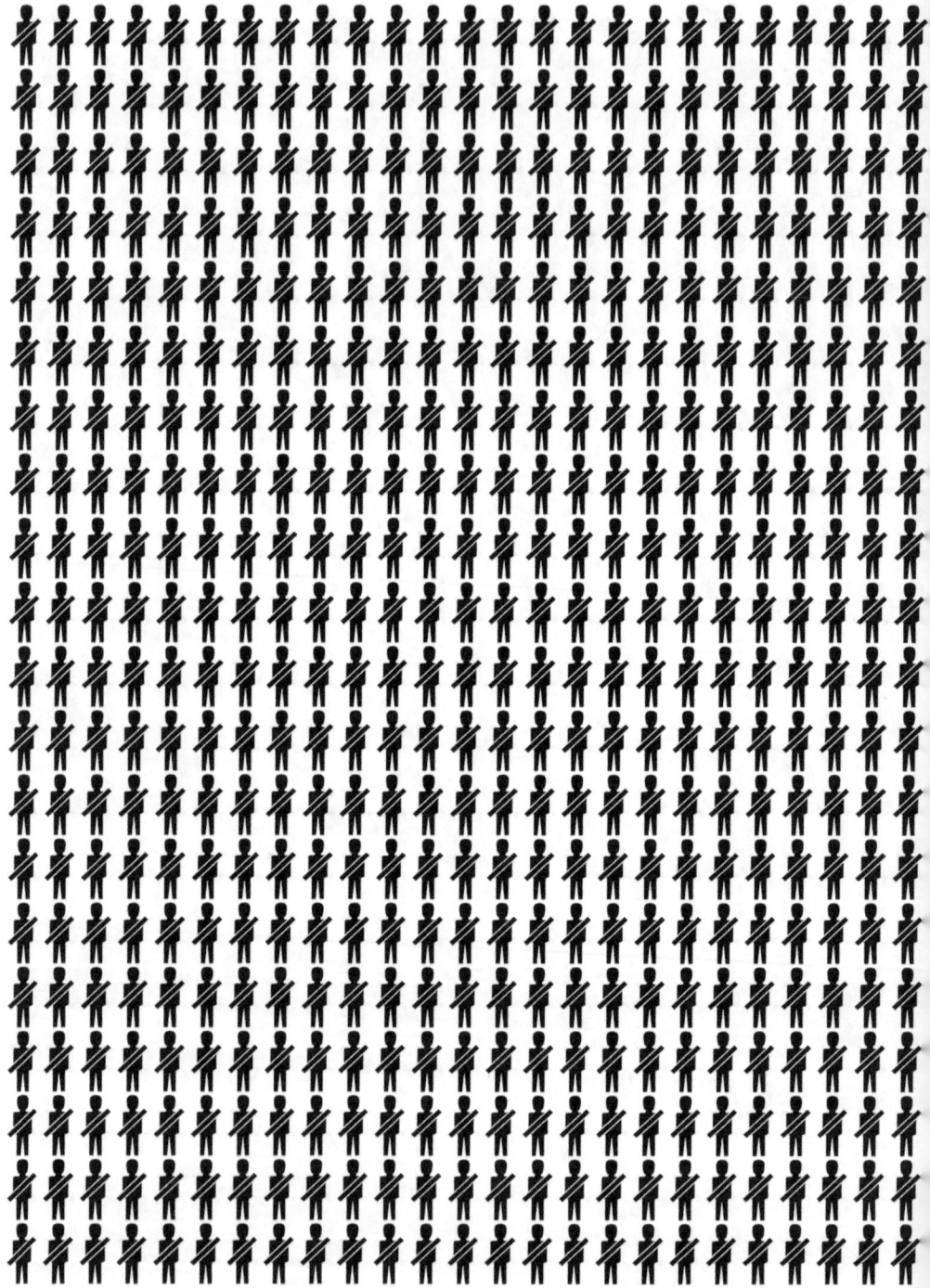

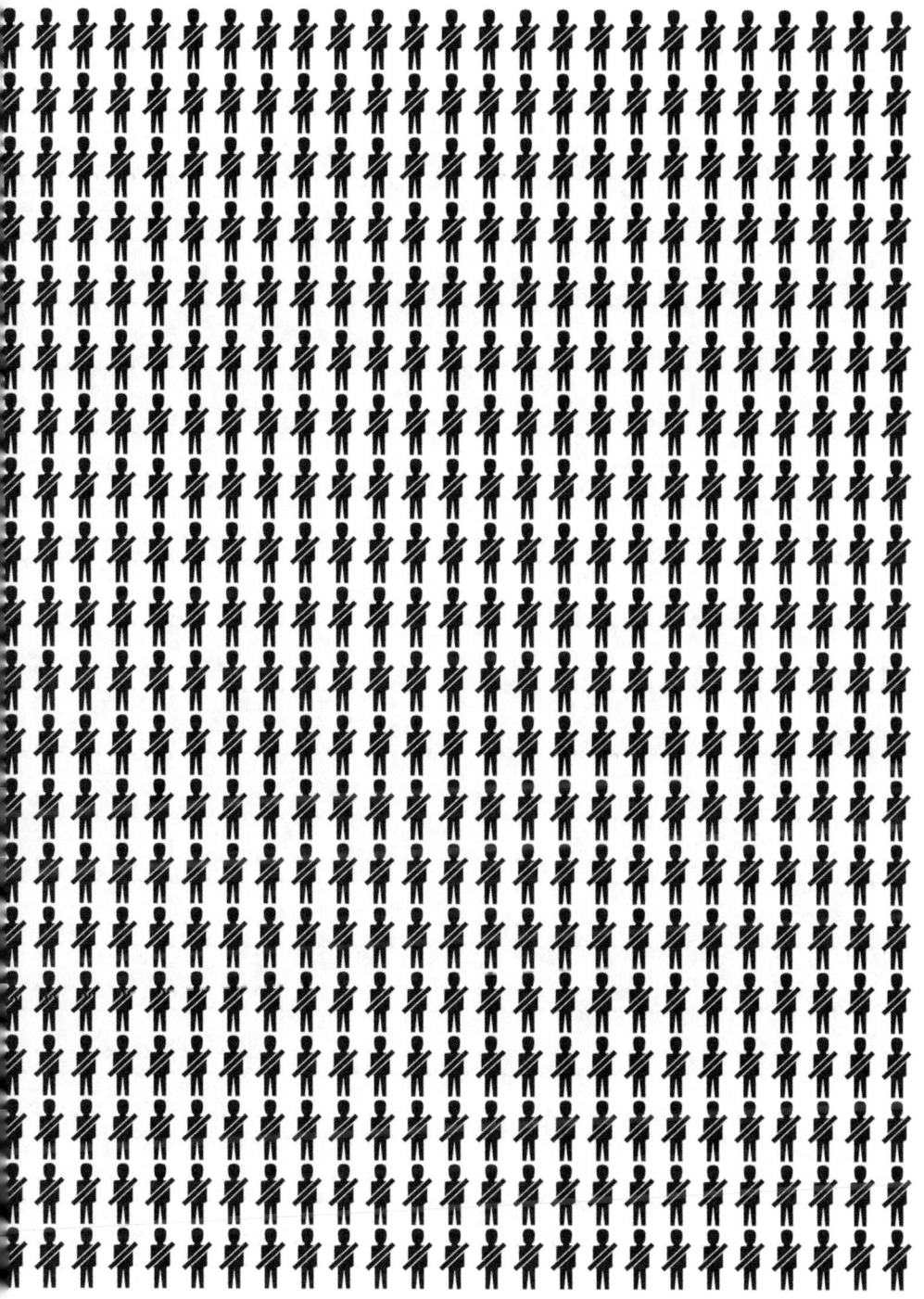

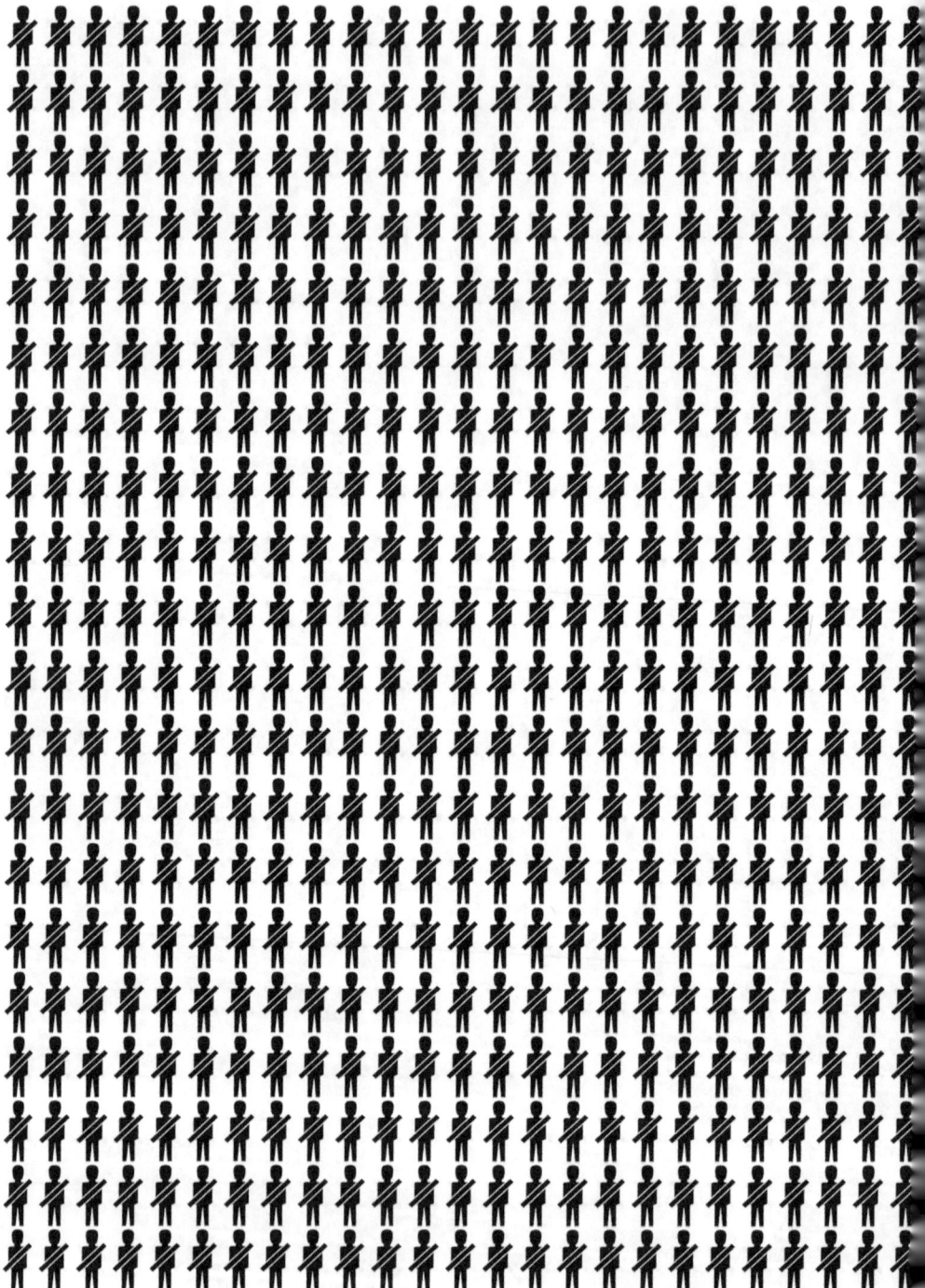

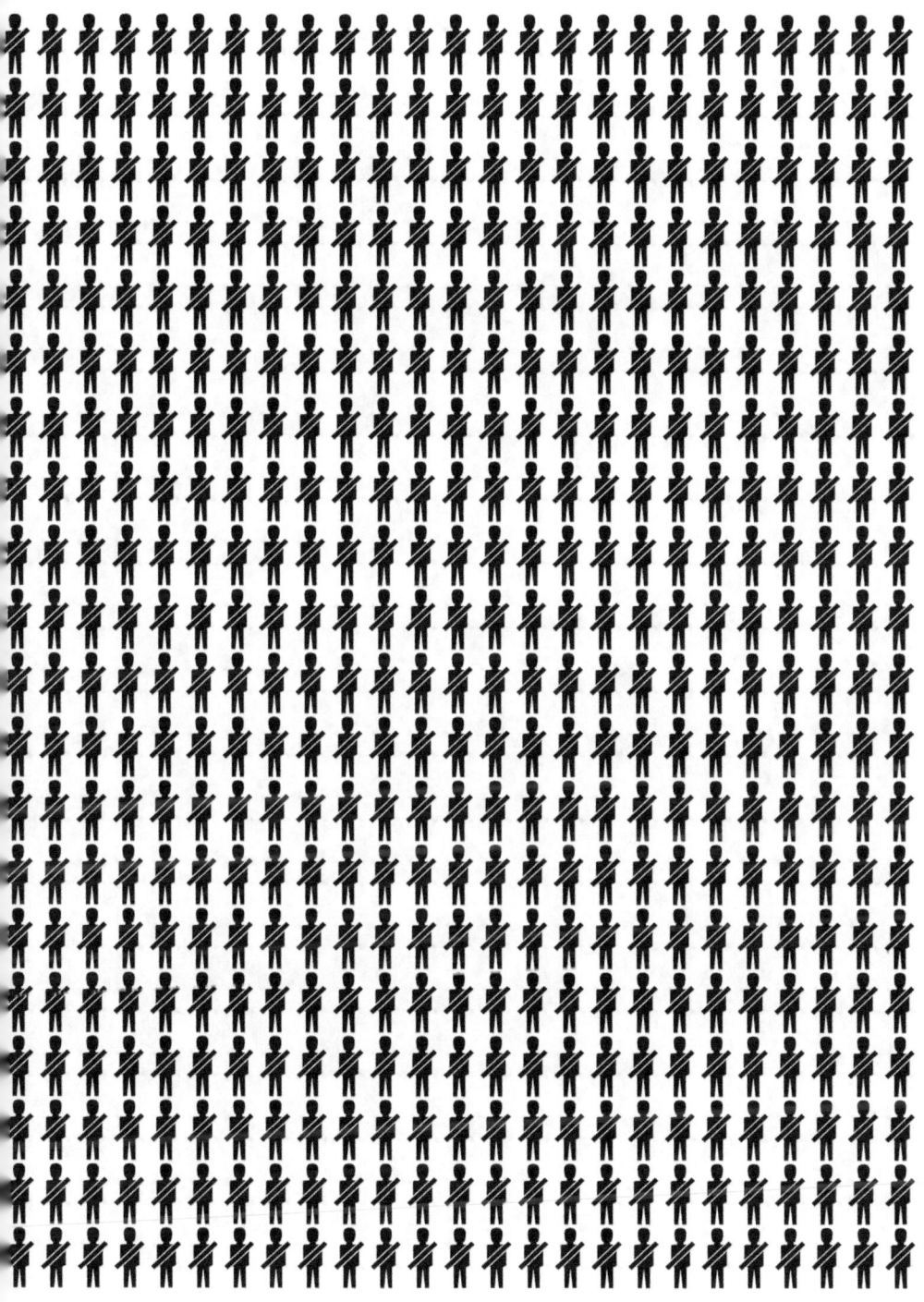

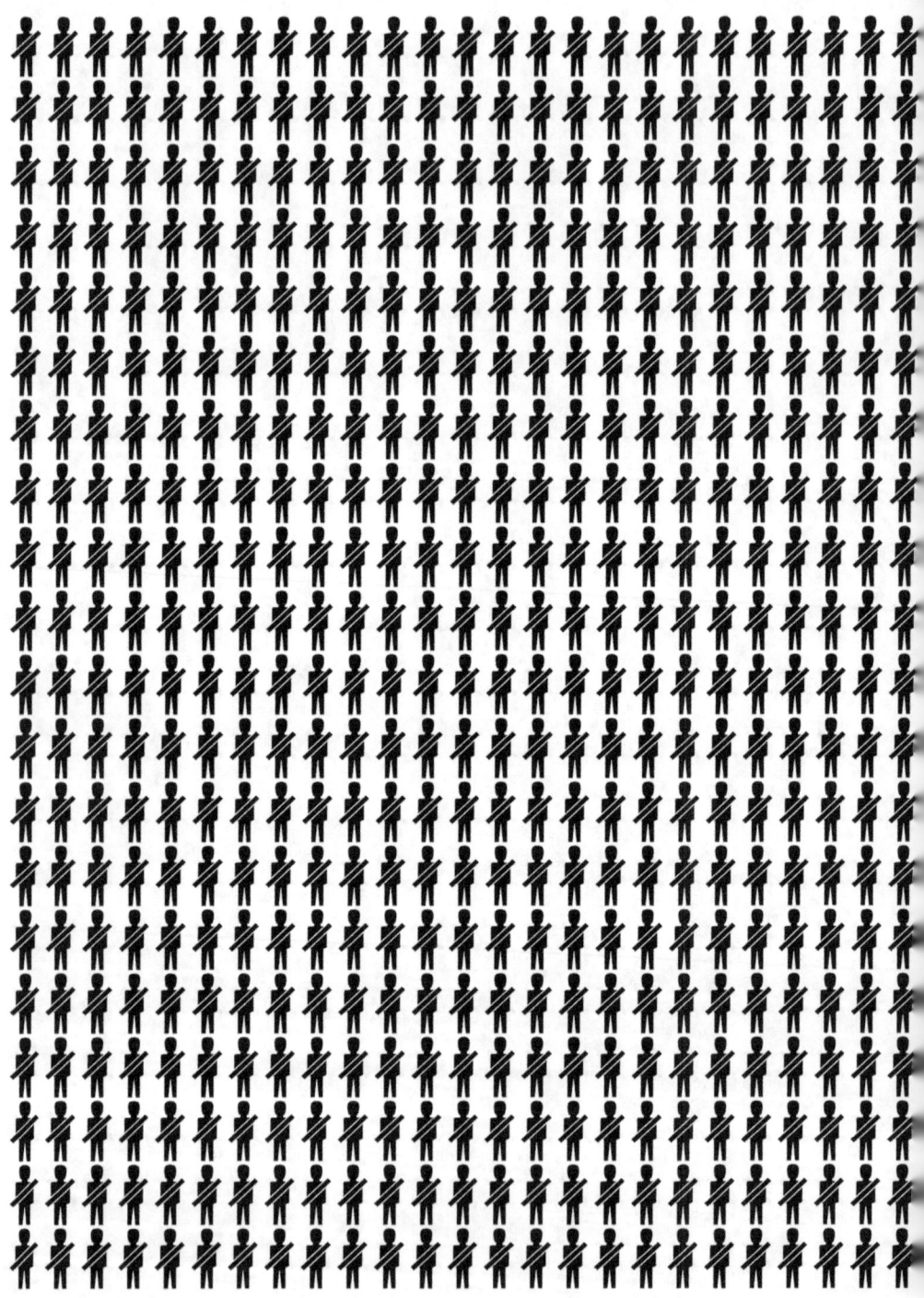

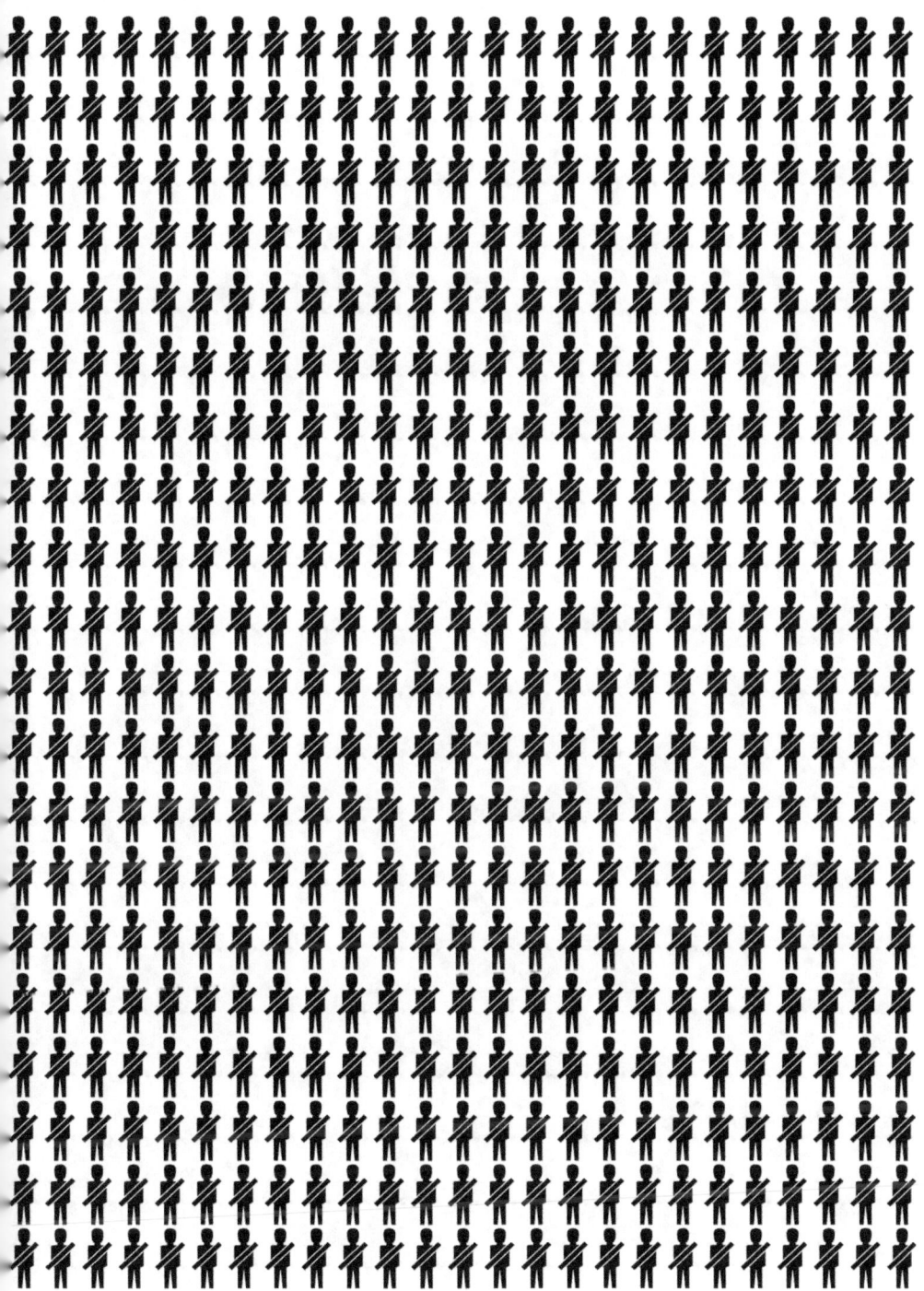

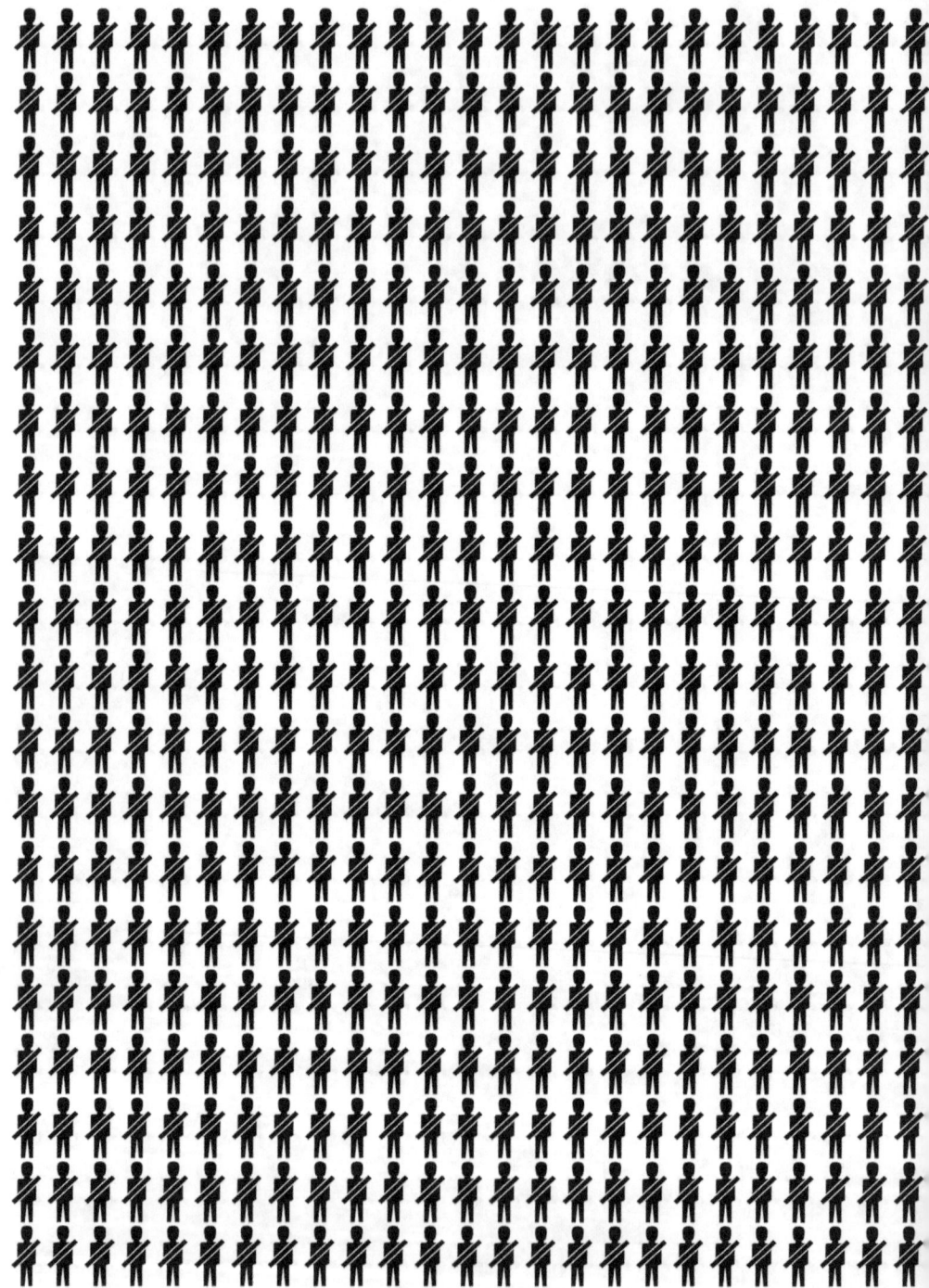

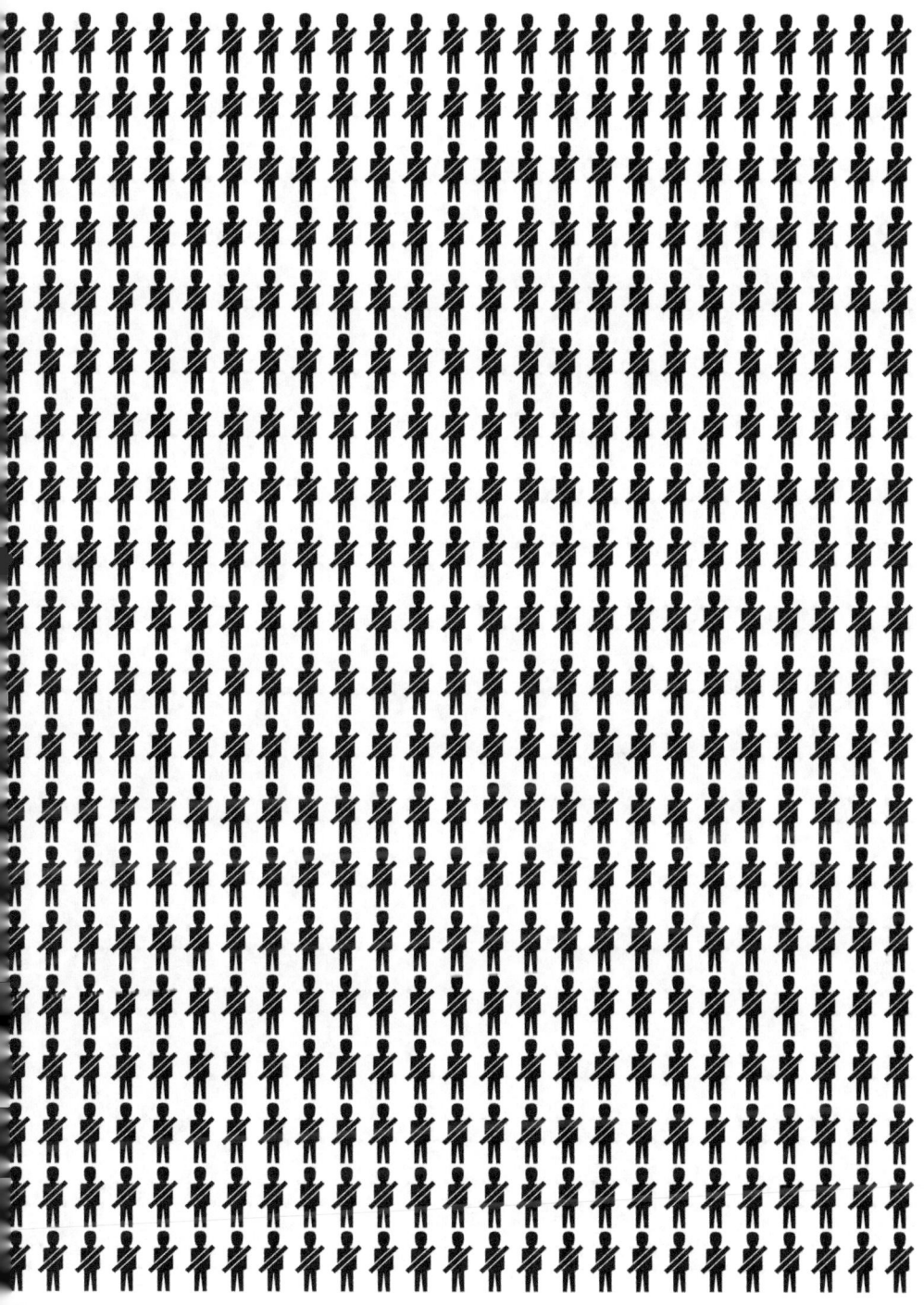

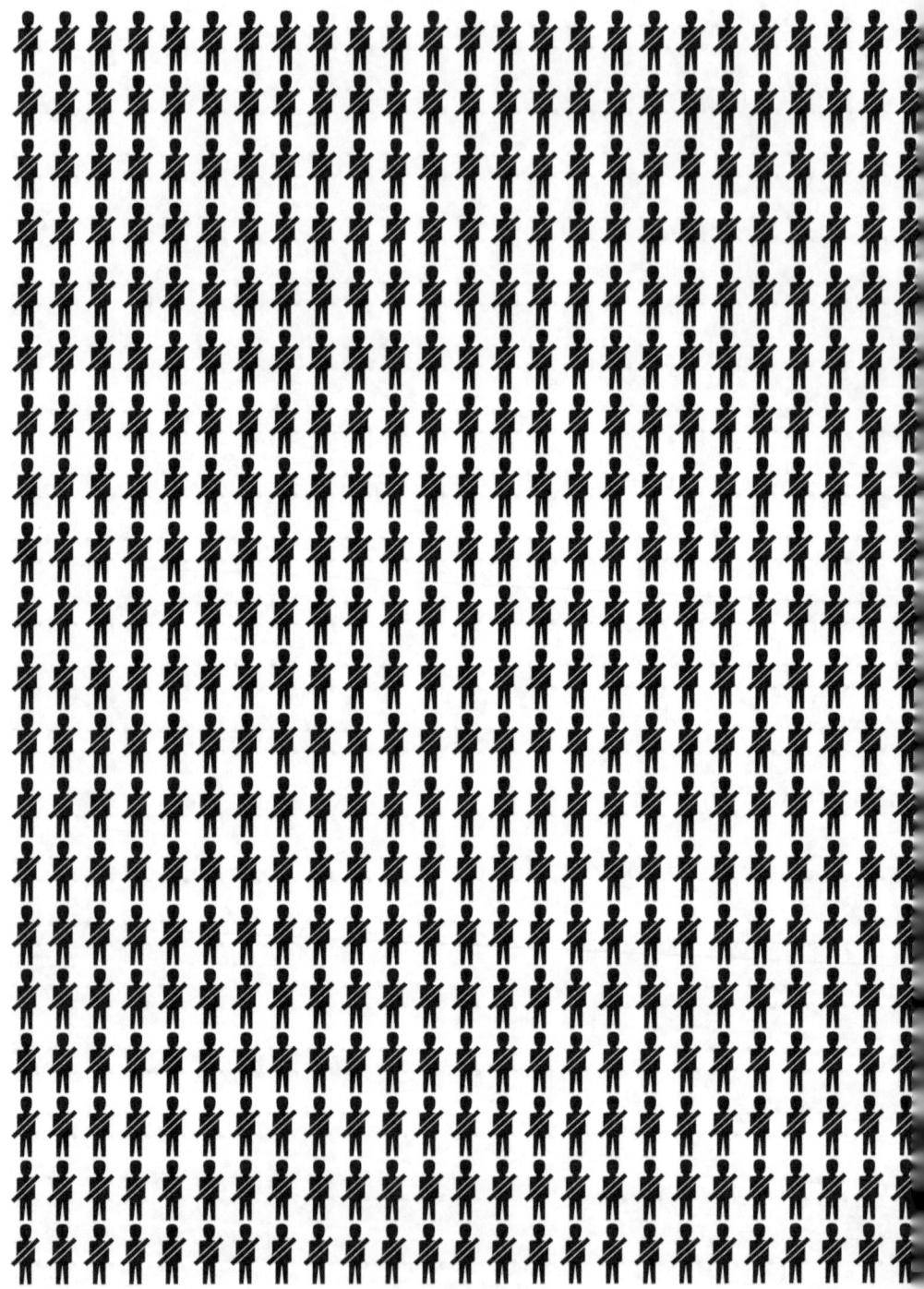

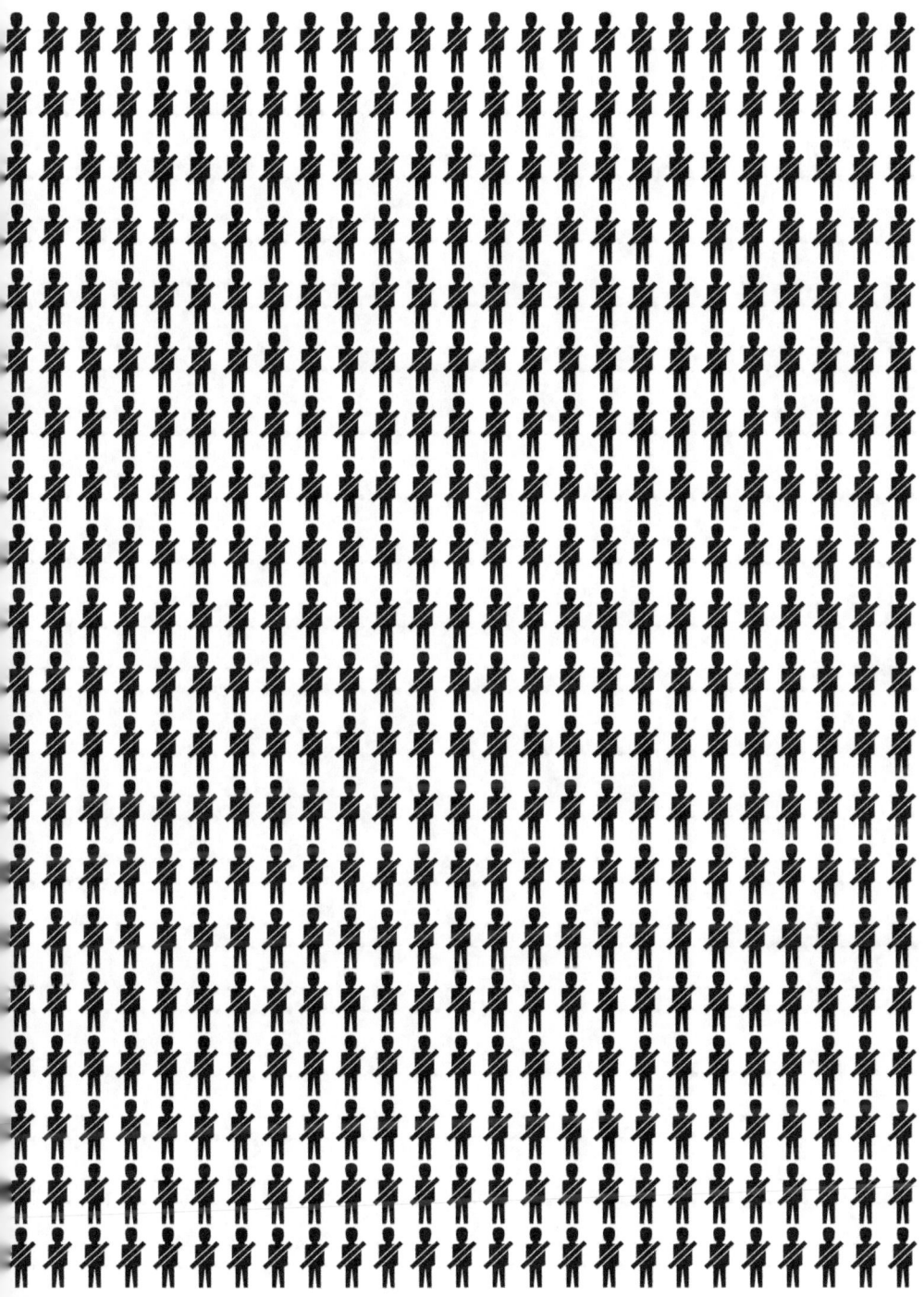

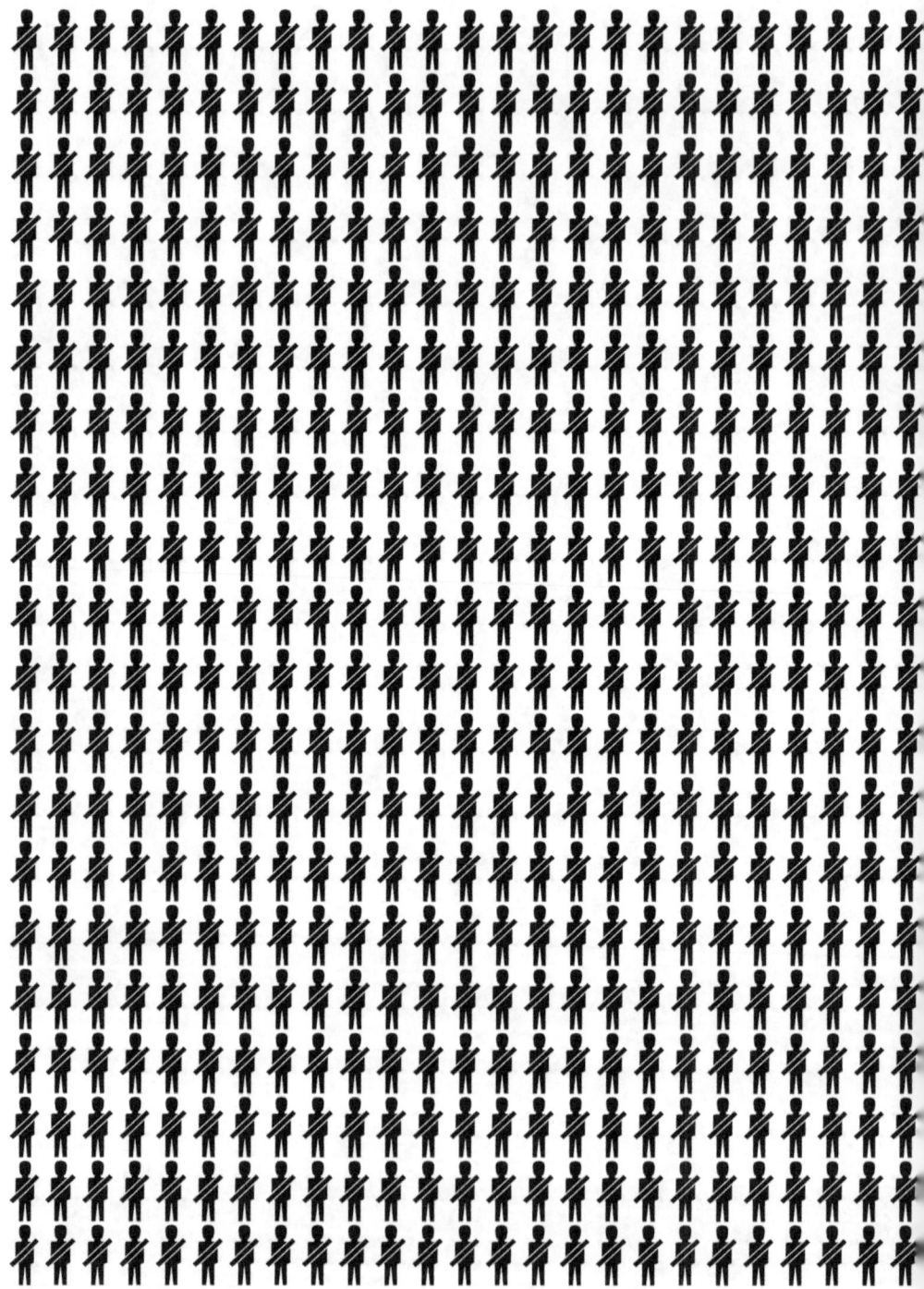

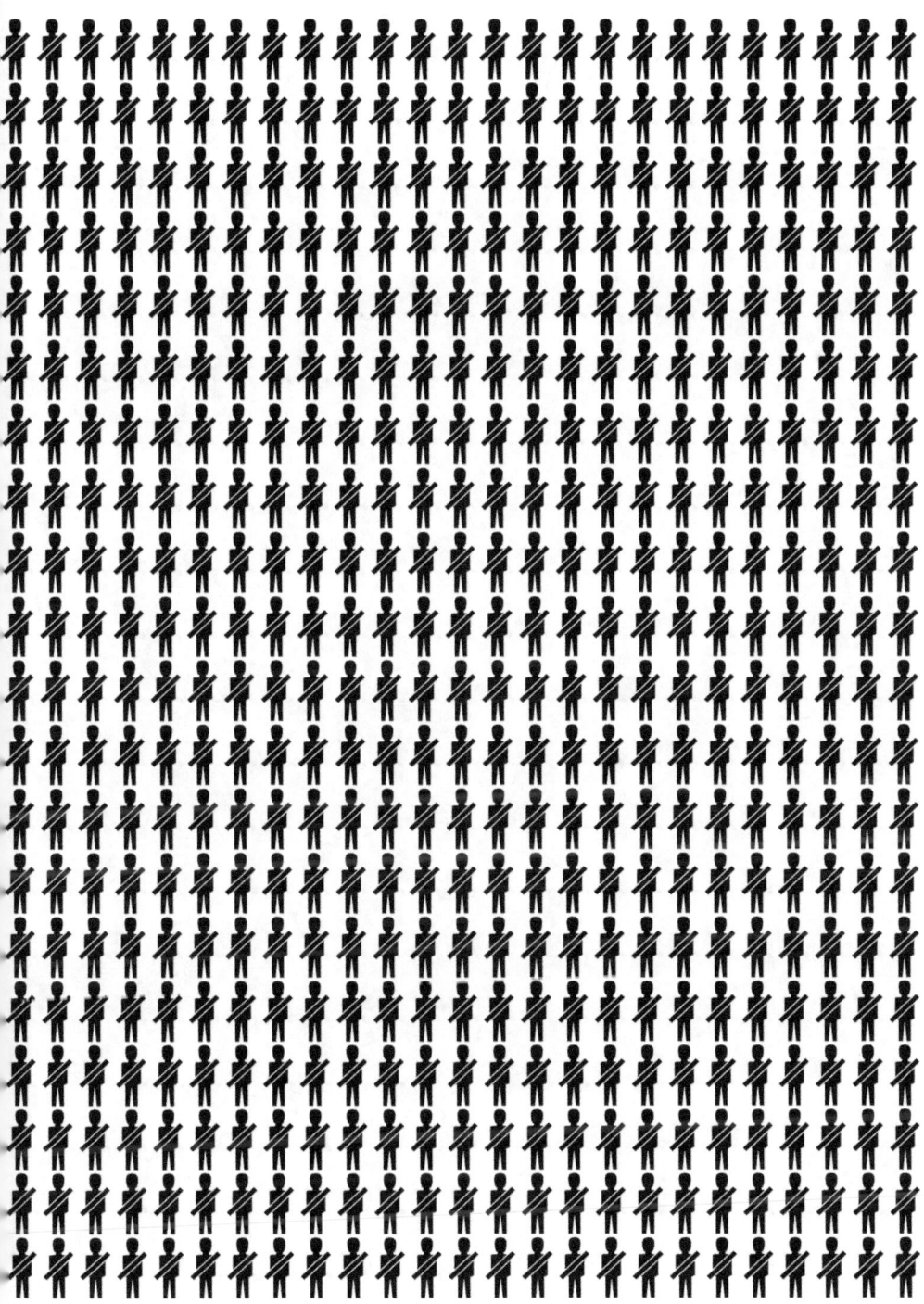

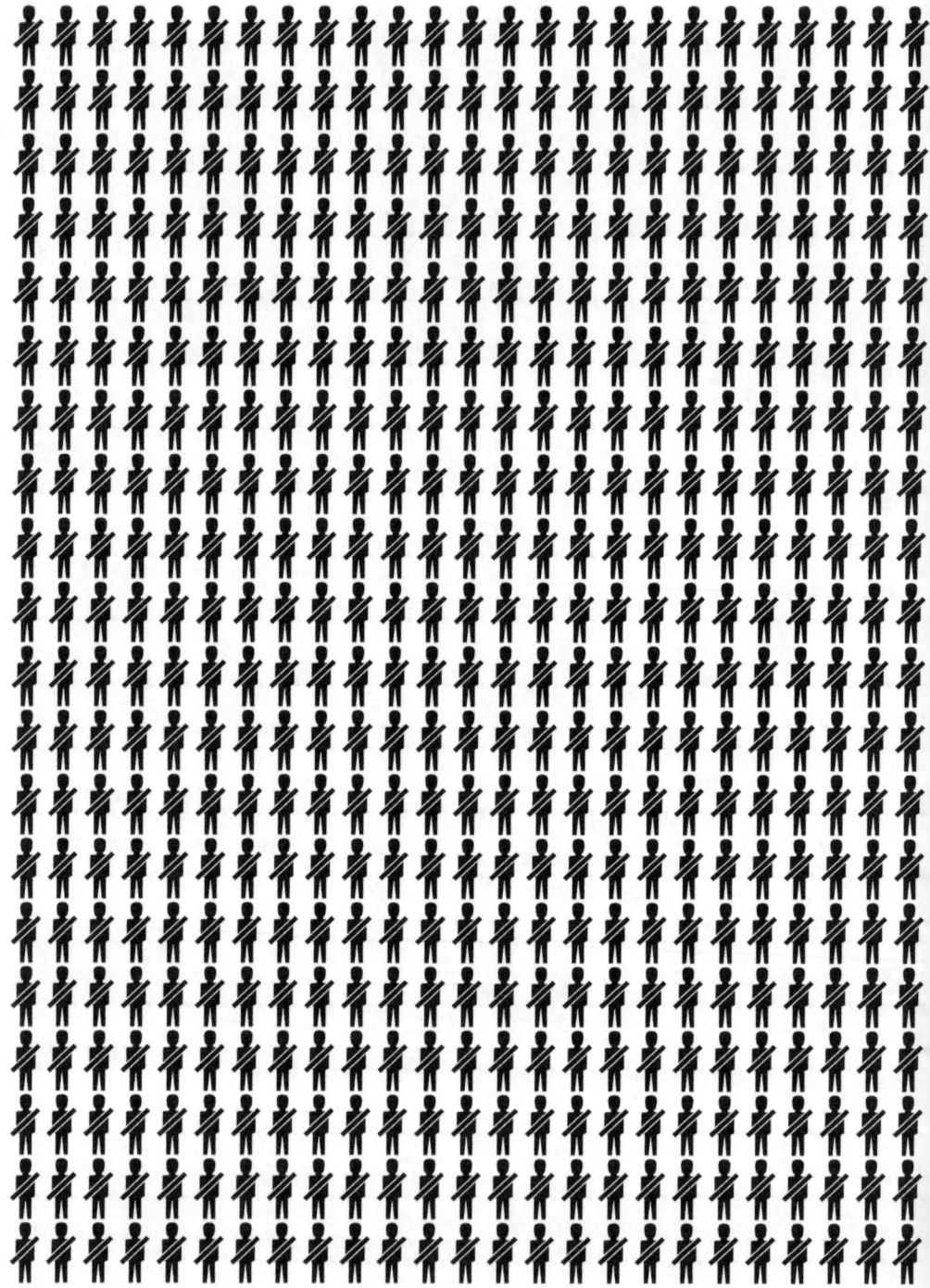

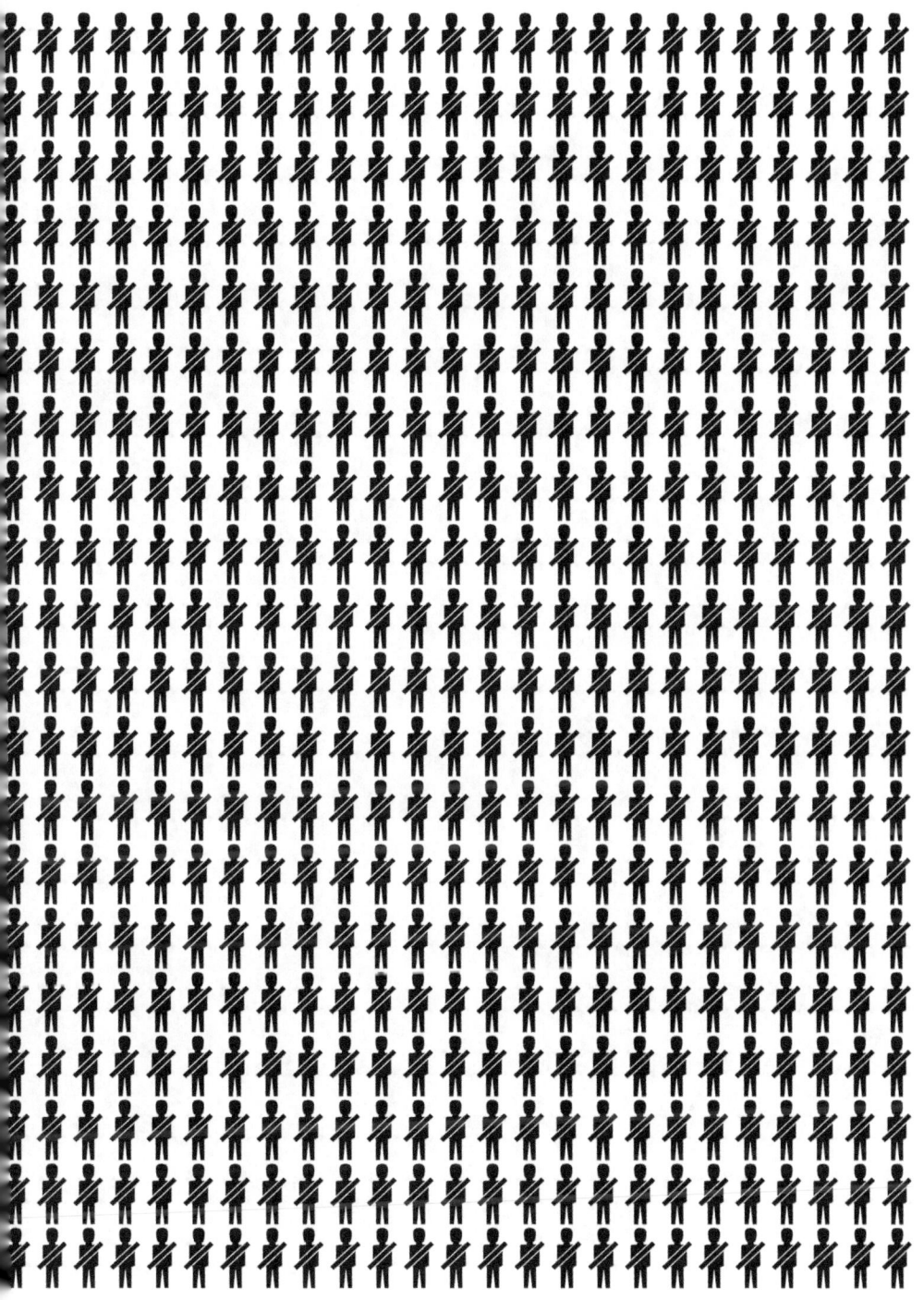

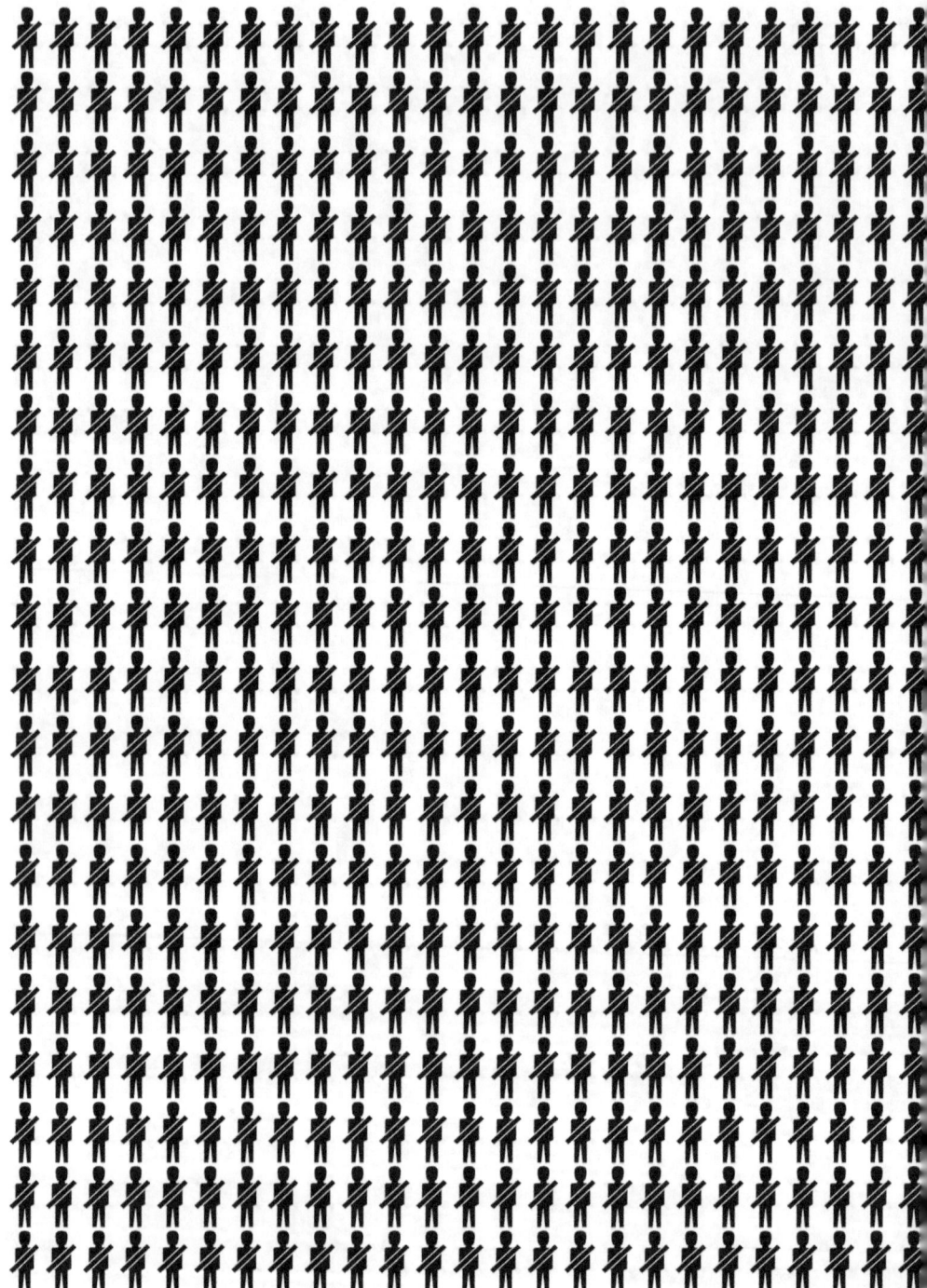

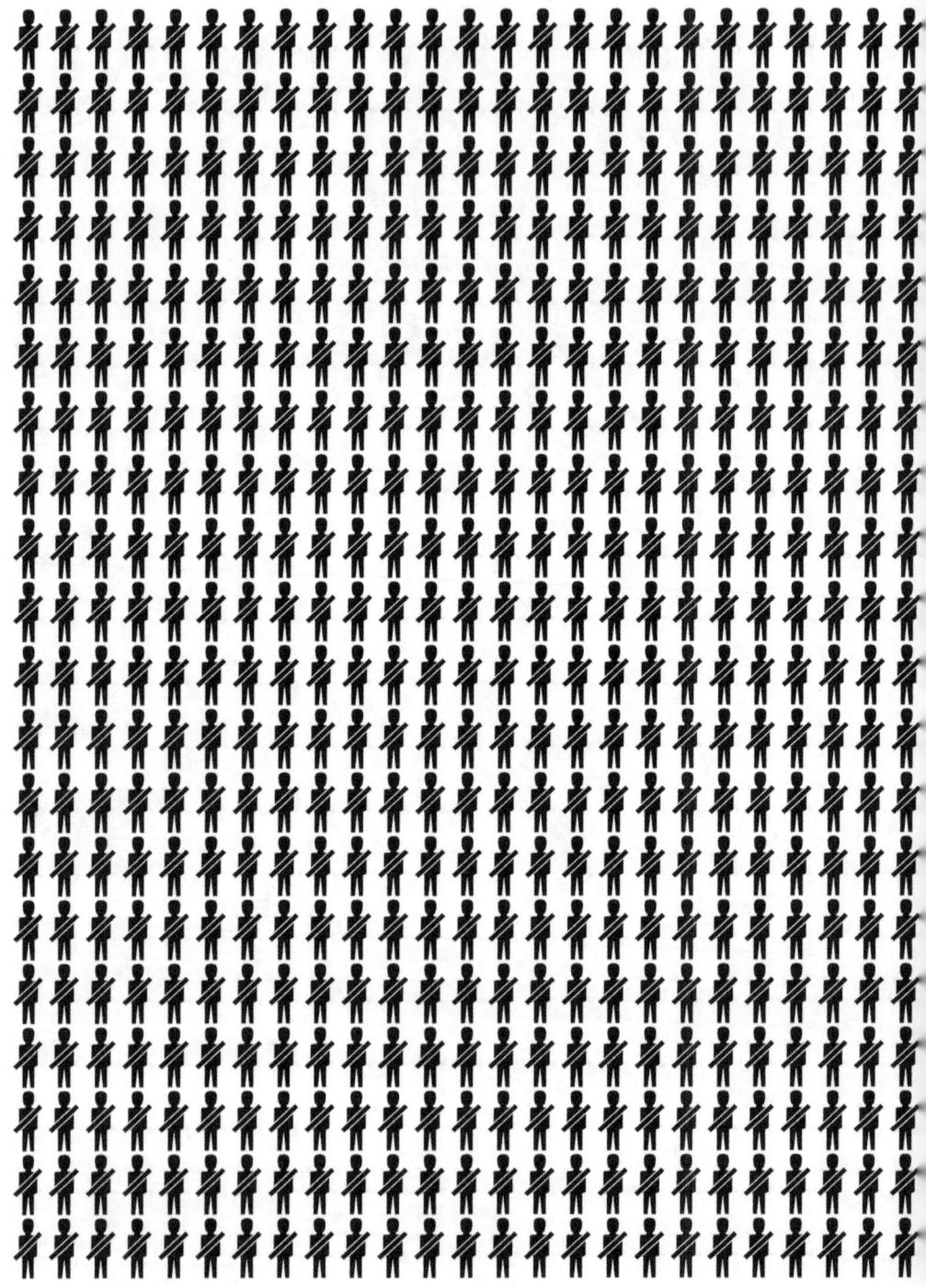

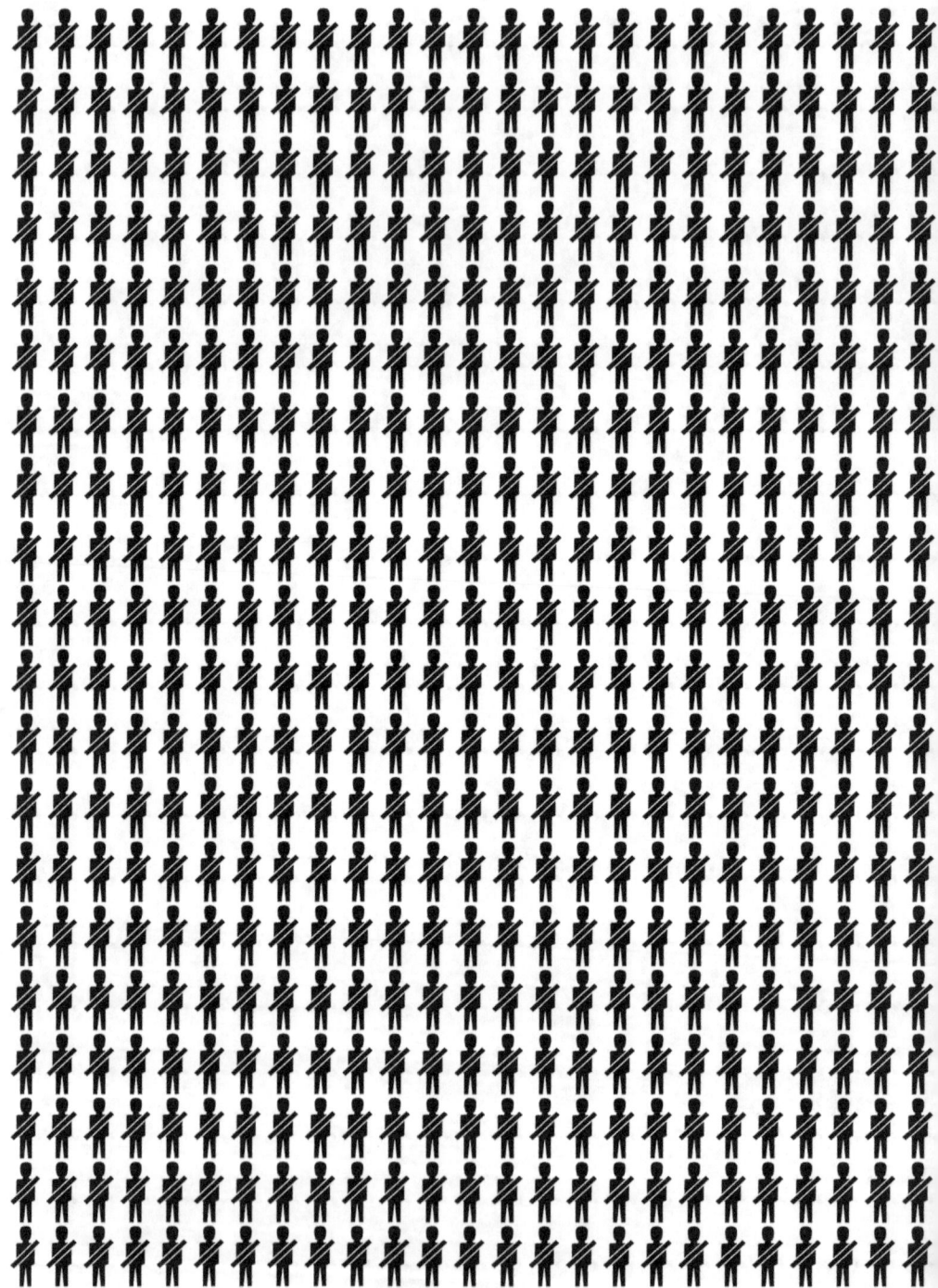

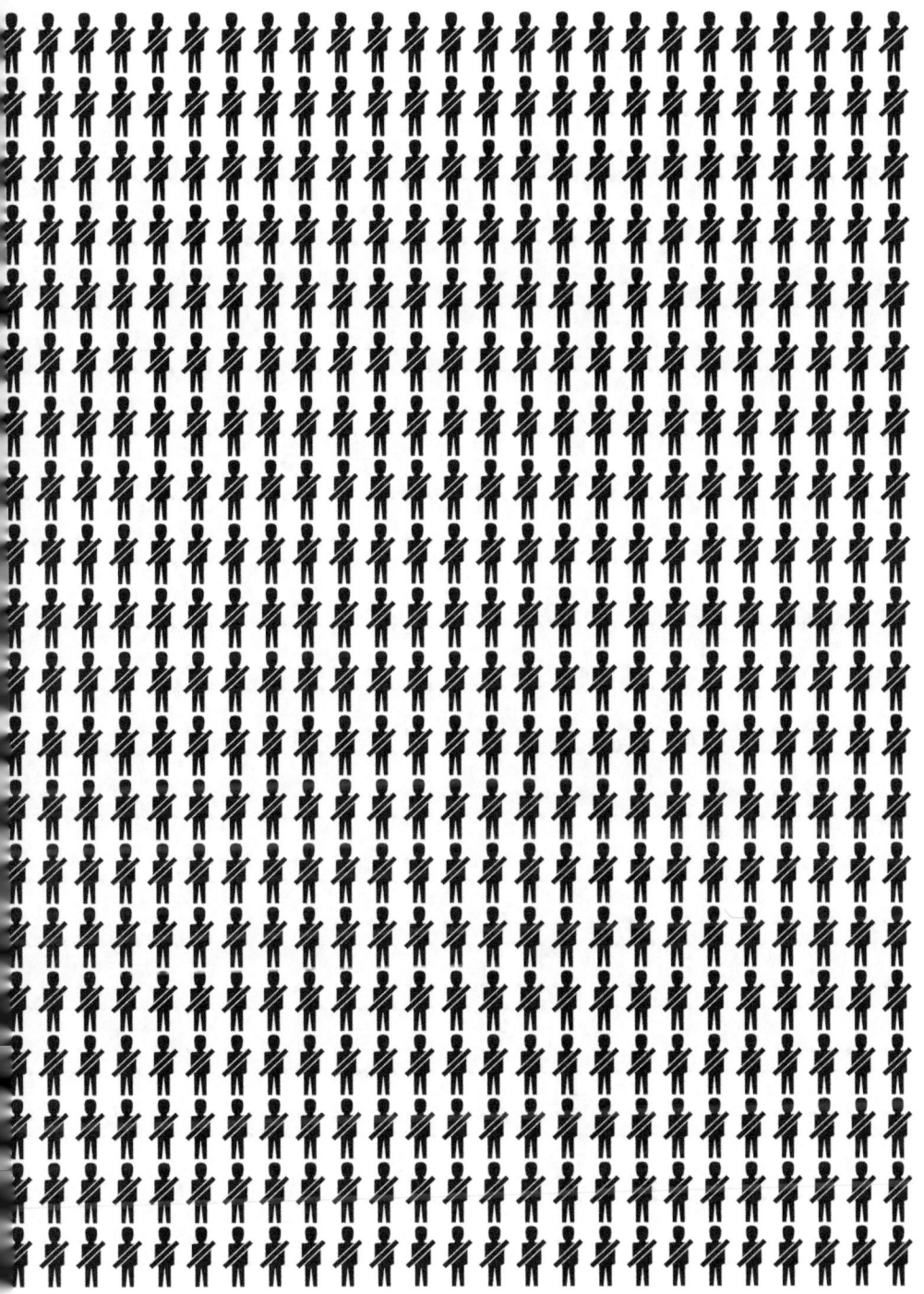

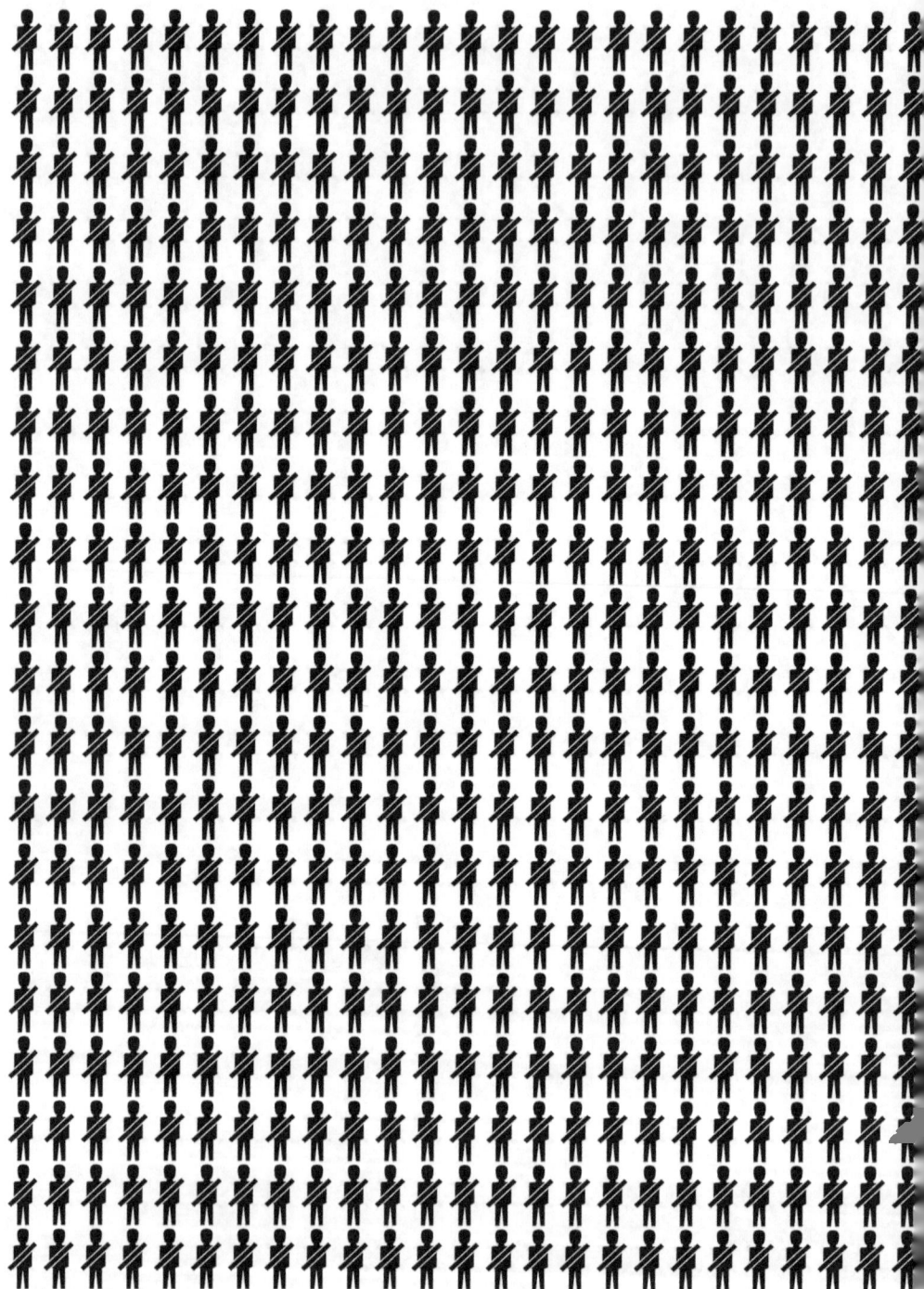

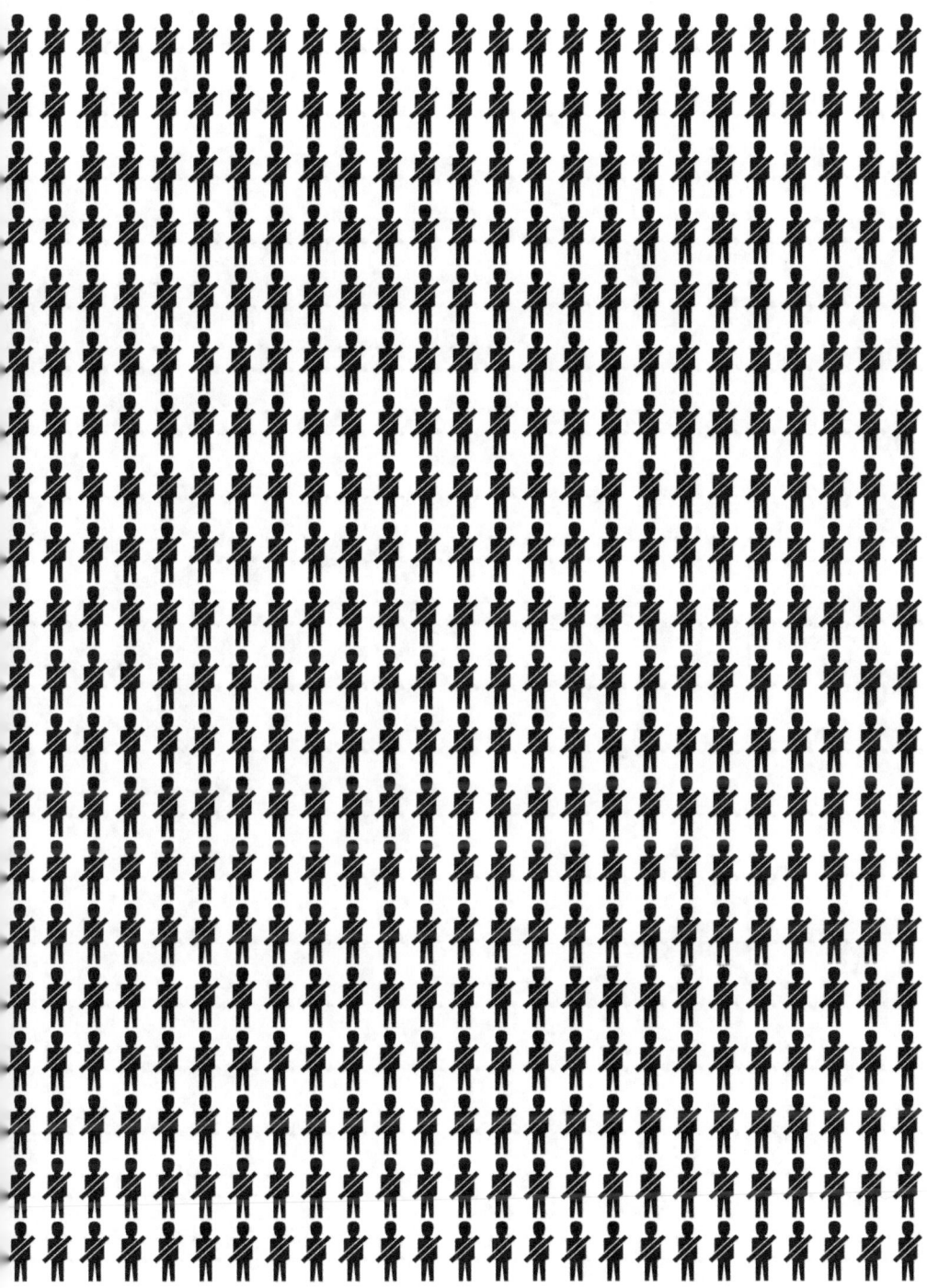

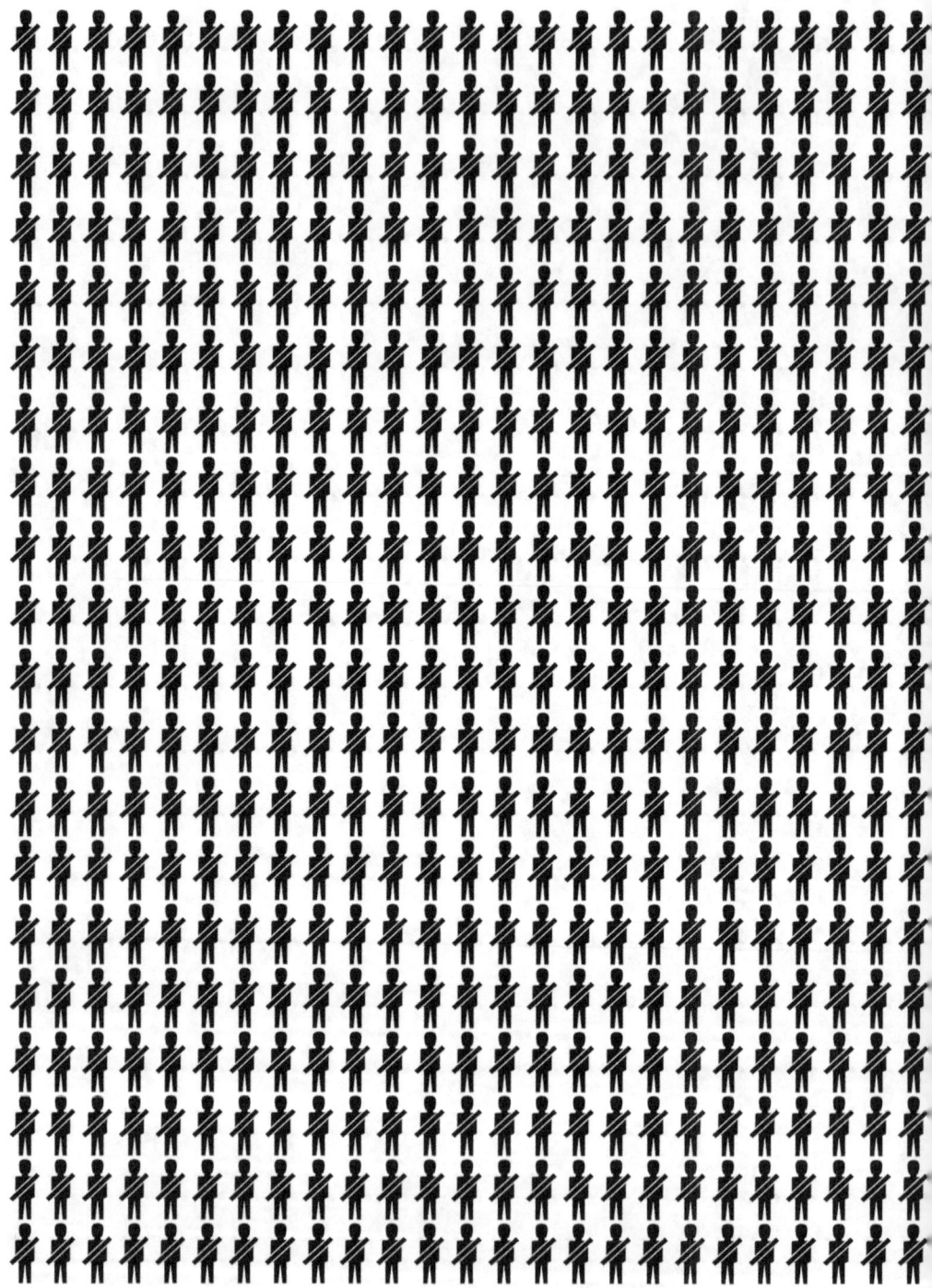

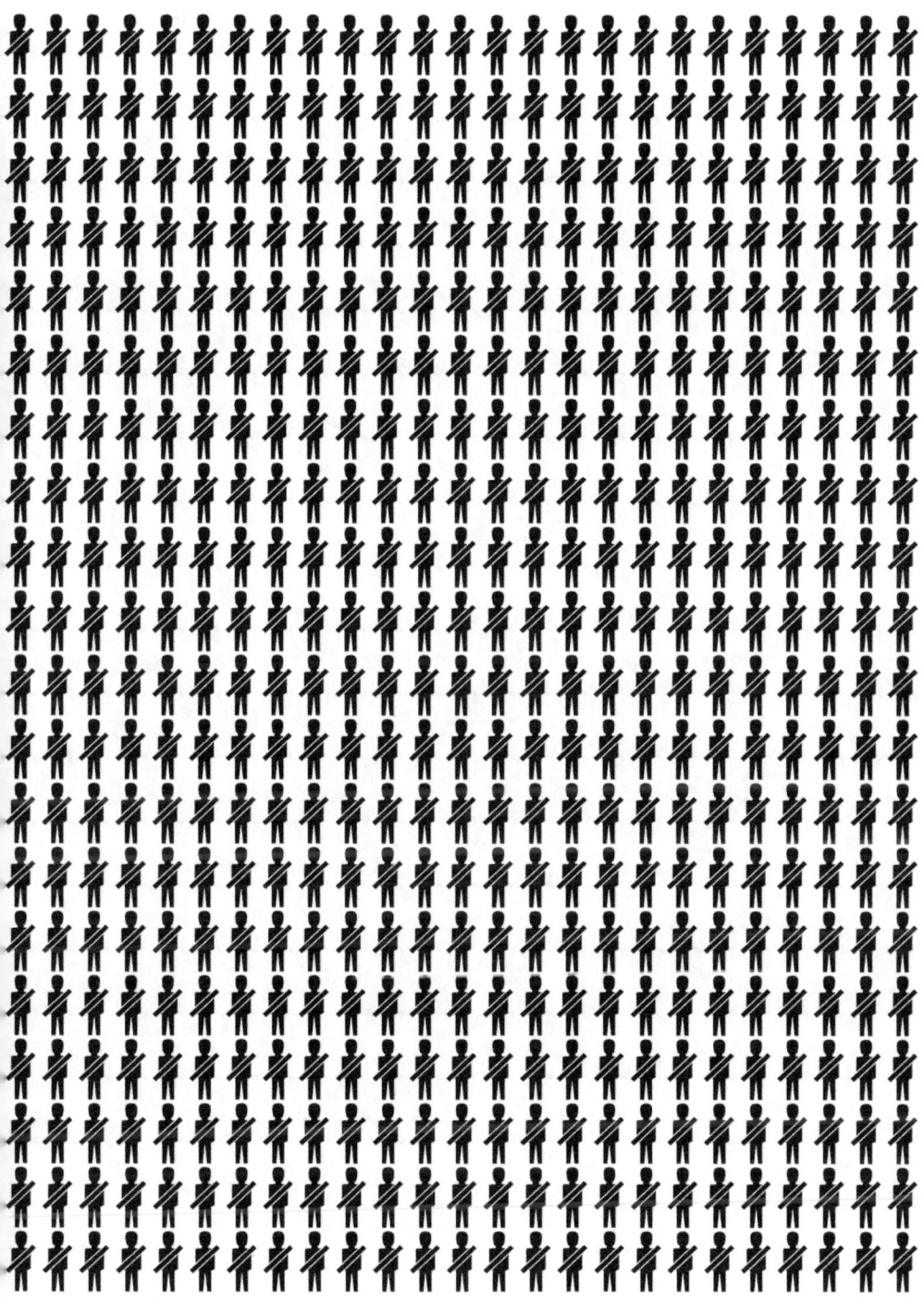

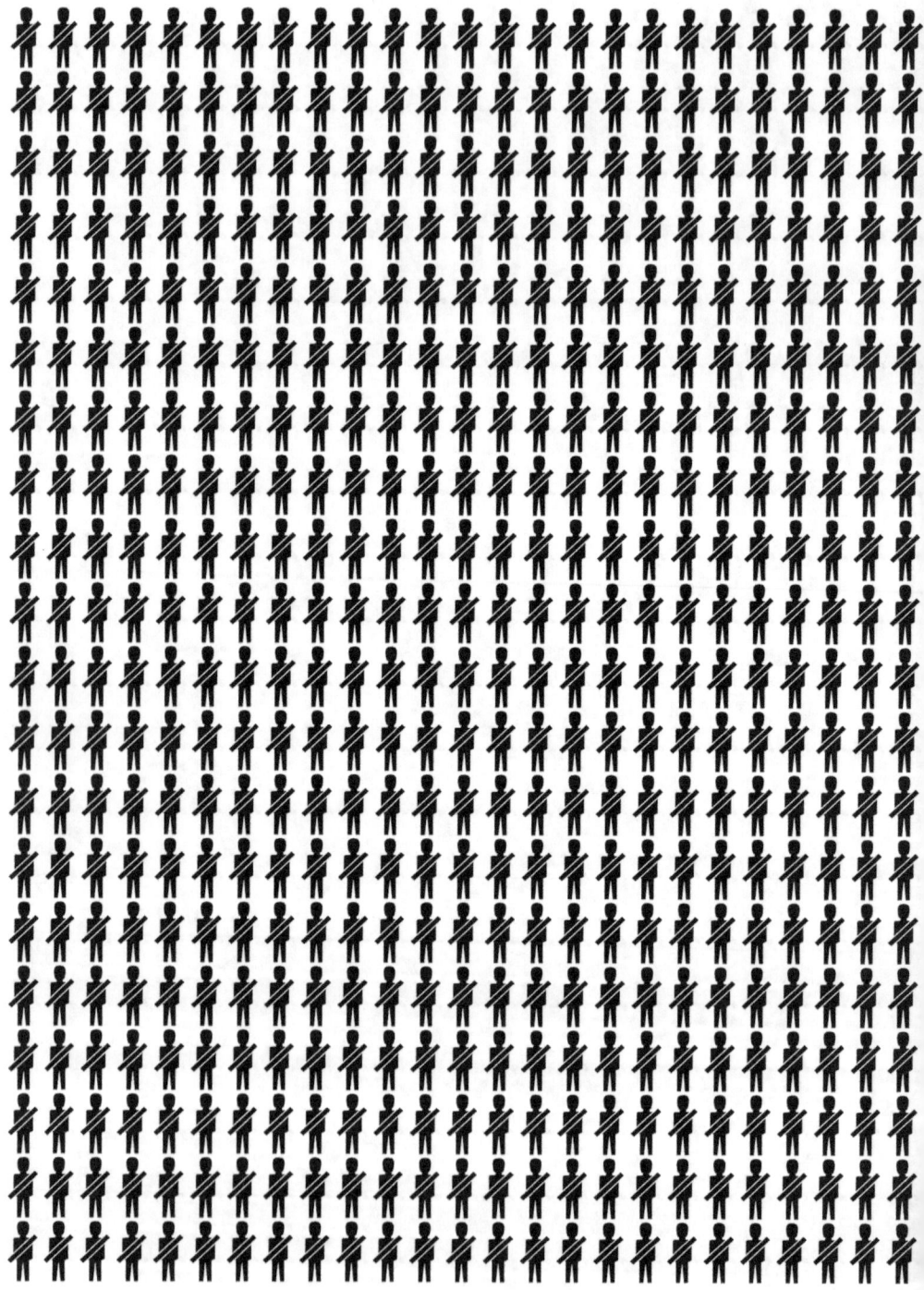

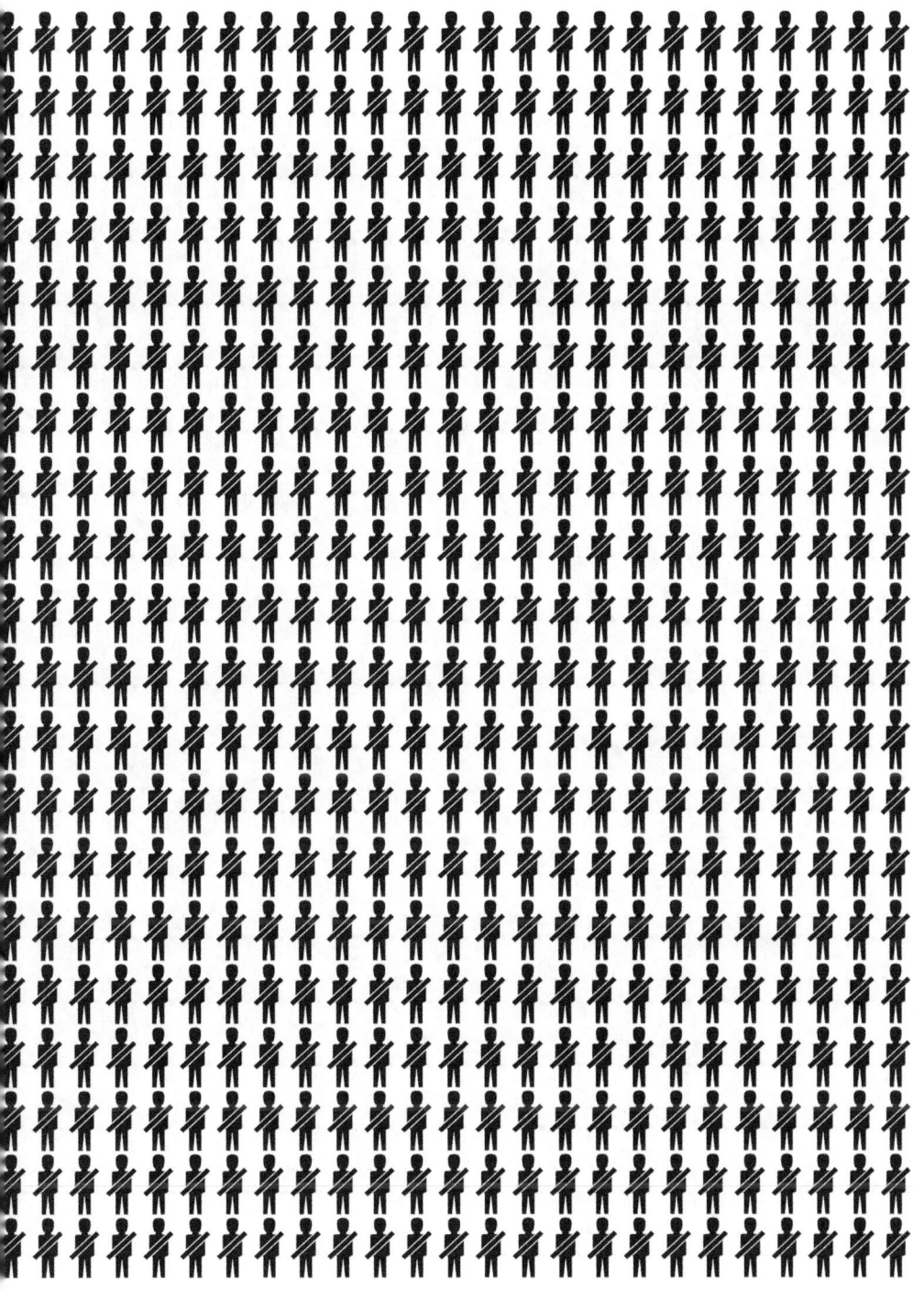

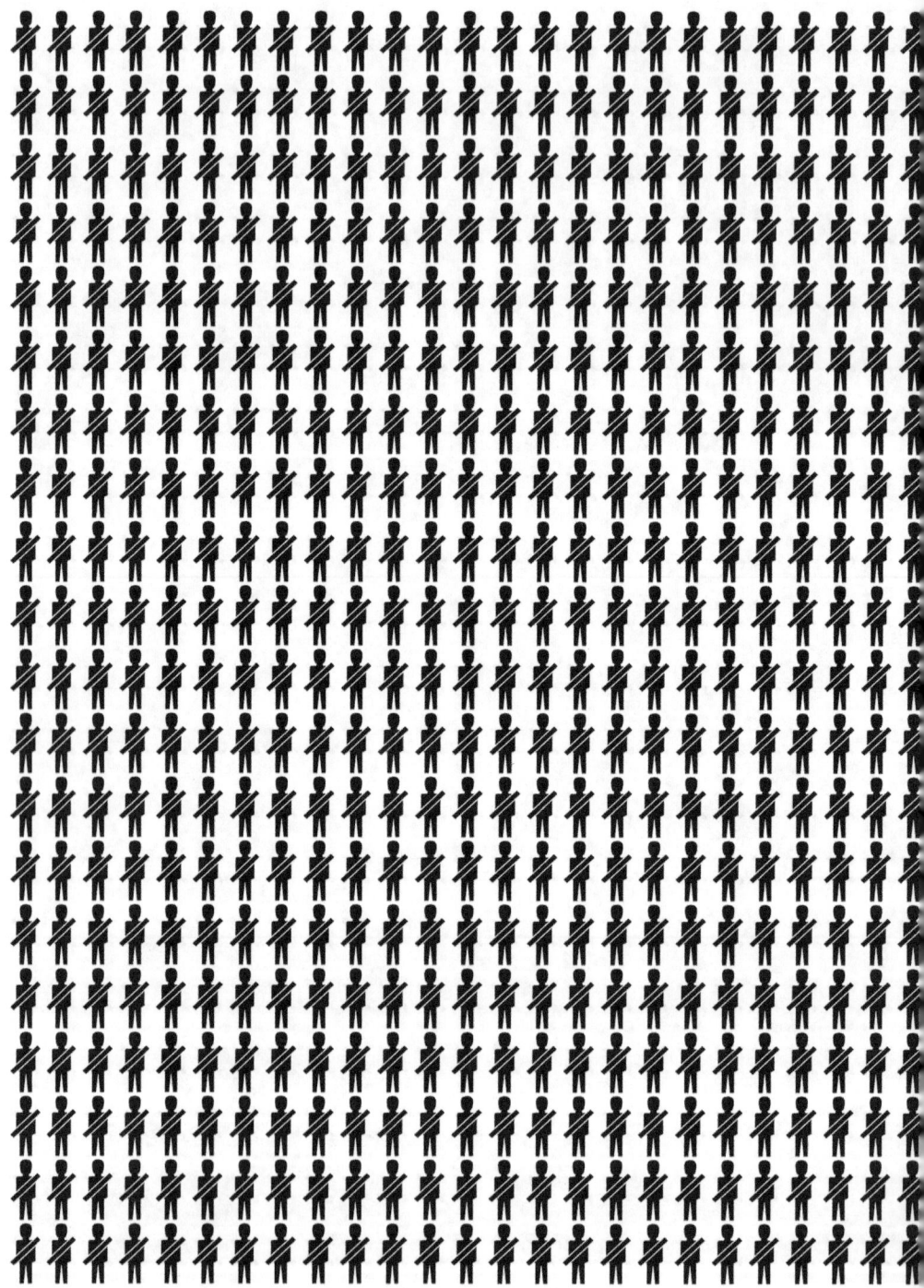

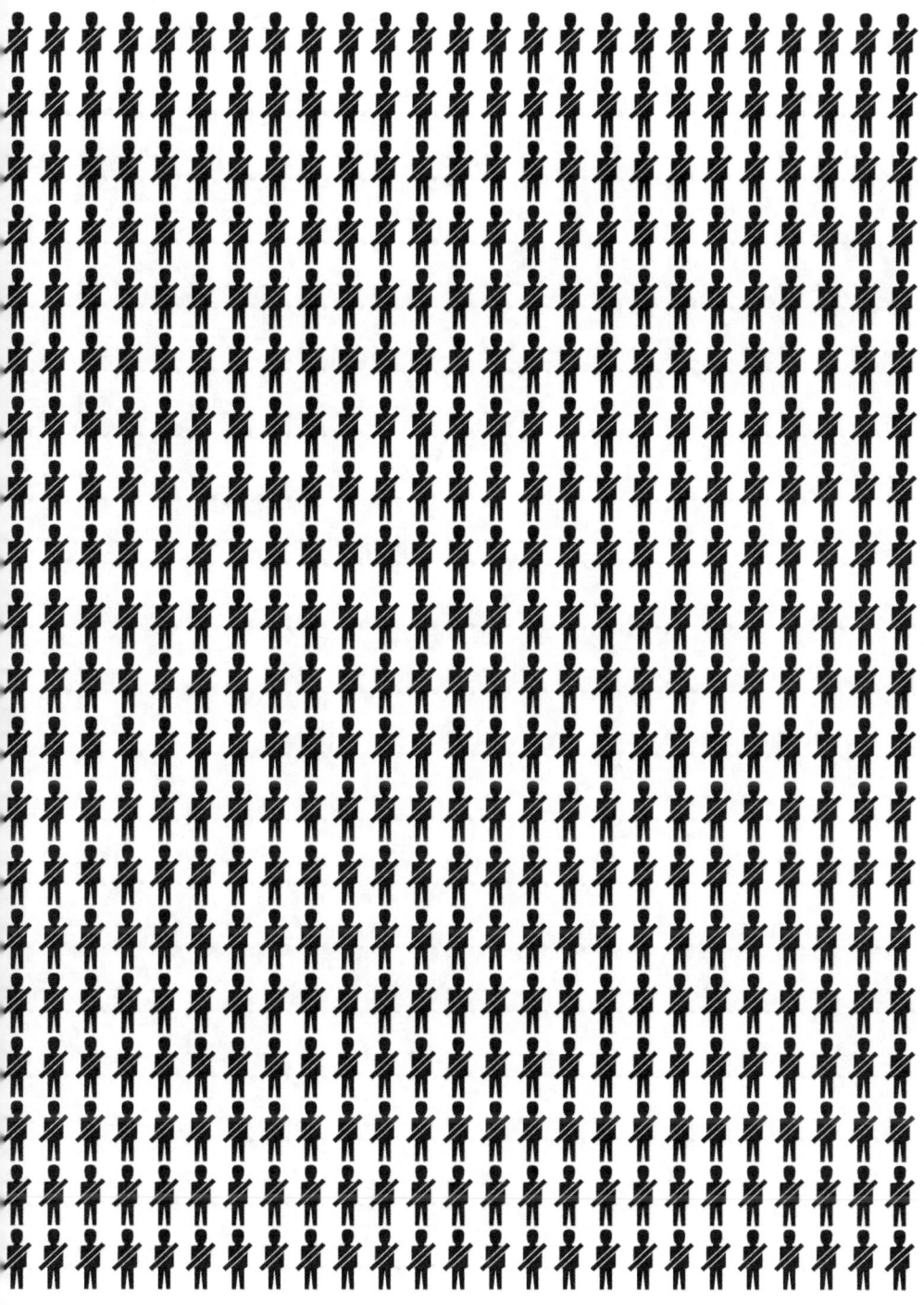

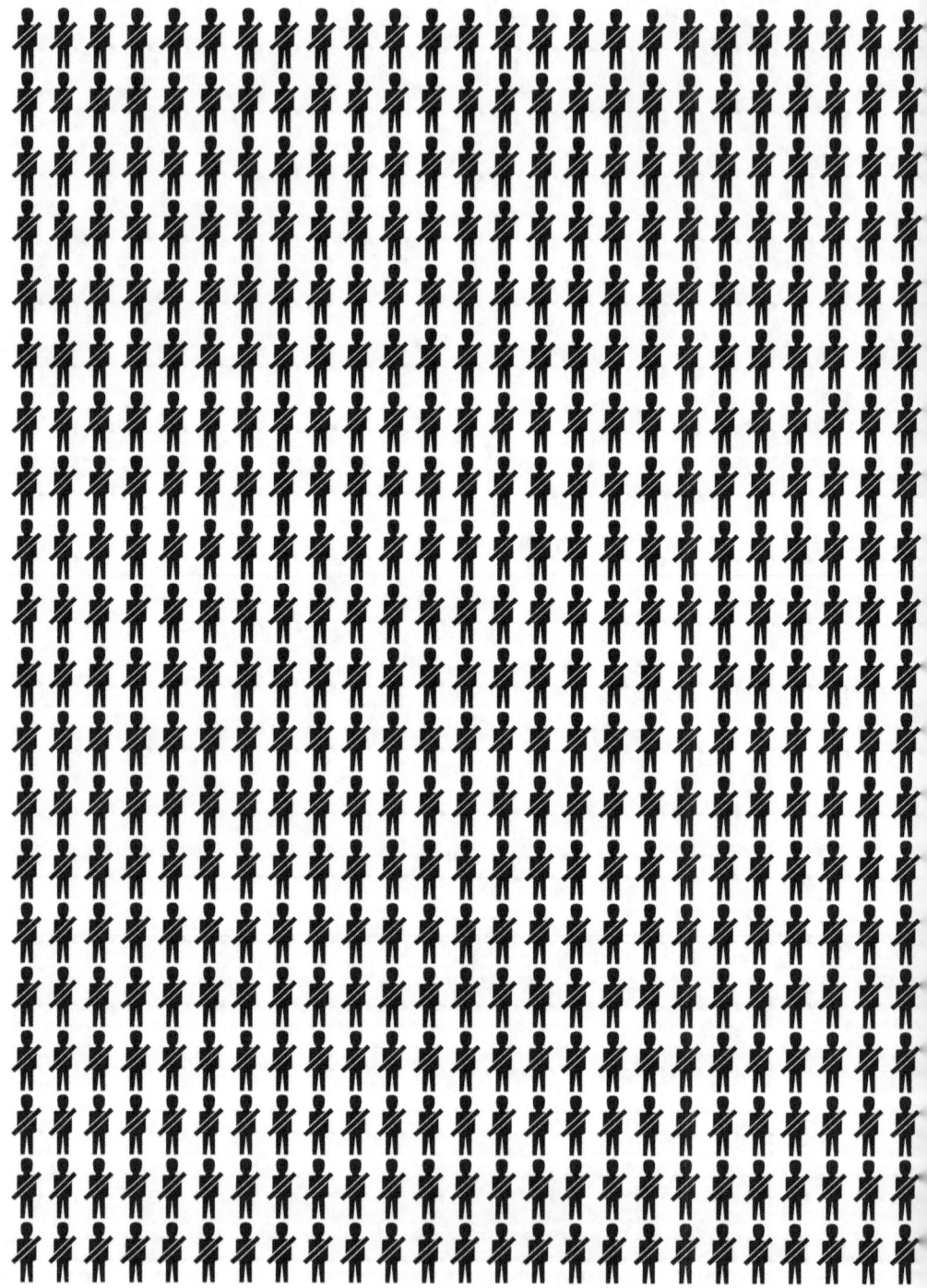

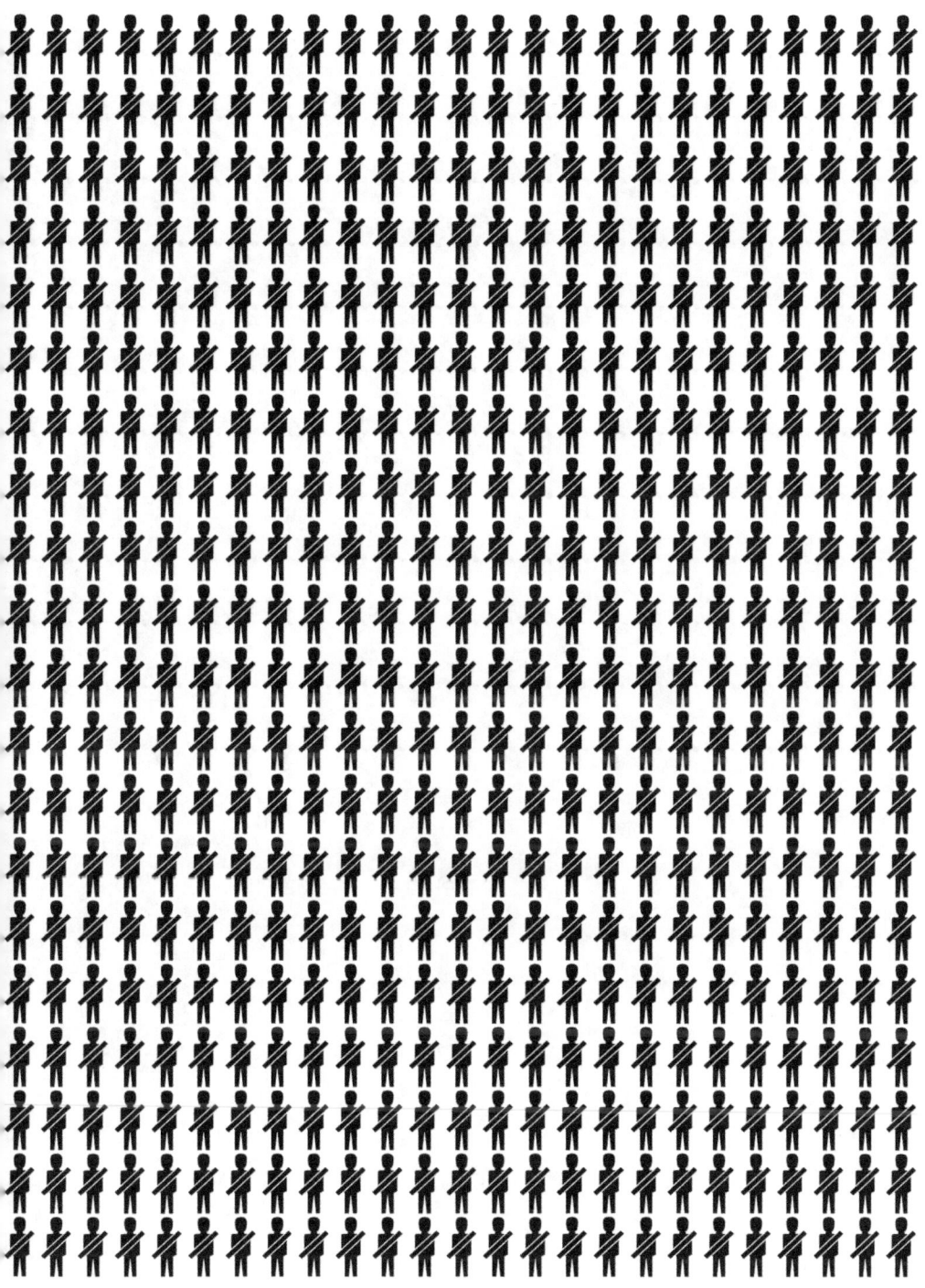

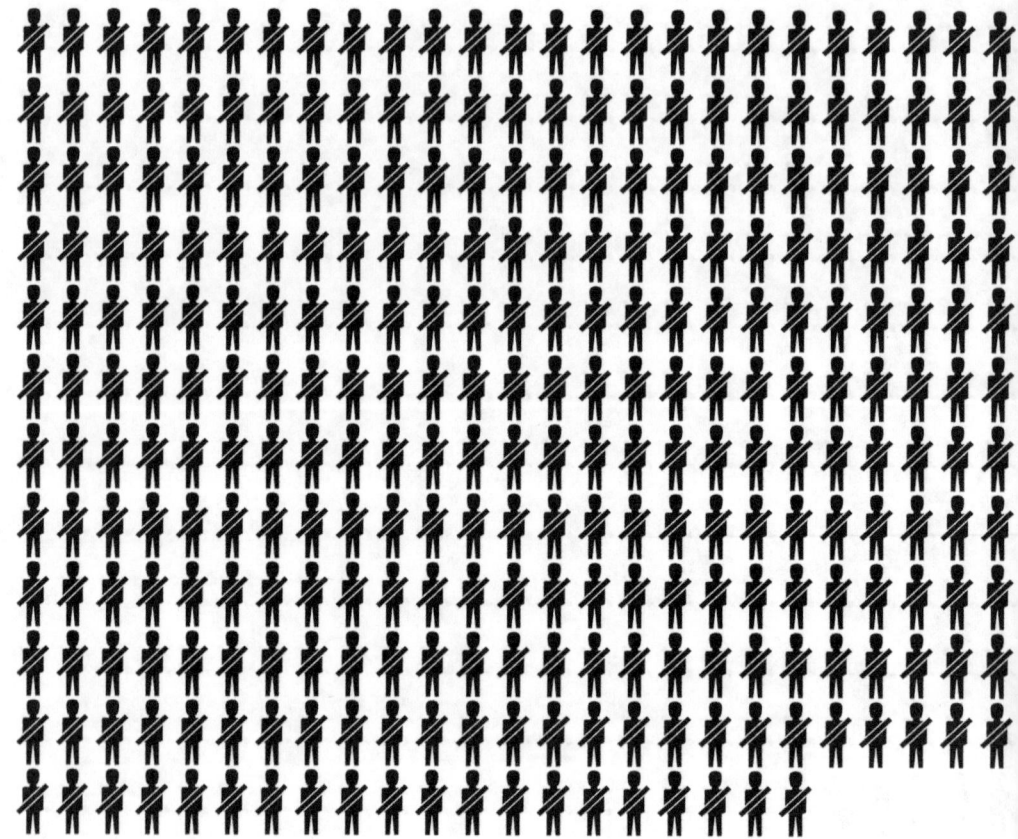

www.ingramcontent.com/pod-product-compliance
Lightning Source LLC
Chambersburg PA
CBHW072133170526
45158CB00004BA/1349